AF775701

HISTORY OF WOMEN IN THE UNITED STATES

HISTORY OF WOMEN IN THE UNITED STATES
Historical Articles on Women's Lives and Activities

Edited by Nancy F. Cott

Series ISBN 3-598-41454-4

HISTORY OF WOMEN IN THE UNITED STATES

Historical Articles on Women's Lives and Activities

14. Intercultural and Interracial Relations

Edited with an Introduction by

Nancy F. Cott
Yale University

K · G · Saur
Munich · New Providence · London · Paris · 1993

Publisher's Note
The articles and chapters which comprise this collection originally appeared in a wide variety of publications and are reproduced here in facsimile from the highest quality offprints and photocopies available. The reader will notice some occasional marginal shading and text-curl common to photocopying from tightly bound volumes. Every attempt has been made to either correct or minimize this effect.

Copyright information for articles reproduced in this collection appears at the end of this volume.

Library of Congress Cataloging-in-Publication Data
History of women in the United States : historical articles on
women's lives and activities / edited with
an introduction by Nancy F. Cott.
p. cm.
Includes bibliographical references and indexes.
Contents: 1. Theory and method in women's history -- 2. Household constitution and family relationships -- 3. Domestic relations and law -- 4. Domestic ideology and domestic work -- 5. The intersection of work and family life -- 6. Working on the land -- 7. Industrial wage work -- 8. Professional and white-collar employments -- 9. Prostitution -- 10. Sexuality and sexual behavior -- 11. Women's bodies -- 12. Education -- 13. Religion -- 14. Intercultural and interracial relations -- 15. Women and war -- 16. Women together -- 17. Social and moral reform -- 18. Women and politics -- 19. Woman suffrage -- 20. Feminist struggles for sex equality.
ISBN 3-598-41454-4 (set)
1. Women--United States--History. 2. Women--United States--Social conditions. I. Cott, Nancy F.
HQ1410.H57 1992
305.4'0973--dc20 92-16765
CIP

Die Deutsche Bibliothek - CIP - Einheitsaufnahme

History of Women in the United States: historical articles
on women's lives and activities / ed. with an introd. by Nancy F. Cott.
- Munich ; New Providence ; London ; Paris : Saur.
ISBN 3-598-41454-4
NE: Cott, Nancy F. (Hrsg.)
Vol. 14. intercultural and interracial relations - (1993)
ISBN 3-598-41468-4

Printed on acid-free paper/Gedruckt auf säurefreiem Papier

All Rights Strictly Reserved/Alle Rechte vorbehalten
K.G. Saur Verlag GmbH & Co. KG, Munich 1993
A Reed Reference Publishing Company

Printed in the United States of America
Printed/Bound by Edwards Brothers Incorporated, Ann Arbor

ISBN 3-598-41468-4 (vol. 14)
ISBN 3-598-41454-4 (series)

Contents

CONTENTS

CONTENTS

Series Preface

In the space of one generation, women's history has become the fastest-growing area of scholarship in U.S. history. Since the resurgence of feminism in the late 1960s and 1970s, insistent questions about the historical meanings of "woman's place" have sowed and reaped a garden of scholarship. Where scholarly works used to be bare of mention of women, academic enterprise has now produced a vigorous growth of books and articles, bringing to light diverse women of every region, race, class and age. This research is marked by a renovating intent that refuses to accept as "human" history a history of men. Interest is lively and debate is stimulating and sought after: attendance at the Berkshire Conference on the History of Women rivals the size of the annual convention of the American Historical Association.

While books in women's history are daily increasing in numbers and strength, as in any fast-developing field the scholarly literature in the form of articles is most expansive and up-to-the-minute. All the history journals now publish articles on women's work, domestic settings, family relations, household matters, female politics and organizations and so forth, and new journals have sprung into being to concentrate on such topics. Women's historians publish in numerous regional and thematic history journals as well as in feminist outlets and in journals of other social science disciplines. This series brings together a collection of outstanding articles from the field, almost all written in the past twenty years and more than half published during the 1980s. It brings together, in volumes organized by topic, essays otherwise widely dispersed. These volumes reprint only articles that originally appeared in journals, not chapters of books; review articles are not included. Articles have been chosen for overall quality and for range. Each one was chosen for one or more of the following reasons: because it is the standard authority on its subject matter; represents an important statement on a topic by a recognized scholar; presages an important book to come; provides a first look at new evidence or new methods; or opens an untapped area or new controversy. Older articles have been reprinted if their data or interpretation have not been surpassed or if they marked an important stage in the historiography, even if since superseded.

The historical coverage of the series extends from the Revolutionary era to the 1960s. The articles themselves are dated from the 1940s through 1988. Volumes are organized by topic rather than time period. Within each volume, the articles are ordered chronologically (with respect to substance), so that the whole can be read as an historical overview. The only exception to this ordering principle is Volume One, on Theory and Method, in which the contents are arranged in order of publication. Within each volume there is an attempt to include articles on as diverse kinds of women as possible. None of the volume topics is regionally or racially defined; rather, all volumes are topically designed so as to afford views of women's work, family lives, and public activities which cut across races and regions. Any volume in the series stands on its own, supplying as full a treatment of a designated subject matter as the scholarly literature will provide. Several groupings of volumes also make sense; that is, volumes two through five all center around domestic and family matters; volumes five through nine consider other varieties of women's work; volumes nine through eleven concern uses and abuses of women's bodies; volumes twelve through fourteen look at major aspects of socialization; and volumes fifteen through twenty include organizational and political efforts of many sorts.

As a whole, the series displays in all its range the vitality of the field of women's history. Aside from imbuing U.S. history with new vision, scholarship in this area has informed, and should continue to inform, current public debate on issues from parental leave to the nuclear freeze. By bringing historical articles together under topical headings, these volumes both represent accurately the shape of historical controversy (or consensus) on given issues and make historians' findings most conveniently available for current reference.

Introduction

When the field of U.S. women's history began to develop in the late 1960s and early 1970s, it focused principally on white, middle-class, Protestant women of the urban Northeast. Some historians from the first made efforts to examine the lives of workingclass women, who were more numerous if less enshrined in American cultural values than their prosperous sisters; but data and interpretations which illuminated the dominant class and image of American womanhood multiplied most readily. Within ten years, however—and more emphatically as the 1980s proceeded—this narrow focus was recognized as such. Its regional, urban, class and ethnic narrowness was no more pronounced than the usual bias of mainstream U.S. history, but women's historians sought explicitly to uncover the history of women in their ethnic and and racial diversity.

One important move, then, was to make plain that periodization based on urbanization and industrialization and concomitant changes in women's work and the household in the early nineteenth century bore a regional bias, toward the urban Northeast. In the South, Midwest and West, most households remained rural for the better part of the nineteenth century, and it was not until 1920 that more than half of the U.S. population lived in "urban" places (defined as population bases of 2500 or more). Another was to recognize that the "image" of appropriate womanhood touted by publicists, moralists, politicians, and other contributors to public discourse was usually (at any given time) far more unitary than the reality of American women, and often unmatched to experience, because it was derived from or proposed to a white, middle-class, urban model. A third move was to focus on the history of women in groups outside the dominant norm: white or black women in the slaveholding South, for instance, or immigrant women in factory jobs; or domestic servants.[1]

Turning the examining lens toward rural women, Hispanic or black women, women of the poor and laboring classes, has resulted in some of the most interesting and innovative work in women's history in the past decade.[2] These investigations have also enabled historians to see that the history of women has been, and must be conceptualized as being, a history of interactions, alliances and conflicts between different kinds of women. Where the first inquiries in women's history tended to look for the features that united women's lives and experiences across divergences of class, race, region, religion and so on, more recent inquiries have evoked the differences of situation, outlook, and possibility among diverse women. The newer focus not only expands the breadth of women's history but also allows a more accurate and critical look at the purported norm of women's experiences.

In this volume, the articles all explore interactions between and among women of differing cultures or races. Perhaps the paradigmatic model of such interaction has been the dynamic between black slave women and white mistresses in the antebellum South, early a magnet of interest. Practitioners of women's history have raised new questions about the maintenance, structure and meaning of the system of black slavery, simply by insisting that women must be distinguished as part of the groups of both slaveholders and slaves. There has been new attention to elite white women's roles as as icons and objects in the patriarchal value system of the white South, and to their double position of subordination to white males and command over black slaves. New distinctions have been drawn between black women's and men's experiences of slavery, especially focusing on black women's efforts to preserve kin ties and intimacy in the face of systematic sexual degradation by white owners. Some of the most interesting work has focused on relations between white mistresses and black slaves, asking to what extent there might have been particular commonality of interest, or particular intesity of conflict, because of their shared gender. The interest in black and white women's interaction during slavery has been further extended to inquiries into the continuing force of racism in later women's history, and also to examination of mistress/servant relationships in the postbellum South and the rest of the United States. For domestic service, more often than not, white women commanding social and economic resources have employed women of class and ethnic or racial identities differing from their own. At successive times in American history, not only the dsecendants of former slaves but also Irish, Asian, and Mexican immigrant women have found their basic employment in domestic service under white mistresses whose values and expectations differed sometimes dramatically from theirs. Besides this, there are several other categories, so to speak, of intercultural or interracial interaction, which can be discerned as characteristic of United States history. One as yet little-developed area is the study of interaction between women of different racial or ethnic groups at work, in fields or factory, where their similarity of economic resources and employment has sometimes, but rarely, brought women together. Another much better explored is that of cultural contact as white settlers moved across the American continent, bumping up against Native American and Hispanic populations who already inhabited the land. Both the attitudes of hostility or empathy between women of the different groups coming in contact, and the impact of United States government policy on sex roles and family structures of subjugated native groups, have commanded scholarly interest. And as in the study of the Southern system of slavery, all these types of interaction between women require the study of interaction between men and women, since the issues of white males' sexual conquests, interracial sex, miscegenation, and intermarriage always become prominent.

Much of the recent literature looks at the Western states. This volume reflects that weight of the historiography, which has collected in part because women's historians turned their attention to the West fairly recently, after ethnic and racial diversity was recognized as central to women's history, and partly because intercultural contact has typically shown up in sharper relief in Western history. Although Native Americans were segregated by the U.S. government on reservations, women of Asian, Latin and European background intermingled in the settlement of the West Coast, and Mexican and Anglo women in the Southwest. White women's intents to aid or educate black, Indian, or Latin women through missionary or similar efforts brought a purposeful kind of intercultural and interracial interaction, also represented by articles in this volume. Historians have looked initially from the point of view of the missionaries or the reformers, since these women often left considerable documentation of their endeavors, but increasingly have tried to recapture the interaction from the point of view of the women being aided—or imposed upon. As a whole, the volume not only shows the diversity of women whose history is currently being investigated, but also delineates intercultural and interracial interaction as a subject with a history of its own.

Notes

[1] *See*, for example, Catherine Clinton, *The Plantation Mistress: Woman's World in the Old South* (N.Y., Pantheon, 1982); Leslie Woodcock Tentler, *Wage-Earning Women: Industrial Work and Family Life in the United States, 1900-1930*, (N.Y., Oxford, 1979); Faye Dudden, *Serving Women: Household Service in Nineteenth-Century America* (Middletown, CT, Wesleyan Univ. Press, 1983).

[2] *See*, for example, Joan Jensen, *Loosening the Bonds: Mid-Atlantic Farm Women, 1750-1850* (New Haven, CT Yale Univ. Pr., 1986); Sarah Deutsch, *No Separate Refuge: Culture, Class, and Gender on an Anglo-Hispanic Frontier in the American Southwest, 1880-1940* (N.Y., Oxford, 1987); Jacqueline Jones, *Labor of Love, Labor of Sorrow: Black Women, Work, and the Family from Slavery to the Present* (N.Y., Basic, 1985); Christine Stansell, *City of Women: Sex and Class in New York, 1790-1860* (N. Y., Knopf, 1986).

Intercultural and Interracial Relations

The Role of Native Women in the Creation of Fur Trade Society in Western Canada, 1670–1830

SYLVIA VAN KIRK

Sylvia Van Kirk provides a major example of how the understanding of history changes when women and minorities are treated seriously. In this article she highlights some of the findings from her pioneering study of the Canadian fur trade, Many Tender Ties. *As she shows, the Canadian fur trade was neither violent nor male-dominated, because the incoming Europeans needed the cooperation of Indians of both sexes for the trade to succeed. Van Kirk's explanation of the activities of Indian women is a model of the feminist scholar's art of "piecing together" information about women from male-focused and ethnocentric sources. Her account does not present a picture of the Canadian fur trade from an Indian perspective, but it does take a giant first step toward a multicultural history.*

The United States fur trade was much smaller and of shorter duration than the Canadian enterprise. American trappers seem to have depended more on their own resources and less on those of American Indians. However, many trappers married Indian women. Perhaps the American mountain man was not in fact the celebrated loner of legend and story. Because research on these questions is just beginning in the United States, it is still too early to tell.

In essence the history of the early Canadian West is the history of the fur trade. For nearly two hundred years, from the founding of the Hudson's Bay Company in 1670 until the transfer of Rupert's Land to the newly created dominion of Canada in 1870, the fur trade was the dominant force in shaping the history of what are today Canada's four western provinces.

This long and unified experience gave rise in western Canada to a frontier society that seems to have been unique in the realm of interracial contact. Canada's western history has been characterized by relatively little violent conflict between Indian and white. I would like to suggest two major reasons why this was so. First, by its very nature, the Canadian fur trade was predicated on a mutual exchange and dependency between Indian and white. The Indian not only trapped the fur pelts but also provided the market for European goods. Until very recently, the fur trade has been viewed as an all-male affair, but new research has revealed that Indian women played an active role in promoting this trade. Although the men

"At the Portage." The Indian family of a Hudson's Bay Company steersman watches while trade goods are being prepared for the portage at Grand Rapids, ca. 1882. From *Picturesque Canada*, vol. 1, edited by George Monro Grant, published by Belden Bros., Toronto, 1882.

were the hunters of beaver and large game animals, the women were responsible for trapping smaller fur-bearing animals, especially the marten whose pelt was highly prized.[1] The notable emergence of Indian women as diplomats and peacemakers also indicates that they were anxious to maintain the flow of European goods such as kettles, cloth, knives, needles, and axes which helped to alleviate their onerous work.[2]

The second factor in promoting harmonious relations was the remarkably wide extent of intermarriage between incoming traders and Indian women, especially among the Cree, the Ojibwa, and the Chipewyan. Indian wives proved indispensable helpmates to the officers and men of both the British-based Hudson's Bay Company and its Canadian rival, the North West Company. Such interracial unions were, in fact, the basis for a fur trade society and were sanctioned by an indigenous rite known as marriage *à la façon du pays*—according to the custom of the country.

The development of marriage *à la façon du pays* underscores the complex and changing interaction between the traders and the host Indian societies. In the initial phase of contact, many Indian bands actively encouraged the formation of marital alliances between their women and the traders. The Indians viewed marriage in an integrated social and economic context; marital alliances created reciprocal social ties, which served to consolidate their economic relationships with the incoming strangers. Thus, through marriage, many a trader was drawn into the Indian kinship circle. In return for giving the traders sexual and domestic rights to their women, the Indians expected reciprocal privileges such as free access to the posts and provisions.[3]

As a result of this Indian attitude, it was soon impressed upon the traders that marriage alliances were an important means of ensuring good will and cementing trade relations with new bands or tribes. The North West Company, a conglomerate of partnerships which began extensive trading in the West in the 1770s, had learned from its French predecessors of the benefits to be gained from intermarriage and officially sanctioned such unions for all ranks (from bourgeois down to *engagé*).[4] The Hudson's Bay Company, on the other hand, was much slower to appreciate the realities of life in Rupert's Land. Official policy formulated in faraway London forbade any intimacy with the Indians, but officers in the field early began to break the rules. They took the lead in forming unions with the women of prominent Indian leaders, although there was great variation in the extent to which the servants were allowed to form connections with native women.[5]

Apart from the public social benefits, the traders' desire to form unions with Indian women was increased by the absence of white women. Although they did not come as settlers, many of the fur traders spent the better part of their lives in Rupert's Land, and it is a singular fact in the social development of the Canadian West that for well over a century there were no white women.[6] The stability of many of the interracial unions formed in the Indian country stemmed partly from the fact that an Indian woman provided the only opportunity for a trader to replicate a domestic life with wife and children. Furthermore, although Indian mores differed from those of the whites, the traders learned that they trifled with Indian women at their peril. As one old voyageur explained, one could not just dally with any native woman who struck one's fancy. There was a great danger of getting one's head broken if a man attempted to take an Indian girl without her parents' consent.[7]

It is significant that, just as in the trade ceremony, the rituals of marriage *à la façon du pays* conformed more to Indian custom than to European. There were two basic steps to forming such a union. The first step was to secure the consent of the woman's relatives; it also appears that the wishes of the woman herself were respected, as there is ample evidence that Indian women actively sought for trade husbands. Once consent was secured, a bride price had then to be decided; this varied considerably among the tribes but could amount to several hundred dollars worth of trade goods. After these transactions, the couple were usually conducted ceremoniously to the post where they were now recognized as man and wife.[8] In the Canadian West, marriage *à la façon du pays* became the norm for Indian-white unions, being reinforced by mutual interest, tradition, and peer group pressure.[9] Although ultimately "the custom of the country" was to be strongly denounced by the missionaries, it is significant that in 1867, when the legitimacy of the union between Chief Factor William Connolly and his Cree wife was tried before a Canadian court, it was found to have constituted a lawful marriage. The judge declared a valid marriage existed because the wife had been married according to the customs and usages of her own people and because the consent of both parties, the essential element of civilized marriage, had been proved by twenty-eight years of repute, public acknowledgement, and cohabitation as man and wife.[10]

If intermarriage brought the trader commercial and personal benefit, it also provided him with a unique economic partner. The Indian wife possessed a range of skills and wilderness know-how that would have been quite foreign to a white wife. Although the burdensome work role of the nomadic Indian woman was somewhat alleviated by the move to the fur-trade post, the extent to which the traders relied upon native technology kept the women busy.

Perhaps the most important domestic task performed by the women at the fur-trade posts was to provide the men with a steady supply of "Indian shoes" or moccasins. The men of both companies generally did not dress in Indian style (the buckskinned mountain man was not part of the Canadian scene), but they universally adopted the moccasin as the most practical footwear for the wilderness. One wonders, for example, how the famed 1789 expedition of Alexander Mackenzie would have fared without the work of the wives of his two French-Canadian voyageurs. The women scarcely ever left the canoes, being "continually employ'd making shoes of moose skin as a pair does not last us above one Day."[11] Closely related to the manufacture of moccasins was the Indian woman's role in making snowshoes, without which winter travel was impossible. Although the men usually made the frames, the women prepared the sinews and netted the intricate webbing which provided support.[12]

Indian women also made a vital contribution in the preservation of food, especially in the manufacture of the all-important pemmican, the nutritious staple of the North West Company's canoe brigades. At the posts on the Plains, buffalo hunting and pemmican making formed an essential part of the yearly routine, each post being required to furnish an annual quota. In accordance with Indian custom, once the hunt was over the women's work began. The women skinned the animals and cut the meat into thin strips to be dried in the sun or over a slow fire. When the meat was dry, the women pounded it into a thick flaky mass, which was then mixed with melted buffalo fat. This pemmican would keep very well when packed into ninety-pound buffalo-hide sacks, which had been made by the women during the winter.[13]

But pemmican was too precious a commodity to form the basic food at the posts themselves. At the more northerly posts, the people subsisted mainly on fish, vast quantities of which were split and dried by the women to provide food for the winter. Maintaining adequate food supplies for a post for the winter was a precarious business, and numerous instances can be cited of Indian wives keeping the fur traders alive by their ability to snare small game such as rabbits and partridges. In 1815, for example, the young Nor'Wester George Nelson would probably have starved to death when provisions ran out at his small outpost north of Lake Superior had it not been for the resourcefulness of his Ojibwa wife who, during the month of February, brought in fifty-eight rabbits and thirty-four partridges.[14] Indian women also added to the diet by collecting berries and wild rice and making maple sugar. The spring trip to the sugar bush provided a welcome release from the monotony of the winter routine, and the men, with their families and Indian relatives, all enjoyed this annual event.[15]

As in other pre-industrial societies, the Indian women's role extended well beyond domestic maintenance as they assisted in specific fur-trade operations. With the adoption of the birch-bark canoe, especially by the North West Company, Indian women continued in their traditional role of helping in its manufacture. It was the women's job to collect annual quotas of spruce roots, which were split fine to sew the seams of the canoes, and also to collect the spruce gum, which was used for caulking the seams.[16] The inexperienced and undermanned Hudson's Bay Company also found itself calling upon the labor power of Indian women, who were adept at paddling and steering canoes. Indeed, although the inland explorations of various Hudson's Bay Company men such as Anthony Henday and Samuel Hearne have been glorified as individual exploits, they were, in fact, entirely dependent upon the Indians with whom they traveled, especially the women. "Women," marveled one inlander, "were as useful as men upon Journeys."[17] Henday's journey to the Plains in 1754, for example, owed much of its success to his Cree female companion who provided him with much timely advice about the plans of the Indians, in addition to a warm winter suit of furs.[18] The Hudson's Bay Company men emphasized to their London superiors the value of the Indian women's skill at working with fur pelts. In short, they argued that the economic services performed by Indian women at the fur-trade posts were of such importance that they should be considered as "Your Honours Servants".[19] Indian women were indeed an integral part of the fur-trade labor force, although, like most women, because their labor was largely unpaid, their contribution has been ignored.

The reliance on native women's skills remained an important aspect of fur-trade life, even though by the early nineteenth century there was a notable shift in the social dynamic of fur-trade society. By this time, partly because of the destructive competition between rival companies which had flooded the Indian country with alcohol, relations between many Indian bands and the traders deteriorated. In some well-established areas, traders sometimes resorted to coercive measures, and in some cases their abuse of Indian women became a source of conflict.[20] In this context, except in new areas such as the Pacific Slope, marriage alliances ceased to play the important function they once had. The decline of Indian-white marriages was also hastened by the fact that fur-trade society itself was producing a new pool of marriageable young women—the mixed-blood "daughters of the country." With her dual heritage, the mixed-blood woman possessed the ideal qualifications for a fur trader's wife; acclimatized to life in the West and familiar with Indian ways, she could also adapt successfully to white culture.

From their Indian mothers, mixed-blood girls learned the native skills so necessary to the functioning of the trade. As Sir George Simpson, governor of the Hudson's Bay Company emphasized in the 1820s: "It is the duty of the Women at the different Posts to do all that is necessary in regard to Needle Work,"[21] and the mixed-blood women's beautiful beadwork was highly prized. In addition to performing traditional Indian tasks, the women's range of domestic work increased in more European ways. They were responsible for the fort's washing and cleaning; "the Dames" at York Factory, for example, were kept "in Suds, Scrubbing and Scouring," according to one account.[22] As subsistence agriculture was developed around many of the posts, the native women took an active role in planting and harvesting. Chief Factor John Rowand of Fort Edmonton succinctly summarized the economic role of native women in the fur trade when he wrote in the mid-nineteenth century: "The women here work very hard, if it was not so, I do not know how we would get on with the Company work."[23] With her ties to the Indians and familiarity with native customs and language, the mixed-blood wife was also in a position to take over the role of intermediary or liaison previously played by the Indian wife. The daughters of the French-Canadian voyageurs were often excellent interpreters: some could speak several Indian languages. The timely intervention of more than one mixed-blood wife saved the life of a husband who had aroused Indian hostility.[24] Indeed, in his account of fur-trade life during the Hudson's Bay Company's monopoly after 1821, Isaac Cowie declared that many of the company's officers owed much of their success in overcoming difficulties and in maintaining the company's influence over the natives to "the wisdom and good counsel of their wives."[25]

In spite of the importance of native connections, many fur-trade fathers wanted to introduce their mixed-blood daughters to the rudiments of European culture. Since the place of work and home coincided, especially in the long winter months, the traders were able to take an active role in their children's upbringing and they were encouraged by company officials to do so.[26] When the beginnings of formal schooling were introduced at the posts on the Bay in the early 1800s, it was partly because it was felt to be essential that girls, who were very seldom sent overseas, should be given a basic education which would inculcate them with Christian virtue.[27] Increasingly, fathers promoted the marriage of their daughters to incoming traders, as the means to securing their place in fur-trade society. In a significant change of policy in 1806, the North West Company acknowledged some responsibility for the fate of its "daughters" when it sanctioned marriage *à la façon du pays* with daughters of white men, but now prohibited it with full-blooded Indian women.[28]

As mixed-blood wives became "the vogue" (to quote a contemporary), it is notable that "the custom of the country" began to evolve more toward European concepts of marriage. Most importantly, such unions were coming to be regarded as unions for life. When Hudson's Bay Company officer J. E. Harriott espoused Elizabeth Pruden, for example, he promised her father, a senior officer, that he would "live with her and treat her as my wife as long as we both lived."[29] It became customary for a couple to exchange brief vows before the officer in charge of the post, and the match was further celebrated by a dram of liquor to all hands and a wedding dance. The bride price was replaced by the opposite payment of a dowry, and many fur-trade officers were able to dower their daughters quite handsomely.[30] Marriage *à la façon du pays* was further regulated by the Hudson's Bay Company after 1821 with the introduction of marriage contracts, which emphasized the husband's financial obligations and the status of the woman as a legitimate wife.

The social role of the mixed-blood wife, unlike that of the Indian wife, served to cement ties within fur-trade society itself. Significantly, in the North West Company, many marriages cut across class lines, as numerous Scottish bourgeois chose their wives from among the daughters of the French-Canadian *engagés* who had married extensively among the native people. Among the Hudson's Bay Company men, it was appreciated that a useful way to enhance one's career prospects was to marry the daughter of a senior officer.[31] Whatever a man's initial motivation, the substantial private fur-trade correspondence which has survived from the nineteenth century reveals that many fur traders became devoted family men. Family could be a source of interest and consolation in a life that was often hard and monotonous. As Chief Factor James Douglas pointedly summed it up: "There is indeed no living with comfort in this country until a person has forgot the great world and has his tastes and character formed on the current standard of the stage . . . habit makes it familiar to us, softened as it is by the *many tender ties* which find a way to the heart."[32]

However, the founding in 1811 of the Selkirk Colony, the first agrarian settlement in western Canada, was to introduce new elements of white civilization that would hasten the decline of the indigenous fur-trade society. The chief agents of these changes were the missionaries and white women.

The missionaries, especially the Anglicans who arrived under the auspices of the Hudson's Bay Company in 1820, roundly denounced marriage *à la façon du pays* as being immoral and debased.[33] But while they exerted considerable pressure on long cohabiting couples to accept a church marriage, they were in no way champions of miscegenation. In fact, this attack upon fur-trade custom had a detrimental effect upon the position of native women. Incoming traders, now feeling free to ignore the marital obligations implicit in the "the custom of the country," increasingly looked upon native women as objects for temporary sexual gratification. The women, on the other hand, found themselves being judged according to strict British standards of female propriety. It was they, not the white men, who were to be held responsible for the perpetuation of immorality because of their supposedly promiscuous Indian heritage. The double standard, tinged with racism, had arrived with a vengeance!

Racial prejudice and class distinctions were augmented by the arrival of British women in Rupert's Land. The old fabric of fur-trade society was severely rent in 1830 when Simpson and another prominent Hudson's Bay Company officer returned from furlough, having wed genteel British ladies.[34] The appearance of such "flowers of civilization" provoked unflattering comparisons with native women; as one officer observed, "this influx of white faces has cast a still deeper shade over the faces of our Brunettes in the eyes of many."[35] In Red River especially, a white wife became a status symbol; witness the speed with which several retired Hudson's Bay Company factors married the English schoolmistresses after the demise of their native wives. To their credit, many company officers remained loyal to their native families, but they became painfully anxious to turn their daughters into young Victorian ladies, hoping that with accomplishments and connections, the stigma of their mixed blood would not prevent them from remaining among the social elite. Thus in the 1830s, a boarding school was established in Red River for the children of company officers; the girls' education was supervised by the missionary's wife, and more than one graduate was praised for being "quite English in her Manner."[36] In numerous cases, these highly acculturated young women were able to secure advantageous matches with incoming white men, but to some extent this was only because white ladies did not in fact make a successful adaptation to fur-trade life. It had been predicted that "the lovely, tender exotics" (as white women were dubbed) would languish in the harsh fur-trade environment,[37] and indeed they did, partly because they had no useful social or economic role to play. As a result, mixed marriages continued to be a feature of western Canadian society until well into the mid-nineteenth century, but it was not an enduring legacy. Indian and mixed-blood women, like their male counterparts, were quickly shunted aside with the development of the agrarian frontier after 1870. The vital role native women had played in the opening of the Canadian West was either demeaned or forgotten.

Notes

1. Sylvia Van Kirk, *Many Tender Ties: Women in Fur Trade Society, 1670–1870* (Norman: University of Oklahoma Press, 1980; Winnipeg, Manitoba: Watson and Dwyer, 1980), pp. 72–73.

2. The most outstanding examples of Indian women who, although not married to whites, were active peacemakers and diplomats, are Thanadelthur, a Chipewyan, and Lady Calpo, a Chinook. See ibid., pp. 66–71, 76–77.

3. The few cases of violent conflict, such as the Henley House Massacre of 1752, were caused by the traders' failure to respect this bargain. See ibid., pp. 41–44.

4. Ibid., p. 28.

5. Ibid., pp. 28–29, 41–42.

6. After an ill-fated venture in 1686, British wives were officially prohibited from traveling to Hudson Bay. It was not until 1812 with the Selkirk settlers that women were again officially transported to Hudson Bay. A French-Canadian woman in 1806 was the first and one of the few white women to come west in the North West Company canoes. See Van Kirk, *Many Tender Ties*, pp. 173–80.

7. *Johnstone et. al.* v. *Connolly*, Appeal Court, 7 Sept. 1869, *La Revue Legale*, 1:280 (hereafter cited as Connolly Appeal Case, 1869).

8. Van Kirk, *Many Tender Ties*, pp. 36–37. For a discussion of the motivation of the Indian women, see chap. 4.

9. This does not mean that sexual exploitation of Indian women was unknown in the Canadian West. Prostitution certainly existed, and the marriage relationship could be abused as in white society.

10. *Connolly vs. Woolrich*, Superior Court, Montreal, 9 July 1867, *Lower Canada Jurist* 11:230, 248.

11. W. Kaye Lamb, ed., *The Journals and Letters of Sir Alexander Mackenzie* (Cambridge, England: Cambridge University Press, 1970), p. 220.

12. Van Kirk, *Many Tender Ties*, pp. 54–55.

13. Ibid., p. 56.

14. Toronto Public Library, George Nelson Papers, Journal, 29 Jan.–23 June 1815. See also Van Kirk, *Many Tender Ties*, pp. 58–59.

15. Van Kirk, *Many Tender Ties*, p. 57.

16. Ibid., p. 61.

17. J. B. Tyrrell, ed., *Journals of Samuel Hearne and Philip Turnor, 1774–1792*, Champlain Society, vol. 21 (Toronto, 1934), pp. 252–53.

18. Van Kirk, *Many Tender Ties*, p. 64.

19. Hudson's Bay Company Archives, B.239/b/79, fols. 40d–41 (hereafter HBCA).

20. Van Kirk, *Many Tender Ties*, pp. 90–91.

21. R. H. Fleming, ed., *Minutes of Council of the Northern Department of Rupert's Land, 1821–31*, Hudson's Bay Record Society, vol. 3 (London, 1940), p. 378.

22. Public Archives of Canada, James Hargrave Correspondence, vol. 21, Hargrave to Christie, 13 June 1832.

23. HBCA, D.5/18, fols. 535d–536.

24. One of the most famous cases was that of James Douglas, a clerk in northern British Columbia, whose high-handed treatment so outraged the Carrier Indians that he might have been killed but for intervention of his mixed-blood wife Amelia and the wife of the interpreter. See Van Kirk, *Many Tender Ties*, pp. 111–13.

25. Isaac Cowie, *The Company of Adventurers* (Toronto: W. Briggs, 1913), p. 204.

26. Van Kirk, *Many Tender Ties*, pp. 97, 99, 106, 131.

27. Ibid., pp. 103–104.

28. W. S. Wallace, ed., *Documents Relating to the North West Company*, Champlain Society, vol. 22 (Toronto, 1934), p. 211.

29. Connolly Appeal Case, 1869, p. 286.

30. Van Kirk, *Many Tender Ties*, pp. 108, 115.

31. Ibid., pp. 108–109.

32. G. P. de T. Glazebrook, ed., *The Hargrave Correspondence, 1821–1843*, Champlain Society, vol. 24 (Toronto, 1928), p. 381.

33. Van Kirk, *Many Tender Ties*, pp. 153–56.

34. They also violated "the custom of the country" by callously casting aside their former mixed-blood partners after the fact. For a full discussion of this episode see Sylvia Van Kirk, "The Impact of White Women on Fur Trade Society," in *The Neglected Majority: Essays in Canadian Women's History* (Toronto: McClelland and Stewart, 1977), pp. 27–48.

35. PAC, Hargrave Correspondence, vol. 21, Hargrave to Charles Ross, 1 Dec. 1830.

36. Glazebrook, ed., *Hargrave Correspondence*, p. 229.

37. Ibid., pp. 310–11.

Honor Ideology, Marriage Negotiation, and Class-Gender Domination in New Mexico, 1690-1846

by
Ramón A. Gutiérrez*

The ways in which societies organize marriage provide us an important window into how economic and political arrangements are construed. When people marry, they forge affinal alliances, change residence, establish rights to sexual service, and exchange property. Besides being about the reproduction of class and power, however, marriage is about gender. The marital exchange of women gives men rights over women that women never gain over men. This feature of marriage provides a key to the political economy of sex, by which cultures organize "maleness" and "femaleness," sexual desire, fantasy, and concepts of childhood and adulthood (Rubin, 1975: 166).

With these theoretical moorings in mind, I present here an essay on the history of marriage in a colonial setting, New Mexico between 1690 and 1846, an environment in which class domination was culturally articulated and justified through hierarchies of status based on race, ethnicity, religion, and gender. My major concern will be to examine the key role that control over marriage choice played in the maintenance of social inequality, focusing on changes in the mode of marriage formation during the period under study—a decline in the incidence of parentally arranged nuptials and an increase in those freely contracted by adolescents on the basis of love and personal attraction. Rather than discussing the roots of these changes abstractly, I will explore how parents and children negotiated their behavior, the disparities of power

---

*Ramón A. Gutiérrez is an Assistant Professor of Latin American and Chicano History at the University of California, San Diego. He is the author of a forthcoming book, ***Honor, Marriage and the Family in Colonial New Mexico.*** He is now undertaking research on Indian slavery in New Mexico and the history of confession in colonial Latin America.
This article was completed while the author was a Fellow at the Center for Advanced Study in the Behavioral Sciences. For financial support, he would like to express his gratitude to the National Endowment for the Humanities FC20029 and the Andrew Mellon Foundation.

LATIN AMERICAN PERSPECTIVES, Issue 44, Vol. 12 No. 1, Winter 1985 81-104
© 1985 Latin American Perspectives

that constrained their actions, and the ambiguities, tensions, and contradictions within the ideological superstructure that gave historical agency meaning.[1]

HISTORICAL SETTING

Once the ancient temples of Mexico City had been leveled and cities of gold had failed to materialize, the business of colonizing Mexico's central plateau began. The 1548 discovery of silver at Zacatecas quickly moved the frontier north and set the pace for the establishment of a rapid succession of towns: Guanajuato, Queretaro, San Luis Potosí, Durango. The far north, the areas we know today as New Mexico, California, and Texas, was explored in the the first half of the sixteenth century by such men as Álvar Núñez Cabeza de Vaca, Fray Marcos de Niza, and Francisco Vásquez de Coronado. Nonetheless, it remained a fantasy of future enrichment in the Spanish imagination until the end of the century. Then, in 1598, Don Juan de Oñate, the son of one of Zacatecas's wealthiest silver miners, mustered 129 soldiers and together with their dependents ventured into the land of the Chichimecas—the fierce nomadic Indian tribes that had effectively curtailed Spanish expansion north—to establish the Kingdom of New Mexico.

Arriving in August of 1598 armed with the cross of Christ and the sword to impose it, the soldier-settlers and friars quickly set about the task of "civilizing" the Indians through baptism, the introduction of European seeds and livestock, and the imposition of Spanish mores of comportment and dress. To ensure the presumed physical and spiritual well-being of New Mexico's Pueblo Indians, they were diviued into 41 *encomiendas* awarded to notables of the conquest. For this "entrustment" to the protection and spiritual care of the Spanish, the natives paid dearly in tribute, labor, and, often, lives (Bloom, 1939: 367-371; Snow, 1983: 347-357).

Though "savages" were all the Spaniards saw when they arrived in the Rio Grande Valley, the word is hardly adequate to describe the Indians living there. Since the thirteenth century, the river basin had been occupied by the compact agricultural villages of the Pueblo Indians. The 90 pueblos—so named by the Spanish because their multistoried dwellings resembled Aztec cities—were economically independent, politically autonomous, and best described as city-states. In 1598 the Pueblo population totaled approximately 60,000. Though several nomadic Indian tribes, notably the Apache and Navajo, hunted in the surrounding plains and mountains, their low level of material culture and social organization spared them the yoke of subjugation until the early 1700s (Dozier, 1950: 43-52).

The years 1598-1680 were brutal ones for the Pueblo peoples. Their food reserves were depleted by the colonists; their lives were disrupted by Spanish labor demands; their religious images were desecrated by the friars and their rituals suppressed. Many saw their kin driven to the point of death; women were raped and children enslaved. In 1680 they formed a confederation and routed the Spanish from the area, a feat that reverberated throughout New Spain and spurred other Indians to similar action. When the fury of the Pueblo Revolt was over, 21 out of 33 Franciscan friars were dead and 380 settlers had lost their lives. The 2,300 white survivors fled south to El Paso (Texas), where they regrouped and remained until 1693 (Bailey, 1940).

Don Diego de Vargas was charged with the reconquest of the territory and in 1693 led 100 soldiers, 70 families, and 18 friars to reestablish Spanish presence in Santa Fe. A second Spanish town, Santa Cruz de la Cañada, was founded in 1695 (Archivo General de la Nación, Historia [hereafter AGN-HIST] 39-5), followed by Albuquerque in 1706 (Bloom, 1935: 48). Colonists who did not live in one of these three towns resided in small dispersed ranches or hamlets situated along the banks of the Rio Grande. The white population in 1700 was perhaps no more than 3,000. The Pueblo population by that year had declined to 15,000 (Dozier, 1950: 122).

The period following the reconquest saw a major readjustment in Indian-white relations. Faced with the realization that there was a limit to the exploitation the Pueblo would tolerate and that they would not be cowed into abandoning their native religious beliefs easily, the crown abolished the encomienda and replaced it with the *repartimiento*, a less onerous rotational labor levy. New Mexico's governors were ordered to observe Indian rights strictly, and the martyrdom of their brothers impressed on the friars that their evangelical zeal would have to be tempered (Meinig, 1974: 27-32; Bannon, 1974: 28-48).

But the problem of extracting labor and wealth from the native population in its various forms remained. The revolt had not altered the practice of using political office as a vehicle for personal enrichment. Someone still had to construct the imposing mission compounds that were to dot the landscape, and the aristocracy's sense of preeminence was still dependent on the labor of others. For these ends, then, a new enemy was necessary. The "Apaches"—as the Spanish called all the nomadic Indians whose hunting grounds bordered on the agricultural settlements of the river basin (Jicarilla, Mescalero, Navajo, Ute, and Comanche)—were quickly defined as Satan's minions; this status made them eligible for "just war." Scores of men, women, and particularly children were brought into Spanish villages enslaved as prisoners of war. Some *genízaros,* as these detribalized Indians became known, were retained in local households for the performance of domestic tasks while others were traded for luxury goods in the mining centers of northern New Spain. The growth of this commerce in captives during the eighteenth century was directly responsible for the constant warfare the kingdom's colonists were to experience (Bailey, 1966: 1-89).

In this environment, the Spanish colonists of the post-reconquest period fashioned a society that they perceived as ordered hierarchically by honor, a prestige system based on principles of inherent personal worth. Honor was a complex gradient of status that encompassed several other measures of social standing such as descent, ethnicity, religion, profession, and authority over land (Tönies, 1953: 12-21). The summation and ordering of these statuses and the pragmatic outcome of evaluations of honor resulted in the organization of society into three broadly defined groups: the nobility, the landed peasantry, and the genízaros.

The status hierarchy did not completely encompass class standing as structured by relations of production. The Pueblo Indians on whose labor and tribute the colonists so heavily relied fell outside the groups to whom honor mattered and refused to accept, cherish, and validate the ideals by which Spanish society organized its interactions. From the colonists' point of view, the physical tasks the Pueblo Indians performed were intrinsically dishonorable and conquest by a superior power itself dishonoring. Obviously, the Pueblo did not consciously share this view. In colonial New Mexico, honor and class were nevertheless interdependent. Social power ultimately gained its effectiveness from the combination of the two (Giddens, 1971: 166-167).

The nobility consisted of 15-20 families that intermarried to ensure their continued dominance. Their sense of aristocracy was rooted in the legally defined honor granted to the kingdom's colonizers by King Phillip II in their 1595 charter of incorporation (Hammond and Rey, 1953: 50). As the colony developed, nobility gained a broader social meaning and was claimed by individuals who acquired large amounts of land, by military officials, and by bureaucrats—wealth and power acting as the determinants of intragroup mobility. By comparison with the titled peerage of central Mexico, New Mexico's nobility at best enjoyed the life of a comfortable gentry (Ladd, 1976). Yet, perhaps because of its isolation—and the attendant belief that it was a cultural oasis in a sea of barbarism—New Mexico's aristocracy considered itself second to none. Bearing Old Christian ancestry, harboring pretensions of purity of blood, and eschewing physical labor, it reveled in its rituals of precedence, in ostentatious display of lavish clothing and consumption of luxury goods, in respectful forms of address and titles. Needless to say, such habits were buttressed by force of arms, wealth, and a legal superstructure premised on the belief that the social order was divinely ordained.

Landed peasants who were primarily of mestizo origin but considered themselves "Spaniards" were next in the hierarchy of honor. They had been recruited for the colonization of New Mexico with promises of land, and in 1700 all enjoyed rights to *merced,* a communal land grant consisting of private irrigated farmlands, house plots, and commons for livestock grazing. By 1800, the progressive subdivision of private plots had resulted in parcels too small for subsistence. Under these circumstances, owners of morseled holdings increasingly turned to wage labor. Their ranks were swelled by persons who had not gained access to land as part of their patrimony. Though the land area of New Mexico may seem boundless, it was constrained by limited water sources, by the previous and competing water and land claims of the Pueblo Indians, and by the resistance to geographic expansion offered by hostile tribes (Leonard, 1970).

Lowest in prestige, dishonored and infamous because of their slave status, were the genízaros, a diverse group of Indians who resided in Spanish towns and performed the community's most menial and degrading tasks. Between 1694 and 1849, 3,294 genízaros entered Hispanic households (Brugge, 1968: 30). Early in the seventeenth century, New Mexicans had been granted the privilege of warring against infidel Indians and retaining them in bondage for ten years as compensation for the costs of battle (Góngora, 1975: 128). Though many genízaros remained slaves much longer, they were customarily freed at marriage. Lack of access to land and the development of emotional dependencies on their masters, by whom in most cases they had been raised, meant that even after manumission genízaros had few options for social mobility. Remaining in the household and employment of their former owners was common.

Genízaros (from the Turkish *yeni,* "new," and *cheri,* "troops") were truly New Mexico's shock troops against the infidel. Stigmatized by their former slavery, lacking kinship ties to the European community, and deemed devious because of their lack of mastery of Spanish, the increasing numbers of free genízaros were segregated in special neighborhoods such as Santa Fe's Barrio de Analco or congregated in new settlements such as Belén (1740), Abiquiu (1754), Ojo Caliente (1754), and San Miguel del Vado (1794). All of these genízaro communities—communities now of landed peasants of genízaro origin—were strategically established along the Indian raiding routes and were to serve Spanish settlements as buffers against attack (Swadesh, 1974: 31-35).

THE IDEOLOGY OF HONOR

Honor was a polysemic word embodying meanings at two different but fundamentally interrelated levels, one of status and one of virtue. Honor was first and foremost society's measure of social standing, ordering on a single vertical continuum those persons with much honor and differentiating them from those with little. Excellence manifested as territorial expansion of the realm was the monarchy's justification for the initial distribution of honor. Yet, "the claim to honor," as Julian Pitt-Rivers (1968: 505) notes, "depends always in the last resort, upon the ability of the claimant to impose himself. Might is the basis of right to precedence, which goes to the man who is bold enough to enforce his claim." The children of the conquistadores gained their parents' honor through ascription and maintained and enhanced it through behavior deemed appropriate to a highly esteemed person.[2]

The second dimension of honor was a constellation of virtue ideals. Dividing the community horizontally along prestige-group boundaries, honor-virtue established the status ordering among equals. Definitions of virtue were gender-specific. Males embodied honor (the sentiment of honor) when they acted *con hombría* (in a manly fashion), exercised authority over family and subordinates, and esteemed honesty and loyalty. Females possessed the moral and ethical equivalent of honor, *vergüenza* (shame), if they were timid, shy, feminine, virginal before marriage and afterwards faithful to their husbands, discreet in the presence of men, and concerned for their reputations. Infractions of the rules of conduct dishonored men and were a sign of shamelessness in women. Shamelessness accumulated around the male head of household and dishonored both the family as a corporate group and all its members.

The maintenance of social inequality was central to the way in which status and virtue were defined to interact, the aim being the perpetuation of the nobility's preeminence. An aristocrat of however low repute was always legally more honorable than the most virtuous peasant. Because precedence at the upper reaches of the social structure guaranteed more material and symbolic benefits, it was usually among the nobility and elites that the most intense conflicts over honor-virtue occurred. Family feuds and vendettas were frequently the way sullied reputations were avenged and claims to virtue upheld.[3]

Consensus seems to have existed among New Mexicans of Hispanic origin regarding the behavior deemed virtuous and worthy of honor. Among the nobility and the peasantry alike, men concerned for their personal and familial repute, judged by how well they resolved the contradictory imperatives of domination (protection of one's womenfolk from assault) and conquest (prowess gained through sullying the purity of other men's women), hoped to minimize affronts to their virtue, thereby maintaining their status. Female seclusion and a high symbolic value placed on virginity and marital fidelity helped accomplish this aim.

Yet only in aristocratic households, where servants and retainers abounded, could resources be expended to ensure that females were being properly restrained and shameful. The maintenance of their virtue was made easier because genízaro women could be forced into sexual service. As slaves they were dishonored by their bondage and could therefore be abused without fear of retaliation, for as one friar lamented in his 1734 report to the viceroy, Spanish New Mexicans justified their rapes saying: "an Indian does not care if you fornicate with his wife because she has no shame [and] . . . only with lascivious treatment are Indian women conquered" (Archivo General de la Nación, Inquisición [hereafter AGN-INQ] 854: 253-256).

Inequalities in power and status kept peasant men from honorably challenging aristocrats. Both because of this disparity in status and because of the excesses of the nobility in asserting their virility, ideals of female virtue were as intensely cherished by peasants. Manuel Alvarez, the United States consul in Santa Fe, alluded to this when he wrote in 1834: "the honorable man (if it is possible for a poor man to be honorable) has a jewel in having an honorable wife" (Manuel Alvarez, personal papers, notebook, New Mexico State Records Center and Archives). Among the peasantry, gender prescriptions undoubtedly had to be reconciled with the exigencies of production and reproduction of material life. The required participation of all able household members in planting and the harvest meant that there were periods when constraints on females of this class were less rigorously enforced. Juana

Carillo of Santa Fe admitted as much in 1712 when she confessed enjoying the affections of two men her father had hired for their spring planting (Archives of the Archdiocese of Santa Fe [hereafter AASF] 51: 735-758). Again, in households where men were frequently absent, such as those of soldiers, muleteers, shepherds, and hunters, cultural ideals were less rigid. The fact that females supervised family and home for large parts of the year, staved off Indian attack, and cared for the group's public rights meant that it was difficult for them to lead sheltered and secluded lives. It was not uncommon for these women to lament that they had been assaulted, raped, or seduced while their husbands or fathers were away from home (AASF 60: 270; Spanish Archives of New Mexico [hereafter SANM] 18: 579; AASF 60: 376).

HONOR AND MARRIAGE

Marriage was the most important ritual event in the life-course, and in it the honor of the family took precedence over all other considerations. The union of two properties, the joining of two households, the creation of a web of affinal relations, the perpetuation of a family's symbolic patrimony—its name and reputation—were transactions so important to the honor-status of the group that marriage was hardly a decision to be made by minors. The norm in New Mexico was for parents to arrange nuptials for their children with little or no consideration of their wishes. Filial piety required the acceptance of any union one's parents deemed appropriate or advantageous.

The 1786 marriage of Francisco Narpa and Juana Lorem in Sandia provides a glimpse of the familial motivations involved in an arranged union. Appearing before the provincial ecclesiastical judge to explain how he had married, Francisco reported: "Having agreed with Juana Lorem that we wished to marry, I asked her grandmother Tomasa Cibaa, and with her permission and that of her relatives, I married." Juana Lorem had a slightly different understanding of the events that led up to her marriage to Francisco. She told the judge, "It is totally false that I agreed to marry the said Francisco. I never wanted to marry the said Francisco. But for fear of my grandmother Tomasa Cibaa I contracted the marriage." Finally, Tomasa Cibaa explained: "I ordered my granddaughter Juana to marry the said Francisco Narpa because he is moderately wealthy, and it is true that I pressured Juana to appear before the priest [for the matrimonial investigation] and say nothing that might provoke questioning." The details of this marriage surface as part of an ecclesiastical investigation into the allegation that the union was incestuous. Francisco had fathered a child by María Quieypas, Juana's mother, and therefore his marriage to Juana was invalid. The marriage was annulled, dotal and patrimonial property were confiscated, the three were publicly flogged, and Narpa was exiled from New Mexico (AASF 64: 706-707; 52: 773-774).

Of course, I do not wish to suggest that arranged marriage was an inflexible rule. The extent to which parental preference for arranged marriage could be enforced was mediated both by the person's status and by each family's particular fertility history. The number of children in a family, their birth order, and their sex dictated the options available to parents to secure their son or daughter an acceptable or advantageous spouse. These and other variables also conditioned the range of filial responses possible—whether a son or daughter acted as if bound by duty or sentiment or resisted or attempted to manipulate the situation so as to appease everyone's concerns.

From a father's point of view, a round of poker is an excellent metaphor for the way in which limited resources (the patrimony) were manipulated to maximize the gains associated with marital alliance. Pierre Bourdieu (1976: 122) has applied this metaphor to the marriage of a family's children. Success at enhancing and perpetuating the family's status is based not only on the hand one is dealt (whether the nuptial candidate is an only child, the eldest of several sons, or the youngest of many daughters) but also the skill with which one plays it (bids, bluffs, and displays). The patrimony was the material resource a father had to apportion among its claimants at strategic moments to maximize reproductive success. Although legally every legitimate child in New Mexico was entitled to an equal share of this wealth, practice varied by class. Aristocratic holders of large landed estates preferred male primogeniture as a way of keeping their property intact. The eldest son, as the heir to the household head's political rights over the group and the person responsible for the name and reputation of the family, was the individual to whom a disproportionate amount of parents' premortem resources was committed. As first in importance, even if preceded by older sisters, he could not suffer a misalliance without lowering the entire family's public rating and diminishing the possibilities of securing honorable partners for his unmarried brothers and sisters. Therefore, he was the child of whom parents expected the most and the child disciplined most severely to ensure obedience but allowed the greatest excesses in other matters. He was also perhaps the most predisposed to bow to duty.

If the eldest son had married well and the family's position had thus been attended to, filial participation in the marriage process was tolerated in subsequent cases. Because younger sons were unlikely to fare as well in the acquisition of marital property and could expect only enough money and movable goods to avoid misalliance, fathers might be more open to their suggestions regarding eligible brides.

Daughters of the nobility were a potential liability on the marriage market, dissipating the material and symbolic patrimony by having their dowries absorbed into their husbands' assets. Every attempt would be made to dispose of nubile females as quickly as possible and at minimal expense. If a daughter experienced a prenuptial dishonor, such as the loss of her virginity, additional resources would have to be committed to secure her an appropriate mate. Thus large amounts of time and energy were spent ensuring that a maiden's sexual shame was being maintained. Undoubtedly, the result was that a woman's freedom to object to a marriage, to express her desires in spouse selection, was more limited than that of her brothers (SANM 10: 4-25, 868-872).

Peasants enjoying rights to communal land grants practiced partible inheritance. Sons were given their share of the family's land when they took a bride and were assigned a certain number of *vigas* ("beams"—a way of dividing the space in a house) in the parental home. If space limitations prohibited such a move, assistance was given in the addition of rooms to the house or the construction of a separate edifice in the immediate vicinity. For females, premortem dowries usually consisted of household items and livestock. Daughters seldom received land rights at marriage because parents fully expected the husband's family to meet this need. The authority relations springing from this mode of property division meant that parental supervision over spouse selection and its timing was as rigidly exercised as among the nobility.

For landless freed genízaros, the institution of marriage itself was of no consequence. Many preferred concubinage, as they held no property to transmit and the alienation from their Indian kin that accompanied enslavement made the issue of perpetuation of family name irrelevant. Wage earners and landless peasants were in a similar situation with regard to marriage. Once children were old enough to leave the familial hearth in search of a livelihood, parental control over their behavior all but ceased. Their only concern in the timing of marriage, if in fact they chose matrimony for cultural reasons, was the necessity to accumulate a nest egg with which to establish a conjugal residence.

MARRIAGE AND THE CHURCH

The settlement of the Kingdom of New Mexico was a joint venture of church and state. In all the remote areas of the Spanish empire in which civilization was to be brought to the Indians, it was by the religious orders, through the institution of missions, that the task was accomplished. Acting as defenders of the Indians, as guardians of community piety and morality, and as a counterpoint to the power of the state, the church at one and the same time legitimated and buttressed the colonial system and challenged certain tenets of its rule. Nowhere was this tension among the authorities of God, of the family head, and of the state clearer than on the issue of marriage.

Until 1776, the Catholic church enjoyed exclusive jurisdiction over the ritual, sacramental, and contractual aspects of matrimony. Ecclesiastical law, articulated as a theory of impediments to marriage, was dominated by two concerns: the prohibition of incest and the determination of the exercise of free will. The latter principle drew on the Roman legal tradition that a nuptial contract was valid only if the parties had given free and absolute consent. The use of persuasion and coercion to arrange marriages of children could place patriarchs in direct confrontation with the church and its clerics.

Arranged marriage was a complex issue for the church. Scripture and canon law were fraught with ambiguities and contradictions on the matter. Christian ideology reinforced the honor code regarding the obedience and personal subordination children owed their parents. "Honor your father and mother," ordered the fourth commandment. "Children, obey your parents in the Lord," enjoined St. Paul in his Epistle to the Ephesians (5:22). The church maintained that the law of nature bound parents and children in a relationship that entailed reciprocal rights and obligations. The authority of man over his wife, children, and servants emanated from God's power over creation, and therefore his was the right to guide and discipline children as necessary. Filial submission, St. Paul promised, would be reciprocated with paternal love, protection, and guidance (Flandrin, 1979: 118-119).

But the vexing question clerics were obliged to ask, in the case of marriage, was when paternal guidance and filial obedience simply became coercion. The issue was of some importance because forced marriages, or those contracted under duress, were invalid. Matrimony was the sacramental union of free will based on mutual consent. Ideally it was the work of God, and "what God has joined together, let no man separate."

The autonomy of individual will, responsibility, and conscience in undertaking marriage was central to Catholic thought. In arranged marriages, in which conflicts between obedience to parents and obedience to one's conscience existed, the will of the individual was to take precedence (Flandrin, 1979: 122). The scriptural basis for limits on the authority of the father and the freedom of Christ's message rested in the following: "Call no man your father upon the earth: for One is your Father, which is in heaven" (Matthew 23:9). And again (Matthew 10:34-37):

> *Think not that I am come to send peace on earth: I came not to send peace, but a sword. For I am come to set a man at variance against his father, and the daughter against her mother, and the daughter-in-law against her mother-in-law. And a man's foes shall be they of his own household. He that loveth father or mother more than me is not worthy of me: and he that loveth son or daughter more than me is not worthy of me.*

A mechanism for the determination that a person was marrying freely existed in canon law. If the slightest hint of coercion surfaced, the local priest had the power to remove the candidate from his/her home for isolation from parental pressures. Once the person's wishes became known, the priest was legally bound either to marry the person, even against parental wishes, or to prohibit a forced union. Don Salvador Martínez of Albuquerque, for example, availed himself of ecclesiastical intervention when he sought Vicar Fray Manuel Roxo's help in his 1761 matrimonial bid for Doña Simona Baldes. Though Martínez had twice asked for Doña Simona's hand in marriage, his proposals had been ignored. Moved by the evidence, the vicar sequestered Doña Simona, who admitted she wanted to be Martínez's bride. The marriage occurred despite parental objections, which may have been due to a gross age difference. Don Salvador was a 62-year-old widower; Doña Simona was only 19 (AASF 62: 311-314).

The freedom that the Catholic church might grant the sexes in the selection of conjugal mates formed the legal foundation for the subversion of parental authority, but, as the experience of all areas of the Spanish colonial empire testifies, the law and its execution were two very different matters. It was not uncommon for clerics charged with the interpretation and execution of canon law to enforce it selectively or to bend its dictates to avoid misalliances or subversion of the social order. If a friar believed an arranged marriage was a good match, he might uphold parental prerogatives and rationalize that the natural authority of a father over his children was in full accord with the will of God.

A variant of such an alliance between priest and parents occurred in Santa Fe in 1710. María Belasquez and Joseph Armijo appeared before Fray Lucas Arebalo that year claiming that her parents would not allow her to marry Joseph. They asked the friar to take María into his custody so that she could express her "true" wishes. María was sequestered but was returned to her father shortly after Joseph left the rectory. Joseph immediately appealed to the provincial ecclesiastical judge, who agreed that Fray Lucas had not upheld the marriage canons of the Council of Trent. The two were sequestered anew and were finally joined in wedlock after affirming their desire to be husband and wife (AASF 60: 680-692).

From the evidence in the ecclesiastical archives, "absolute" legal liberty to choose a spouse meant, in fact, freedom to select a mate from *within* one's class and ethnic group. No examples exist in the Archives of the Archdiocese of Santa Fe of clerics' sanctioning a cross-class marriage over parental objections. The church might subvert the particular authority of parents, but it would not subvert the social order at large.

CULTURAL CONTRADICTIONS AND THE DIALECTICS OF SOCIAL ACTION

Marriage was a ritual event with meanings derived from several interrelated and interpenetrating ideologies. For the state, it was a way of perpetuating status and property inequalities in their hierarchical order. In Christian thought, it prefigured the love between Christ and the church and was of necessity the union of free wills. The sacrament preserved community morality by providing a sanctioned arena for the expression of sexual desires. The emotions of parents and children regarding affinity and connubiality figured in behavior, as did fertility histories and demographic realities.

The cultural system in which marriage was enmeshed was diverse and divisive, resting on symbols that were ambiguous and polysemic. The head and the heart were two such equivocal symbols that synthesized beliefs about hierarchy, honor, and desires and translated them into behavior. According to the native cognitive model of New Mexicans, behavior was the outcome of interplay between several realms. Individual actions were the result of mediation between external forces, such as social rules, values, and chance, and internal physical drives, such as sentiments and emotions.

External factors were comprehended through the head. Reason, probity, and the conscience were perceived to be located there. The head was the symbol of personal and collective honor. The king's honor was exhibited through a crowned head, the honor of the bishop through his miter. Honor and precedence were paid by bowing one's head, taking off one's hat, or (for women) covering one's head. Decapitation was a dishonorable punishment. Honor challenges were frequently initiated by a slap to the face. Manuel Martín of San Juan in 1766 punished his daughter for bearing an illegitimate child by cutting off all her hair; a bald head was to serve the community as a sign of her shamelessness (SANM 9: 943). Catholic priests cut a tonsure in their hair as a sign of their vow of chastity and pledge to sexual purity (Pitt-Rivers, 1977: 23).

Just as the head was the source of reason, its antithesis, emotion, was rooted in the heart. The heart was the organ through which "natural" urges were experienced and heartfelt. "I wish to marry for no other reason than to serve God and because it comes forth from my heart, without it being the result of any other motivation," said Sebastiana de la Serna of her 1715 marriage bid (AASF 61: 209). For Fray José de la Prada, concupiscence sprang from the heart. Writing the governor of New Mexico concerning the sexual laxity of his congregation, Prada complained that "their customs and heathen friskiness have sunk very deep roots into their hearts" (SANM 15: 617). Another friar in a sermon on lust warned his congregation of the metabolic repercussions of an unregulated heart. "It is from the heart that we must displace this monster of sensuality . . . it is the cause of so many sudden deaths, infectious disease, and numerous maladies of the liver" (Archivo General de la Nación, Hacienda [hereafter AGN-HACIENDA] 29-8: 2).

The heart as a natural symbol for love had been enmeshed in the popular consciousness of Western Europeans since at least the thirteenth century (Huizinga, 1949: 77-84). The songs and poetry of courtly love diffused to the New World cast the heart as the well of sentiment. As roving troubadours performed their medieval romances in New Mexico's villages, the motifs of their repertoire—the all-consuming love that tormented the courtier, the impossible desires of an inferior man for a married lady, the discovery of an adulterous liaison that ended in death for the two lovesick individuals—certainly resonated in the imaginations of young and old alike (Campa, 1946: 29-90; Espinosa, 1915: 446-560).

The tensions between external forces and personal desires symbolized as conflicts between the head and the heart, between reason and sentiment, between collective responsibility and individual will, provided Hispanics in New Mexico with a variety of options and explanations for their behavior. One sees in the 1715 statements of Sebastiana de Jesús of Santa Fe the equivocation over such ideals. Appearing before the local priest to complete the matrimonial investigation necessary so that she could be joined in wedlock with Gerónimo Ortega, she was asked if she truly wanted to marry. She said:

> *When the mother who raised me, whose name is Lucía Ortis, asked me about the marriage the first time, I said no, I did not want to marry; but later, so that my mother would not be angry I said yes. But now, the desire to marry him does not spring from my heart... and having heard that the father of Gerónimo de Ortega has become a public ward in Santa Fe, I refuse to marry him. And if I marry him it will be only because my mother forces me to. I must do as she wishes, and will do it only to please her.... I do not wish to marry, it is not of my heart.... Before it was not of my heart and it is even less so now.*

Fray Antonio Miranda was uncertain whether Sebastiana was being forced into matrimony, so he ordered a new declaration taken. When asked again, she said blankly that she wanted to marry Gerónimo "of my absolute liberty" (AASF 61: 209-212).

The individuals, be they clerics, family heads, or bureaucrats, who articulated the ideals of marriage formation that opposed arranged marriage to marriage choice, hierarchy to egalitarianism, had a vested interest in presenting the cultural system as rigidly circumscribed by these dichotomies. In reality, much behavior fell along a continuum of which these oppositions were the extremes. After all, our information on these prescriptions comes largely from litigation before the civil and ecclesiastical courts, which established the outer limits of proper conduct. In their daily lives, individuals negotiated their behavior pragmatically in dynamic relationships with one another using the ideals of the cultural system as anchors. Thus, for example, on the continuum between arranged marriage and marriage choice, children of the aristocracy may all have their marriages arranged; children of the peasantry may vary between the two forms depending on their sex and birth order;

and genízaros, wage laborers, and landless peasants would be relatively free to choose their own partners (Drummond, 1980: 352-374).

The dialogue that undoubtedly occurred between the generations while negotiating a marriage match was seldom voiced and rarely recorded. Folk songs alone give us a hint of the interaction that must have been central to the selection process. "The Recent Bride," an early nineteenth-century song from Taos (Works Progress Administration, New Mexico Folklore Collection, 5-5-19 #26), explores the tensions between parents and children over marriage choice. Parents, having themselves at one time perhaps experienced the same feelings, can articulate the child's view but do so negatively, casting duty and sentiment, reason and passion, paternal love and romantic love as irreconcilable. The parental objective is clearly the subversion of individualistic filial behavior. By describing the consequences of ignoring parental counsels, they hope to have their expectations fulfilled:

A recent bride and woe is me
I weep the livelong day
To think I'm wed so unhappily
Nothing can my fate allay.

Before I wed my mother dear
Did try to turn me from my course,
Her counsels wet with many a tear
I now regret with great remorse.
But willful was I, I paid no heed
And God has fully punished me,
But willful was I, I paid no heed
And God has fully punished me.

For my husband I have found to be
A man who drinks and drinks and drinks,
He has already forgotten me
Of his young bride he never thinks....

In "La Señora Chepita" (Campa, 1946: 203), the nature of the generational conflict is more explicit:

Oh what times these are Señora Chepita;
Oh what things are happening these days!
Laboriousness is no longer prized,
Misery engulfs us all,
Progress itself is lost.
Oh what times these are Señora Chepita!

In my time commerce bleated
And the crafts with much to do.
Lovers were always constant,
No woman was ever false.
Women in times past
Spent their time only caring
For their children, husbands and servants
And of none did they gossip.

Today it is common to see
That honor is snatched from one another
In others defects are found
While ignoring one's own, Señora Chepita.
If a young man made a conquest
He would hide it with just reason
So that none would know
The secrets of his heart.

From the parents' point of view presented above, their society is orderly and rule-bound, whereas that of the new generation is chaotic and ruleless. The song is not a statement of fact. If we took them literally, the folk songs in which the older generation laments the shortcomings of the new—a lament so common in every historical period—would lead us to believe that society was constantly in a state of breakdown. These songs are instead comments about what parents would like their children to do. Parents refuse to legitimate the norms that guide filial behavior by denying that such norms exist. The songs express parental displeasure. They attempt to persuade sons and daughters to conform to parental ideals and do things the way they used to in "the good old days" (Yanagisako, 1980: 56).

The bishop of Durango in 1823 attested to the fact that children, though constrained in their marital options, did not sit by passively and always accept parental will. They manipulated the symbols of marriage, of honor and love, to obtain a desired spouse. Given the bishop's concern that maidens were being deflowered as part of youthful schemes "undertaken to facilitate" marriages that might otherwise have been unacceptable to parents (AASF 53: 790), we can speculate on what actions may have been taken by adolescents. A young man and woman might be aroused by a genuine love for one another and desire matrimony. Fearing that parents would object to a union, they might devise a ploy to maneuver an acceptable solution within the limits of their familial honor preoccupations. The woman might allow her virginity to be taken, claim that her honor had been sullied, and demand marriage simply as a way of forcing parents to consider a mate who might otherwise never have been ideally acceptable. The discourse in such a case would take place entirely in the idiom of honor, but only because this strategy allowed the parties to maneuver within the parental value system. Such ploys were popular resolutions to conflicts of honor in Golden Age Spanish theater (Larson, 1977: 17-37).

Parents and children negotiated with different amounts of power. The dynamics of the process were clearly skewed in favor of the elders in both conscious and unconscious ways. Sons and daughters were familiar with the options available to them in marriage formation and knew exactly what was expected to ensure property transmission, to satisfy the requirements of the family's symbolic patrimony, and to avoid scandal and ostracism. Norms and the authority of custom buttressed parental prerogatives, as did the socialization process. Personal "tastes" were learned in infancy and reinforced through avoidance of contact with certain persons. Thus a child's desire for a certain mate was just as much the result of interaction with persons of similar status, race, education, and subcultural traits as it was of "individualistic" urges (Bourdieu, 1976: 140-141).

SOCIAL CHANGE

From the years following the reconquest to the early 1770s, the Kingdom of New Mexico was peripheral to the empire. Isolated on the northern margins of New Spain, the colony's only link to "civilization" was a yearly mule train to Mexico City, which traveled over several thousand miles of territory inhabited by hostile Indians. New Mexico contained no significant mineral deposits, its population's material culture was rudimentary, and its cash-crop production (wheat, cotton, corn, pine nuts) was insignificant. In fact, had the Franciscan order not pleaded passionately before the crown for the privilege of converting New Mexico's Indians, colonists might never have been sent there in the first place (Adams, 1954: 3-4).

The isolation of the province slowly began to crumble in the 1760s. Frightened by the increasing levels of Russian, Anglo-American, and French encroachment into Texas, New Mexico, and California, King Charles III ordered a series of economic, military, and administrative reforms, commonly known as the Bourbon reforms, to safeguard the territory.

The reform project began in 1765 when the Spanish Royal Corps of Engineers was sent to the northern frontier of New Spain to map the area thoroughly, to identify its mineral and hydraulic resources, to assess the feasibility of textile production, to propose methods for increasing agricultural production, and to outline the military changes necessary to fortify the frontier (Fireman, 1977). On the basis of the expedition's recommendations, northern New Spain was reorganized in 1776 into one military and administrative unit called the Internal Provinces. New presidios were constructed to ward off foreign attack, and vigorous campaigns were staged to subdue the "Apaches," who made trade and communication difficult. It was precisely in this period that permanent settlements were finally established in California, the first mission being built in 1769 at San Diego (Bannon, 1974: 143-190).

The crown believed that New Mexico could be retained as part of the empire only through fuller integration into the market economy centered in Chihuahua. To achieve this aim, trade and travel restrictions were abolished, New Mexican products were given sales tax exemptions, and agricultural specialists, veterinarians, and master weavers were sent to the area to upgrade local production and improve the competitive position of the kingdom's products. Within a few years the frequency of mule trains to and from Chihuahua increased, money began to circulate more widely, and new colonists from north-central Mexico migrated into the area (AGN-HIST 25-31: 252-253; 25-36: 297; Archivo General de la Nación, Californias [hereafter AGN-CALIF] 17-7: 228; 17-10: 325-327; SANM 10: 931-933, 1020-1037; Escudero, 1832: 37-38).

Imperial economic reforms coincided with a period of demographic growth in New Mexico, which resulted in intense land pressure. Between 1760 and 1820, the Spanish and mixed-blood population of New Mexico grew from 7,666 to 28,436. By the 1780s, many of the land grants to the initial colonists were insufficient for subsistence. A few new *mercedes* were conceded in the late 1780s, but not enough to meet the population's needs. Governor Fernando de la Concha noted this in his 1796 report to the commandant of the Internal Provinces and estimated that there were 1,500 individuals without land to till (AGN-CALIF 17-7: 226). The inevitable upshot of this situation was the expansion of wage labor. A comparison of the occupational structures of the kingdom in 1790 and 1827 reflects this expansion of wage laborers. In 1790, Albuquerque had an adult working population of 601. Farmers constituted 65 percent (391), 25 percent (151) were craftsman, and 10 percent (58) were day laborers. By 1827, 610 persons were listed as full-time workers: 66 percent (397) were farmers, 14 percent (85) craftsmen, and 19 percent (113) day laborers. The 1790 census of Santa Fe listed 413 individuals with occupations. Farmers represented 85 percent (350), craftsmen 7 percent (28), and day laborers 8 percent (34). By 1827, of 846 workers, 55 percent (467) were farmers, 12 percent (101) craftsmen, and 31 percent (264) day laborers. An expansion of the day-laborer category in both size and proportion also occurred in Santa Cruz during this period (SANM 12: 319-502; Carroll and Villasana Haggard, 1942: 88). The end result of the Bourbon reforms and the land pressure that accompanied them was the expansion of socially autonomous forms of labor and increased mobility for a significant portion of the population.

To complete the picture of changes that occurred in the last quarter of the eighteenth century, we must also examine church-state relations as they affected New Mexico. During the reign of Charles III many of the formal aspects of the Patronato Real, the partnership between church and state that had been so effective in the colonization of the Americas, were abolished. The religious orders, perceived as independent and powerful because of their relationship to the indigenous population, were first to lose their privileged status. In New Mexico, where the Franciscan friars and the area's governors had battled incessantly since the 1600s over the extent to which each could exploit Indian land and labor, the Bourbon attack on clerical rights put an end to the feud. The missions were gradually secularized; where 30 friars had administered the sacraments in 1760, by 1834 none remained (Weber, 1982: 43-82).

The loosening of the Franciscans' grip on the population of New Mexico, part and parcel of the growth of secularism and the diffusion of rationalism throughout Europe and its colonies, bred an indifference toward moral theology, the scriptures, and the authority of priests. One of the first changes one notes in this increasingly secular society is a linguistic change in the ecclesiastical marriage records. Whereas between 1690 and 1790 most individuals married ostensibly "to save my soul" (AASF 61: 404), "to serve God and no other reason" (AASF 61: 68), or motivated by similar religious convictions, after 1790 nuptial candidates are moved by "the growing desire we mutually have" (AASF 66: 18) and by "the urges of the flesh, human wretchedness and the great love we have for each other" (AASF 79: 122). Increasingly, individuals mention personal desires such as love as the reason for marriage.

The Bourbon reforms and the growth of a landless population dependent on wage labor for its reproduction had increased social differentiation. This in turn brought into open question the ideological consensus that had formerly existed between the nobility and the landed peasants regarding ascribed honor as a sign of social status premised on family origin and control over means and instruments of production. For free genízaros, mestizos who could not boast of "Spanish" origin, and landless peasants, honor was of little material consequence. Their social status was obtained primarily through individual achievement; under such circumstances patriarchal control over marriage formation was of no functional significance. After all, parental sanction for arranged marriage was effective because familial honor carried with it property and social privileges. Once children were able with their own wages to accumulate the necessary resources to establish a household, and could not in any way count on significant inheritance of property, generational relations were placed on a new footing.

Examining the period from 1690 to 1848, the major change that occurred in marriage formation was an increased preference for unions based explicitly on romantic love over those arranged by parents pursuing economic considerations. This change was not sudden; it was an ongoing process. Love matches were possible from the earliest days of Spanish settlement but occurred infrequently among the landed classes concerned for the perpetuation of their patrimonies. Children had plenty of parental counsels, ballads, folktales, laws, and sermons to make them realize the disastrous consequences of placing desires over reason.

The history of marriage in a colonial social formation such as New Mexico reveals the centrality of patriarchal control for generational, gender, and class forms of domination. Arranged marriages that enhanced honor provided the nobility and the landed peasantry with a tool by which to protect their status in an unequal society. The various ideologies by which gender and class hierarchies were comprehended and legitimated, however, were not monolithic and static. The partnership between the church and state so instrumental in the conquest of Latin America created distinct views on the meaning of marriage. Though the positions of church and state frequently converged, differences between them enabled children to challenge parental authority without danger to the social order. Similarly, the meanings attached to the system of status and prestige varied by class and changed in response to larger economic forces that themselves transformed relations of production and the power relations between church and state. By the 1800s, the material underpinnings of the honor code had been eroded, creating the conditions that allowed individual urges such as romantic love to exert greater influence on marriage formation.

NOTES

1. The generalizations presented in this article are derived from extensive reading of documents in the Archives of the Archdiocese of Santa Fe, the Spanish Archives of New Mexico, and the Mexican Archives of New Mexico (deposited at the New Mexico State Records Center and Archives, Santa Fe, sections of the Archivo General de la Nación in Mexico City that pertained to New Mexico (Historia, Provincias Internas, Inquisición, Californias, Hacienda), and the folklore collections housed at the Museum of New Mexico in Santa Fe and the University of New Mexico's Zimmerman Library in Albuquerque. The major portion of my source material dates from 1690 to 1846 and is primarily court cases heard by the civil and ecclesiastical authorities on seduction (or the loss of female virtue), affronts to a person's honor, parental opposition to marriage, impediments to matrimony, dowry negotiations, concubinage, rape, adultery, spouse mistreatment, and divorce. By examining points at which behavior deviated from prescriptions, I have attempted to reconstruct the society's ideals. Where my evidence is thin, I have been forced to turn to Mexican proscriptive literature that, though not produced by New Mexico's residents, was undoubtedly available to its literate members and reflected the broader cultural milieu of New Spain. Readers desiring more extensive documentation of my sources should consult Gutiérrez (1980).

2. A general understanding of honor can be obtained from Peristiany (1966), Campbell (1976), Bourdieu (1977), Martínez-Alier (1974), Schneider (1971), Kirshner (1978), García Valdecasas (1948), Gutiérrez (1980, 1984), and Pitt-Rivers (1977).

3. No one has yet adequately explained the origins of honor-virtue. Its history is ancient in the Mediterranean as a cultural template for the maintenance of hierarchy through endogamy and precepts concerning the sacred. Honor antedates Christianity, yet their moral and ethical ideals coincide on many points. The most intelligent discussion of the origins of honor is found in Schneider (1971).

REFERENCES

Adams, Eleanor B.

1954 *Bishop Tamaron's Visitation of New Mexico, 1760*. Albuquerque: Historical Society of New Mexico.

Bailey, Jesse B.

1940 *Diego de Vargas and the Reconquest of New Mexico*. Albuquerque: University of New Mexico Press.

Bailey, Lynn Robinson

1966 *Indian Slave Trade in the Southwest*. Los Angeles: Westernlore Press.

Bannon, John F.

1974 *The Spanish Borderlands Frontier, 1513-1821*. Albuquerque: University of New Mexico Press.

Bloom, Lansing B.

1935 "Albuquerque and Galisteo: Certificate of their founding." *New Mexico Historical Review* 10: 48-50.

1939 "The Vargas Encomienda." *New Mexico Historical Review* 14: 367-371.

Bourdieu, Pierre
1976 "Marriage strategies as strategies of social reproduction," pp. 117-144 in R. Forster and C. Ranum (eds.) *Family and Society*. Baltimore, MD: Johns Hopkins University Press.
Brugge, David M.
1968 *Navajos in the Catholic Church Records of New Mexico 1694-1875*. Window Rock, AZ: The Navajo Tribe.
Campa, Arthur L.
1946 *Spanish Folk-Poetry in New Mexico*. Albuquerque: University of New Mexico Press.
Campbell, J. K.
1976 *Honor, Family, and Patronage: A Study of Institutions and Moral Values in a Greek Mountain Community*. New York: Oxford University Press.
Carroll, H. Bailey and J. Villasana Haggard (eds.)
1942 *Three New Mexico Chronicles*. Albuquerque, NM: Quivira Society.
Dozier, Edward
1950 *The Pueblo Indians of North America*. New York: Holt, Rinehart and Winston.
Drummond, Lee
1980 "The cultural continuum: A theory of intersystems." *Man* 15: 352-374.
Escudero, Juan Agustín
1832 *Noticias estadísticas del estado de Chihuahua*. Mexico City: Juan Ojeda.
Espinosa, Aurelio M.
1915 "Romancero nuevomejicano." *Revue Hispanique* 33: 446-560.
Fireman, Janet R.
1977 *The Spanish Royal Corps of Engineers in the Western Borderlands: Instrument of Bourbon Reform, 1764 to 1815*. Glendale, CA: Arthur K. Clark.
Flandrin, Jean-Louis
1979 *Families in Former Times: Kinship, Household, and Sexuality*. Cambridge: Cambridge University Press.
García Valdecasas, Alfonso
1948 *El hidalgo y el honor*. Madrid: Revista de Occidente.
Giddens, Anthony
1971 *Capitalism and Modern Social Theory*. Cambridge: Cambridge University Press.
Góngora, Mario
1975 *Studies in the Colonial History of Spanish America*. Cambridge: Cambridge University Press.
Gutiérrez, Ramón A.
1980 "Marriage, sex, and the family: Social change in colonial New Mexico, 1690-1846." Ph.D. dissertation, University of Wisconsin, Madison.
1984 "From honor to love: Transformation of the meaning of sexuality in colonial New Mexico," in Raymond T. Smith (ed.) *Interpreting Kinship Ideology and Practice in Latin America*. Chapel Hill: University of North Carolina Press.
Hammond, George and Agapito Rey
1953 *Don Juan de Oñate: Colonizer of New Mexico, 1595-1628*. Albuquerque: University of New Mexico Press.
Huizinga, Johan
1949 *The Waning of the Middle Ages*. Garden City, NY: Doubleday.

Kirshner, Julius

1978 *Pursuing Honor While Avoiding Sin.* Milan: Quaderni di "Studi Senesi."

Ladd, Doris M.

1976 *The Mexican Nobility at Independence, 1780-1824.* Austin: University of Texas Press.

Larson, Donald R.

1977 *The Honor Plays of Lope de Vega.* Cambridge, MA: Harvard University Press.

Leonard, Olen E.

1970 *The Role of the Land Grant in the Social Organization and Social Processes of a Spanish-American Village in New Mexico.* Albuquerque, NM: Calvin Horn.

Martínez-Alier, Verena

1974 *Marriage, Class, and Colour in Nineteenth-Century Cuba.* Cambridge: Cambridge University Press.

Meinig, D. W.

1974 *Southwest.* New York: Oxford University Press.

Peristiany, J. G.

1966 *Honor and Shame: The Values of the Mediterranean.* Chicago: University of Chicago Press.

Pitt-Rivers, Julian

1968 "Honor," pp. 503-511 in *the Encyclopedia of the Social Sciences,* 2nd ed. New York: Macmillan.

1977 *The Fate of Shechem, or The Politics of Sex.* Cambridge: Cambridge University Press.

Rubin, Gayle

1975 "The traffic in women: Notes toward a political economy of sex," pp. 157-210 in Rayna Reiter (ed.) *Toward an Anthropology of Women.* New York: Monthly Review Press.

Schneider, Jane

1971 "Of vigilance and virgins: Honor and shame and access to resources in Mediterranean societies." *Ethnology* 10: 1-23.

Snow, David H.

1983 "A note on encomienda economics in seventeenth-century New Mexico," pp. 347-358 in Marta Weigle (ed.) *Hispanic Arts and Ethnohistory.* Albuquerque: University of New Mexico Press.

Swadesh, Frances Leon

1974 *Los primeros pobladores: Hispanic Americans of the Ute Frontier.* Notre Dame: University of Notre Dame Press.

Tönnies, Ferdinad

1953 "Estates and classes," pp. 12-21 in R. Bendix and S. Lipset (eds.) *Class, Status and Power: A Reader in Social Stratification.* New York: Basic Books.

Weber, David J.

1982 *The Mexican Frontier 1821-1846.* Albuquerque: University of New Mexico Press.

Yanagisako, Sylvia

1980 "Time, ambiguity, and the norms of filial relations." Paper presented at the Conference on Theoretical Perspectives on Kinship in Latin America, sponsored by The Social Science Research Council and The American Council of Learned Societies.

CROSS-CULTURAL MARRIAGES IN THE SOUTHWEST: THE NEW MEXICO EXPERIENCE, 1846–1900

DARLIS A. MILLER

APPROXIMATELY 75,000 SPANISH-SPEAKING PEOPLE were living in the Southwest at the time of the American conquest in 1846. Although sharing a common language, religion, and Iberian heritage, they were not culturally homogeneous but were separated into several population centers, each with its distinct culture. Different dates for migration and settlement as well as geographic isolation, environmental conditions, and Indian populations contributed to the diversity among Hispanic societies in Texas, California, Arizona, and New Mexico.[1]

Similarly, each center of population developed its pattern of assimilation of Anglo-American culture. The adjustment made by Nuevo Mexicanos, for instance, was different from that made by Californios. But in each area, cross-cultural marriages between Hispanic women and Anglo men contributed to the assimilation process. Recent sociological studies have emphasized the important role that intermarriage plays in assimilation. It is used as an index of social distance and has been called the "crucial test of acceptance of one group by another."[2] In all sections of the Southwest, continuous and intimate contact between Hispanic and Anglo spouses helped to bridge cultural differences and eventually led to partial assimilation of some wives and their offspring into Anglo society.

Despite claims of one writer, who attributes cross-cultural marriages to Anglo-American land hunger,[3] Hispanic women were valued by Anglo men for many reasons: as helpmates, links to powerful Hispanic families, and as mothers, companions, and lovers. Still, women who married Anglo men typically were forced to adjust to changing environments, primarily because exogomous marriages

0028-6206/82/1000-0335 $2.50/0
© Regents, University of New Mexico

disrupted primary group relationships and thus undermined the cohesiveness of Hispanic society.

Although cross-cultural marriages occurred throughout the Southwest, scant information is available concerning their frequency, quality, or socioeconomic impact.[4] Jane Dysart, in her study of Hispanic women in San Antonio, gives the most complete in-depth analysis of mixed marriages in Texas. She found that interethnic marriages between high-status Hispanic women and Anglo men were relatively frequent in San Antonio, where at least one daughter in almost every mid-nineteenth-century upper-class Hispanic family married an Anglo. This unleashed a process of assimilation that resulted in the Americanization of Anglo-Hispanic families; in the vast majority of cases, sons and daughters of high-status mixed marriages married non-Hispanos.[5]

Similar in-depth studies of cross-cultural marriages are lacking for others areas of the Southwest. Still, some writers offer intriguing theories about mixed unions that need to be substantiated and expanded by further research. James Officer, for example, has suggested that cross-cultural marriages in Tucson helped establish amiable relations between Hispanos and Anglos following American acquisition of that region in 1853. In later years, descendants of these mixed unions linked the two ethnic groups and "helped maintain good relations . . . in Tucson down to the present day."[6]

Mixed marriages may have muted ethnic hostility in other areas of the Southwest as well. Carey McWilliams suggests that the few hundred American and European entrepreneurs who infiltrated California during the 1820s and 1830s became "hispanicized Anglos," marrying daughters of the California elite, joining the Catholic Church, hispanicizing their names, and accepting Mexican citizenship.[7] But the assimilation of these men into Hispanic society was incomplete; at the time of American conquest, Anglo Americans enthusiastically supported the new regime and encouraged their Hispanic in-laws to collaborate with the invader. Moreover, Anglo sons-in-law imparted subtle lessons in Americanization through their wives—daughters of such elite families as the Yorbas, Sepúlvedas, Bandinis, and Picos—and these ethnic alliances assured limited cultural fusion.[8] Research is sparse concerning cross-cultural marriages in California for later years; Leonard Pitt points out, however, that marriage alliances in southern California contributed to a mixed cultural elite that was still evident in the 1880s.[9]

Few scholars of the Southwest, then, have systematically studied cross-cultural marriages. And only Dysart concentrates on Hispanic women and the role they played in mixed unions. For all areas of the Southwest, detailed information is needed concerning the frequency of intermarriage, the social class of spouses, and the tensions and stresses accompanying these unions. To shed light on these and other factors, this paper will focus on intermarriage in nineteenth-century New Mexico, emphasizing the assimilation process and the nature of social change as it affected Hispanic women. To a limited extent, women who intermarried became culturally uprooted because of the physical mobility of Anglo husbands. By focusing on New Mexico, a territory having the largest Spanish-speaking population in the Southwest in 1846, it will be possible to establish a basis for comparison with other areas.

At the time of American conquest, an estimated 60,000 Spanish-speaking settlers—four-fifths of all Spanish-speaking people in the Southwest—resided in New Mexico.[10] The Anglo-American population was considerably smaller. After Mexico achieved independence and opened its borders to foreigners in the 1820s, Anglo merchants and adventurers began trickling into the territory so that by the 1850s there was an Anglo population of between 500 and 1200 people.[11] Arriving without wives or relatives, many early Anglo settlers married into the territory's elite Hispanic families. Two daughters of the wealthy Jaramillo family, for example, married respectively Charles Bent, first Anglo governor of New Mexico, and Christopher "Kit" Carson, famous fur trapper and explorer. Henry Connelly, a Kentuckian who became well known as a merchant and later as Civil War governor of New Mexico, married into the influential Perea family, while Charles Beaubien of French-Canadian heritage married a daughter of the prominent Lovato family.[12] These marriages tied an intruding foreign population to the ruling class of New Mexico and smoothed transition to American rule.

At the time of American conquest, New Mexico was a highly stratified society in which a small wealthy class (ricos) controlled social, economic, and political power. Most New Mexicans were

Miguel Otero, Jr., with his second wife, Maud Frost Otero; Otero was the son of a Hispanic father and an Anglo mother. He married twice, both times to Anglo women. Courtesy Special Collections Department, University of New Mexico.

illiterate and poor (pobres), subsisting in small rural villages or working on large ranches. Many were held in debt peonage, which meant virtual labor for life to a wealthy land owner.[13] After American takeover, Hispanic elite were forced to share political and economic power with Anglos, but Hispanos continued to be powerful in politics and business into present times.[14]

The first significant influx of Anglos in the American era came during the Civil War, when more than two thousand Union soldiers—members of the California Column—marched from the Pacific Coast to New Mexico to help expel Confederates who had invaded the territory. More than three hundred California veterans remained in New Mexico after their discharge, adding significantly to the Anglo population.[15] Following the war, New Mexico experienced steady population growth, partly as a result of high birth rates but also because a slow but steady trickle of Anglo-American immigrants turned into a vigorous stream after railroads entered the territory in 1879.[16]

Perhaps the most distinctive characteristic of the small Anglo community in New Mexico through the 1870s was its sex-ratio imbalance. Anglo men typically arrived in New Mexico without wives or families, and in early territorial days an Anglo woman was a rare sight. This sex imbalance encouraged unions between Anglo men and Hispanic women, though other factors also contributed to the high frequency of interethnic marriages. Despite cultural and physical differences, for example, the predominant Hispanic culture had no sanctions against mixed marriages, and many Hispanic families welcomed Anglos into their homes, thus filling a void for the newcomers caused by loss of intimacy and family life.[17] In addition, potential barriers to intermarriage were eliminated due to the isolation of Anglos from more restrictive eastern mores. Nonetheless, Anglo Americans were color-conscious and generally chose lighter-skinned women for mates. But this practice paralleled the Hispanic custom of equating lighter skin with higher social class.[18] Certainly differences in skin color did not prevent social intermingling and intermarriage; socially isolated Anglo men welcomed friendships and social contacts within the Hispanic community.

It is true that European and American visitors to New Mexico in the early years were highly critical of Hispanic society, although they reserved their harshest judgements for lower-class customs and mores. These observers frequently recorded in letters and diaries the alleged sins as well as virtues of New Mexican women. Many criticized the women's attitudes about marriage vows and their general moral laxity; others were shocked by their immodest attire.[19]

Opinions varied regarding the physical attractiveness of Hispanic women. A twenty-nine-year-old private stationed in New Mexico during the Civil War expressed distaste for Mexican women whom he described "as black as the ace of spades and ugly as sin." But other troopers agreed with the soldier-correspondent who listed the "sunny smiles of the Castilian beauties" as one of the pleasures to be enjoyed in the small town of Mesilla.[20] Moreover, Hispanic women were universally praised for their kindness and hospitality.[21] Although Anglos viewed their society as superior to that of Hispanos, the many Anglos who married New Mexican women indicated their need and regard for the latter.

Because Anglo migration to New Mexico during territorial days was preponderantly male, cross-cultural marriages were almost exclusively between Hispanic women and Anglo men. From early days of Spanish settlement, however, interethnic unions had characterized New World society. Many Spanish conquistadores legally married Indian women while others took them as mistresses. The presence of Spanish-speaking mulattoes in the colonial Southwest reflects similar unions between blacks and Hispanos.[22]

In post-Civil War New Mexico, cross-cultural unions other than between Anglo males and Hispanic females were rare, although some of the most prominent Hispanic men in territorial New Mexico were married to Anglo women, as for example, Miguel A. Otero and J. Francisco Chávez, each of whom served as territorial delegate to Congress.[23] Occasionally Spanish-speaking men of lesser status wed Anglo women or lived in informal relationships with Indian women. Census returns also reveal other interethnic unions. In the small mining community of Silver City, for instance, there resided in 1880 a Chinese laundryman who was married to an Hispanic woman and also an Hispanic laundress who had wed a black man.[24] Still, throughout the nineteenth century, cross-cultural marriages most frequently occurred between Anglo men and Spanish-speaking women.

Nancie Gonzáles correctly stated more than a decade ago that during the early years after American conquest "intermarriage between Anglo men and Mexican women was apparently quite common and not restricted to any particular social class."[25] Manuscript census schedules for 1870 and 1880 indicate that the overwhelming majority of married Anglo men residing in the territory were married to Hispanic women. Census data for 1870 for three small towns in sprawling Doña Ana County in southern New Mexico testify to the frequency of mixed unions. In the town of Las Cruces, 90 percent of married Anglo men were married to Hispanos; in Mesilla, 83 percent; in Doña Ana, 78 percent. A decade later percentages had declined to 69 percent and 50 percent for Las Cruces and Mesilla respectively, while Doña Ana—a small Hispanic community inhabited by only four married Anglo males—now registered 100 percent.[26]

In the territorial capital of Santa Fe, where large numbers of Anglos resided in 1870, 63 percent of Anglo family men were united in mixed marriages. On the other hand, the mining town of Silver City, inhabited mainly by unattached Anglo males, recorded a low percentage of married men wed to Hispanos—33 percent in 1870 and 23 percent in 1880.[27]

Data concerning military personnel also support the contention that cross-cultural marriages were not uncommon. Most soldiers who arrived in the territory during the Civil War were bachelors, and many who settled in New Mexico after mustering out of the service married Hispanic women. To cite but three examples: Lt. John E. Oliphant of New York married Helena Martínez in Las Cruces one month prior to his discharge; Pvt. Patrick Higgins, an Irishman, married a fourteen-year-old Hispanic girl in a Catholic ceremony at Mesilla two years before he mustered out of the service; and Lt. Albert J. Fountain, stationed at Fort Fillmore, fell in love with sixteen-year-old Mariana Pérez and married her while he was still a soldier.[28]

Nearly two hundred California veterans are listed in the 1870 New Mexico census; over half lived as single men or in households lacking women of marriageable age. Of the eighty-nine who lived in households that included their wives or women of marriageable age, ten were married to Anglo women, while seventy-nine were married to or living with Hispanic women.[29] These figures tend to support an observation made by a Santa Fe resident that in the years immediately after the war "so few of the Americans were married . . . that a married man was an exceptional man."[30] Yet the typical veteran who did marry, wed a Spanish-speaking woman.

Although many Anglo men who journeyed to New Mexico in the 1820s and the 1830s married into elite Spanish families, military records and census returns indicate that mixed marriages in subsequent years were not limited to upper-class members. Among the laboring and artisan class who entered mixed unions were farm laborers, carpenters, blacksmiths, miners, butchers, cooks, and numerous small farmers. The women who married these men frequently came from humble surroundings. Margaret Estrada performed housework in private homes and local hotels before marrying a small Lincoln County farmer. Felipa Montoya worked as a servant in a private residence in Belen before she wed a stage coach driver. María Baca was a laundress at Fort Craig during the Civil War and later married an Anglo rancher and farmer. Not infrequently these women were left destitute upon the death of their husbands. Cruzita Apodaca, a case in point, took in washing and ironing to maintain herself after her blacksmith-husband, Joseph D. Emerson, died in Socorro.[31]

For many New Mexican women, a rise in social status accompanied marriage to an Anglo. The latter generally—but not always—had more money to spend than his Hispanic counterpart and usually was better educated. Because income and literacy rates provide indirect means to assess opportunities for socioeconomic mobility, data from selected areas can shed light on this aspect of interethnic unions.

In one rural precinct bordering the Tularosa River in southern New Mexico, the average Anglo and Hispanic settler reported modest wealth in 1870. Oral tradition handed down through several generations of Tularosa dwellers affirms that when the area was settled in the 1860s, all the settlers—Anglo and Hispanic alike—were poor. The 1870 census tends to confirm this observation. Although Perfecto Armijo, a local merchant, listed his personal assets at three thousand dollars, the vast majority of Hispanos either failed to declare assets or claimed personal assets below three hundred dollars. Anglo men living in the precinct who had Spanish-speaking wives tended to have assets in excess of five hundred dollars.[32]

Educational levels in territorial New Mexico were abysmally low; the vast majority of Hispanic men and women could neither read nor write. New Mexican women who formed cross-cultural unions with Anglos generally were slightly better educated than their sisters who married endogamously. Literacy data from Santa Fe in 1870 shows that in Precinct 3, 62 percent of women in mixed unions were illiterate compared to 87 percent who married Hispanos. In Precinct 4, the figures were 74 percent and 84 percent respectively. But a great educational chasm separated men whom Hispanic women chose to marry. Only 8 percent of Anglo men who had intermarried in Precinct 3 and 9 percent in Precinct 4 were totally or partially illiterate, while the percentages for married Hispanic men were 72 percent and 69 percent respectively. If sociologists are correct in citing ability to read and write as an index of power and social standing, it is apparent that women who married into the Anglo community enhanced their opportunity for social and economic mobility.[33]

One prime factor affecting rates of intermarriage was the degree of social contact between members of different ethnic groups. Upper-class Hispanic women were less restricted than their nonelite sisters in seeking opportunities to establish social relationships with Anglo outsiders. From the days of earliest contact, social intercourse was common between Anglo men and the Hispanic elite. They exchanged visits, attended the same parties, and danced at the same bailes. Social life in Santa Fe during territorial days has been described as "a hybrid product" of a joint upper-class society.[34]

Lower-class Spanish-speaking women, nonetheless, had the opportunity to establish social relationships with Anglo newcomers. Small towns adjacent to military posts staged frequent dances where local women fraternized with soldiers. One lonely trooper reported that dances were fine amusements as "the Mexican gals are very gay."[35] Then, too, women employed as camp laundresses had ample opportunity to mingle with the troops. Because there were so many "loose women" hovering around military camps, an order issued during the Civil War stated that only married women be employed as laundresses. At least one Hispanic laundress thereafter entered into a written contract with a soldier that they live together as man and wife, though they were not officially married. Upon being discharged three years later, the soldier tore up the contract, left his "wife," and went off to Texas.[36]

The lives of some military laundresses reflected the easy morality characteristic of Hispanic society that shocked Anglo visitors in early territorial days. Describing New Mexico in the 1850s, U.S. Attorney W.W. H. Davis lamented that "probably there is no other country in the world claiming to be civilized, where vice is more prevalent among all classes of the inhabitants. . . . The standard of female chastity is deplorably low, and the virtuous are far outnumbered by the vicious."[37]

In Hispanic culture, an official system of morality demanded formal marriages, but folk practices accepted informal unions that church and state officials reluctantly tolerated. Moreover, social class shaped standards of morality. A double standard in upper-class society demanded legal marriage and chastity for women but allowed men to keep mistresses and flaunt their sexual prowess. In lower-class society, the double standard merged with folk custom that sanctioned greater sexual freedom for women.[38]

Evidence of informal unions and easy morality is scattered in a number of sources—local legislative records, church documents, census schedules, and military pension files. The territorial legislature occasionally enacted laws that legitimatized the offspring of unmarried parents, as in the case of Juana María Gonzáles and John F. Collins, former territorial Indian superintendent and owner of the *Santa Fe Gazette*.[39] Moreover, local priests recorded in baptismal records that certain children were "natural" rather than legitimate offspring of their parents.[40]

Although researchers must use manuscript census schedules judiciously, these records can provide leads for untangling community attitudes towards sex and morality. The fact that certain enumerators in 1880 described the relationship between the head of household and a woman as husband and wife did not necessarily mean that the two had been formally married. The accuracy of the relationship rested to some degree on the moral perspective of the enumerator. Most enumerators—Anglo and Hispanic alike—made infrequent use of the word "mistress" in defining a woman's relationship to the head of household, but the census taker for the predominantly Anglo mining town of Silver City repeatedly made use of that term, revealing his more puritanical approach to informal unions.[41]

Upon the deaths of military men, wives and other survivors became eligible for federal pensions. In the course of investigating their claims, federal agents recorded personal histories of many Hispanic women, and these files contain rare insights into intimate relations. Testimony by Hispanic women reveals that some had borne children out of wedlock prior to their marriage to Anglo husbands. Felipa Montoya, to cite one example, stated that she had never married prior to her marriage to a soldier in the California Column, although she had given birth to four children: two children shared the same Hispanic natural father, while two different Hispanos fathered the remaining two children.[42]

Several veterans of the California Column entered into common law marriages with Hispanic women after they left the service. One old soldier later stated in a deposition that after the war "it was very common for ex-soldiers and Mexican women to live together years before marriage and in many instances not marry until the law suggested."[43] The Dutchman Linklain Butin of Pinos Altos lived for seven years in such an arrangement with his wife Candelaria, who gave birth to two children during those years. When the old soldier became seriously ill in 1876, he and Candelaria were legally married though Linklain died a few days after the marriage. Several years later, when Candelaria applied for a widow's pension, she testified that "we had all the time we were living together intended to get married but kept putting it off thinking to be married by a Catholic priest[.] But we seldom saw one and we never had any spare money to go to one until finally he was taken sick[.] So we were married while he was on his death bed by the justice of the peace so that our children might not suffer from our failure to do so."[44]

When Butin and other members of the California Column arrived in New Mexico, they discovered a society that differed from theirs in language, customs, and mode of living, and these differences had considerable bearing on the nature of cross-cultural marriages. The traditional center of life in territorial New Mexico was the isolated village with its patron saint standing guard over the health and wealth of the community. Margaret Mead has stated succinctly that "to be Spanish American is to be of a village."[45] It was from the village that an individual gained identity, rather than from a larger national or cultural entity, and an intricate webb of kinship fused village members into a cohesive and supportive folk society.

To be Hispanic American, again quoting Margaret Mead, "is to belong to a *familia*."[46] Spanish culture valued large families, and in New Mexico extended families, consisting of parents, children, and a wide circle of relatives, were common. The familia did not reside always under the same same roof but frequently consisted of several households in proximity that together functioned as a unit.

The Hispanic family was patriarchal in structure; authority of the father—and of the oldest male—was unquestioned. In return, the patriarch owed loyalty to the family and was responsible for its welfare. This paternalistic and authoritarian institution demanded submissiveness in women who were regarded by males as irrational, childlike, and in need of strong discipline. The appropriate role for a woman was as housekeeper and mother because her interests centered on producing children and caring for the family. Although census records reveal that some Hispanic women worked outside the home, chiefly as laundresses, servants, and occasionally as teachers, there was no basic alteration in prescribed sex roles throughout the nineteenth century. Women were family oriented and expected to stay at home.[47]

Despite other differences, Anglo and Hispanic societies were both masculine oriented and each assigned subordinant roles to women. Submissiveness in Hispanic wives suited Anglo men since this behavior was also prescribed in Anglo society. Unfortunately, diaries, letters, and journals written by Hispanic women are rare, making it difficult to assess the impact that interethnic marriages had on Hispanic women. To pose one important question, did marriage to an Anglo male force Spanish-speaking women to alter role expectations? Based on available evidence, the answer apparently is no. The vast majority of Hispanic women who married

Anglo men cared for children and households.[48] It should be noted, however, that although Anglo men expected women to be submissive, they also valued women as helpmates and companions. These Anglo-oriented values may have placed subtle pressures on women to modify traditional behavior and indeed may have increased their power and independence.[49]

Although the quality and essence of family life within a cross-cultural marriage cannot be restructured with absolute certainty, it is possible to speculate on what it meant to be an Hispanic woman married to an Anglo man. Interethnic marriages tend to break down cultural differences and to cause partial assimilation of one or both partners into their spouse's society. Researchers have pointed out, however, that ethnic identities are hardy things, difficult to erode, and, certainly, New Mexico proved to be no melting pot.[50] Still, Hispanic women who married Anglo husbands experienced subtle pressures for change that women who married in the traditional manner did not encounter. And although the first foreigners to enter New Mexico in the 1820s may have blended into Hispanic society, newcomers who arrived following annexation toiled to re-establish social institutions and the amenities that they had known in former homes. Rather than being assimilated into Hispanic society, Anglo husbands became agents for social change.

Possibly the greatest strain many women endured in cross-cultural marriages was their physical removal from village and familia. Nineteenth-century American society was extremely mobile; pioneers moved from one section of the country to another to exploit natural resources and to build new careers in distant and oftentimes unsettled regions. Anglo men who migrated to the territory and subsequently married Hispanic women were themselves examples of this mobile society, and their restlessness continued in New Mexico. Their Hispanic wives frequently found themselves in regions distant from former homes when they accompanied husbands to isolated ranches, raw mining camps, and even to regions outside the territory. These women were separated not only from Hispanic friends and relatives but oftentimes from female companionship as well.

Silver City, which emerged in 1870 as a rough mining camp in southwestern New Mexico, illustrates the isolation all women experienced who followed husbands in their search for quick wealth. When the census was recorded for that year, the camp had a population of eighty people, the overwhelming majority of whom were Anglo males. Two Anglo-American women accompanied their husbands to the mines, while four Hispanic women resided there, one of whom was married to an Anglo miner. Conditions were similar in the nearby mining camp of Ralston where in 1870 six Hispanic women were living with Anglo men in nuclear households. The camp was devoid of Anglo women.[51] In both camps Hispanic women were deprived of the rich religious life and kinship ties that animated and strengthened traditional society.

Some Spanish-speaking wives followed Anglo husbands beyond the borders of the territory. Yeneca Montoya married her Anglo husband in 1865 in the small town of Sapello forty miles east of Santa Fe; at the time of her death thirty-two years later she was living at Tascosa, a lawless town in the Texas Panhandle. Children born to Juana Barela testify to the mobile life that she led following her marriage to miner John Van Order at Silver City in 1879. Her first child was born in Clifton, Arizona, her second in Chihuahua, Mexico, and the following two in El Paso, Texas, and Morenci, Arizona. Juana herself died in 1910 at Salomonville in Arizona territory. Occasionally Hispanic women accompanied their soldier-husbands eastward after leaving the service. Tersita Vigil of Las Cruces, for example, married Capt. Thomas P. Chapman in 1864 and subsequently moved with him to Iowa and then Nebraska where they settled on a homestead. Following his death in the seventies, Tersita returned to New Mexico.[52]

Like other frontier women, Hispanic wives who moved to sparsely populated regions commonly were left to fend for themselves when Anglo husbands were absent for long periods of time. This was true of women who lived in the small agricultural community of Mimbres, some twenty miles northeast of Silver City, since the men of that community frequently journeyed to distant mines or to the county seat to attend district court.[53] Although the town had a total population of 180 in 1870 and had ceased to exist as a viable community by the following decade, its brief history illustrates conditions affecting assimilation in cross-cultural marriages. Mimbres was inhabited in 1870 by fifty adult Hispanic women, forty-three adult

Hispanic men, five adult Anglo women, and forty-one adult Anglo men. Fourteen of the latter were married to Hispanic women while five had Anglo wives. Some Mimbres women who had intermarried may have had relatives among the town's Hispanic population, but the large number of Anglos undoubtedly had a stronger Americanizing influence on women of mixed marriages than on those who had married endogamously.[54]

In Mimbres, as elsewhere, the ethnic tendency to congregate meant that Anglo men frequently socialized with other Anglos, and their Hispanic wives therefore came into greater contact with non-Hispanic values. Moreover, at least fourteen Mimbres residents had served in the California Column, and they retained their identity as "Column Men" or "California boys" for the rest of their lives. This unique martial bond strengthened the Anglo community and to some extent neutralized the lack of familial ties among Anglos, as for example, when Helena and John E. Oliphant chose Josiah Hull, a former soldier in the California Column, as a godparent for their youngest son, rather than choosing, say, a Hispanic relative. Moreover, several former soldiers, including Oliphant, persuaded relatives to join them in New Mexico, thus providing further reinforcements for the Americanization of their families.[55]

The ethnic tendency to club together is vividly reflected in settlement patterns as disclosed in manuscript census returns. Census enumerators were instructed to list adjacent households consecutively, and even allowing for errors of omission their tabulations reveal the ethnic composition of a community or district. To cite but one example, about 640 individuals resided in Precinct 4 of Lincoln County in 1870. Seventeen were adult Anglo men, ten of whose names are listed seriatim in the census for that year. Of the ten Anglos living in close proximity, five were married to Hispanic women and one to an Anglo woman. Since households in this rural precinct were widely dispersed, Hispanic women in mixed marriages were more likely to have Anglos rather than Hispanos for their nearest neighbors. In addition, the five Anglo-Hispanic families lived in nuclear households, bereft of additional Hispanic relatives who might have counterbalanced the Americanizing influence on Spanish-speaking wives and their children.[56]

Anglos not only settled in proximity, they jointly worked to change

New Mexico society so that it more closely resembled that found in more settled portions of the United States. Anglo men married to Spanish-speaking women helped spearhead the drive for public education that arose in the territory in the 1870s and 1880s, although some sent their children east for schooling, a procedure greatly accelerating the process of assimilation. In addition to tax-supported education, Anglo men sponsored public lyceums, organized musical and theatrical events, joined fraternal lodges and veterans organizations—all of which served as vehicles for community improvement as well as forums for political discussion. Clearly, substantial numbers of Anglo men who wed New Mexican women formed primary social and fraternal ties with other Anglos, thereby exerting pressure upon their families to assimilate into Anglo society. Thus, Hispanic wives frequently participated in fraternal activities organized by their Anglo husbands. By 1890, for example, a ladies' auxiliary of the Grand Army of the Republic had been formed in Las Cruces. All but two of its forty-two members were either Anglo women or Hispanic wives and daughters of Anglo men.[57]

Husbands also placed pressures on Hispanic wives to adopt Anglo-American health practices. One army sergeant stationed at Fort Craig had the post doctor attend his Hispanic wife during pregnancy. When she went to nearby La Mesa to be among her family for final delivery, her husband insisted that the post doctor continue to see her at the family home.[58]

Although large numbers of mixed marriages endured until the death of one partner, some ended in divorce. Divorce was not very common in the Spanish Southwest because of strong religious sanctions against it, and, although no statistical study has been made, available evidence indicates that Hispanic women who married Anglo men were more likely to experience divorce than New Mexican women married within the Hispanic community. Some divorces came after Anglo husbands abandoned their Hispanic wives. Francisca Taylor of Mesilla, for example, was granted a divorce from her husband after the courts judged Robert Taylor guilty of "Cruelty and Abandonment."[59]

A second woman abandoned by her Anglo husband was Rosario Catanach. The daughter of a Kentucky-born father and a Hispanic mother, Rosario had married David Catanach in 1867 at the age of fifteen. Over the next fifteen years, Rosario gave birth to thirteen children, including three pairs of twins. Living in Santa Fe, Rosario experienced a mental breakdown after the premature birth of her last child during the spring of 1881. One son James reported that David deserted his wife a few months after her illness and subsequently went to Lincoln County where he established a ranch. A second son John believed the cause of separation was his father's hard drinking—"he would be drunk for a week at a time"—rather than his mother's breakdown. A third son Archibald felt that the separation was caused by his grandparents; they took Rosarîo to their home after she became ill, claiming that David was not providing her proper care. Although Catanach was granted a divorce in 1885, he subsequently deeded property he owned in Santa Fe to Rosario and her children. He later left the territory and never again saw his children.[60]

If divorce was more common among women who intermarried, so too was the potential for internal stress during times of ethnic conflict. One of the most notorious lawless episodes in New Mexico's history involved the Socorro vigilantes who split the town of Socorro into two armed camps pitting Anglos against Hispanos. In 1880 Socorro was a thriving community of about 1300 people located on the Rio Grande river seventy miles south of Albuquerque. Gold and silver had been discovered in nearby mountains, and the town was full of prospectors and drifters looking for new opportunities.

The tragedy that led to violent ethnic conflict occurred Christmas Eve 1880 when three brothers by the name of Baca, nephews of the leading Hispanic merchant in the city, killed the editor of the local newspaper. The machinery of the law was in the hands of Hispanos, who backed the powerful Baca family in protecting the brothers. Subsequently, a vigilante group was formed by Anglo members of the community, headed by Col. E. W. Eaton, veteran of the Civil War who was himself married to an Hispanic woman. The vigilantes held daily meetings, and membership became practically compulsory for Anglos of any standing in the community. The 1880 census for Socorro lists the names of 109 Anglo men, ten of whom were married to Anglo women and sixteen married to

Hispanos. Unfortunately a complete vigilante membership list is unavailable so that it becomes difficult to assess the impact of Hispanic wives on vigilante membership. The fact that Colonel Eaton led the vigilantes, however, indicates that ethnic loyalties of Hispanic wives had minimal effect in determing actions of their Anglo husbands. But undoubtedly ethnic conflict placed a terrible strain upon Hispanic women and their children.[61]

Despite conflicts and tensions, marriage to an Anglo started the process of assimilation for Spanish-speaking women and their offspring. The degree of Americanization that occurred varied according to local circumstances and personalities of husband and wife. Some wives adopted an Anglo mode of living but retained Spanish customs, becoming bicultural in the process. Others took up certain external features of American culture but, for all intents and purposes, remained wedded to the traditional folk society.[62]

Scarcity of literary and oral sources, however, complicates efforts to understand the process of assimilation, and manuscript census schedules, though revealing much about household organization and residential practices, shed very little light on the degree to which individuals have accepted an alien culture. One key to the assimilation process rests with the second generation. What happened to the children of mixed marriages? Hispanic influences were undoubtedly great in early years of childhood, as parents generally had children baptized in the Roman Catholic Church and selected godparents from Hispanic friends and relatives. In many instances, households included one or more members of the mother's family.[63] At the same time, however, children underwent a variety of experiences that aided assimilation into Anglo society. Spanish was not universally spoken in the home, and it is probable that many children of mixed unions learned English as their first language.[64] Also helping to assimilate children into their father's ethnic group were attendance at schools, visits by Anglo relatives, and the presence of English-speaking neighbors.[65]

Choice of marriage partners by the second generation no doubt strengthened identification with either the mother's or the father's ethnic group. After sifting through countless marriage and baptismal records, one discovers that no single pattern emerged in New Mexico, as it did in San Antonio, relative to marriage patterns among children of Anglo-Hispanic unions. The majority of children born of intercultural marriages who can be traced in church and civil records in one county—Doña Ana—married into Hispanic society. This appears to be true of upper-class children as well as those born into families of modest means.[66] However, variations are many.

Children of mixed marriages frequently married individuals who were themselves the products of cross-cultural unions, while numerous families of mixed ancestry had sons and daughters who married into each of the ethnic groups. María Silva and David Wood of Las Cruces, for example, produced at least one daughter who married an Hispano as well as a son and a daughter who each married offspring of mixed unions. Francisca Lujan and Henry Cuniffe, on the other hand, raised at least three daughters who married Anglos, while a fourth daughter married the Hispanic sheriff of Las Cruces. In few families did all sons and daughters marry into Anglo society, whereas several families can be located whose children married entirely within the Hispanic ethnic group.[67]

Cross-cultural marriages occurred in all areas of the Southwest, bringing changes to the lives of many Hispanic women and accelerating the rate of Americanization. A decade ago, a prominent scholar challenged western historians to focus their research on the meeting of cultures in the West, to analyze and define the dynamic interaction between different peoples, as a means of providing new and fruitful insights into the settlement of the American West.[68] To understand fully the role that mixed unions played in this process, detailed studies for each major settlement area are needed. In addition, oral histories must be collected from families resulting from intermarriages. In this manner it may be possible to develop clearer perceptions of the quality of mixed marriages and to assess more carefully the tensions placed on Hispanic women who entered such unions.

Scholars generally agree that by the beginning of the twentieth century some degree of Americanization had been experienced throughout the Spanish Southwest. As one recent interpreter of this region has stated, "by a process of accretion, American ways made inroads."[69] When further studies of mixed unions are completed, it will probably be apparent that these marriages played a significant role in this process and that the New Mexico experience was reflected in varying degrees throughout the Southwest.

NOTES

1. See Rodman W. Paul, "The Spanish-Americans in the Southwest, 1848–1900," in *The Frontier Challenge: Responses to the Trans-Mississippi West*, ed. John G. Clark (Lawrence: University of Kansas Press, 1971), pp. 32–34. The best overviews of Hispanic societies in the Southwest, emphasizing their diversity, are Carey McWilliams, *North From Mexico: The Spanish-Speaking People of the United States* (New York: Greenwood Press, 1968); Matt S. Meier and Feliciano Rivera, *The Chicanos, A History of Mexican-Americans* (New York: Hill and Wang, 1972); Paul, "The Spanish-Americans in the Southwest."

2. See for example Leo Grebler, Joan W. Moore, and Ralph Guzman, *The Mexican American People: The Nation's Second Largest Minority* (New York: Free Press, 1970), pp. 405–6; Frank G. Mittelbach, Joan W. Moore, and Ronald McDaniel, *Intermarriage of Mexican-Americans*, Mexican-American Study Project, No. 6 (Los Angeles: University of California, 1966), pp. 1, 5. Quote is from Husuf Dadabhay, "Circuitous Assimilation Among Rural Hindustanis in California," *Social Forces* 33 (December 1954): 141. Although there are many definitions for the term assimilation, here it means to become more like the contact group.

3. Mittelbach, Moore, and McDaniel, *Intermarriage*, p. 45.

4. Few studies have been completed on intermarriage in the nineteenth century. Most sociologists have focused their research on twentieth-century intermarriages. But see conference paper by Richard M. Bernard, "Intermarriage Patterns Among Immigrants and Natives of Wisconsin, 1850–1920" (paper presented at the Ninth Annual Conference on Social-Political History, 1976).

5. Jane Dysart, "Mexican Women in San Antonio, 1830–1860: The Assimilation Process," *Western Historical Quarterly* 7 (October 1976): 370–72. Such was not the case in rural and isolated regions along the lower Rio Grande, however, where, according to Jovita Gonzáles, descendants of Anglo-Hispanic families attended school in Mexico and merged into Hispanic culture. Jovita Gonzáles, "Social Life in Cameron, Starr, and Zapata Counties" (Master's thesis, University of Texas, Austin, 1930), pp. 69–70.

6. James Officer, "Historical Factors in Inter Ethnic Relations in the Community of Tucson," *Arizoniana* 1 (Fall 1960): 13–14. For a recent study of intermarriage in northern New Mexico that stresses the fact that intermarriages contributed to, or were signs of, amiable relations between Hispanos and Anglos, see Rebecca McDowell Craver, *The Impact of Intimacy: Mexican-Anglo Intermarriage in New Mexico, 1821–1846*, Southwestern Studies, No. 66 (El Paso: Texas Western Press, 1982).

7. McWilliams, *North From Mexico*, p. 90.

8. McWilliams, *North From Mexico*, pp. 90–91; Leonard Pitt, *The Decline of the Californios: A Social History of the Spanish-Speaking Californians, 1846–1890* (Berkeley & Los Angeles: University of California Press, 1966), pp. 110, 125.

9. Pitt, *Decline of the Californios*, pp. 267–68.

10. McWilliams, *North From Mexico*, p. 52. Estimates of the number of His-

panos in the Southwest may need to be refined. See Oscar J. Martínez, "On the Size of the Chicano Population: New Estimates, 1850–1900," *Aztlán* 6 (Spring 1975): 43–67.

11. Robert W. Larson, *New Mexico's Quest for Statehood, 1846–1912* (Albuquerque: University of New Mexico [UNM] Press, 1968), p. 71.

12. James M. Lacy, "New Mexican Women in Early American Writings," *New Mexico Historical Review* [NMHR] 34 (January 1959): 50; Ralph Emerson Twitchell, *The Leading Facts of New Mexican History*, 5 vols. (Cedar Rapids, Iowa: Torch Press, 1912), 2: 273, 391. María Ignacia Jaramillo was the common-law wife of Charles Bent.

13. Paul, "Spanish Americans," p. 36. Communities in northern New Mexico lacked class stratification, however, and were characterized by equalitarian relations among residents. See Paul Kutsche, ed., *The Survival of Spanish American Villages*, The Colorado College Studies, No. 15 (Colorado Springs: Colorado College, 1979), pp. 15–17.

14. For a summary of the political and economic development of New Mexico until statehood, see Howard R. Lamar, *The Far Southwest, 1946–1912: A Territorial History* (New York: W. W. Norton and Co., 1970).

15. Darlis A. Miller, "A Civil War Legacy: Californians in New Mexico" (Ph.D. dissertation, UNM, 1977), p. 60.

16. Lamar, *Far Southwest*, p. 107.

17. Miller, "Civil War Legacy," p. 19. Oral history records that shortly after American takeover (and presumably after the Taos uprising of January 1847), relations between the people of Taos and Anglo soldiers were very friendly because the Americans provided protection against hated Indian raiders. "Then it was that many friendships were begun which resulted in the marriage of some of these soldiers with Spanish families, making for mutual appreciation" (Lorin W. Brown, *Hispano Folklife of New Mexico: The Lorin W. Brown Federal Writers' Project Manuscripts* [Albuquerque: UNM Press, 1978], p. 64).

18. Dysart, "Mexican Women," pp. 367–68.

19. Beverly Trulio, "Anglo-American Attitudes Toward New Mexican Women," *Journal of the West* 12 (April 1973): 229–39; W. W. H. Davis, *El Gringo: or New Mexico and Her People* (1857; reprint ed., New York: Arno Press, 1973), pp. 221–22.

20. Miller, "Civil War Legacy," pp. 38–39.

21. Lacy, "New Mexican Women," p. 41. See also Robert C. and Eleanor R. Carriker, eds., *An Army Wife on the Frontier: The Memoirs of Alice Blackwood Baldwin, 1867–1877* (Salt Lake City: University of Utah Library, 1975), p. 59; Martha Summerhayes, *Vanished Arizona: Recollections of the Army Life of a New England Woman* (Glorieta, N. Mex.: Rio Grande Press, 1970), p. 144.

22. Francisco Terán, "The Conquistadors' Ladies," *Américas* 28 (February 1976): 12–18; Jack D. Forbes, "Black Pioneers: The Spanish-Speaking Afroamericans of the Southwest," *Phylon* 27 (Fall 1966): 233–46.

23. Carolyn Zeleny, *Relations Between the Spanish-Americans and Anglo-*

Americans in New Mexico: A Study of Conflict and Accommodation in a Dual-Ethnic Situation (New York: Arno Press, 1974), p. 319; Tibo Chavez, "Colonel Jose Francisco Chavez, 1833–1904," *Rio Grande History* 8 (1978): 7.

24. U.S., Department of Commerce, Bureau of the Census, *Tenth Census of the United States, 1880*, Grant County, New Mexico, Population Schedules, National Archives (NA) Microfilm No. T 9, reel 1.

25. Nancie L. González, *The Spanish-Americans of New Mexico: A Heritage of Pride* (Albuquerque: UNM Press, 1967), p. 80. Recent scholarship states erroneously that "intermarriage was not a common phenomenon, but rather restricted to marriages between *ricos* and Anglos designed to serve their common economic and political interests" (Alvin R. Sunseri, "Anglo Attitudes Toward Hispanos, 1846–1861," *Journal of Mexican American History* 3 [1973]: 77).

26. Thirty-three Anglo males resided in Las Cruces in 1870; eighteen were married to Hispanic women, and two were married to Anglo women. In 1880 sixty-one Anglo males resided there; eighteen were married to Hispanic women, and eight to Anglo women. Thirty-eight Anglo males resided in Mesilla in 1870; nineteen were married to Hispanic women, and four to Anglo women. Ten years later, sixty Anglo males resided in Mesilla; twelve were married to Hispanos, and twelve to Anglos. In 1870 eleven Anglo males lived in the village of Doña Ana; seven were married to Hispanic women, and two had married Anglo women. In 1880 six Anglo males lived in Doña Ana; four were married to Hispanic women, but none was married to an Anglo. U.S., Department of Commerce, Bureau of the Census, *Ninth Census of the United States, 1870*, Doña Ana County, New Mexico, Population Schedules, NA, Microfilm Publication 593, reel 1; *Tenth Census, 1880*, Doña Ana County. Mixed marriages were identified by place of birth in conjunction with surnames of spouses.

27. *Ninth Census, 1870*, Santa Fe County, reel 4; *Ninth Census, 1870*, Grant County, reel 1; *Tenth Census, 1880*, Grant County, reel 1.

28. John D. Oliphant and Patrick Higgins, Pension Application Files, Civil War Series, Records of the Veterans Administration, Record Group (RG) 15, NA; Arrell Morgan Gibson, *The Life and Death of Colonel Albert Jennings Fountain* (Norman: University of Oklahoma Press, 1965), p. 23.

29. Miller, "Civil War Legacy," p. 338.

30. Lycurgus D. Fuller, Pension Application Files, RG 15, NA.

31. For occupations of men who intermarried, see entries for New Mexico in the 1870 and 1880 census. For women mentioned in this paragraph, see respectively Pension Application Files for Henry C. Brown, Allen Buchanan, Henry Hays, and Joseph D. Emerson, RG 15, NA. During the 1860s, Vincenta Fresquez escaped from peonage to live with an Anglo soldier in Las Cruces. She was later arrested by the sheriff of Doña Ana County and returned to her master, Cristobal Ascarate of Mesilla, to repay a debt contracted by her mother. Ascarate forced Vincenta to work with a chain fastened to her leg (Testimony of Sergeant John W. Carey, 20 April 1864 and Testimony of Vincenta Fresquez, 21 April 1864,

Letters Received by the Office of the Adjutant General, Main Series, 1861–1870, RG 94, NA Microfilm Publication M-619, roll 284).

32. *Ninth Census, 1870*, Lincoln County, precinct 4, reel 2.

33. But see Harvey J. Graff, *The Literacy Myth: Literacy and Social Structure in the Nineteenth-Century City* (New York: Academic Press, 1979). Percentages were computed from data recorded for precincts 3 and 4, Santa Fe County (*Ninth Census, 1870*).

34. Zeleny, *Relations Between the Spanish-Americans and Anglo-Americans*, p. 315. For a good discussion of conditions affecting rates of intermarriage, see Robert K. Merton, "Intermarriage and the Social Structure: Fact and Theory," in *The Blending American: Patterns of Intermarriage*, ed. Milton L. Barron (Chicago: Quadrangle Books, 1972), p. 15.

35. Ernest Marchand, ed., *News From Fort Craig, New Mexico, 1863. Civil War Letters of Andrew Ryan, with the First California Volunteers* (Santa Fe: Stagecoach Press, 1966), p. 72.

36. Henry Hays, Pension Application Files, RG 15, NA. Laundresses and their soldier-husbands lived in a highly stratified military society. A wide gulf separated commissioned officers from all other military personnel, and this caste system extended to wives and children. Because of the nature of their work, Anglo and Hispanic laundresses at frontier posts had ample opportunity for social intercourse, and social isolation from officers' wives generated a unique female world where ethnic differences had less impact than social class.

37. Davis, *El Gringo*, pp. 220–21.

38. Woodrow Borah and Sherburne F. Cook, "Marriage and Legitimacy in Mexican Culture: Mexico and California," *California Law Review* 54 (May 1966): 960–61.

39. "An Act for the Legitimation of Juana Francisca Collins, daughter of John F. Collins and Juana Maria Gonzales," 25 December 1869, Records of the Territorial Legislative Assembly, Territorial Archives of New Mexico [TANM], State Records Center and Archives [SRCA], Santa Fe, reel 4.

40. Baptismal Books, San Albino Church, Mesilla, N. Mex.

41. *Tenth Census, 1880*, Grant County, reel 1.

42. Allen Buchanan, Pension Application Files, RC 15, NA.

43. Linklain Butin, Pension Application Files, RG 15, NA.

44. Linklain Butin, Pension Application Files, RG 15, NA. A former private in the California volunteers declared that he had three natural children by a Hispanic woman whom he later married after obtaining a divorce from his previous wife. See Edwin L. Elwood, pension Application Files, RG 15, NA.

45. Margaret Mead, ed., *Cultural Patterns and Technical Change* (New York: New American Library, 1955), p. 152.

46. Mead, *Cultural Patterns*, p. 153.

47. For discussion of Hispanic families, see Mead, *Cultural Patterns*, pp. 153–57; Dysart, "Mexican Women," pp. 366–67; R. Griswold del Castillo, "La Familia

Chicana: Social Changes in the Chicano Family of Los Angeles, 1850–1880," *Journal of Ethnic Studies* 3 (Spring 1975): 42–43; Robert Staples, "The Mexican-American Family: Its Modification Over Time and Space," *Phylon* 32 (Summer 1971): 179–92. For a more optimistic view of women's independence, see Janet Lecompte, "The Independent Women of Hispanic New Mexico, 1821–1846," *Western Historical Quarterly* 12 (January 1981): 17–35.

48. This conclusion is based on pension application files of the California veterans who married Hispanic women as well as census returns for counties of Doña Ana, Grant, Lincoln, Santa Fe, and Socorro.

49. For corroboration of this point in the field of literature, see Cecil Robinson, *With The Ears of Strangers: The Mexican in American Literature* (Tucson: University of Arizona Press, 1963), pp. 84, 93.

50. Ithiel de Sola Pool, "Plural Society in the Southwest: A Comparative Perspective," in *Plural Society in the Southwest*, ed. Edward H. Spicer and Raymond H. Thompson (Albuquerque: UNM Press, 1972), p. 323; Marc Simmons, *New Mexico: A Bicentennial History* (New York: W. W. Norton and Co., 1977), p. 164.

51. *Ninth Census, 1870*, Grant County, reel 1. Ralston had a population of 174, which included eighteen Hispanic men and eleven Hispanic women (six of the latter were married to Anglos).

52. For women mentioned in this paragraph, see the Pension Application Files of Theodore Briggs, John Van Order, and Thomas P. Chapman, RG 15, NA.

53. See, for example, John E. Oliphant, Pension Application Files, RG 15, NA. Oliphant, who was living in Mimbres with his wife Helena Martinez in 1870, had been gone a month prospecting and working in the mines at Ralston before he returned home and subsequently died of an unknown illness.

54. *Ninth Census, 1870*, Grant County, reel 1.

55. John E. Oliphant, Pension Application Files, RG 15, NA. Oliphant's children were sent east to live with Anglo relatives after their father's death.

56. *Ninth Census, 1870*, Lincoln County, reel 2.

57. Miller, "Civil War Legacy," pp. 339–43, 346–51; Phil Sheridan Post Day Book, Grand Army of the Republic, p. 41, Branigan Library, Las Cruces, N. Mex. It has not been possible to identify the ethnic origin of all auxilliary women married to Anglo men.

58. See statement of Robert A. Christian, 19 March 1866, Southern District of New Mexico, Department of New Mexico, Records of the United States Army Continental Commands, 1821–1920, RG 393, NA.

59. Civil and Criminal Records (1878–1881), Doña Ana County Records, Doña Ana County, N. Mex., p. 339.

60. David N. Catanach, Pension Application Files, RG 15, NA; Civil and Criminal Records (1884–1885), Doña Ana County Records, p. 45; Deed Book R, Santa Fe County Records, SRCA, p. 410.

61. *Tenth Census, 1880*, Socorro County, reel 3; Chester D. Potter, "Reminiscences of the Socorro Vigilantes," ed. by Paige W. Christiansen, NMHR 40

(January 1965): 23–54. Eventually, one Baca brother was hanged by the vigilantes, one was killed trying to escape jail, and one was acquitted in a court of law.

62. Margarita Romero, "descendant of the great dons of Spanish New Mexico," who married Robert Taylor, a young railroad engineer, exemplifies those Hispanic women who functioned effectively in both Anglo and Hispanic cultures (George Fitzpatrick, "Doña Margarita: Symbol of Lifestyle Now Gone," *Albuquerque Journal*, 14 November 1976. This is not the same Robert Taylor who abandoned his wife.). Dolores Fields and Alvina Walters of Tularosa, on the other hand, are examples of those women who remained tied to traditional Hispanic culture (Interview with Antonio Candelario, 31 May 1977, Las Cruces, N. Mex.).

63. See *Ninth Census, 1870*, and *Tenth Census, 1880*; Baptismal Books, San Albino Church, Mesilla, N. Mex.

64. See family history compiled by Arthur R. Curule, December 1977, New Mexico State University (in possession of the author); Brown, *Hispano Folklife*, p. 8.

65. Census records for the city of Las Cruces indicate that the majority of school-age children of mixed marriages were attending school (*Ninth Census, 1870*, Doña Ana County, reel 1, and *Tenth Census, 1880*, Doña Ana County, reel 1).

66. In addition to sources already cited, the following were utilized in tracing cross-cultural marriages in Doña Ana County: Doña Ana County Church Records (Marriages and Baptisms), Microfilm Collection, Church of Jesus Christ of Latter-day Saints, Salt Lake City, Utah; Marriage Records, 1870–1921, Doña Ana County Records.

67. Diversity characterized marriage patterns in the third generation as well. Grandchildren of mixed unions on occasion married into the opposite ethnic group as did their own mother or father, the offspring of the original mixed union. Leopoldo Reinhard of German extraction, for example, married Francisca Montes; their daughter May wed Horace Hickerson, also of German descent. The Hickerson's daughter Pauline subsequently married Felipe López. But the reverse also occurred. A son of Mariana Pérez and Albert J. Fountain wed an Hispano, while a child of this new union married into the Anglo community.

68. Jack D. Forbes, "Frontiers in American History and the Role of the Frontier Historian," *Ethnohistory* 15 (Spring 1968): 203–35.

69. Simmons, *New Mexico*, p. 164.

Race, Sex, and Region: Black Women in the American West, 1850–1920

Lawrence B. de Graaf

The author is professor of history in California State University, Fullerton.

THE EXPERIENCES OF BLACKS IN THE settlement of the American West have received considerable attention from scholars in the last decade, but little of the literature deals with black women. This omission is partly rooted in the oversight by historians of the role of women in general, but it may also reflect an uncertainty as to the perspective from which to treat the topic. Women's history, western history, and black history have each developed distinct interpretations. Scholars need to ask: Did black women have essentially the same experiences as white women? Were their experiences dictated more by race or class or region? This article attempts to answer these questions by first analyzing the demographic characteristics of western black women and then by comparing their experiences with those of white women.

How "the West" is defined is crucial to the conclusions reached about black women. Most blacks residing west of the Mississippi River from the frontier era to the early twentieth century were in Missouri, Texas, Arkansas, Louisiana, and Oklahoma. Their history was dominated by southern institutions growing out of slavery and its aftermath, and several scholars have argued that their experiences should be interpreted on the basis of class rather than race.[1] In the remainder of the West, however, blacks were much less numerous, and their relations with whites were as likely to have been shaped by the frontier experience as by southern institutions. This study will omit the trans-Mississippi states with a predominantly southern culture and concentrate primarily on blacks living in the Rocky Mountain and Pacific Coast states (Arizona, New Mexico, Utah, Nevada, Colorado, Idaho, Montana, Wyoming, Washington, Oregon, and California) and secondarily on those living in states and territories of the Great Plains outside the South (North Dakota, South Dakota, Nebraska, Kansas, Minnesota, and Iowa).

The most outstanding feature of blacks in the West was their small number. In relation to whites, black women, like men, made up a miniscule portion. There were only 392 black women in the non-slave states west of the Mississippi in 1850, and they comprised less than three-tenths of one percent of the area's total female population. Black women never reached one percent of the females in the Mountain and Pacific states through 1920. Only in Kansas did they become a substantial segment of the total population, composing 5.3 percent in 1870 and 4.6 percent in 1880.[2] When compared to Asian immigrants, however black women assume greater numerical significance. Because Chinese immigrants and Japanese prior to 1910 were overwhelmingly male, black women outnumbered Asian females in the Mountain and Pacific states from 1880 through 1910. East of the Rockies, they were the largest female minority in most states.[3]

---

[1]See especially Jonathan M. Wiener, "Class Structure and Economic Development in the American South," *American Historical Review*, LXXXIV (1979), 970–992; Eugene D. Genovese, *Roll, Jordan, Roll: The World the Slaves Made* (New York, 1974).

[2]U.S. Bureau of the Census, *Negro Population in the United States, 1790–1915* (Washington, D.C., 1918; reprint 1969), 29, 33; U.S. Bureau of the Census, *Historical Statistics of the United States: Colonial Times to 1957* (Washington, D.C., 1960), 12; U.S. Bureau of the Census, *Negroes in the United States, 1920–1932* (Washington, D.C., 1935), 13; U.S. Census Office, *Ninth Census*, Vol. 1: *Statistics of the Population of the United States* (Washington, D.C., 1872), 606–609; U.S. Census Office, *Tenth Census*, Vol. 1: *Statistics of the Population of the United States* (Washington, D.C., 1883), 542–545.

[3]Black females were undoubtedly not as numerous as Indian women in the West until the early 1900s, when they exceed them in the Pacific states. There are no reliable figures on Native Americans until 1900. Censuses from 1870 through 1890 limited their enumeration to "Civilized Indians." Even this group outnumbered black women

TABLE I
WHITE AND BLACK SEX RATIOS IN ROCKY MOUNTAIN AND PACIFIC COAST STATES, 1850–1920

Females per 1,000 Males	1850	1860	1870	1880	1890	1900	1910	1920
Black	199	456	635	707	635	766	828	758
White	593	456	682	707	735	805	792	884

SOURCES: U.S. Census Office, *Seventh Census of the United States: 1850* (Washington, D.C., 1853), xlii, xliv; *Population of the United States in 1860* (Washington, D.C., 1864), 593–595; *Ninth Census* (Washington, D.C., 1872), I, 606-609; *Tenth Census* (Washington, D.C., 1883), I, 542–545; *Report on the Population of the United States at the Eleventh Census* (Washington, D.C., 1895), Part I, p. 488; *Twelfth Census of the United States, 1900: Population* (Washington, D.C., 1902), Part II, xxii, xxiv; U.S. Bureau of the Census, *Thirteenth Census of the United States, 1910: Abstract* (Washington, D.C., 1913), 24, 100; *Thirteenth Census of the United States, 1910: Population—General Report and Analysis* (Washington, D.C., 1913), I, 267, 269–271; *Fourteenth Census of the United States, 1920: Population* (Washington, D.C., 1920), II, 108.

Despite their great difference in number, black and white females shared several characteristics. Both were generally less numerous than their male counterparts.[4] For both black and white women the sexual disparity was greatest in the early stages of frontier settlement, though in the case of blacks this was true only west of the Rockies. In California in 1850 there were only 90 black females in a total population of 962 blacks. Wide discrepancies between black women and men existed in Montana in the 1860s, Arizona during the 1880s, and states whose settlements long retained rural frontier characteristics, particularly Wyoming.[5]

In their urban-rural settlement patterns, however, black women were quite different from whites. Throughout the

in the West. No separate figures were published for persons of Mexican or Latin origin during this period. The probability that their female population was considerably larger than that of black women is supported by noting that the total population of New Mexico alone, which was at least fifty percent of Latin origin and had a sexual balance similar to that of blacks, was six times the Negro population of the Mountain and Pacific West from 1900 through 1910.

[4]On the scarcity of white women, see T. A. Larson, "Women's Role in the American West," *Montana*, XXIV (1941), 5; and Mary W. Hargreaves, "Women in the Agricultural Settlement of the Northern Plains," *Agricultural History*, L (1976), 179.

The more common method of expressing sex ratios, especially in census works, is males per 100(0) females. This figure is explicit for the relative number of males but only suggestive of the relative female population. Therefore, all sex ratios used in this article have been calculated to express the number of females per 1000 males.

[5]*Seventh Census*, xlii–xliv; *Tenth Census*, I, 542–545; *Eleventh Census*, I, 488.

predominantly rural West, black women concentrated in urban communities to a much greater degree than white females. In 1860, 46 percent of California's 1,259 black women lived in San Francisco, Sacramento, and Marysville, and they continued to reside mostly in urban communities through the late nineteenth century. By 1900, when racially comprehensive, urban-rural statistics first appeared, the concentration of black women in towns and cities, when contrasted with white women and the total population, showed striking differences.[6]

Since black women were more numerous than males in urban populations nationwide, their concentration in western cities was not unusual. But the percentage of women residing in towns and cities in the West exceeded that of the North or South. Black women were particularly evident in some large cities. They composed a majority of blacks in Los Angeles from 1900 through 1920 and in Denver from 1900 through 1910. They also had consistent majorities in smaller cities with large servant populations, such as Pasadena and Berkeley. East of the Rockies, women made up the greater part of the black population in several large Kansas cities.[7] Conversely, black women were much less evident than black males in rural areas. They numbered only 500 per 1,000 males in 1900, 547 in 1910, and 367 in 1920.[8]

Concentration in urban areas gave western black women a strikingly lower childbearing rate than those elsewhere, particularly in the South. Between 1900 and 1920, there were less than half as many Negro children per 1,000 women in the West as in the South; within larger cities the rate was even lower.[9] Yet the proportion of black women in the West who married was among the highest of any region. In Los Angeles, at the turn of

[6]U.S. Census Office, *Population in 1860, passim.* Rural-urban data on black women are not available in subsequent censuses until 1900. The states of the Mountain and Pacific West with the largest urban centers, California and Colorado, contained over seventy percent of black females in that area between 1870 and 1890. References to individual black women during this period are almost entirely to women in an urban setting.

[7]*Negro Population, 1790–1915,* 152, 156–157, 182, 184; *Fourteenth Census: Population,* II, 108.

[8]*Negro Population, 1790–1915,* 154; *Negroes in U.S., 1920–32,* 81; *Fourteenth Census: Population,* III, 74–1144.

[9]*Negro Population, 1790–1915,* 288, 290, 295–297; *Negroes in U.S., 1920–32,* 202, 204. The regional differences are even more pronounced when children under 5 per 1,000 *married* black women are claculated. In 1900 the South had 888, the West 398; in 1910, these regions had ratios of 757 and 315, respectively.

TABLE II
PERCENT OF BLACK FEMALES AND WHITE FEMALES IN URBAN AREAS OF ROCKY MOUNTAIN AND PACIFIC COAST STATES, 1900–1920

	Total Population			Black Female			White Female		
	1900	1910	1920	1900	1910	1920	1900	1910	1920
West	40.7	48.8	56.2	74.9	83.3	83.8	43.8	51.7	55.3
Mountain	32.3	36.0	36.4	73.7	77.6	73.5	36.0	39.3	38.9
Pacific	46.4	57.0	62.4	76.1	87.4	88.8	49.0	59.5	65.0

SOURCES: U.S. Bureau of the Census, *Negro Population 1790–1915* (Washington, D.C., 1918), 32–33, 154; U.S. Bureau of the Census, *Negroes in the United States, 1920–1932* (Washington, D.C., 1935), 81; U.S. Bureau of the Census, *Fourteenth Census of the United States, 1920: Population* (Washington, D.C., 1922), III, 74–1144.

the century, single women were so scarce that black men "inspected" incoming trains for possible mates. The dearth of children may also have reflected a higher median age among western black women.[10] In the frontier stage of settlement, and in many urban areas, women between the mid-twenties and forties comprised the largest age groups, thus placing many of them beyond the prime age for childbearing.[11]

This demographic profile suggests that a cultural pattern emerged among western black women which differed significantly from that in the South. The greater age, smaller families, and urban concentration of black women were least evident in areas adjacent to the South and most pronounced on the Pacific Coast. Apparently, many of those making the longest migrations west were a select class of blacks already living in the North, or southern blacks who were able and willing to break with their traditional culture. In either case, black women in the West, particularly California, considered themselves to be an elite. Rudolph Lapp has observed that Gold Rush blacks "were in many ways exceptional and represented a higher degree of initiative, aggressiveness and tenacity than most Americans, black or white."[12]

[10] *Negro Population, 1790–1915*, 247; *Negroes in U.S., 1920–32*, 151–152; Louis Robinson, "Richest Negro Family," *Ebony*, XVIII (Dec. 1962), 154–155.

[11] *Negro Population, 1790–1915*, 182.

[12] Rudolph M. Lapp, *Blacks in Gold Rush California* (New Haven, 1977), 269. A similar thesis is advanced in Douglas H. Daniels, "Pioneer Urbanites: San Francisco Blacks from 1850 to World War II" (Ph.D. dissertation, University of California, Berkeley, 1975).

The small number and select nature of black women in the West may be attributed in part to certain aspects of black culture, especially the strength of the family. The importance which black women attached to family unity and kinship ties discouraged movement over long distances.[13] The conditions of frontier life only reinforced this disinclination to migrate. In several respects the West was "a heaven for men and dogs but a hell for women and oxen."[14] The journey west was dreary and dangerous. Biddy Mason and her three children walked a grueling route from Mississippi via Missouri to San Bernardino, herding sheep much of the way. Clara Brown at the age of fifty-five traveled from St. Louis to Denver on the back seat of a covered wagon. Margaret Frink observed in the Humboldt Sink "a Negro woman . . .tramping along through the heat and dust, carrying a cast iron bake stove on her head, with her provisions and a blanket piled on top . . .bravely pushing on for California."[15]

The few reminiscences by black women of life on the frontier complained of the desolate environment and the primitive eating and living conditions. Williana Hickman recalled her first impression of Nicodemus, Kansas: "The family lived in dugouts. We landed and once again struck tents. The scenery to me was not at all inviting, and I began to cry."[16] Another black woman, a participant in the Oklahoma land boom of 1889, remembered life in a dugout: "it was terrible how those people had suffered to get to the homes they did not own. Some had died on the way. . . . The few left who took part in those times . . . do not wish to mention it, they were so disappointed." One Oklahoma woman recalled going to a nearby town to do domestic work to

[13]This theme has been particularly developed by Herbert Guttman, *The Black Family in Slavery and Freedom, 1750–1925* (New York, 1977). The Kansas exodus of 1879 is cited by Guttman as an example of black family stability contributing to migration to the West (*Ibid.*, 435–436). However, elsewhere he emphasizes the black woman's fear of being separated from kin as a strong restraint on blacks leaving the South in the decades after Emancipation. *Ibid.*, 209, 212–213, 264–265.

[14]This oft-cited comment first appeared in Noah Smithwick, *The Evolution of a State, or Recollections of Old Texas Days* (Austin, 1900), 15.

[15]Margaret Frink, *Adventures of a Party of California Gold Seekers* (Oakland, 1897), 92, as quoted in Lapp, *Blacks in Gold Rush*, 30; William L. Katz, *Black People Who Made the Old West* (New York, 1971), 88, 99.

[16]Topeka *Daily Capitol*, Aug. 29, 1937, as quoted in Glenn Schwendemann, "Nicodemus: Negro Haven on the Solomon," *Kansas Historical Quarterly*, XXXIV (1968), 14.

keep the family alive while the men cleared the land for farming.[17]

To such tales of hardship black women could add complaints about their isolation from other black communities and from social functions that were particularly important to them. White women had similar complaints about frontier isolation, but the small number of black women made their plight even more acute. In most parts of the West, blacks lived apart from white society, yet they had little social life in their own communities. Emma Ray, a black missionary in Seattle, described the feeling of black women in much of the West when she wrote, "There were but few of our own people in Seattle when we came in 1889 and at times I got very lonely."[18]

While sharing feelings of isolation with white women, western black women had very different experiences in the West in the areas of legal restrictions and social discrimination. Some blacks who moved to what they believed was free territory in the West still found themselves enslaved. Slavery remained a legal institution in Utah until 1862.[19] Although California's constitution prohibited slavery, owners were allowed to retain slaves "in transit" through the state, as the celebrated case of Biddy Mason revealed, and a few California black women reportedly remained in a state of servitude as late as 1872.[20] Black women and men also faced legal restrictions ranging from efforts to exclude all blacks from settlement or land purchase to denials of civil rights, public transit, and suffrage in several western states. Emancipation ended legal efforts to bar blacks from the West, but sporadic local efforts to exclude or drive them out were reported into the early twentieth century. In the 1850s and '60s most western states prohibited them from testifying against a

---

[17]Arthur L. Tolson, "The Negro in Oklahoma Territory, 1889–1907: A Study in Racial Discrimination" (Ph.D. dissertation, University of Oklahoma, 1966), 17–18.

[18]Emma P. Ray, *Twice Sold, Twice Ransomed: Autobiography of Mr. and Mrs. L. O. Ray* (Chicago, 1926), 40; Robert Athearn, *The Coloradans* (Albuquerque, 1976), 28–29.

[19]Ronald G. Coleman, "Blacks in Utah History: An Unhuman Legacy," in Helen Papanikolas, ed., *People of Utah* (Salt Lake City, 1976), 117, 112; *Seventh Census*, xliii–iv; *Population in 1860*, 595.

[20]Dorothy Gray, *Women of the West* (Millbrae, Calif., 1976), 64–66; Lapp, *Negroes in Gold Rush*, 8–9, 121.

white person. On stagecoaches in Kansas and Colorado and streetcars in San Francisco, black women were even either denied public transit or forcibly ejected and left to fend for themselves.[21]

Black women also struggled with a rising tide of social discrimination in places of business. The black press in the Los Angeles area carried frequent stories of exclusion or denial of service to blacks in the early twentieth century, and there is little reason to believe that these conditions were not typical of the status of blacks throughout the West. Restaurants outside the black community frequently refused to serve blacks, theatres refused them admission, and some department stores denied them service. They could not rent rooms in most hotels. Public recreation facilities were either closed to blacks, opened on a limited and segregated bases, or separately constructed in black and white neighborhoods.[22] These discriminations affected such daily activities of black women as shopping, and much of the resistance to such practices was initiated by them.

The earliest significant protests of black women took the form of individual law suits during the 1860s against the denial of civil rights. In California a black woman filed one of the first successful suits for the right to testify against a white person. Several black women, including the celebrated Marry Ellen ("Mammy") Pleasant, were ejected from San Francisco streetcars and filed suits which eventually compelled the streetcar lines to allow Negroes to ride.[23] In the late nineteenth century, several western states passed civil rights laws, and black women were conspicuous in using them to sue theatres for excluding them.

[21]Eugene Berwanger, *The Frontier against Slavery: Western Anti-Negro Prejudice and the Slavery Extension Controversy* (Urbana, 1967), 118; William L. Katz, *The Black West* (Garden City, 1971), 58; Elmer R. Rusco, *"Good Time Coming?" Black Nevadans in the Nineteenth Century* (Westport, Conn., 1975), 207–209, 211; Delilah L. Beasley, *The Negro Trail Blazers of California* (Los Angeles, 1919; reprint, New York, 1969), 56–65. The reluctance of some western states to guarantee blacks equal legal rights is illustrated by the defeat of civil rights legislation in Nevada as late as 1959 and 1961.

[22]"Colored Californians," *Crisis*, VI (Aug. 1913), 194; *San Francisco Examiner*, June 4, 1903; *California Eagle*, April 27, 1918, Sept. 13, 1919; Anna G. Hedgeman, *The Trumphet Sounds: A Memoir of Negro Leadership*, 30–31, as quoted in Gerda Lerner, ed., *Black Women in White America* (New York, 1972), 489–490. Segregation in public recreational facilities in the North and West was only beginning by 1920 and became more widespread and institutionalized in the next decade.

[23]Lapp, *Negroes in Gold Rush*, 207; *San Francisco Elevator*, Oct. 26, 1866; W. Sherman Savage, *Blacks in the West* (Westport, Conn., 1976), 152–153.

Some women went beyond court suits in combating exclusion from restaurants. In 1916, Sadie Cole, upon being charged fifty cents for a five cent glass of buttermilk, began a campaign to remove the "Negroes not wanted" signs.[24] A black female in Riverside inaugurated California's first suit against exclusion from municipal swimming pools, while black women's groups in Los Angeles raised money for separate playgrounds.[25] Black women seldom felt free from popular prejudice against dark skin. Occasionally such prejudice took ironic forms. When a white women's club in Oakland sponsored a talk by Booker T. Washington, most black women were excluded because the white clubwomen "did not desire the attendance of a 'large body of colored persons. . . .' " The press was yet another vehicle for prejudice. In 1915 the *Los Angeles Times*, in conducting a women's subscription contest with automobiles for prizes, announced that "no colored ladies are eligible."[26]

Some historians of women may complain that none of these conditions was unique to females. Some forms of discrimination, particularly the denial of voting rights before the Fifteenth Amendment, were unique to males. But the fact that both men and women faced discrimination and prejudice did not lessen the impact of such action on the lives of black women in the West. The same point pertains to the struggle of black women to overcome illiteracy and gain an education. This task was not as formidable in the West as in the South, for western black women had a markedly higher rate of literacy than did those in other regions.[27] This was no doubt a consequence of the select nature of the population, but it may also have reflected the

---

[24] *California Eagle*, Nov. 4, 1916, May 18, Aug. 3, Sept. 21, 1918. Other authors have suggested similar patterns of discrimination elsewhere in the West. Rusco, *Good Times*, 205–206; Athearn, *Coloradans*, 172; Beasley, *Negro Trail Blazers*, 241. See also *California Eagle*, June 6, 1914, Sept. 30, 1916.

[25] *Los Angeles Citizens Advocate*, April 2, 1921; *California Eagle*, Nov. 16, 1918.

[26] *Los Angeles Record*, Jan. 6, 1903; *San Francisco Examiner*, Jan. 8, 1903; "Along the Color Line," *Crisis*, X (May 1915), 12.

[27] In 1860 the vast majority of the nation's blacks were illiterate, but only 26 percent of black women in the West were so classified. *Eighth Census: Population*, 594–595; Census Office, *Eighth Census of the United States: Mortality and Miscellaneous Statistics* (Washington, D.C., 1866), 508. From 1870 through 1920 western blacks of both sexes had rates of illiteracy several percent below those of northern blacks and only one-third to one-fifth those of southern blacks. *Negro Population, 1790–1915*, 419; *Negroes in U.S., 1920–1932*, 243.

greater educational opportunities which the West offered to women. Girls tended to have slightly higher rates of school attendance than boys throughout the West by the early twentieth century. This pattern was most pronounced among blacks, and black girls in that region by 1920 had a higher rate of school attendance than those in any other section. The West was the only part of the nation in which over half of the high-school-aged black girls were in school.[28] There are also indications that many black families allowed their daughters to stay in school through their teens while sending their sons to work, thus following the "farmer's daughter" pattern.[29]

The relatively open access of black women to education should not be overstated, however. Black girls, like boys, faced formidable legal obstacles to their obtaining any schooling. Several western states and territories simply closed off educational opportunities for blacks. Laws passed in the 1850s and 1860s barred the admission of blacks to white public schools and made little provision for separate ones. The extent to which this policy was enforced is illustrated by the case of Sarah Lester, a light-skinned San Franciscan who "passed" into the city's only high school in 1858 by virtue of high grades but was expelled when a white newspaper discovered her race.[30] By 1880, court suits and legislation had gained admission for blacks to integrated schools in most western states. However, a few states either allowed local school segregation, particularly common in Kansas, or mandated a segregated school system, as did Arizona.[31]

The end of exclusion or legal segregation still left black girls with impediments to education. Loneliness weighed heavily on those entering all-white schools. Even in states with substantial

[28] Page Smith, *Daughters of the Promised Land* (Boston, 1970), 224; *Thirteenth Census*, I, 1116–1117; *Fourteenth Census: Population*, II, 1055–1057.

[29] This characteristic of black families is discussed in E. Wilburn Bock, "Farmer's Daughter Effect: The Case of the Negro Female Professions," *Phylon*, XXX (Spring 1969), 17–26.

[30] Rusco, *Good Time*, 80; James Guinn, *History of California and Extended History of Los Angeles and Environs* (Los Angeles, 1915), I, 384; Lapp, *Gold Rush*, 169–172.

[31] Gilbert T. Stephenson, *Race Distinctions in American Law* (1910; reprint, New York, 1969), 177–189; Charles S. Mangum, Jr., *The Legal Status of the Negro* (Chapel Hill, 1940), 79–82. By 1930, New Mexico and Wyoming also sanctioned local school segregation, but these states allowed blacks into white schools during most of the period covered in this article.

black populations, Negro girls found themselves lone representatives of their race in some schools. The first black girl to graduate from a San Francisco high school was the only Negro in a class of 1,500. A generation later, her daughter was the only black graduate of a class of several hundred.[32] Ostracism and discrimination made racial isolation more painful. Black girls were occasionally prevented from taking examinations and were referred to by teachers as "dirty," "shiftless," and "a menace to the community." Students in a Calexico high school refused to allow the black female valedictorian to sit on the commencement platform.[33]

Despite these continuing obstacles, black girls often excelled in school. Their concentration in cities gave them access to long school years which many whites in rural areas did not have. As early as 1890 in the West, a higher percentage of black girls than whites attended schools for six months or more.[34] Some black girls achieved exceptional honors, leading graduating classes in scholarship despite being the only or one of the few blacks in the school. But they also showed a higher tendency than white girls to drop out of school before graduation.[35]

As teachers, western black women had similar experiences of hardship and accomplishment. Teaching was the most accessible profession to black women, and as long as black students were denied entry to white schools in the West, black women were responsible for much of their education. Although men are credited with setting up black schools in gold rush California, a majority of the teachers were black women. Elizabeth Thorn Scott opened the first black schools in Sacramento and later in Oakland. Other women opened private schools in San Francisco and taught in Sacramento, Oakland, and Red Bluff. The end of separate schools in most western states, however, signalled the

[32]Beasley, *Negro Trail Blazers*, 121, 186.

[33]*California Eagle*, May 13, 1916; *Los Angeles Evening Express*, Dec. 2, 1919; "Along the Color Line," *Crisis*, VII (Dec. 1913), 63.

[34]*Eleventh Census: Population*, II, 169. The disparity in school terms between rural and urban schools resulted in native-born whites of native parentage (who lived largely in rural areas) having a considerably lower percent of children in school six months or more than either foreign-born whites or native whites of foreign parentage in 1890 (the only census with such data). *Eleventh Census: Population*, II, xxviii–ix.

[35]Berlinda Davison, "Educational Status of the Negro in the San Francisco Bay Region" (M.A. thesis, University of California, Berkeley, 1921) 40–43.

near demise of black women teachers. At the turn of the century, there were only 15 black female teachers west of the Great Plains, and the vast majority of them west of the Mississippi were in Kansas or other states which had segregated school systems.[36] In nonsegregated states, positions opened primarily in predominantly Negro school districts. Both of these patterns raised the issue of whether black women should acquiesce in segregated schools for the employment benefits they offered. Many teachers resolved this question by viewing black schools as an opportunity to improve the education of their race. Kansas blacks abandoned their fight for integrated schools in 1880 on the grounds that the presence of "educated black men and women . . . would greatly benefit our society as well as excite a laudable emulation in our children."[37]

Teachers comprised the elite of black working women, but their numbers were small in comparison to the total number employed outside the home. In fact, a greater percentage of black women were employed than other American women. Nationwide teenage and adult black female "breadwinners" composed 40 to 50 percent of their population between 1890 to 1920; among white women, 12 to 25 percent were so employed; among Indians and Asians, 15 to 16 percent.[38] These conditions prevailed in the West as elsewhere. While forming less than one percent of the female population of the census West, black women composed two percent of its women workers. Married black women were twice as likely to be employed as married Indians or Asians; five times as likely as white women.[39] For many white women, moreover, employment was a brief interlude between school and marriage; for some middle-class

[36]Beasley, *Negro Trail Blazers*, 173–178, 123; Lapp, *Negroes in Gold Rush*, 184; *San Francisco Elevator*, July 5 and 16, 1867; Delilah Beasley, "California Colored Women Trail Blazers," in Hallie Q. Brown, ed., *Homespun Heroines and Other Women of Distinction* (Xania, Ohio, 1926), 241–242; U.S. Census Office, *Twelfth Census of the United States: Special Report, Occupations* (Washington, D.C., 1904), 226–422.

[37]Nell I. Painter, *Exodusters: Black Migration to Kansas after Reconstruction* (New York, 1977), 50.

[38]U.S. Bureau of the Census, *Statistics of Women at Work* (Washington, D.C., 1907), 12, 20; U.S. Bureau of the Census, *Fourteenth Census of the United States, 1920: Population*, IV: *Occupations* (Washington, D.C., 1923), 362, 744.

[39]Fourteenth Census, *Population*, IV, 362.

whites it became a symbol of independence from Victorian norms of domesticity. But among black women, work was sheer necessity which neither age nor marriage would change. Black men and women generally extolled the Victorian ideal of the female as homemaker and mother, but male unemployment, restricted job opportunities, and low wages made working wives essential.[40]

Black male and female workers were concentrated in the lowest occupational strata. From 1890 to 1920 seven out of eight black women employed in the United States were in agriculture or domestic service. Outside the South, however, few black women engaged in farming. In 1890, throughout the West, only 476 were so employed, 2.4 percent of the region's black farmers. By 1920, some 1,084 worked in agriculture, comprising 6.3 percent of western blacks in that occupation. In no decade did farmers and farm laborers in the West compose over two percent of working black women.[41] The hardships of prairie and arid-land farming and the cost of equipment discouraged many, and competitive sources of farm labor left little demand for black women. In 1910, some 967,333 of them nationwide worked as farm laborers, but only 276 were in the Plains states and only 30 in the Mountain and Pacific states. Black women, more than men, seem to have equated farming with slavery.[42] Therefore, western black women generally worked in domestic service.

In the late nineteenth century, a majority of all working women earned their money in domestic service. According to several historians, in 1870 over half of the female labor force in the Mountain and Pacific states was so employed.[43] While no data on occupations and race were published until 1890, other

[40]David M. Katzman, *Seven Days a Week: Women and Domestic Service in Industrializing America* (New York, 1978), 81–84; U.S. Census Bureau, *Women at Work*, 13, 15, 20–22.

[41]*Eleventh Census: Population*, II, 348–349; *Twelfth Census: Occupations*, 155–157; *Fourteenth Census: Population*, IV, 878–1048; Lorenzo Greene and Carter G. Woodson, *The Negro Wage Earner* (Washington, D.C., 1930), 39.

[42]Schwendemann, "Nicodemus," 16–19; *Negro Population, 1780–1915*, 507–508; U.S. Bureau of the Census, *Thirteenth Census of the United States, 1910: Population*, IV: *Occupation Statistics* (Washington, D.C., 1914), 468–534. Mark Reisler, *By the Sweat of Their Brow: Mexican Immigrant Labor in the United States, 1900–1940* (Westport, 1976), chap. 4; Charlotta Bass, *Forty Years* (Los Angeles, 1960), 12–13.

[43]Larson, "Women's Role," 5; Mary P. Ryan, *Womanhood in American: From Colonial Times to the Present* (New York, 1975), 218.

evidence from earlier years indicates that western black women were much more concentrated in that occupation. A black San Francisco editor explained in 1866:

> For the colored servants there are few other occupations open, and from the effects of generations of servitude, we are compelled to acknowledge the humiliating fact that a majority of our people are better fitted for that kind of labor than any other.[44]

The few references to black women in southern California prior to 1890 mention them as domestic servants. Most women participating in the Kansas exodus worked as washerwomen or servants to augment family incomes.[45] The employment patterns of western black women after 1890 reveal a continuing concentration in domestic jobs with only token numbers in most other areas. Up to half of all those working were servants; laundress was the second largest occupation.

The concentration of black women in domestic service contrasted sharply with the occupational opportunities of white women throughout the West. The trend among white women was clearly away from domestic service into professions and retail sales and office work. Black women, on the other hand, remained a tiny fraction of white-collar employees, while composing an increasing minority of domestic workers. That servant, laundress, dressmaker, and midwife were four of the leading occupations of western black women indicates both the low status and pay of their work, and its increasing obsolescence.[46]

The conditions of domestic work aggravated its low status. Servants complained about the monotony, subservience, isolation, and degrading social stigma of their work. While some were hired specifically to cook, wash, keep house, or care for children, most were employed as general housekeepers who performed all of those tasks. Black women were much more likely to be confined to domestic service for years and to continue it after being married and having families of their

---

[44] *San Francisco Elevator*, March 16, 1866.

[45] Painter, *Exodusters*, 153–257; Harris Newmark, *Sixty Years in Southern California, 1853–1913* (Boston, 1930), 120.

[46] Katzman, *Seven Days*, 289–290.

TABLE III
PERCENT OF BLACK FEMALES IN SELECT OCCUPATIONAL CATEGORIES IN THE ROCKY MOUNTAIN AND PACIFIC COAST STATES, 1890–1920

	Total Females				Black Females			
	1890	1900	1910	1920	1890	1900	1910	1920
Domestic Service	48.1	43.6	36.6	27.9	92.2	90.8	87.4	85.3
Business/Clerical	6.7	11.4	20.9	33.0	0.4	0.6	1.2	3.1
Professional	15.5	15.7	17.3	19.9	1.9	2.6	2.8	3.8

SOURCES: U.S. Bureau of the Census, *Eleventh Census: Population*, II, 348–353; *Twelfth Census: Occupations*, 154–155, 158–163; *Fourteenth Census: Population*, IV, 54, 878–1048; *Thirteenth Census: Population*, IV, 48–49, 468–534.

own. The latter condition upset some black men who complained that black women working outside their own homes lessened respect for their race and invited discriminatory treatment. Women, on the other hand, most resented "the social stigma which rightly or wrongly attaches to it. It savors to them of the degradation of their slavery days."[47] One employer summarized the relationshp between mistress and servant: "My servant is hired to do whatever she is told to do and to be at anytime subject to my command."[48]

Economic rewards for domestic work were meagre through the late nineteenth century, but were superior to the earnings of black servants in many other parts of the country. California domestics earned between $20 and $30 a month in the 1880s and 1890s, as compared to only $10 a month in the South. By the 1920s, Los Angeles was second only to New York in the wages its servants received. The western black press advertised for women, and a few black employment agencies were established primarily to secure servant jobs.[49] However, white em-

[47]Isabel Eaton, "Special Report on Negro Domestic Service in the Seventh Ward, Philadelphia," in W.E.B. Du Bois, *The Philadelphia Negro* (Philadelphia, 1899), 467; Katzman, *Seven Days*, 246–247; *California Eagle*, Jan. 23, 1915.

[48]Quoted in Katzman, *Seven Days*, 150; Eaton, "Report on Negro Domestic Service," 444; Elizabeth R. Haynes, "Negroes in Domestic Service in the United States," *Journal of Negro History*, VIII (1923), 426–428.

[49]Katzman, *Seven Days*, 55, 246–247; Haynes, "Negroes in Domestic Service," 422, 424–425; George Hamilton Fitch, "Races and Labor Problems in California," *Chautauquan* XXXIV (1897), 431; *San Francisco Elevator*, March 16, 1866; *Oakland Sunshine*, Dec. 21, 1907; *Los Angeles New Age*, June 26, 1914.

ployers made few efforts to attract black women to the West, probably because they had an ample supply of servants from other groups. Therefore, female servants never became the dominant element in the West's black labor force or population that they were in northern cities.

Managing "hotels" and running "tonsorial palaces" were among the most prestigious businesses operated by black women in the West. Boardinghouses were one of the earliest and most widespread Negro enterprises in the West, and one of the few to obtain substantial white patronage. By 1900, seventy "hotels" west of the Mississippi were run by blacks, quite a few by women.[50] The most famous of such women was Mary Ellen ("Mammy") Pleasant. Born a slave, she was sent to Boston, married into wealth, and brought her money to California in 1849 or 1850 where she either opened a boardinghouse or gained fame as a cook and later purchased one. She had augmented her wealth by the 1860s through operating boardinghouses, investing in mining stock, and loaning money at high interest. She made several contributions to the San Francisco black community, including filing an early suit for access to streetcars, assisting runaway slaves, placing blacks in servant jobs, and allegedly helping fund the Atheneum Institute, a cultural and civic center. After 1870 she withdrew from the community to become either companion to or housekeeper for a wealthy white man. As such she allegedly invested his money and had access to many powerful figures before his mysterious death and subsequent rumors of her practicing voodoo cast her into disrepute.[51]

Less dramatic but more frequently cited by contemporary

---

[50] Savage, *Blacks in West*, 122–123.

[51] This person is so entangled with legend that historians do not agree on her last name. The most scholarly biography is W. Sherman Savage, "Mary Ellen Pleasant," in Edward T. James *et al.*, eds., *Notable American Women* (3 vols., Cambridge, 1971), III, 75–76. Helen Holdredge, *Mammy Pleasant* (New York, 1953) is the only detailed biography but it is undocumented and probably exaggerates both her influence over white men and her following in the black community. This summary has also relied on Olive W. Burt, *Negroes in the Early West* (New York, 1969), 80–83; Francis Lortie, *San Francisco's Black Community, 1870–1890* (San Francisco, 1976), 11, 14, 24–27; James de T. Abajian, comp., *Blacks in Selected Newspapers, Censuses and Other Sources: An Index to Names and Subjects* (3 vols., Boston, 1977), III, 75–76; Lapp, *Blacks in Gold Rush*, 100; Lerone Bennett, Jr., "The Mystery of Mary Ellen Pleasant," *Ebony*, XXXIV (April 1979), 90–96.

blacks as examples of upward mobility were women who combined domestic service and real estate investment. In the late nineteenth century, several black women in Los Angeles who worked as laundresses or home nurses either invested their earnings in land or became brokers for blacks seeking housing. When migration escalated real estate values, they made substantial profits.[52] Most celebrated of these entrepreneurs was Biddy Mason. Following her successful suit for freedom, she worked for a Los Angeles physician as a midwife and nurse, and at his suggestion, invested $250 in what became the downtown business district. By 1896, her total estate was estimated at $300,000. She also gained fame for her philanthropic work and support of the first African-Methodist Episcopal Church (A.M.E.).[53] Her counterpart in Colorado was "Aunt" Clara Brown, also an ex-slave, who came to Denver in 1859 and subsequently established herself as a laundress in Central City. By the late 1860s she had acquired houses or lots in five Colorado towns as well as gaining a reputation for religious work and philanthropy. Like Mammy Pleasant, she encountered adversities that left her penniless at her death.[54]

Western black women also operated hairdressing establishments, and after the turn of the century, it became their most celebrated business. In Carson City, Nevada, the only beauty parlor was run by a black woman, and black women were in similar work in nineteenth-century Los Angeles, Pasadena, and San Francisco. The business gained greater popularity when Madame C. J. Walker began marketing products for lightening complexion and growing and straightening hair. By the second decade of the twentieth century there were black hairdressers in every state west of the Mississippi except North Dakota. The

---

[52] Beasley, *Negro Trail Blazers*, 244; Newmark, *Sixty Years in Southern California*, 138; *Los Angeles Times*, Feb. 17, 1909. Newmark confuses two early Los Angeles black women, "Aunt" Winnie Ownes and Biddy Mason, whose children married and assumed the former name. Both were examples of black women who made money in real estate while working in service jobs.

[53] Donna Mungen, *Life and Times of Biddy Mason: From Slavery to Wealthy California Laundress* (N.p., 1976); Gray, *Women of West*, 66–67; *Los Angeles Times*, Feb. 12, 1909; Miriam Matthews, "The Negro in California from 1789 to 1910: An Annotated Bibliography" (Berkeley, 1955), xxiii–iv.

[54] Kathleen Bruyn, *"Aunt" Clara Brown: Story of a Black Pioneer* (Boulder, Colo., 1970), 55–81, 101, 148; LeRoy R. Hafen, ed., *Colorado and Its People* (4 vols., New York, 1948), II, 220–221, 564–565.

black press was filled with ads for hair treatments, and Madame Walker was lecturing throughout the West on her product as the secret to wealth for black women.[55] It seems tragic that a black enterprise was built on de-Africanizing women's features, but many black women relied on such devices to give them the self respect denied by white society.[56]

The West did provide a few black women with professional opportunities that were uncommon elsewhere. In the early twentieth century at least two western black newspapers were edited by women. There are occasional references to female preachers as early as the 1850s. In 1916, Los Angeles hired its first Negro policewoman. After moving to Hollywood in the early twentieth century, the motion picture industry provided black women with numerous jobs as servants and a few semi-professional careers as hair stylists and modistes. But film provided only marginal employment to black actresses. Many of the best "Negro" roles were filled by whites in blackface.[57] One of the few blacks to obtain work as an actress prior to the 1920s was Madame Sul-te-Wan. She had performed in Negro vaudeville in the East, but her efforts to obtain an acting job were repeatedly rebuffed until she was offered a role in "The Clansman." Temporarily fired on the allegation that she had provoked black protest against that film, she continued making pictures for the next two decades, but she would later note of her career that "I don't work long enough to buy a handkerchief."[58] Such was the lot of one of the few black women to enter the West's most glamorous profession.

Similar obstacles confronted black women seeking employment in sales or as secretaries. Most women hired for such

[55] N. F. Mossell, *The Work of the Afro-American Woman* (Freeport, N.Y., 1894), 24; *Pacific Coast Appeal*, Dec. 21, 1901; *California Eagle*, Sept. 25, 1915; *Negro Population, 1790–1915*, 521–522; Manuscript Report of the Census of Los Angeles County, 1870, Bancroft Library; *San Francisco Elevator*, May 17, 1873.

[56] Ray, *Twice Sold*, 36. Emma Ray emphasizes her love for fine clothes and false hair as a mask for her poverty and her lack of self-direction as a young woman.

[57] Bass, *Forty Years*, 30; Abajian, *Blacks in Selected Newspapers*, I, 221–222, 649, 716; Beasley, *Negro Trail Blazers*, 242; *California Eagle*, Nov. 25, 1916, April 10, 1925; Carleton Moss, "The Negro in American Films," *Freedomways*, III (1963), 136–137; Thomas Cripps, *Slow Fade to Black: The Negro in American Films, 1900–1942* (New York, 1977), 97.

[58] Beasley, *Negro Trail Blazers*, 239–240; *California Eagle*, July 27, 1916; Cripps, *Slow Fade*, 130, 254, 271–272, 282–283, 295.

positions were native whites. Los Angeles County Hospital did not admit black women to nurses' training until 1918, and then only in the face of a threatened strike by white nurses. In 1916, a black girl who applied for a job as librarian in Spokane was rejected by a board that expressed amazement that "a colored girl should presume to ask such a privilege."[59] From Minnesota to California blacks complained of exclusion from sales and office work. As in other occupations, there were exceptions. One Los Angeles department store replaced its Asian help with Negroes in 1917, and two Bakersfield women were managing milliner and stenographer-bookkeeper for a department store.[60] But that such cases were exceptional only emphasizes that the West offered few more economic opportunities to black females than did other sections of the nation.

Among the experiences which black women had primarily as women, the greatest concern revolved around their image in sexual affairs and their consequent treatment by both white and black men. In some respects, this problem was not as serious in the West as in the South. There was little rape or sexual abuse of black females by white males, and derogatory references to Negro immorality and criminality were usually aimed at the entire race, not specifically at females. However, the fear of being stereotyped as "bad" was omnipresent among western black women, as evidenced by numerous references to "vicious elements," vice, and prostitutes. Prostitution among black women in the West deserves consideration less as a condition which was widespread than as a potential image which many of them feared could be imposed upon all of them.

On the antebellum frontiers, black prostitutes seem to have been scarce. Delilah Beasley reported that "very few of the free women of color went astray during the wild days of the gold rush," a remarkable fact compared to the "lawlessness among

---

[59] *Los Angeles Times*, July 18, Oct. 28, 1918; *California Eagle*, May 6, 1916. The U.S. census for 1920 does not provide data on librarians for all states, but the three Pacific states had one black librarian out of 1,611; four Plains states 4 out of 1,230.

[60] Abajian, *Blacks in Selected Newspapers*, III, 723; *California Eagle*, Nov. 3, 1917, June 22, 1918; A. W. Hunton, "The Club Movement in California," *Crisis*, V (Dec. 1912), 9.

the men and women of the opposite race." Later scholars have largely corroborated her observations. Manuscript censuses report few or no black prostitutes in California cities, although there were many brothels.[61] By the end of the century, however, there are indications that the number of black women following that pursuit in some western cities may have been out of proportion to their population. "Negresses" are noted as a distinct subgroup of prostitutes in San Francisco, with a separate section of brothels. West Oakland's black community became notorious for its prostitutes. A Seattle paper complained in 1899 that " 'Eastern' harlots were giving all Negro women a bad name." Blacks both staffed and ran brothels in Los Angeles by the early twentieth century, and vice was a frequent concern of that city's black press and women's organizations.[62] In other frontier areas, black prostitutes do not seem to have been "disproportionately" present, for they followed black males to areas that had few other black women, allowing them sexual pleasure without crossing racial lines. The larger cowtowns had black bagnios, and as black soldiers moved about the frontier, prostitutes followed. The small black population could make it seem that a few black prostitutes were far greater in number, as occurred in Nevada from 1870 through 1880.[63]

That black women did not turn to prostitution in greater numbers is remarkable in light of the pressures on them to do so. While a few black women on the frontier may have chosen

---

[61] Beasley, "California Colored Women," 240; Lortie, *San Francisco Black Community*, 13–14; Lapp, *Negro in Gold Rush*, 110, 113–114.

[62] *Seattle World*, Jan. 4, 1889; Herbert Asbury, *Barbary Coast* (New York, 1933), 255, 257, 269; Jesse Kimbrough, *Defender of the Angels: A Black Policeman in Old Los Angeles* (London, 1969), 36–39, 122–124; Robert C. Francis, "A Survey of Negro Business in the San Francisco Bay Region" (M.A. thesis, University of California, Berkeley, 1928), 20.

[63] Erwin N. Thompson, "The Negro Soldier and His Officers," in John M. Carroll, ed., *The Black Military Experience in the American West* (New York, 1971), 182; Kenneth W. Porter, "Negro Labor in the Western Cattle Industry," *Labor History* X (1969), 327. Nevada manuscript censuses enumerated 4 black prostitutes in 1870 and 6 in 1880. Both numbers seem trivial compared to the 138 prostitutes in Virginia City alone in 1870, yet in both decades they amount to 1 black prostitute for every 30 black women in the state, significantly higher than the 1:50 ratio for Virginia City's total female population in 1870. George M. Blackburn and Sherman L. Ricards, "The Prostitutes and Gamblers of Virginia City, Nevada: 1870," *Pacific Historical Review*, XLVIII (1979), 245; Rusco, *Good Time*, 137, 202; U.S. Census Office, *Ninth Census*, Vol. II: *Vital Statistics* (Washington, D.C., 1886), 648; *Negro Population, 1790–1915*, 149–50.

that career for its economic rewards, most black women became prostitutes out of necessity. Los Angeles blacks in the decade after 1910 attributed nearly all their prostitution and crime to poverty. A study of that city's black delinquents found the average family of seven was subsisting on only two-thirds of the income which the federal government regarded as minimum for comfortable living. In some cases blacks turned to prostitution for material refinements. Emma Ray recalls a black prostitute in Seattle who declined pleas to quit that life on the grounds that she did not have good clothes "and if she did not have good clothes, no one would recognize her."[64] The chance that black girls would come into contact with prostitutes was greater than for many other young women since the vice centers of several cities were located in or near black communities. When Charlotta Bass in 1918 visited Imperial City, one of the few remaining red light districts in southern California, she was appalled at "the sight of cabins of prostitution right next door to homes where little Negro children played" and by city officials who "seem to think what is going on is all right."[65]

While prostitution does not seem to have been significantly more prevalent among blacks than other women in the West, it was widely associated with vice and a negative image for black women. Between 1910 and 1920 the Los Angeles black press campaigned against Chinese gambling dens and commercialized vice, and charged that by condoning such immorality, the city was allowing "macks, pimps, and whores . . . to be heralded as our leading colored citizens."[66] Some spokesmen warned that any loss of virtue could affect the image of all black women. Attorney E. Burton Ceruti told the first colored nursing students who entered the Los Angeles County Hospital:

> The enemies of our race have often sought to wound us and weaken us by reflections upon the virtue of our women . . . [and] it may be that temptation will come to you as it does at times to every woman

[64] Ray, *Twice Sold*, 84–85; Blackburn and Ricards, "Prostitutes and Gamblers," 246; *California Eagle*, Nov. 25, 1916; Homer K. Watson, "A Study of the Causes of Delinquency among Fifty Negro Boys Assigned to Special Schools in Los Angeles" (M.A. thesis, University of Southern California, 1923), 40–42.

[65] Bass, *Forty Years*, 49–50.

[66] *California Eagle*, June 12, 1915, March 15, 1919.

worthy. Whensoever . . . the suggestion is born, you . . . will recall that you are the representative of a great people whose honor is at stake and whose reputation is now on trial.[67]

Similar concerns would preoccupy many of the social organizations which black women established in the West.

Social group activities were an indispensible antidote to the hardships in the lives of black women, and their development in the West was similar to that in other sections. Through most of the nineteenth century, these activities were centered in the churches. Women were responsible for much of their fund raising, often by holding festivals or cultural events to attract whites. They were also founders of several churches in the West. Biddy Mason helped establish and for years was sole support for the first A.M.E. church in Los Angeles; Clara Brown offered her home to the earliest Methodist Church in Aurora, Colorado. Much of the charity work among the Negro poor in western towns was done either by religiously motivated black women or ladies' missionary associations. By the end of the century, such groups had raised money for the first of several homes for the aged or working girls that black churches would support in California.[68]

In some cities, benevolent or literary societies were established as early as the 1850s. By the end of the century these had evolved into black women's clubs as part of the reaction of middle-class blacks to their exclusion from white society and as a result of black women having different needs for organization than white women. Black women's clubs were less concerned with suffrage, unions, and national or global issues than with meeting community needs and particularly with raising the standards of black women and families to offset accusations of immorality.[69] In 1899, Oakland black women formed the Fannie Jackson Coppin Club, apparently the first of the most typical

---

[67] *California Eagle*, Sept. 20, 1920.

[68] Bruyn, *'Aunt' Clara Brown*, 44, 159; Lapp, *Negro in Gold Rush*, 164; Beasley, "California Colored Women," 243–244; *The Forum* (April 18, 1908), 3; *California Eagle*, March 24, 1917.

[69] Abajian, *Blacks in Selected Newspapers*, I, 74: Eleanor Flexner, *Century of Struggle: The Woman's Rights Movement in the United States* (Cambridge, Mass., 1959), 186–188; Lerner, *Black Women*, 437, 440–441.

variety of black women's clubs in the West. After 1902, they appeared in such widespread cities as Butte and Tacoma, and several were set up in Oakland and Los Angeles. In 1906 the California clubs created a State Federation of Colored Women's Clubs, and by 1920 several other western states had similar federations.[70]

The functions of most black women's organizations are epitomized by the Sojourner Truth Industrial Club of Los Angeles. Established to provide a home for orphans and unwed women, it trained them in domestic arts and service, and helped them to cultivate "intellectual and moral culture." Its building, completed in 1913, was both a home for "self-supporting girls" and a community center. The club emphasized training in service to build character and promote the dignity of all labor. The lectures, teas, and lessons in needlecraft enabled black society women to obtain a sense of recognition as community leaders and cultured females. This mixture of homeless girls and elite women served both as "a pioneer in welfare work" and an outlet for the energies of the "grander dames of the ghetto."[71]

Other black women's organizations tried to assist the large domestic servant population. The Woman's Day Nursery Association, formed in Los Angeles in 1908, cared for the children of working mothers and provided homes for those whose mothers lived with their employees or were indigent. Several other cities had "Mothers Clubs" for needy mothers and children, and by 1920 at least two other organizations had been established in southern California to improve the wages and working conditions of domestic servants.[72] Many clubs empha-

---

[70] Abajian, *Blacks in Selected Newspapers*, III, 441; Hunton, "Club Movement in California," 90–91; *Colored Directory of the Leading Cities of Northern California: 1916–17* (Oakland, 1917), 73–77. The author expresses appreciation to Miriam Matthews, Vivian Osborne Marsh, the East Bay Negro Historical Society, and Deborah Major and the San Francisco African-American Historical and Cultural Society for information on California women's clubs. Similar contact with persons prominent in black women's organizations in other western states is needed for a complete history of such groups.

[71] Articles of incorporation of the Sojourner Truth Industrial Club, California State Archives; Sojourner Truth Industrial Club, *Golden Anniversary, 1905–1954* (Los Angeles, 1954); Beasley, *Negro Trail Blazers*, 228; Cripps, *Slow Fade*, 109; "Some Facts concerning Sojourner Truth Home," box 838: Lecture Engagement file, Booker T. Washington Papers, Library of Congress.

[72] Haynes, "Negroes in Domestic Service," 435; Hunton, "Club Movement in California," 90; *Los Angeles Tribune*, April 5, 1914; *California Eagle*, May 16, 1914; Aug. 2, 1919.

sized the development of musical, literary, and artistic talents but coupled this goal with a desire to work "for the interest and uplift of humanity." Black women also became increasingly active in protest and political groups, at least one of which, the Los Angeles-based Women's Civic and Protective League, was exclusively female.[73]

The role of black women in the suffrage movement offers perhaps the clearest test of the relative importance of race, sex, and region in shaping their experiences. All suffrage victories prior to World War I came in western states, giving women there an aura of being especially conscious of their rights, and the West an image of progressive attitudes toward females.[74] If regional influences were paramount, women's suffrage should have been an important cause to western black females. From a racial standpoint, however, they had strong reasons for not making suffrage a major concern. Since the shattering of the alliance between white women and blacks with the passage of the Fifteenth Amendment, suffrage leaders had ignored injustices to blacks, justifying their attitude by noting the need for southern support.[75] Then, too, most black women were of the working class and were seldom as concerned with the franchise as were middle- and upper-class whites. This gulf widened because of the insistance of many western suffragists that only the "right" women be involved in the movement. Denver suffrage meetings made unwelcome those "women who were not intelligent and respectable."[76] Many western black women inferred that they did not meet those criteria since suffragists frequently justified enfranchising white women on the grounds that they deserved

---

[73]Beasley, *Negro Trail Blazers*, 234–235; *California Eagle*, Dec. 14, 1918; *Colored Directory of Northern California: 1916–17*, 72.

[74]T. A. Larson, "Dolls, Vassals and Drudges–Pioneer Women in the West," *Western Historical Quarterly*, III (1972), 13–14; Beverly Beeton, "Women Suffrage in the American West, 1869–1896" (Ph.D. dissertation, University of Utah, 1976), 56–58, 160–173.

[75]Aileen S. Kraditor, *The Ideas of the Woman Suffrage Movement, 1890–1920* (Garden City, 1970), 114, 158; S. Jay Walker, "Frederick Douglass and Woman Suffrage," *Black Scholar*, IV (1973), 28–29.

[76]Quoted in Beeton, "Woman Suffrage," 206; William Chafe, *Women and Equality: Changing Patterns in American Culture* (New York, 1977), 124; T. A. Larson, "Montana Women and the Battle for the Ballot," *Montana*, XXIII (1973), 32.

the vote more than some "ignorant" classes that already had it. Indians, Chinese, and Negroes were most frequently referred to in this vein.[77]

Nevertheless, some black women did participate in western suffrage campaigns and political activities. Most frequently mentioned was Naomi Anderson of Kansas, who was an official colored representative of the National American Woman's Suffrage Association in the West and played an active role in the campaigns in Kansas in 1894 and California in 1896. In the latter state, her efforts found support from the Afro-American Women's League. Sarah M. Overton was a leader in suffrage organizations in San Jose for many years and toured the state in 1911 to organize black support for the suffrage amendment. Outside California, however, there is little record of black activity in the suffrage movement. A few did become active in politics after receiving the vote. Colorado black women set up Republican clubs in 1894, and one woman became an officer in the Republican State League. Subsequently, another black woman in that state was twice a candidate for the legislature.[78]

The participation of western black women in temperance and prohibition movements paralleled their activities in suffrage. Here, too, there were reasons for them to avoid involvement. Prohibition sentiment was strongest in rural areas of the West, where few black women lived. Most large cities were "wet" strongholds, and black areas were close to establishments that depended on liquor. A Los Angeles observer found many church-going black women opposing prohibition because "it makes business dull when a town goes dry."[79] Negro women had been attracted to the early temperance movement by its religious orientation and its concern with homeless girls and vice districts, but the movement's interest in such activities declined as the leadership shifted its allegiance to the Anti-Saloon League with

---

[77] Elizabeth C. Stanton, Susan B. Anthony, Matilda J. Gage, Ida H. Harper, *History of Woman Suffrage* (6 vols., reprint, New York, 1969), V. 77.

[78] *Ibid.*, IV, 490, 494–499; Beasley, *Negro Trail Blazers*, 323; Jessie Fauset, "Out of the West," *Crisis*, XXVI (Nov. 1923), 18; *Woman's Era*, I (June 9, 1894), 18; Adella H. Logan, "Colored Women as Voters," *Crisis*, V (Sept. 1912), 243.

[79] *California Eagle*, Nov. 24, 1917; Athearn, *Coloradans*, 159–161; Joseph R. Gusfield, *Symbolic Crusade: Status Politics and the American Temperance Movement* (Urbana, 1963), 100–105.

its singular goal of legal prohibition. Black men were probably more strongly opposed to prohibition than to suffrage. A final deterent was that white temperance leaders, like suffragists, refused to take a stand against southern racial violence, a position that was especially highlighted by the exchange between Frances Willard and Ida Wells-Barnett in the 1890s.[80]

These conditions did not prevent some black women from participating in temperance campaigns. Emma Ray's missionary zeal led her into the Women's Christian Temperance Union in both Washington and Kansas. Naomi Anderson was as active in temperance work in Kansas as she was in suffrage. The California Dry Federation had Sadie Cole of Los Angeles on its executive board and several prominent black women on that city's local unit.[81] Most of these people worked in predominantly white organizations, as the black community did not encourage temperance groups. Emma Ray established a WCTU unit in an A.M.E. church in Seattle only to have its pastor persuade members to leave the organization because it conflicted with their duty to the church. Black women were admitted to western WCTU chapters, but whites did not actively solicit their membership. The Los Angeles Dry Federation had a superintendent for blacks, but the California WCTU had no such position, even though it had unions for various European immigrants and a Department of Oriental Work.[82] In sum, suffrage and temperance were important issues to a few individual black women, but they did not command the attention that racial rights or social uplift did.

The message of these experiences is clear: The activities and roles of black women in the West were shaped primarily by their being black and only to a limited degree by their residence in western states or their sex. The West was an influence mainly in that its remoteness limited the size of the black population and

[80] Gusfield, *Symbolic Crusade*, 72, 108–109; *California Eagle*, Jan. 23, 1915, Oct. 28, Nov. 18, 1916, Alfreda M. Duster, ed., *Crusade for Justice: Autobiography of Ida B. Wells* (Chicago, 1970), 150–151; Mrs. Dorcas Spencer, *The History of the WCTU of Northern and Central California* (Oakland, 1913), chaps. 12–13.

[81] Monroe Majors, *Noted Negro Women: Their Triumphs and Activities* (Reprint, Freeport, N.Y., 1971), 85; Ray, *Twice Sold*, 68, 113; Beasley, *Negro Trail Blazers*, 241; *Los Angeles Tribune*, Oct. 11, 1914; *California Eagle*, Oct. 21, 1916.

[82] Spencer, *WCTU in California*, 122–123; Beasley, *Negro Trail Blazers*, 132; Ray, *Twice Sold*, 71; Majors, *Noted Negro Women*, 85; *California Eagle*, Oct. 21, 1916.

hence precluded the formation of large racial communities. However, there is little evidence that black women were affected by the West in the manner that its influence has generally been perceived. Few black women were associated with the traditional frontier roles of farming, mining, cattle raising, or military service. The experiences of most western black women resembled those of black women in the northeastern states. They had superior educational opportunities in the Pacific states, and they were less subject to sexual abuse by whites in the West than elsewhere. But in civil rights, social exclusion, employment opportunities, access to public facilities, and contact with derogatory racial images, black women who hoped for greater freedom in the West were likely to be disappointed.

Some scholars have tried to equate the experiences of women and blacks by defining women as a minority group, presuming that a key to understanding both groups was that each suffered differential and unequal treatment.[83] This approach has several shortcomings. There is no comparison between the actual suffering or extent of oppression of black compared to white women in the West or elsewhere. The denial of basic rights, social ostracism, and segregation were common conditions for many black women, and these abuses had no equivalent in the lives of most white women. The latter could often improve their condition by marriage to persons of influence or wealth, or by white-collar jobs, avenues usually closed to blacks.[84]

Black women in the West did share many aspirations of middle-class white women. Black servants complained of their work detracting from their domestic functions. Some western society women retired from club and civic activities in order to devote their energies to child-rearing. While domesticity was not the dominant norm for black women, many seem to have wished it were.[85] However, there are also significant differences between the gender experiences of black and white women. Most black women in the Victorian era did not experience

---

[83]Chafe, *Women and Equality*, 4. A classic statement of this position is Helen Hacker, "Women as a Minority Group," *Social Forces*, XXX (Oct. 1951), 60–69.

[84]Chafe, *Women and Equality*, 51–52; Gerda Lerner, "Women in American History," *Journal of Social History*, I (1969), 58.

[85]Guttman, *Black Family*, 167; Beasley, *Negro Trail Blazers*, 228; Haynes, "Negroes in Domestic Service," 391–392.

domesticity as middle-class white women did. Black women were often compelled to become breadwinners and thus could not function only as homemakers and mothers. Therefore, it is doubtful that moving to the frontier had the same upsetting effect on them that historians contend it had on white women.[86] Finally, the lives of many black women were preoccupied with the basic problem of survival for their families and their race, and their attitudes were primarily fixed on their status as blacks rather than as women.[87]

Though western black women had their lives shaped primarily by race, they did not constitute a distinct class defined by their economic position, which in turn determined much of their life. The situation of black women in the West cannot be compared to that of southern blacks under the hegemonic control of the planter class or the caste system of sharecropping and segregation which succeeded it. Most western black women could choose to live in urban areas and avoid farming, but this was a choice denied to most southern black women. While a disproportionate number of black women had to work and were concentrated in domestic jobs, there is no evidence that this situation was created or perpetuated by white employers in the West in order to make black women an available servant class. White employers had other sources of servant labor. Many blacks combined their occupation as domestics with other pursuits, and some achieved wealth and a status within their own communities which transcended the boundaries of class.[88]

But if western black women escaped confinement in an economic class, they could not escape white attitudes of indifference and a stigma of inferiority which restricted their opportunities and ignored their accomplishments. In their quest for

[86]Ryan, *Womanhood*, 139–142, 186–187; Johnny Faragher and Christine Stansell, "Women and Their Families on the Overland Trail to California and Oregon, 1842–1867," *Feminist Studies*, II (1975), 153.

[87]Lerner, *Black Women*, xxv; Robert Staples, "The Myth of the Black Matriarchy," *Black Scholar*, I (Feb. 1970), 13.

[88]Jonathan Wiener has similarly contended that southern blacks faced "formal and informal obstacles to the free market in labor" which blacks experienced in the North, and therefore the latter group should not be included in a class interpretation of black conditions in the late nineteenth century. Wiener, "Class Structure and Economic Development," 984.

white-collar jobs, access to public facilities, and social respect, western black women repeatedly found themselves judged by their color rather than their abilities. Such experiences could only make race, in the words of Chicago sociologist William J. Wilson, a "far more salient and important issue in shaping their sense of group position than their economic class position."[89]

However distinguished black women may have become, they received virtually no recognition for their accomplishments from whites. This attitude is epitomized by the *Who's Who among Women in California,* which was published in 1922. Although black women in that state had entered several professions, participated in civic and wartime activities, and had established numerous social organizations, this work does not mention a single black woman or group.[90] Black women would long remain an invisible segment of western society whose lives and accomplishments would remain known only within the confines of their race.

[89] William J. Wilson, *The Declining Significance of Race* (Chicago, 1978), 21.
[90] *Who's Who among the Women of California, 1921–22* (San Francisco, 1922).

Frontierswomen's Changing Views of Indians in the Trans-Mississippi West

by Glenda Riley

MHS Photo Archives

Stereograph by Bailey, Dix & Mead in 1882 at Sitting Bull's camp at Fort Randall, Dakota Territory, showing a woman from the fort visiting with Sitting Bull, his wife, and several children.

Copyrighted, 1882, by Bailey, Dix & Mead.

As women moved westward in the nineteenth century, like whites in general, they carried with them deeply ingrained images and preconceptions of American Indians in the trans-Mississippi West. As women, they also labored under a set of images and preconceptions of females in the nineteenth century that in turn influenced and shaped their views of Indians. As a result, they tended to emphasize and react to certain aspects of Indian culture, society, and value systems. And they responded, at least initially, in exactly the ways expected of properly indoctrinated nineteenth century white women.

A crucial change in this response pattern appeared frequently as frontierswomen interacted with various Indian peoples and as they realized their own resilience in facing the harsh demands of living in the West. Both experiences quite often challenged the prevailing view of what constituted "real" Indians and "true" women. Many frontierswomen began to eschew these stereotypes in favor of a more authentic relationship with American Indians. They began to trade and to interact socially with Indians, and sometimes they even expressed affection for and sympathy toward some of them.

Contemporary American and European writers, however, failed to record these changes. Journalists and novelists fed the anti-Indian prejudices of their reading publics with fictionalized accounts of brutal and primitive savages who preyed especially on the women who dared to venture into their domain. When women's own accounts were printed they were usually "penny dreadfuls" or narratives of captivity that further inflamed white hatred of Indians.[1]

Encouraged by profitable sales and enthusiastic readers, authors willingly responded with increasingly dramatic accounts of what were

---

1. Roy Harvey Pearce, "The Significance of the Captivity Narrative," *American Literature*, 19 (1947): 1-20; and Richard Van Der Beets, "The Indian Captivity Narrative as Ritual," *American Literature*, 43 (1972): 548-562. One investigator has argued that these captivity narratives sold so well because they "focused on Indian brutality" which "served to justify the extermination of the Indian" who "still inhabited and defended the lands which whites coveted." James A. Levernier, "Indian Captivity Narratives: Their Functions and Forms" (Ph.D. diss., University of Pennsylvania, 1975), 27.

termed Indian "depredations," particularly those perpetrated upon pure and passive womenfolk. One anthology of women's horror stories, for example, waxed eloquent on the subject:

> The very sight of Indians were terrible to many women on the frontier. The savages could not be looked upon without calling to mind the horrid work of the tomahawk and the scalping-knife—the desolated home and the butchered relatives.[2]

And James Fenimore Cooper responded to the tradition with captivity segments such as those found in *The Last of the Mohicans.*[3]

Much can be learned about the tastes and prejudices of the nineteenth century reading public from a tale such as Abbie Garner-Sharpe's *The Spirit Lake Massacre*, an inflammatory account of the "massacre" of her family, which she sold in the souvenir shop that she established in the same cabin where the "depredations" occured.[4] And there is no doubt that women who traveled the Overland Trail and settled in frontier communities felt genuine fright at the thought of meeting Indians. But in women's personal writings about their frontier experiences a much different portrait of frontierswomen and Indians emerges than that presented in the captivity narratives and the sensational fiction published by the popular press. Frontier realities forced women to examine themselves, their roles, their views of Indians, and Indian culture in a new light. As a result, women related to Indians in ways that were ignored or blurred in captivity narratives and women acted in their own lives in ways that contradicted the stereotypes of frontierswomen created by popular writers. Reading frontierswomen's diaries, journals, letters, memoirs, and reminiscences is the

2. John Frost, *Pioneer Mothers of the West; Or, Daring and Heroic Deeds of American Women* (Boston: Lee and Shepard, 1875), 22.

3. David T. Haberly, "Women and Indians: *The Last of the Mohicans* and the Captivity Tradition," *American Quarterly*, 28 (Fall 1976): 431-443; and Donald L. Kaufman, "The Indian as Media Hand-Me-Down," in Gretchen M. Bataille and Charles L.P. Silet, *The Pretend Indians: Images of Native Americans in the Movies* (Ames: Iowa State University Press, 1980), 24-25.

4. Abie Gardner-Sharpe, *The Spirit Lake Massacre and the Captivity of Miss Abie Gardner* (Des Moines: Iowa Printing Co., 1885).

only valid way to learn how they perceived themselves and their relationships with American Indians.

FRONTIERSWOMEN'S personal documents were seldom written for publication. They were daily records of significant events, usually expressing her on-the-spot feelings and reactions, and had no reading public other than herself or perhaps her family "back East" or in Europe. The diaries women kept on the Overland Trail, the journals and daybooks of women settlers, the accounts by army wives, and the records of female missionaries used here represent experiences throughout the trans-Mississippi West from the mid 1830s to the end of the nineteenth century, and they include several unpublished statements of women who were involved in violent white-Indian conflicts. Not written as treatments of Indians and with no particular vested interest to promote, these documents reflect the attitudes and feelings of a cross-section of western women who typically had only casual and intermittent contact with Indians, rather than the more prolonged and intense experience women missionaries and teachers had with native groups. Trail diaries especially illuminate how women's reactions to Indians changed as they moved westward, while women missionaries' accounts, for example, express deeply ingrained and fairly inflexible perceptions of Indians, a reflection of their sense of mission and clearly unrèpresentative of frontierswomen in general.

Before turning to these women's statements, it is essential to understand the prejudicial attitudes that influenced most of them. That era's strong anti-Indian ideology originated during America's colonial years when attempts to enslave, acculturate, or assimilate American Indians faltered because of difficulties or resistance and when many concluded that Indians should eventually be exterminated. Later generations of Americans elaborated on that theme. They created the stereotypic category "Indian," which lumped together over 2,000 native cultures and described them as savages, infidels, heathens, and barbarians. In the whites' view, these

Indians were "bad"; naked, dirty, mean, rapacious, and hostile, they fully deserved destruction by the progressive and civilized white society.[5]

At the same time, some whites pointed out that Indians possessed admirable qualities—bravery, courage, simplicity—that white society often lacked and that some Indians could be friendly and courteous toward the invading whites. There must, then, be at least some "good" Indians. This positive image, however, failed to remove the ultimate necessity of extermination. Too many Americans believed that Indians were impossible subjects for acculturation or even successful coexistence.[6]

Europeans also developed an ambivalent image of Indians. As Ray Allen Billington has explained, European writers defined "good" and "bad" Indians in moral terms: "good" Indians were friendly to whites, and "bad" Indians were not. Racist depictions of Indians by Americans, however, encouraged Europeans in the nineteenth century to believe that "the Noble Savage was a myth; the true red man was more beast than man, unfit to associate with Civilized Christians." As Europeans increasingly visualized the West as a land of savagery, they began to agree with those Americans who advocated the extirpation of Indians. Indians pervaded nineteenth century American and European literature, revealing more about American whites' attitudes than Indians' lives and providing European readers with vicarious thrills, courtesy of the American West. Coopermania, as Billington termed it, became powerful on both sides of the ocean.[7]

5. Roy Harvey Pearce, *The Savages of America: A Study of the Indian and the Idea of Civilization* (Baltimore: Johns Hopkins University Press, 1965), 3-5; and Frederick Turner, "The Terror of the Wilderness," *American Heritage*, 28 (1977): 59-62. See for example Robert F. Berkhofer, Jr., *The White Man's Indian* (New York: Alfred A. Knopf, 1978), 2, 23-28.

6. Ibid., 28-30.

7. Ray Allen Billington, *Land of Savagery, Land of Promise: The European Image of the American Frontier in the Nineteenth Century* (New York: W. W. Norton & Company, 1980), 5, 26, 30, 106; Nancy B. Black and Bette S. Weidman (eds.), *White on Red: Images of the American Indian* (Port Washington, New York: Kennikat Press, 1976), 1-2; Billington, "Cowboys, Indians and the Land of Promise: The World Image of the American Frontier" (Opening Address, 14th International Congress of Historical Sciences, San Francisco, August 22-29, 1975), 5.

Consequently, by the time American and European migrants started west images of inferior native peoples who were bad, hostile, and vicious swirled in their heads alongside enigmatic visions of superior native beings who were friendly, kind, and courageous. The dominant image of Indian inferiority, however, induced most migrants' expectations to be negative. Their nerves taut with fearful anticipation as they finally set foot on the trail, the emigrants let their psyches become geared up by expecting the worst at the hands of the American Indians. Harriet Smith commented that she was "naturally. . . somewhat afraid" when she spied her first Indians, for she immediately recalled to her mind her grandfather's tales of Indians during the War of 1812. Virginia Reed Murphy also recorded the terror her grandmother had instilled in her with frequent recitals of the "fearful deeds of the savages."[8]

Once on the trail, these migrants lived in an even more intense climate of myth and rumor. "We hear many stories of Indian depredations," one woman reported; another mentioned that "there is great tails [*sic*] about the indians."[9] Another wrote that "Printed circulars have been distributed informing the emigrants of many Indians' depredations," and one woman gleaned her information from animal bones used as bulletin boards. "We see writing on bones every day stating the deeds of the Indians." A few days later she added, "Here we saw a bone stating that Indians had run off 27 mewls & horses."[10]

Yet another woman described talk she heard by a fireside in the middle of Colorado "Indian country" in 1864:

> The conversation naturally, under the circumstances, centered on Indian stories, Indian

8. Harriett A. L. Smith, "My Trip Across the Plains in 1849," California State Library, Sacramento; Virginia Reed Murphy, "Across the Plains in the Donner Party (1846). A Personal Narrative of the Overland Trip to California," *Century Magazine*, 42 (July 1891): 409.

9. Diary of Jane Augusta Gould, 1862, Iowa State Historical Society; and Diary of Louisa Miller Rahm, 1862, Bancroft Library, University of California, Berkeley.

10. Margaret A. Frink, *Journals of the Adventures of a Party of California Gold-Seekers* (Oakland, California: n.p., 1897), 28; and Lucene Pfuffer Parsons, "The Women in the Sunbonnets," 1850, Stanford University Libraries, Palo Alto, California.

MHS Photo Archives

Homesteaders in eastern Montana with materials to build a substantial structure on their land. Homestead women, as with their predecessors on the overland journey, often saw themselves in a secondary position to men, thereby living out a part of the role set forth in the definition of "true womanhood."

> attacks, crossing the plains, etc., and as the night wore on they grew more and more eloquent—it seemed to me they were gifted with an *awful* eloquence on that particular subject.[11]

The emigrants' anxieties understandably set them up to mistake a variety of occurrences for Indian attacks.[12] Olivia Holmes's notation was common: "We got up a little excitement about the Indians but it did not amount to anything, only to frighten...us women folks." In one instance, a ferry rope splashing in the water sounded like Indians to the women, and on other occasions a deer, a lost dog returning to camp, and some U.S. soldiers making noise in their tent camp became threatening Indians. Quite often wolves created Indian scares in a camp. Maria Schrode recorded that one man's wife thought "some wolves was Indians and she screamed louder than the wolves howled and frightened some of us considerably." Sometimes flocks of birds started the trouble. Mary Powers, for example, wrote that "the Indians that had so frightened us were nothing but a flock of filthy bussards." And frequently emigrants themselves generated the scare. When two young women playfully rushed through the dark at a young man on the fringe of camp, they were appalled to see him dash into camp and raise an Indian alarm in unreasoning fright.[13]

Such scares and alarms, although they frightened both men and women, were generally believed to be especially taxing to female migrants. Margaret Hall Walker noted: "Those groundless scares in the night were very exasperating to Pa. They made the women nervous and sick." Harriet Ward believed that the

11. Mallie Stafford, *The March of Empire Through Three Decades* (San Francisco: Geo. Spaulding & Co., 1884), 126-127.

12. Robert L. Munkres, "The Plains Indian Threat on the Oregon Trail before 1860," *Annals of Wyoming*, 40 (1968): 212-215.

13. Diary of Olivia Holmes, 1873, Bancroft Library; Journal of Catherine Amanda Washburn, 1853, Huntington Library, San Marino, California; Ward G. DeWitt and Florence Stark DeWitt (eds.), *Prairie Schooner Lady: The Journal of Harriet Sherrill Ward, 1853* (Los Angeles: Westernlore Press, 1959), 46; Ada Millington, "Journal Kept While Crossing the Plains," 1862, Bancroft Library; Journal of Maria Schrode, 1870, Huntington Library; Mary Rockwood Powers, "A Woman's Overland Journal to California," 1856, California State Library; and Susan Parrish, "Westward in 1850," Huntington Library.

false attacks were worse than the real thing: "I hardly think we ever suffer quite as much when anything of this kind really happens as we do in the anticipation," she wrote. And Emily Fitzgerald concurred: "For a few moments, I think, we women with our helpless little children suffered as much as if the Indians had really come."[14]

In this state of nearly constant agitation, both male and female travellers readily blamed Indians for any misfortune. When cattle stampeded, Mary Warner indicated that the guards assumed the cause to be Indian treachery. Katherine Dunlap explained that when their stock wandered it was "natural" to think it had been stolen by Indians, as they were often seen "skulking around the camps." When she saw her first Indians, Lucy Sexton noted that "they were mounted, and one of them on a fine American horse, undoubtedly stolen." And Emily Horton offered a harsh judgment when some of the men brought a bleached skull into camp: It was "all there was to show that one of our race had perished far from home. No doubt death was caused by savages."[15]

AS WOMEN EMIGRANTS viewed American Indians through this prejudicial veil, they contended with the conditioning they had undergone as nineteenth century females. Society attributed to women, as it did to Indians, a superior and inferior nature. The superior side of women's character derived primarily from their supposedly exceptional moral abilities, the quality that cast them in the role of moral guardians of the home and family and included a cluster of other ascribed traits. They were kind, gentle, passive, religious, domestic, pure, and refined. On the other

14. Margaret Hall Walker, *The Hall Family Crossing the Plains* (San Francisco: Privately Printed by Wallace Kibbee & Son, 1952), 13; DeWitt and DeWitt (eds.), *Prairie Schooner Lady*, 46; Erwin N. Thompson, "The Summer of '77 at Fort Lapwai," *Idaho Yesterdays*, 21 (1977): 14.

15. Diary of Mary Eliza Warner, 1864, Bancroft Library; Journal of Katherine Dunlap, 1864, Bancroft Library; Lucy Sexton, *The Foster Family, California Pioneers* (Santa Barbara, California: Press of the Schauer Printing Studio, Inc., 1925), 123; and Emily McCowen Horton, *My Scrap-book* (Seattle, Washington: n.p., 1927), 17.

hand, they were inferior because of their obvious physical weakness and assumed intellectual limitations. They had small brains and weak muscles, and they were helpless, childlike, non-assertive, indecisive, and unable to protect themselves.[16]

Having listened all their lives to these descriptions of the female character, most women internalized them and carried them westward. Their own self-concepts, especially their view of themselves as the guardians of morality—the protectors of ethics and civilization—tended to shape their perceptions of Indians as uncivilized, morally deficient, and brutalized by their primitive existence and their understanding of themselves as the harbingers of civilization.[17]

Women's imputed superiority thus often encouraged them to emphasize, and even become obsessed with, the Indians' inferiority. Accordingly, negative views of Indians frequently dominated the early pages of most women's diaries and journals. The women often expressed disappointment when they met their first Indians and disillusionment at the ragged, unkempt appearance of the Indians that did not match the befeathered image they had expected. Kate Furness wrote that they were "very ugly," and Sarah Herndon dismissed her first Indian as being "very disappointing as the 'Noble Red Man' we read about." The Indians' lack of clothing often shocked women and drew their comments. Mary Sandford recorded that "the Indians were nude save for a throw over one shoulder, and a strap around the

16. Carl N. Degler, *At Odds: Women and the Family in America from the Revolution to the Present* (Oxford: Oxford University Press, 1980), 26-27, 30-31, 150-151, 283, 351-353; Ann Douglas, *The Feminization of American Culture* (New York: Alfred A. Knopf, 1979), 8-10, 45-48, 56-60, 68-76; John Mack Faragher, *Women and Men on the Overland Trail* (New Haven: Yale University Press, 1979), 94-97; Gerda Lerner, *The Majority Finds Its Past: Placing Women in History* (New York: Oxford University Press, 1979), 25-28, 162-165, 185-186n; and Glenda Riley, "The Subtle Subversion: Changes in the Traditionalist Image of the American Woman," *The Historian*, 32 (February 1970): 210-227, and *The Origins of the Feminist Movement in America* (St. Charles, Missouri: Forum Press, 1973), 1-13.

17. Leslie A. Fiedler, *The Return of the Vanishing American* (New York: Stein and Day, 1968), 24, 177; Julie Roy Jeffrey, *Frontier Women: The Trans-Mississippi West, 1840-1880* (New York: Hill and Wang, 1979), 33-34; and Ronald J. Quinn, "The Modest Seduction: The Experience of Pioneer Women on the Trans-Mississippi Frontier" (Ph.D. diss., University of California-Riverside, 1977), i-iii, 8-9, 11, 15, 18, 23, 30, 39, 45-50.

loins." Mary Staples noted that their "clothing was very scant," Sallie Maddock that they were "mostly naked," Margaret Hecox that they frequently came "to our camp in a perfectly nude state," and Harriet Smith that she was "a little streaked for he had nothing on but a blanket and great earrings and bracelet, all brass."[18]

Even when the Indians *were* dressed, women's assessments tended to be derogatory. After seeing her first Indians, Caroline Richardson wrote that they were "drest in their 'peculiar costome.'" Another woman observed that although "some are nearly naked, some dressed most fantastically," and another that they were "decorated in the extreme of Indian dandyism." When the Indian attire simulated white styles, however, women viewed it more positively. A group of Sioux who were "neatly dressed" in an approximation of white fashion struck Hecox as "clean and wholesome in appearance." And when Maria Norton encountered Indians dressed "with pants and caps," she judged them to be "the most respectable that we have seen."[19]

Women frequently disparaged various American Indian groups for being unclean, dirty, and even filthy. To Maddock they were "disgusting and dirty looking," to Staples "a filthy set," and to Mary Jane Guill "a filthy and dirty set of Indians."[20] As one women put it, "the romance of Indian life will not

18. Kate McDaniel Furness, "From Prairie to Pacific," California State Library; Sarah R. Herndon, *Days on the Road: Crossing the Plains in 1865* (New York: Burr Printing House, 1902), 73; Mary Fetter Hite Sandford, "A Trip Across the Plains," 1853, California State Library; Reminiscences of Mary Pratt Staples, ca. 1886, Bancroft Library; Sallie Hester Maddock, "The Diary of a Pioneer Girl," 1849, California State Library; Margaret M. Hecox, *California Caravan: The 1846 Overland Trail Memoir of Margaret M. Hecox* (San Jose: Harlan-Young Press, 1966), 40; and Fleming Fraker, Jr. (ed.), "To Pike's Peak by Ox Wagon: The Harriet A. Smith Day-Book," *Annals of Iowa*, 35 (Fall 1959): 132.

19. Journal of Caroline L. Richardson, 1856, Bancroft Library; Leo M. Kaiser and Priscilla Knuth (eds.), "From Ithaca to Clatsop Plains: Miss Ketcham's Journal of Travel," Part II, *Oregon Historical Quarterly*, 62 (December 1961): 368; Mrs. B. G. Ferris, *The Mormons at Home* (New York: Dix & Edwards, 1856), 13; Hecox, *California Caravan*, 32; and Maria J. Norton, "Diary of a Trip Across the Plains in '59," Bancroft Library.

20. Maddock, "Diary of a Pioneer Girl"; Reminiscences of Mary Staples; and Mary Jane Guill, "The Overland Diary of a Journey From Livingston County, Missouri, to Butte County, California," 1860, California State Library.

bear a closer inspection—they are neither more or less than filthy savages."[21]

Many women associated the Indians' uncleanliness with some Indians' disconcerting habit of eating insects. When Angeline Ashley observed Utah Indians pulling wings off locusts and harvesting them in sacks, she decided that "they are very low Indians and very ugly looking." Another woman, watching an Indian woman eat lice from her husband's head while feeding him a few of the choice ones, wrote that the Indians were contemptible objects due to the "extreme indolence of their nature, the squalid conditions in which they live. . .and the general imbecility of their intellects." Helen Stewart indicated that she would prefer that visiting Indians avoid her camp altogether. "They are the durtyist creatures I ever saw," she wrote. "They will pick the lice out of there [*sic*] head and eat them."[22]

Many women also seemed to associate peculiar odors with Indians. They noted smelling a nearby Indian camp or their own horses and dogs responding with presumed fear to the smell of an Indian.[23] One woman phrased it delicately when she wrote that the "effluvia arising from their persons is none of the sweetest." Another was more direct: "they were simply, and only, painted, dirty and nauseous-smellin savages."[24]

Even though they were already of the opinion that American Indians lived a life deficient in certain basic areas, many women stood in near shock when they discovered that many Indians spoke little or no English. With obvious dismay, Ellen Adams remarked that "Some of the Indians could not understand a single word of English." And when an Indian

21. Ferris, *Mormons at Home*, 68.

22. Angeline Jackson Ashley, "Diary—Crossing the Plains in 1852," Huntington Library; Mrs. D. B. Bates, *Incidents on Land and Water* (Boston: James French and Company, 1857), 151-152; and Diary of Helen Marnie Stewart Love, 1853, Huntington Library.

23. Hecox, *California Caravan*, 29; and Thompson, "Summer of '77," 11.

24. Mary C. Fish, "Across the Plaines in 1860," Bancroft Library; and Frances M. A. Roe, *Army Letters From an Officer's Wife, 1871-1888* (New York: D. Appleton & Co., 1909), 10.

could manage a few words of the whites' language, women often recorded it, sometimes with derision.[25] "They do not understand any of our language," one woman reported, "and when they can speak a word of it they seemt to think that they have done something very smart."[26]

Puzzlement, derision, and outright racism characterized many women's assessments of Indian customs. The sight of Indian villages moving on pole carts pulled by dogs or with the sticks of wigwams on ponies amused some, and other women found curious the Indian custom of burying their dead above ground. Marie Nash called the burial custom a "sad sight," but others minimized its significance, seeing it as simply a practical means to protect graves from being pillaged and bodies from being mutilated by wolves. Some women had so little respect for Indian burial customs that they entered burial grounds to collect beads to string and wear as ornaments.[27]

Indian mating practices drew such notice that some women seemed obsessed with a need to chronicle every French trader they met who had an Indian wife and "half-breed" children. Amused by it all, Mary Fish quipped when she met one French trader, "the Frenchmen go for amalgamation," and when she saw another with a dozen wives she joked that he was simply "fond of a plural number." Another woman wrote that the children of one such marriage seemed "playful and happy," but Maria Norton found the idea an abomination: "the greatest absurdity," she penned, ". . . was for a white man to live with black dirty squaws."[28]

25. Ellen Tomplins Adams, Diary, 1863; Journal of Esther Bell Hanna, 1852, Bancroft Library; and Guill, "Overland Diary."

26. Kaiser and Knuth, "From Ithaca to Clatsop Plains," 368.

27. Guill, "Overland Diary"; Norton, "Diary of a Trip"; DeWitt and DeWitt, *Prairie Schooner Lady*, 78; Diary of Marie Nash, 1861, California State Library; Diary of Helen Carpenter, 1856, California State Library; and Millington, "Journal."

28. Fish, "Across the Plaines"; Frances H. Sawyer, "Overland to California," 1852, Bancroft Library; and Norton, "Diary of a Trip."

Erroneously concluding from their often superficial observations that Indian males crassly traded ponies and other goods for wives, many women became further distressed. "I was somewhat shocked to think of such a loose state of morals," Mary Bailey wrote in 1852. Yet, if an Indian male attempted to trade ponies for *them*, women generally took the matter lightly. Emily Horton recorded her sarcastic reply to an Ottawa Indian's proposal: "I was too unsophisticated to appreciate the honor." In a similar situation, Harriet Smith jested, "I thought I would wait untill some one would give Unc a lot of ponies for me and I would go and stay awhile with them then run away, and then we would have some ponies." Mary Warner jokingly noted in her diary that "Uncle Chester traded Aunt Lizzie off for two ponies but she would not go." And Catherine Bell wrote home that "There was an Indian chief offered Charlie two of his best ponys for me, dont you think he ought to have traded?"[29]

Despite occasional amusement, women generally deplored the manner in which Indian men treated Indian women. When they witnessed men taking money from women who had earned it by selling their own handiwork, riding while women walked, or expecting women to carry the load while they went unburdened, white women judged Indian men to be detestable and contemptible.[30] These inaccurate perceptions of the low status of Indian women also added a new dimension to frontierswomen's forebodings regarding captivity, and they nervously guarded themselves and their children. "I have no desire to go among the Indians in that way," one asserted, and another confessed that she had her son watch her when she fetched water so that Indians would not carry her off and that she protectively

29. Mary Stuart Bailey, "A Journal of the Overland Trip From Ohio to California," 1852, Huntington Library; Horton, My Scrap-book, 17; Fraker, "To Pike's Peak," 134; Diary of Mary Warner; and Letter from Catherine Jane Bell to Julia (no identity given), October 31, 1859, Oroville, California, Bancroft Library.

30. Millington, "Journal"; and Harriet Bunyard, "Diary of a Young Girl," 1868, Huntington Library.

gathered her children in her arms whenever Indians approached. Similarly, when Mary Caples saw Indians "dressed in their long macinaw blankets, with eagle feathers in their hair," she worried that "they would kill us all, and take my baby in captivity."[31]

GIVEN THESE NEGATIVE and usually imprecise interpretations of Indian ways, it is little wonder that many women initially concluded that the Indians' character must be of the lowest order and deserved a harsh assessment. Epitaphs such as "hard-hearted & cruel people," "too devilish for any human beings," "most treacherous mortals on earth," and "too indolent to exert themselves much" were not unusual.[32] Although the Pawnee she met appeared friendly, Georgia Willis Reed insisted that "they are noted cowards, but if they get you in their power, your situation is critical." When Lucy Sexton saw a band of peaceful Pawnee routed by a small number of their Sioux enemies, she was moved to sarcasm: "A brave nation, truly. One hundred and fifty of them vanquished by 13." A peace treaty with the Sioux, Helen Carpenter believed, was not worth the paper "once an Indian begins to feel ugly, and aching for a 'scrap.'" Another woman harshly concluded that Nebraska Indians were unfit "to inhabit such beautiful soil as we are now traveling through."[33]

Even when frontierswomen learned that most American Indians did not intend to seize them, their children, or their scalps, their indigation toward Indians continued. It irked many women that Indians were, in Sarah Royce's words, "evidently desirous of getting something out of us if they could." Complaints were legion against Indian groups who

31. Kaiser and Knuth, "From Ithaca to Clatsop Plains," 262; Miriam D. Colt, *Went to Kansas; Being a Thrilling Account of an Ill-Fated Expedition* (Watertown: L. Ingalls & Co., 1862), 136, 61; and Mary Jane Caples, "Overland Journey to California," 1911, California State Library.

32. Martha Ann Minto, "Female Pioneering in Oregon," 1849, Bancroft Library; Emeline L. Fuller, *Left By the Indians. Story of My Life* (Mt. Vernon, Iowa: Hawk-Eye Steam Print, 1892), 29; Margaret W. Chambers, *Reminiscences* (No place: n.p., 1903), 45; and Bates, *Incidents on Land and Water*, 156.

33. Diary of Georgia Willis Read, 1850, California State Library; Sexton, *The Foster Family*, 127-128; Diary of Helen Carpenter; Diary of Mrs. Nicholas Harrison Karchner, 1862, California State Library.

begged and stole from the whites. The phrases "thieving people," "somewhat troublesome," and "troubled by beggin Indians" appeared many times in women's writings.[34] Although Indians often asked for sugar, meat, flour, coffee, other foodstuffs, and tobacco, apparently frontierswomen seldom questioned why once self-sufficient groups needed to beg. And instead of attempting to understand the Indians' conceptions of hospitality, they more often viewed Indians as sly, disgusting, or pesky.[35] One caustically wrote, "They are the greatest beggars I ever saw. I do wonder if they are hungry."[36] Other women were even more acrimonious. "The better Indians come to camp to pay us a visit," wrote Mary Jane Guill, and "always stay till after supper I suppose it is fashionable for them to stay." Mallie Stafford scornfully noted: "Two large powerfully built warriors, in all the glory of red paint, buckskin, beads, feathers, dignity and general magnificence, condescended to honor our humble camp with a call—a call long enough to eat up and devour everything we had cooked, that being an immense pot of beans and bacon." Notations of concern appeared in women's journals about the safety of their livestock, expressing the fear that a particular group of Indians intended to steal their animals. But the women did not question why American Indians might want or need the emigrants' stock.[37]

Paradoxical as it seems, frontierswomen who disparaged Indians also recognized the presence of

34. Sarah Royce, *A Frontier Lady* (New Haven: Yale University Press, 1932), 50; Augusta Tabor, "Cabin Life in Colorado," 1884, Bancroft Library; Rebecca Hildreth Nutting Woodson, "A Sketch of the Life of Rebecca Hildreth Nutting Woodson and Her Family," 1909, Bancroft Library; and Guill, "Overland Diary."

35. Journal of Mary Hall Jatta, 1869, Bancroft Library; Catherine Margaret Haun, "A Woman's Trip Across the Plains, from Clinton, Iowa, to Sacramento, California, by way of Salt Lake City," 1849; and Diary of Helen Love.

36. Herndon, *Days on the Road*, 235.

37. Guill, "Overland Diary"; Stafford, *The March of Empire*, 117; Bunyard, "Diary of a Young Girl"; Journal of Catherine Washburn; Sawyer, "Overland to California"; Mattie Walker, "A Brief History of the William B. Walker Family," California State Library; Leo M. Kaiser and Priscilla Knuth (eds.), "From Ithaca to Clatsop Plains: Miss Ketcham's Journal of Travel," Part I, *Oregon Historical Quarterly*, 62 (September 1961): 258; and Journal of Katherine Dunlap.

Women on the frontier took on many of the same chores they did in more settled regions, but their new environment, such as shown in this photo taken on the western plains at the turn of the century, forced women to reject aspects of the stereotyped "cult of domesticity" that challenged the realities of frontier life.

MHS Photo Archives

"good" Indians. Although whites in general detected favorable qualities in American Indians, white women had a special reason to search out some superior characteristics in the Indians they met. Women had learned to think of themselves as weak, helpless, and incapable of protecting themselves. Their own men, of course, could defend them to a certain degree, but many women seemed to feel dependent on the nobility and strength of character of the "primitive savage," for the Indians could decide whether or not to injure women through thievery, sexual assault, or outright warfare. Therefore, many frontierswomen sought out a glimmer of nobility, a hint of kindness, an indication of intelligence in the native peoples they confronted. In this way, women occasionally found positive aspects in the physical appearance, character, and customs of some Indian people.

Even the women who were most vitriolic regarding the ugliness, filth, and odor of Indians also described some of them with such phrases as "an imposing sight in the wilderness," "good-looking," "fine-looking," and "noble-looking."[38] Other women depicted some Indians as "grave" and "stately," with "the appearance of wealth and independence," and as "tall, strongly made" with "firm features, light copper color, cleanly in appearance, quite well dressed in red blankets."[39] A few women punctuated their derogatory character assessments of Indians with words such as "industrious" and "intelligent," and one spoke of "mannerly conduct" and "a degree of refinement" that she had not expected to find among "just Indians."[40]

38. Hecox, *California Caravan*, 28; Haun, "A Woman's Trip"; Diary of Georgia Read; Diary of Charlotte Pengra, 1853, Huntington Library; and Lucy Rutledge Cooke, *Covered Wagon Days: Crossing the Plains in 1852* (Modesto, California: Privately published, 1923), 30.

39. Eliza Spalding Warren, *Memoirs of the West: The Spaldings* (Portland, Oregon: March Printing Co., 1916), 13; Elizabeth L. Lord, *Reminiscences of Eastern Oregon* (Portland, Oregon: The Irwin-Hodgson Co., 1903), 42; Lodisa Frizzell, *Across the Plains to California in 1852* (New York: New York Public Library, 1915), 18.

40. Barsina French, "Journal of a Wagon Trip," 1867, Huntington Library; Cynthia J. Capron, "Life in the Army," *Journal of the Illinois State Historical Society*, 13 (October 1920): 367; Diary of Charlotte Pengra; Journal of Katherine Dunlap; and Hecox, *California Caravan*, 33.

The women also praised the Indians' abilities, commenting on the ingeniousness of their underground wigwams, the beauty of their needlework, and the high quality of their handiwork. Susan Magoffin went so far as to suggest that Indian postnatal practices were wiser than those undergone by "ladies in civilized life."[41]

A large number of frontierswomen believed that Indians would respond to fair treatment by whites. Others credited the respect, courtesy, friendliness, and willingness to share food with the Indians as important elements that insured the safety of their party. "Evidently our hospitality and courteous treatment won their hearts," Lavinia Porter wrote, "for they showed no signs of hostility to us. In fact from their general demeanor they rather inspired us with a confidence which seemed to sanction our presence in their midst."[42]

Some women began to blame white men for "Indian troubles" because the men exploited kindly Indians or treated them unfairly. Mary Hopping bitterly termed two men who paid an irate Indian counterfeit money for moccasins "smarties" and looked contemptuously on a young woman who asked for a scalp as a trophy from an Indian-hunting expedition. Lavinia Porter claimed in her reminiscence of the overland journey that she remonstrated in vain with the men in her party who teased and played tricks on visiting Indians. In another instance, Pauline Wonderly criticized emigrants who first refused to pay a "reasonable" toll to Indians who had constructed a bridge across the Elk Horn River, and then killed eleven Indians in the ensuing fight. Later par-

41. Parsons, "Women in the Sunbonnets"; Frizzell, *Across the Plains*, 25; Journal of Esther Hanna; see also Emma Shepard Hill, *A Dangerous Crossing and What Happened on the Other Side: Seven Lean Years* (Denver: Bradford-Robinson Printing Co., 1924), 82; Juliette Fish Walker, "Crossing the Plains," *Noticas*, 16, 2, (1970): 4; Susan S. Magoffin, *Down the Santa Fe Trail and Into Mexico: The Diary of Susan Shelby Magoffin, 1846-1847* (New Haven: Yale University Press, 1926), 68.

42. Diary of Rachel C. Rose, 1852, California State Library; Nancy A. Hunt, "By Ox Team to California," Bancroft Library; Furness, "From Prairie to Pacific"; Sandford, "A Trip Across the Plains"; Walker, *The Hall Family*, 28; Journal of Esther Hanna; Lavinia H. Porter, *By Ox Team to California: A Narrative of Crossing the Plains in 1860* (Oakland, California: Oakland Enquirer Publishing Co., 1910), 67.

ties, she prophesied, would have to pay for the "meaness of the men of that train."[43]

MANY WOMEN were ambivalent toward the Indians, an ambivalence founded in women's perceptions of their own weakness and the danger Indians posed. Ada Vogdes's journal reflected this equivocalness. An army wife at Fort Laramie in the late 1860s, she repeatedly wrote in her journal that she was "frightened to death." One night she awoke to imaginary Indian war whoops—actually two drunk cooks—and repeatedly declined her husband's invitations to explore with him the area surrounding the fort. Yet, when a council meeting with Indian leaders followed a dramatic false alarm of attack, she noted Red Cloud's "pleasant smile," Big Bear's "most splendid chest, and shoulders, I ever laid my eyes upon," and Red Leaf's "fatherly looking countenance, & one to whom you would go in trouble, were we in different circumstances." Although Vogdes remained in "constant fear" whenever she left the fort, she also enjoyed becoming "quite a *belle* amongst the red men of the Plains."

When Vogdes moved to Fort Fetterman she complained, "This frontier life is terrible for a nervous excitable person as I am, and it seems as if I could not endure it much longer. For nearly two years the Indians have been the bane of my existence." At Fetterman she mistook a soldier returning late from one of the laundresses' quarters as an attacking Indian, and she shuddered with fear at the sight of Cheyenne Indians outside her windows. Yet, Indian leaders who came into the fort impressed her. Of Red Dog she wrote: "...[he] had nothing on but the skin in which he was born...I never saw such shoulders, arms, & legs, & hands...his legs were equally as fine looking." After sitting with him at a small table she

43. Mary E. Hopping, "Incidents of Pioneer Life As I Remember and As I Have Been Told," 1982, California State Library; Porter, *By Ox Team*, 79; Pauline Wonderly, *Reminiscences of a Pioneer* (Placerville, California: El Dorado County Historical Society, 1965), 4.

wrote that although it would seem strange to an easterner to see her with "this naked man," it did not seem strange to her at all. "I am not shocked if I see them with no clothes on," she added.[44]

This ambivalence, partly the result of indoctrination regarding the contradictory natures of Indians and women, paradoxically also resulted from the gradual erosion of those societally induced attitudes. Women, interacting with Indians, soon learned that Indians were neither as "good" nor as "bad" as the stereotype suggested. Most women discarded the concept of a stereotypic "Indian" and recognized instead that many different types and qualities of native peoples lived throughout the West.

Lavinia Porter, for example, recounted the usual tales of begging Indians infested with vermin and lazy Indian men who expected women to do all the work, and degraded Indians with low moral standards. Like Vogdes, she was frequently "speechless with fright" and suffered extreme anxiety due to exposure to the "dangers of savage life." Yet, increasingly interspersed with these statements were Porter's accounts of helpful and kindly Indians. When an Indian returned the emigrants' wandering cattle to them she mused that, "It truly seemed to us in our long journey traveling alone that the Indians watched over us." At another point she wrote that an Indian traveled with them for three days as a scout and guide, which "went to prove that there was honor among these savage tribes of the wilderness."[45]

Harriet Ward not only overcame her own dread of Indians, but also maintained that many other women experienced a similar reaction. "I have conversed with many ladies," she declared, "and they all appear happy and in good health." Although at one point Ward wrote that she felt uneasy knowing that "hostile" Indians "infested" the mountains and at another time that a few Indian groups they met were "wild," "miserable," and "not to be trusted," she felt confident enough in general not to lose any sleep

44. Journal of Ada Adelaide Vogdes, 1866-1872, Huntington Library.

45. Porter, *By Ox Team*, 26-27.

over the matter. "We encamped beside the mountain, with not a living being near us except the Indians, who, they say, are watching all our movements," she wrote. "We staked our horses near the tent," she went on, "and all laid ourselves down to sleep, which we enjoyed nicely."[46]

Many alterations in women's attitudes about Indians coincided with changes in their attitudes about themselves. They learned that their imputed ability to civilize was only one of a myriad of skills demanded of them on the frontier. Moreover, they discovered that neither they nor society suffered disaster if they could not fully exercize their role of cultural conservator. They washed clothes on the Sabbath, listened to oaths, and came into contact with gambling, drinking, and polygamy, yet life went on. Frontierswomen quickly realized that their value to society did not erode under these circumstances; it took a new direction. Many accepted new functions and roles, driving teams, performing trail work, walking for miles over rough terrain, handling weapons, helping make decisions, and making significant economic contributions.[47]

Women began to suspect that their ascribed inferiority was no more rock-bound than their imputed superiority was proving to be. There was not one recorded case of a woman's brain swelling and cracking from new demands, as had been predicted. Instead, western women grew strong, assertive, and confident. They realized that with their talents and skills they might play some role in shaping their lives, protecting themselves and their children, and determining their ultimate survival in the West.

If women's primary value was not as civilizers, they no longer needed to emphasize the inferior aspects of Indian character. And if women were not really weak and incompetent, their safety did not depend on the Indians' benevolence and superior

46. DeWitt and DeWitt, *Prairie Schooner Lady*, 87, 123, 144, 158, 166.

47. Glenda Riley, *Women on the American Frontier* (St. Louis, Missouri: Forum Press, 1977), 3-4, and "Women in the West," *Journal of American Culture*, 3 (Summer 1980): 314-318.

Photo by Stanley J. Morrow, 1879, Hullman Collection, MHS Photo Archives

Wolf Voice, Gros Ventre. Frontierswomen were often frightened and shocked when they first saw the armed and "nearly nude" Indian warriors who visited forts and white encampments.

qualities. These realizations, added to their discovery that American Indians were people rather than demons, created further contradictions in women's assessments of Indians. How women really interacted with American Indians was vastly different from the story usually told.

Most frontierswomen learned to discriminate between Indian groups, realizing that each possessed different qualities, and to reject the stereotype of "Indian" as an amorphous grouping of people. Women almost always recorded their first sighting of an Indian, but they did so with little knowledge of Indian tribes and territories. Soon, however, they turned to more specific descriptions, such as "we are now in the Pawnee nation" or "we are now in the Sioux nation."[48]

Frontierswomen also learned that Indians not only varied from tribe to tribe and from region to region, but also from era to era. A group of Indians who might have been friendly to whites in the 1840s might have experienced the ravages of white migration so thoroughly by the 1850s that they had become belligerent instead.[49] Mary Pelham recorded a frequent complaint regarding changes for the worst among Indian groups: "How these Indians have changed. Not simple and childlike any more. Until that year (1853) very few had ever seen a white man and seldom a white woman or child. They never tired of watching us and our ways of living."[50]

Some women recognized that the growing pressure of white population on the frontier caused such alterations in Indians' behavior, a pressure that increasingly drove Indian groups into armed combat with each other over dwindling resources as well as into violent attempts to stem white incursions. Kate Furness explained that when she encountered her first Indians just across the Missouri River they were engaged in a war with the Sioux because they "encroached on their hunting-grounds and killed the buffalo."[51]

48. Journal of Elizabeth Julia Goltra, 1853, Bancroft Library.

49. Jean Webster, "The Myth of Hardship on the Oregon Trail," *Reed College Bulletin*, 24 (January 1946): 34.

50. Mary Hall Pelham, "The Indians," in Walker, *The Hall Family*, 29.

51. Minnie Lee Cardwell Miller, "The Road to Yesterday," 1937, Bancroft Library; and Furness, "From Prairie to Pacific."

Huffman Collection, MHS Photo Archives

An Indian child playing "house" while her family visits a white rancher in eastern Montana. Indians frequently camped on white ranchers' doorsteps during visits or when bartering goods. These contacts provided white women with a much more realistic perspective on Indian families and especially Indian women.

These intertribal wars quite often worked to the whites' advantage because Indians attacked each other rather than the encroaching whites.[52] But when Indian groups did turn their attention to opposing white expansion or exacting various types of compensation from whites, not all women meekly accepted Indian demands.[53] There are numerous cases of newly confident women resisting Indian intrusions. Lavinia Porter refused a request for bread only to have bleeding scalps thrust under her nose for her to count and admire. When she refused to retreat, her would-be oppressor muttered "white squaw no fear" and departed. On one occasion, Susanna Ede evicted an Indian interloper from her kitchen by threatening to pour hot grease on him, and on another by raising a pot of boiling water to throw on the trespasser. A Mrs. Kirchner simply tore her belongings out of the hands of pilfering Indians.[54]

Many frontierswomen went beyond resistance to violence in repelling impositions by Indians. Barsina French's mother took turns standing guard with the men to protect the party's stock from marauding Indians. Another woman defended her horses and mules by spending a long night on the roof of her stable shooting at a band of Pimas. Eliza Egbert guarded some wagons by brandishing an empty pistol in the faces of some Pawnee and ordering them to depart or be shot. Mary Ann Davidson threatened an abusive Indian with a poker. And when Susie Van De Wiele's husband asked her if she were afraid of the Indians surrounding their camp she calmly replied, "No, give me a pistol."[55]

52. Polly Jane Purcell, "Autobiography and Reminiscence of a Pioneer," Newberry Library; and Sandford, "A Trip Across the Plains."

53. Susan H. Armitage, "Women's Literature and the American Frontier: A New Perspective on the Frontier Myth," in L. L. Lee and Merrill Lews (eds.), *Women, Women Writers, and the West* (Troy, New York: Whitson Publishing Company, 1979), 5-11.

54. Porter, *By Ox Team*, 56; Barbara Baker Zimmerman and Vernon Carstensen, "Pioneer Woman in Southwestern Washington Territory: The Recollections of Susanna Maria Slover McFarland Price Ede," *Pacific Northwest Quarterly*, 66-67 (October 1976): 143, 147; and Bessie L. Lyon, "Hungry Indians," *Palimpsest*, 9 (October 1928): 366.

55. French, "Journal of a Wagon Trip"; Christiane Fischer, "A Profile of Women in Arizona in Frontier Days," *Journal of the West*, 16 (July 1977): 43; Diary of Eliza Ann Egbert, 1852, Bancroft Library; Mary Ann Ferrin Davidson, "An Autobiography and a Reminiscence," *Annals of Iowa*, 37 (Spring 1964): 256; and Susie P. Van De Wiele, "Travels and Experience in America with army and Indian reminiscences," Newberry Library.

ALL FRONTIERSWOMEN, of course, did not become involved in altercations with Indians. Many women routinely traded trinkets, clothing, and foodstuffs with Indians, engaging in somewhat of a collegial relationship in their mutual attempt to wrest sustenance from the frontier environment. Both on the trail and in their new homes many frontierswomen personally exchanged needles and thread, foods they had processed, articles of clothing, and trifles with Indians who bartered fresh foods in return. White women frequently mention American Indian men and women bringing them butter, eggs, potatoes, corn, pumpkins, melons, strawberries, blackberries, venison and other fresh meats and fish, and dried salmon.[56]

Some women also became interested in obtaining specialized Indian products and crafts for themselves. Lucy Cooke, at first much in awe of the Indians, became an expert trader and by the end of her trail experience had collected a fine cache of furs. Other women grew skillful at bartering for buffalo hides and robes, pants made of antelope and elk hides, moccasins, baskets, and beadwork. Cynthia Capron was delighted with a watertight Indian basket she purchased for one dollar, and Eveline Alexander considered a war shield she bought "quite a valuable trophy." Even Ada Vogdes, who had spent so much of her time being fearful of the Indians, learned local dialects and successfully traded with Indians. "I rushed around all day to get a blanket worked with beads which I succeeded in doing," she wrote triumphantly.[57]

---

56. Sarah J. Cummins, *Autobiography and Reminiscences* (La Grande, Oregon: La Grande Printing Co., 1914), 42; Saunders, "The Whitman Massacre"; Journal of Alimra Neff Beam Enos, 1858-1866, Bancroft Library; Mrs. M. S. Hockensmith, "Diary of a Trip Overland From the Mississippi to California," 1866, Bancroft Library; Reminiscences of Julia L. Hare, California State Library; Hopping, "Incidents of Pioneer Life"; Frink, *Journals*, 46; Diary of Louise Rahm; Sawyer, "Overland to California"; Guill, "Overland Diary"; and Journal of Catherine Washburn

57. Cooke, *Covered Wagon Days*, 66; Mary Horne, "Migration and Settlement of the Latter Day Saints," 1884, Bancroft Library; Martha M. Morgan, *A Trip Across the Plains in the Year 1849* (San Francisco: Printed at Pioneer Press, 1864), 7, 12, 15-16; Ellen McGowen Biddle, *Reminiscences of a Soldier's Wife* (Philadelphia: J. B. Lippincott Co., 1907), 83; Cynthia J. Capron, "Life in the Army," 369; Sandra L. Myres (ed.), *Cavalry Wife: The Diary of Eveline M. Alexander, 1866-1867* (College Station: Texas A&M University Press, 1977), 102; and Journal of Ada Vogdes.

Many women also hired Indian men, women, and children to perform household chores, such as chopping wood, drawing water, and washing dishes and clothes.[58] Despite the common rumor that Indians wanted to capture white children, numerous women entrusted their children to the care of American Indian women and men.[59] Rachel Wright believed that the key to such favorable relations with Indians rested with the whites. Indians were "an advantage rather than otherwise," she explained, "as they were not only willing but glad to work if they were left free, well treated and properly paid for their labor."[60]

In time, social intercourse flourished among some frontierswomen and American Indians. Accounts by women who initially had been very apprehensive of Indians frequently described pleasant visits to Indian camps.[61] "We often visited Indian camps," Allene Dunham wrote. "They always treated us to a piece of dried buffalo, or venison, or some other kind of meat." Another woman reported that the Indians she visited were "really friendly." We had "quite a dish of conversation," she noted after visiting some Indian women.[62] These developing relationships, business and social, often fostered among frontierswomen an acceptance of Indian women and genuine admiration of and affection for them. Harriet Ward clearly contradicted her earlier attitudes when she jotted in her diary how "surprised" her acquaintances would be "to see me writing so quietly in the wagon alone. . . with a great, wild looking In-

58. Mary E. Ackley, *Crossing the Plains and Early Days in California* (San Francisco: Privately printed, 1928), 66; Caroline D. Budlong, *Memories. Pioneer Days in Oregon and Washington Territory* (Eugene, Oregon: Picture Press Printers, 1949), 36; and Fraker, "To Pike's Peak," 137.

59. Sandra L. Myres (ed.), "Evy Alexander: The Colonel's Lady at Ft. McDowell," *Montana the Magazine of Western History*, 24 (Summer 1974): 32-34; and Diary of Caroline Phelps, 1830-1860, Iowa State Historical Society.

60. Rachel Elizabeth Wright, "The Early Upper Napa Valley," 1928, Bancroft Library.

61. Diary of Malvina Virginia Manning, 1862, Bancroft Library; and Louise Sophia Gellhorn Boylan, "My life story. Reminiscence of German settlers in Hardin County, 1867-1883," Iowa State Historical Society.

62. E. Allene Taylor Dunham, *Across the Plains in a Covered Wagon* (n.p., n.d.), 7; and Ferris, *Mormons at Home*, 24.

dian leaning his elbow on the wagon beside me, but I have not a single fear except that they may frighten the horses."[63] Often, as women relaxed enough to genuinely like some Indians, they even expressed happiness at their arrival and sorrow at their departure: "We have parted with white folks that we did not regret so much," one woman insisted.[64]

Gradually, some women made fast, personal friends with some Indians. When Mary Hodgson began trading with and entertaining her Indian neighbors, they responded by bringing "beautiful baskets and elaborate moccasins worked with beads and feathers" as presents. Similarly, when Alice Baldwin helped Indian women crimp and wave their hair, she discovered that "thereafter the Indian women were my firm friends, and rendered me various favors and kindnesses." An Indian man, who Caroline Phelps took into her home as a nurse for her children, gained her family's love so much that after his death they "cryed for poor John... as much as though he had been a relative." Such close friendships with Indians were possible, Leola Lehman believed, once whites realized that the Indians were afraid of white people because of the terrifying stories they had heard. She befriended one Indian woman and came to "like and respect her as one of the best women" she had ever known. When Lehman left the Indian region, she wrote, "I was glad to be back among my own people but had learned to like the Indians. I was no longer afraid and understood that many of their ways that seemed strange to me were caused by fear of white people."[65]

Even women who had suffered white-Indian conflicts or captivity still expressed positive feelings toward individual Indians. Some claimed that "friendly" Indians had saved them from harm, and

63. DeWitt and DeWitt, *Prairie Schooner Lady*, 78.

64. Hopping, "Incidents of Pioneer Life"; and Diary of Eliza Egbert.

65. Mary A. Hodgson, "The Life of a Pioneer Family," 1922, California State Library; Robert C. and Eleanor R. Carriker (eds.), *An Army Wife on the Frontier: The Memoirs of Alice Blackwood Baldwin, 1867-1877* (Salt Lake City: Tanner Trust Fund, University of Utah Library, 1975), 79; Diary of Caroline Phelps; and Leola Lehman, "Life in the Territories," *Chronicles of Oklahoma*, 41 (Fall 1963): 373-375.

Photo by Bailey, Dix & Mead. MHS Photo Archives

Officers and their "ladies" at Fort Randall, Dakota Territory, in 1882, on what the photographer called a "Morning Visit" to Sitting Bull's encampment.

others wrote of Indians who treated them decently and respectfully during a violent outbreak. Minnie Carrigan, taken captive in the New Ulm uprising in 1862, fondly wrote of two Indian women who cared for her. "It seems wrong for me to call those two Indian women squaws," she wrote, "for they were as lady-like as any white women, and I shall never forget them." Of another American Indian family who aided her she wrote, "Their conduct toward me was so considerate that I really liked them."[66]

Considering the evolution of some frontiers-

66. Cummins, *Autobiography*, 37; Saunders, "The Whitman Massacre"; Diary of Mary Richardson Walker, 1848, Huntington Library; and Wilhelmina B. Carrigan, *Captured by the Indians: Reminiscences of Pioneer Life in Minnesota* (Forest City, South Dakota: Forest City Press, 1907), 11, 16. For a similar account see Ruth S. Thompson, "The Tragedy of Legion Valley," 1928, Bancroft Library.

women's emotional ties to Indians, it is little wonder that many began to feel sympathy for the Indians' plight, often focusing their concern on whites' unjust treatment of Indians. "Is it right," Miriam Colt queried, that white men paid Indians "three dollars for a buffalo robe, worth twelve at home?"[67] Many women believed that repeated foolish and thoughtless actions by whites turned Indians into "demons" driven to "avenge grievances or broken promises."[68] As Mary Tatum grumbled:

> The heart grows sick with the repeted tale of wrongs and broken promises by the whites & government why must it be so why must the poor untutored readman [*sic*] suffer so from the whites who feel that they are so much further along[?][69]

Many women, upset that American Indians often lacked adequate food and clothing, pitied them and gave them what they could. After attempting to help twenty hungry Indians, Vogdes lamented, "I did pity these poor things paddling around in the cold & snow." A hungry Indian coughed so hard when Lois Murray refused his begging that she later wrote, "If I could have called him back, I would have given him bread." Claiming that she never turned a needy Indian away again, Murray railed against whites who abhored and mistreated Indians.[70]

Like Murray, many women blamed unprincipled white frontiersmen for their difficulties with Indians, but they indicted others as well; they accused government agents, renegade Frènchmen, Union and Confederate soldiers, Catholic priests, and particularly Mormons of corrupting or inciting American In-

67. Colt, *Went to Kansas*, 67.

68. Furness, "From Prairie to Pacific"; and Lord, *Reminiscences*, 142-145.

69. Diary of Mary Ann Tatum, 1870, Iowa State Historical Society.

70. Journal of Katherine Dunlap; Myres, *Cavalry Wife*, 117; Margaret E. Archer Murray, "Memoir of the William Archer Family," Part I, *Annals of Iowa*, 39 (Summer 1968): 368; Journal of Ada Vogdes; and Lois L. Murray, *Incidents of Frontier Life* (Goshen, Indiana: Ev. United Mennonite Publishing House, 1880), 92-93.

dians.[71] Sympathetic women also considered possible solutions to the dilemma of white-Indian relations. Some argued for United States government intervention, but others believed that as teachers, missionaries, and advocates they could help solve the problems.[72] Less optimistic women, like Margaret Carrington, held that Indians had few options: "abandon his home, fight himself to death, or yield to the white man's mercy." After the attack in 1866 on Ft. Kearny, Carrington disparaged the anti-Indian newspapers that hastily judged the situation "with all the embellishment and accuracy which wood engraving affords while theories of blame were devised by those who never saw a live Indian out of a city show."[73]

DESPITE HAVING EVIDENCE to the contrary, nineteenth century eastern and European literature, poetry, drama, informational books, textbooks, newspapers, magazines, sermons, and lectures supported the traditional image of the fierce, rapacious Indian and the weak, victimized white woman. Yet, of the one hundred and fifty diaries, journals, memoirs, and letters studied here, one hundred and thirteen recorded no

71. Annie Argyle, Cupid's Album (New York: M. Doolady, 1866), 89; Mary Butler Renville, *A Thrilling Narrative of Indian Captivity* (Minneapolis: Atlas Company's Book and Job Printing Office, 1863), 43; Caples, "Overland Journey"; Eleanor Taylor, "Ross Kin: Early Settlers of the West," 1978, Bancroft Library; Mrs. M.A. Rogers, "An Iowa Woman in Wartime," Part I, *Annals of Iowa*, 35 (Winter 1961): 525; Warren, *Memoirs*, 177; Dunham, *Across the Plains*, 11; Narrative of Nancy N. Tracy, 1880, Bancroft Library; and Ruth Peterson (comp.), "Across the Plains in '57," told by Nancy Campbell Lowell, California State Library.

72. Journal of Maria Schrode; Alice C. Fletcher, *Historical Sketch of the Omaha Tribe of Indians in Nebraska* (Washington: Judd & Detweiler, 1885), 12; Letters from Annie K. Bidwell to Colonel Pratt, April 26, 1904, and Senator George C. Perkins, March 11, 1904, in the Annie K. Bidwell Collection, California State Library; Ann Archbold, *A Book for the Married and Single, the Grave and the Gay: And Especially Designed for Steamboat Passengers* (East Plainfield, Ohio: Printed at the Office of the "Practical Preacher," 1850), 168-169; Walker, Diary; and Allie B. Busby, *Two Summers Among the Musquakies* (Vinton, Iowa: Herald Book and Job Rooms, 1886), 19.

73. Margaret I. Carrington, *Ab-sa-ra-ka, Home of the Crows: Being the Experience of an Officer's Wife on the Plains* (Philadelphia: J. B. Lippincott & Co., 1868), 184, 219.

trouble with Indians, twenty-two noted minor problems, and only fifteen reported major difficulties.[74]

A comparable sample of men's sources indicates support for the women's contentions on the relative absence of Indian attacks, but the frontiersmen's sources do indicate that men believed that gender had much to do with women's reactions to Indians. In almost twenty different topic areas mentioned in the men's and women's sources used in this study, men disagreed more than agreed with the women.[75] Most frontiersmen, by role and function, concerned themselves more than frontierswomen did with details of wagons, terrain, directions and maps, finances, land purchase and clearing, crops, equipment, and innumerable other technical and mechanical matters. While they often meticulously described a watering place or campground, a ford or ferry, a land purchase, a crop failure, a harvest, or a house-raising, men seldom touched on birth and child care, processing and cooking foodstuffs, producing and washing clothes, or other domestic affairs.[76] Even when the company consisted entirely of men, male writers mentioned domestic labor and arrangements only in passing. Edwin Hillyer, for example, was bemused by the sight of men cooking. "Who'd a thunk it, three months ago," he wrote, "that they

74. Other scholars who have also argued that the Plains Indian threat was vastly exaggerated are Robert L. Munkres, "The Plains Indian Threat on the Oregon Trail before 1860," *Annals of Wyoming*, 40 (1968): 193-221; and John D. Unruh, *The Plains Across: The Overland Emigrants and the Trans-Mississippi West, 1840-1860* (Urbana: University of Illinois Press, 1979), 9, 135-136, 156-200, 386, 395-396, 408-409.

75. These topic areas included cooking, washing, childbirth, child care, land purchase, land utilization, crops, finances, politics, and social life as well as the appearance, morality, customs, living arrangements, crafts, and warfare of Indians. These topics were compared both for relative frequency of mention and change in attitudes toward them over time.

76. A comparison of men's and women's documents from the same family collection graphically illustrates this point. Although both male and female family members experienced the same western region during the same time period, the emphases and perceptions in their writings are noticeably different. See, for example, the Bourn-Ingalls Family Papers, 1865-1958, Bancroft Library; the DeWitt Family Papers, ca. 1848-1867, Bancroft Library; the Kenyon Family Letters, 1856-1865, Iowa State Historical Society; the Alice L. Longley Collection, Division of Museum and Archives, Des Moines, Iowa; or the Parsons Letters, Northampton Historical Society, Northampton, Massachusetts. See also Faragher, *Women and Men on the Overland Trail*, 103-105, 128-133.

would see John and Ed away out on the plains... cooking over a bush fire?" He later wrote cryptically, "I baked bread. Yes I made and baked bread."[77]

In contrast, female writers concentrated on their continual responsibility for and interest in domestic proceedings. Women frequently listed a diverse catalog of domestic tasks interspersed with recipes, directions for producing goods such as soap or butter, descriptions of childbirth and care, comments on basic as well as fashionable clothing, and numerous remarks on other related subjects.[78] Women's sources, however, did tend to converge with men's in the areas of scenery, weather, meeting old neighbors, making new friends, loneliness and homesickness, illness, deaths, disasters, political events, entertainments, schools and churches, and other items of joint concern.[79]

There were also overlaps in men's and women's views of American Indians. Men emphasized the size and appearance of Indian villages, the number and

77. John O. Holzhueter (ed.), "From Waupun to Sacramento In 1849: The Gold Rush Journal of Edwin Hillyer," *Wisconsin Magazine of History*, 49 (Spring 1966): 222, 228. Other examples of men in all-male expeditions who slighted domestic topics include "Across the Plains in 1850," *Annals of Iowa*, 9 (October 1910): 447-483; Louise Barry (comp.), "Charles Robinson—Yankee '49er: His Journey to California," *Kansas Historical Quarterly*, 34 (Summer 1968): 179, 186; Alonzo Delano, *Life on the Plains and among the Diggings* (Ann Arbor: University Microfilms, 1966); "Journal of A. W. Harlan While Crossing the Plains in 1850," *Annals of Iowa*, 11 (April 1913): 32-62; Diary of Charles Glass Gray, 1849-1850, Huntington Library; Howard Stansbury, *An Expedition to the Valley of the Great Salt Lake* (Ann Arbor: University Microfilms, 1966); Fancher Stimson, "Overland Journey to California by Platte River Route and South Pass In 1850," *Annals of Iowa*, 13 (October 1922): 402-440; Milo Milton Quaife (ed.), *Across the Plains in Forty-nine* (Chicago: The Lakeside Press, 1948); Everett Walters and George B. Strother (eds.),

"The Gold Rush Diary of Henry Tappan," *Annals of Wyoming*, 25 (July 1953): 113-139; and Walker D. Wyman (ed.), *California Emigrant Letters: The Forty Niners Write Home* (New York: Bookman Associates, 1952).

78. Reminiscences of Kitturah Belknap; Dunham, *Across the Plains*; Diary of Eliza Egbert; Diary of Jane Augusta Gould; Haun, "A Woman's Trip"; Virginia W. Ivins, *Pen Pictures of Early Western Days* (Keokuk, Iowa: n.p., 1905); Sarah Welch Nossaman, "Pioneering at Bonaparte and Near Pella," *Annals of Iowa*, 13 (October 1922): 441-453; Diary of Caroline Phelps; and Diary of Mary St. John, 1858, Iowa State Historical Society. See also Faragher, *Women and Men on the Overland Trail*, 121-133.

79. Here again, the best illustration of the convergence of men's and women's writing on similar topics is to compare documents produced by members of the same family. The Reminiscences of Kitturah Belknap; Haun, "A Woman's Trip"; and Nossaman, "Pioneering at Bonaparte and Near Pella," are also cases of women who combine detailed commentary on domestic topics with many remarks of a more general nature.

strength of Indian groups, the amount and types of weapons in evidence, the quantity and quality of horses, and items important in their defense against potential intertribal attacks. And men had a distinct, overriding interest in their own weapons, military organization, and ability to resist Indian incursions.[80] Women, while recognizing the need for defense, mentioned it less often than men and occasionally even joked about it at the men's expense. Viewing her well-armed husband's bowie knife and pistols, Lucy Cooke caustically wrote, "Hope he won't hurt himself."[81] And after watching the men of her family fire fifty shots to kill one cow Maria Schrode wryly penned in her journal, "We think the Indians would be in great danger if they should attack us."[82] Women were much more inquisitive about the Indians' domestic organization, marital customs, child raising practices, and crafts.[83]

80. Barry, "Charles Robinson," 179, 186; Margaret S. Dart, "Letters of a Yankee Forty-Niner," *The Yale Review*, 36 (June 1947): 657-665; Delano, *Life on the Plains*, 165-170, 203, 211, 218-219, 273; Howard R. Egan (ed.), *Pioneering The West 1846 to 1868: Major Howard Egan's Diary* (Richmond, Utah: Howard R. Egan Estate, 1917), 23-24, 29; "Emigration From Iowa to Oregon in 1843," *Iowa Journal of History and Politics*, 10 (July 1912): 415-430; Gilbert Drake Harlan, "The Diary of Barber Harlan," Part I, *Journal of the West*, 3 (April 1964): 148-153, 156-157; Holzhueter, "From Waupun to Sacramento," 219-231; David M. Kiefer (ed.), "Over Barren Plains and Rock-Bound Mountains," *Montana the Magazine of Western History*, 22 (October 1972): 20-29; Charles W. Martin, "Joseph Warren Arnold's Journal of His Trip to and From Montana, 1864-1866," *Nebraska History*, 55 (Winter 1974): 477-491, 530-535; Edward O. Parry (ed.), "Observations on the Prairies: 1867," *Montana the Magazine of Western History*, 9 (October 1959): 25-28; James E. Potter (ed.), "The Missouri River Journal of Leonard W. Gilchrist, 1866," *Nebraska History*, 58 (Fall 1977): 282-283, 286-287, 290, 293-294; James A. Pritchard, *The Overland Diary of James A. Pritchard* (Denver: The Old West Publishing Co., 1959), 58, 109; and Gary C. Stein (ed.), "Overland to California," *American History Illustrated*, 12 (May 1977): 26-36.

81. Cooke, *Covered Wagon Days*, 58.

82. Sandra L. Myres, *Ho For California! Women's Overland Diaries from the Huntington Library* (San Marino, California: Huntington Library, 1980), 271.

83. Mrs. H. J. Clarke, "A Young Woman's Sights on the Emigrant's Trail, 1878," Bancroft Library; Ferris, *Mormons at Home*, 22-24; Frizzell, *Across the Plains*, 25; Hill, *A Dangerous Crossing*, 82; Journal of Esther Hanna; Magoffin, *Down the Santa Fe Trail*, 68; Diary of Virginia Manning; Parsons, "Women in the Sunbonnets"; and Walker, "Crossing the Plains," 4.

THERE IS A SIGNIFICANT contrast with men's and women's accounts of their interactions with Indians. Men described meeting and smoking the pipe with "chiefs," while women wrote of visiting with "squaws" and closely observing their cooking methods, dress, and children.[84] Differences are also evident in the men's reports of trading with Indians primarily for guns, ammunition, and horses, while women reported trading for clothing, furs, and foodstuffs.[85] Men's writings reflect their worry over protecting their animals from Indians, while women's writings show a great deal more concern about protecting their children.[86] Although men often observed that Indians were naked, oddly dressed, polygamous, fond of intermarrying with French settlers, unclean, begged, ate insects, or spoke little or no English, their judgments of such practices were generally terse.[87] Women not only recounted these customs and behaviors, but also seemed compelled

84. Contrast Stansbury, *An Expedition to the Valley of the Great Salt Lake*, 254-256; and Reuben G. Thwaites (ed.), *Early Western Travels* (Cleveland, Ohio: The Arthur H. Clark Co., 1905), 152-153, with Dunham, *Across the Plains*; and Ferris, *Mormons at Home*, 24.

85. Contrast "Across the Plains in 1850," 468-469; Egan, *Pioneering the West*, 47; Pritchard, *Diary of James A. Pritchard*, 104; and Thwaites, *Early Western Travels*, 145, 149, with Cooke, *Covered Wagon Days*, 66; Guill, "Overland Diary"; Hopping, "Incidents of Pioneer Life"; Diary of Louisa Rahm; and Journal of Ada Vogdes.

86. Contrast "Across the Plains in 1850," 472; Egan, *Pioneering the West*, 174; "Journal of A. W. Harlan," 55, 60; Merrill J. Mattes and Esley J. Kirk (eds.), "From Ohio to California in 1849: The Gold Rush Journal of Elijah Bryan Farnham," *Indiana Magazine of History*, 46 (September and December 1950): 407-409; Pritchard, *Diary of James A. Pritchard*, 127; Stansbury, *An Expedition to the Valley of the Great Salt Lake*, 81, 233, 239; and Stimson, "Overland Journey to California," with Caples, "Overland Journey"; Colt, *Went to Kansas*, 61, 136; Florence Call Cowles, *Early Algona. The Story of Our Pioneers, 1854-1874* (Des Moines: The Register and Tribune Co., 1929), 111; Frink, *Journals*, 82; and Margaret A. Kelley, "Notes on Pioneers," California State Library.

87. Barry, "Charles Robinson," 179-188; Truman W. Camp, "The Journal of Joseph Camp, 1859," *Nebraska History*, 46 (March 1965): 32-35; "Journal of A. W. Harlan," 51; Kiefer, "Over Barren Plains," 18-21; Martin, "Joseph Warren Arnold's Journal," 472-477; Mattes and Kirk, "From Ohio to California," 300-301, 307-308; Byron N. McKinstry, *The California Gold Rush Overland Diary of Byron N. McKinstry* (Glendale, California: The Arthur H. Clark Co., 1974), 223-224; Potter, "The Journal of Leonard Gilchrist," 291; Pritchard, *Journal of James A. Pritchard*, 73, 96-98; Raymond W. Settle (ed.), *The March of the Mounted Riflemen* (Glendale, California: Arthur H. Clark, 1940), 40-43, 56-57, 60-61, 72-73, 82-89, 114-115, 150-153, 160-161, 188-191, 202-205, 210-211, 221-224, 229-233, 236, 240-243, 247-255, 262-265, 280-281, 300-301, 306-315, 320-321, 338-339; and Burton J. Williams (ed.), "Overland to the Gold Fields of California In 1850," *Nebraska History*, 50 (Summer 1969): 142-145.

to express their shock, disapproval, and indignation, often at great length.[88]

Rumors and scares of Indian "depredations" affected both men and women. Both quickly learned to distinguish between tribes, found qualities to admire and to disparage in the types of Indians they encountered, and frequently recorded their impressions of the dress and physical appearance of the Indians. But men's writings seldom demonstrated much change in attitude or perception. Usually commited from the outset to an adversarial relationship with American Indians, most men had little motivation or opportunity to know Indians or to develop sympathetic feelings for them.[89] An exception, Alonzo Delano, came to believe that whites created nine-tenths of the trouble with Indians. But even he concluded that peaceful coexistence was impossible and that as inferiors the Indians would have to yield to whites. Howard Egan, another exception, found at least one "good" Indian who he brought back to Salt Lake City with him as a servant. Thomas White's report that he lost any sympathy he may have had for Indians after a few days of contact with the "hateful wretches" represents a much more common opinion among men, as does Randolph Marcy's consistent evaluation of Indians as "marauding and erratic savages."[90]

88. Bailey, "Journal of an Overland Trip"; Diary of Helen Carpenter; Fish, "Across the Plaines"; Guill, "Overland Diary"; Diary of Helen Love; Millington, "Journal"; Minto, "Female Pioneering"; Norton, "Diary of a Trip"; Journal of Caroline Richardson; and Sandford, "A Trip Across the Plains."

89. Although almost all of the male sources examined showed evidence of a lack of change in male attitudes toward Indians, particularly good examples are Elisha Brooks, *A Pioneer Mother of California* (San Francisco: Harr Wagner Publishing Co., 1922); James E. Enos, ca. 1892, "Recollections of the Plains," Newberry Library; Diary of Charles Glass Gray; Randolph B. Marcy, *Thirty Years of Army Life on the Border* (Philadelphia: J. B. Lippincott, 1963); Stansbury, *Expedition to the Valley of the Great Salt Lake*; and Quaife, *Across the Plains*. See McKinstry, *California Gold Rush Overland Diary*, 92-94, 98-101, for an example of one of the few male emigrants who realized that the adversary stance of frontiersmen was frequently unnecessary and even humorous.

90. Delano, *Life on the Plains*, 309, 319-320; Egan, *Pioneering the West*, 185; Oscar O. Winther and Gayle Thornbrough (eds.), *To Oregon in 1852: Letter of Dr. Thomas White* (Indianapolis: Indiana Historical Society, 1964), 12; Randolph B. Marcy, *A Hand-Book for Overland Expeditions* (New York: Harper and Brothers, 1859), 200, 211; and Marcy, *Thirty Years of Army Life*, 47.

This photograph of the "Old Simonson Ranch on Pumpkin Creek," taken by the great frontier photographer Laton A. Huffman in 1882, shows a typical frontier ranch scene: A ranch house that has grown by additions over the years and the women who "kept house" in the rough plains environment.

Huffman Collection, MHS Photo Archives

Over two-thirds of the women's writings, however, manifested process and change.[91] Women commonly expressed sentiments similar to Georgia Reed Murphy's, who although terrorized by Indian tales before leaving home later wrote, "let me say that we suffered vastly more from fear of the Indians before starting than we did on the plains."[92] Yet western women's diaries and letters were not sought out and published as were western men's, nor were women asked to become newspaper correspondents or authors. As women, they were not welcomed on the lecture platform or the lyceum circuit. Moreover, the interviews, sketches, and essays on frontier life cranked out by male writers largely ignored women. And few people asked Indians about their feelings.

During an era when Americans considered women and Indians inferiors, it is not surprising that their personal interpretations of western events would be ignored. But there might be a deeper reason that Americans clung so tenaciously to a deprecating view of these two groups. Most nineteenth century Americans could *not* replace their prejudicial images of women and American Indians with an accurate view, one that recognized them as rational and capable beings. Such a revision would have upset not only prevailing concepts, but also questioned those related discriminatory actions that society inflicted on women and Indians. Because they needed to perpetuate traditional views that justified their prejudicial actions, nineteenth century Americans could not observe nor accept what was actually transpiring between women and Indians in the trans-Mississippi West.

91. Although almost two-thirds of the women's sources showed evidence of favorable changes in female attitudes toward Indians, particularly good examples are Ackley, *Crossing the Plains*; Carriker and Carriker, *An Army Wife on the Frontier*; Cooke, *Covered Wagon Days*; DeWitt and DeWitt, *Prairie Schooner Lady*; Fraker, "To Pike's Peak"; Reminiscences of Julia Hare; Hodgson, "Life of a Pioneer Family"; Hopping, "Incidents of Pioneer Life"; Horne, "Migration and Settlement"; Ivins, *Pen Pictures of Early Western Days*; Diary of Rachel Rose; Van De Wiele, "Travels"; and Journal of Ada Vogdes.

92. Murphy, "Across the Plains," 409.

Consequently, the nineteenth century bequeathed to the twentieth century a selective interpretation of the experiences of women and Indians. That many twentieth century people must have shared the needs and prejudices expressed by nineteenth century people is indicated by their willing acceptance and continued perpetuation of these myths. Many people would agree, particularly those who are women and Indians, that the time is past due for a reassessment of the attitudes and the data that underwrote the inaccurate presentation of this chapter in the history of the American West.

GLENDA RILEY is Professor of History and Coordinator of Women's Studies at University of Northern Iowa and the author of numerous articles on the history of women in the West. This article is part of a book-length study that is scheduled for publication by University of New Mexico Press in late 1984.

A Complex Bond: Southern Black Domestic Workers and Their White Employers

Susan Tucker

Alice Walker, in *Meridian*, shows a young black protagonist summing up her knowledge of white women in order to decipher what her lover could possibly see in someone as undesirable as a white girl. She has had very few first-hand dealings with white women and draws instead upon the memories of her grandmother, a former domestic, and her mother, who has occasionally worked for whites:

> For she realized what she *had* been taught was that nobody wanted white girls except their empty-headed, effeminate counterparts—white boys. . . . As far back as she could remember it seemed something *understood:* that while white men would climb on black women old enough to be their mothers—"for the experience"—white women were considered sexless, contemptible and ridiculous by all. . . . They were clear, dead water.
>
> Her mother, though not a maid, had often worked for white families near Christmastime in order to earn extra money, and she told her family—in hushed, carefully controlled language . . . about the lusty young sons. . . .

Susan Tucker is a Fellow at the Newcomb College Center for Research on Women, Tulane University. Trained as a librarian, she has worked since 1978 in the gathering and compiling of bibliographic material on the relationship of southern domestic workers and their employers. In 1980 she began recording oral memories of and about these two groups of women in the Gulf South. Some of the interviews conducted on this project will be published in 1988 by Louisiana State University Press. This article grew out of early efforts to analyze and write about these recorded memories after six years spent transcribing and editing amidst mothering and other domestic and professional jobs. *For their willingness to discuss ideas and for their help in the editing of this paper, she is sincerely grateful to Beth Willinger, Newcomb College; Barbara Ewell, Loyola University; and the editors of* FRONTIERS.

> But what had her mother said about white women? She could actually remember very little, but her impression had been that they were frivolous, helpless creatures, lazy and without ingenuity. Occasionally one would rise to the level of bitchery, and this one would be carefully set aside when the collective "others" were discussed. Her grandmother—an erect former maid who was now a midwife—held strong opinions, which she expressed in this way: 1. She had never known a white woman she liked after the age of twelve. 2. White women were useless except as baby machines which would continue to produce little white people who would grow up to oppress her. 3. Without servants all of them would live in pigsties.[1]

This paper explores such remembrances, and the corresponding remembrances by white women of black women. For all but the last two decades, southern women, white and black, have primarily been known to one another as Meridian knew of white women—through a domestic worker. She, more than any other person in the segregated South, witnessed the very personal lives of both blacks and whites. She thus became the key person through whom each race claimed to know the other. This paper, then, asks, How do black female domestic workers and their white employers remember one another? And what do these memories tell us about past race relations among southern women?

Data for this research was gathered between 1979 and 1985. Extensive, open-ended interviews were conducted with 100 black and white women: domestic workers, children of domestic workers, employers, and children of employers, all born between 1880 and 1960 in an area that runs from Baton Rouge, Louisiana, to Pensacola, Florida. Because I grew up in this area—the Gulf South—and because much of my personal and professional commitment to change in the South stems from witnessing the life of a black domestic worker, I wanted to know if memories of and about domestic workers had affected the views of others. I specifically asked questions designed to record the interviewees' lifelong memories of each other. I wanted to look closely at how two groups of southern women viewed themselves and each other in terms of race and sex. I conducted all the interviews with white women and a little over half the interviews with black women; the remaining interviews with black women were conducted by Mary Yelling, a black interviewer. Interviewees were selected through the help of social service agencies, churches, college alumnae associations, relatives, friends, and friends of friends.[2]

To study the relationships of black and white southern women involves dissecting a complicated entanglement of race relations and economics. In particular, to study black female domestics and their white female employers involves examining the meaning of frequent contact between two groups of women separated by race and class and yet connected by long years of knowing one another. For within the entanglement of race relations, economics, and power struggles based upon race and economics there grew a complex bond of mutual dependence and mutual distrust, and sometimes, a guarded but nevertheless remembered affection.

Within this complex bond many southern women came to know each other. For example, during the 1950's and 1960's, when I was growing up, half of all working black women in my hometown of Mobile, Alabama, were domestic workers.[3] Until 1968, I had never spoken to a black female who was not either a domestic herself or the daughter, niece, or granddaughter of a domestic.

Until this time, for me as well as many other southern white and black women, the white home was our only meeting place. This was certainly true for upper- and upper-middle-class whites and for the many families of black domestics. But this was also true for middle-class blacks who, like Meridian's mother, made extra money by serving at parties, taking in wash, or other tasks; and for lower-middle-class and working-class whites, who took their clothes to washwomen and often had a "day worker" come in once a week to clean their homes.

Even less well-off white families could afford domestics, because black women had little other choice of employment. As late as 1945, it required only half as large a family income to employ a servant in the South as it did in other parts of the country;[4] the South was long known as a white housewives' utopia.

For southern women, this "utopia," resting as it did on the labor of black women, had other meanings as well. Most important, perhaps, was the symbolic one, for the "utopia" was rooted in the Old South and in the person of the ever-giving, nurturing, and loyal "Mammy." The South retained little of the plantation life so romanticized in film and novels, but it did retain power over blacks and a relatively elite lifestyle, in that it could employ black women for low wages. The domestic, then, was often used to illustrate how the Old South worked at its best.

For example, in one of my first interviews, a white woman stood angrily by her mantelpiece and began telling me how she did not care to do the interview, how no one would ever understand past ties between whites and blacks. Pointing up to a family portrait, she said:

> See that little girl hanging up there? That was Grandmother. And she had a slave named Annie. Well, Annie came with Grandmother and they lived here. Her mother had died when she was a little girl and she was an only child and she was devoted to Annie.
>
> And when the war was over, the Civil War, Annie was right there in the house with them. And, of course, they had everything stripped from them. They didn't have anything. They were poor.
>
> All right, Annie went out and got herself a job and brought her pay home to help buy the groceries, to feed the children in the family for Grandmother. And Annie is buried in our cemetery lot right now. She was part of the family. She stayed with the family all the rest of her life. And she went out when everything was gone to get work, and brought money home to help Grandmother. Now that's true! And how do you explain it?

How does one explain it, except to see these as two individual women, black and white, whose legend of mutual help persists until today? The problem is, of course, to document also the legends told by black domestics and the children of black domestics, in order to hear more than just one side of each legend.

Still, I did find Annie's marker in the cemetery. "Annie Johnson," it reads simply, "1840-1920." There is no indication on the gravestone, as there is on others in this same cemetery, of her status as mammy, nurse, or companion. There is no indication that she was, as the legend passed down through the white family has it, anything other than a part of the family.

In Katherine Anne Porter's story, "The Old Order," the white child Sophia Jane assigns her beloved servant and companion a birthdate and marks it in the family Bible:

> . . . inserting it just below her own. "Nannie Gay," she wrote in stiff careful letters, "(black)," and though there was some uproar when this was discovered, the ink was long since sunk deeply into the paper, and besides no one was really upset enough to have it scratched out. There it remained, one of their pleasantest points of reference.[5]

I prefer Sophia Jane's demarcation of Nannie, *within* the family, but (black). I prefer it because it more accurately reflects how most, if not all, domestics became a part of the white family: first, in slavery, "inserted" there by whites; and later, "inserted" there by economic conditions that left them little other choice.

My interviewee's remembrance, however, is a significant one, and one that I was to hear in various forms in other interviews. Her argument, joining white employer and black domestic in the care and protection of one another, was a favorite example used to illustrate the harmonious ways of the Old South, particularly as remembered by older white women. Such stories were often carried further by white women, and to a lesser extent by black women, to illustrate how white employers and black domestics shared a common distaste for and distrust of men. Such stories discussed husbands who were alcoholics or otherwise neglectful of responsibilities. Two white women told me that it was only with black domestics that they felt free to relate their grievances. Black domestics spoke of revelations of infidelity, drug addiction, financial losses, and incest. With black women, such "secrets" were "safe"—according to the racial etiquette that ensured that what went on in the white home would never be mentioned by a black to another white. But they were also "safe" because until recently white women have not acknowledged that such problems existed at all levels of society. White women seem to have felt that black women—who lived in a society said to be violent—would understand and comfort. In response, white women felt they helped black women in their struggles with abusive men. One white woman described a call at night from a black domestic leaving her husband: "Mother was more than glad to help. She saw this woman as her 'sister' in a common struggle that centered around religion, but also on attitudes toward men, in general."

Black women may have felt a similar security in telling their marital problems to someone outside their own community. Their descriptions of such conversations, however, had a less secretive tone. Instead, they spoke humorously of men—white and black—as "half-people," "boys," "playing at life." Speaking of her own husband and the husband of her employer, one black woman reflected:

> Was he worse than my husband? . . . If you put each one of 'em in a sack, I think they would fall out together. There's a very few good men. It's a very few.

Black women revealed less in these confidential exchanges because as they correctly saw, shared gender did not erase the fact that most white women did not wish to change a system in which their own standard of living rested upon the cheap labor of all blacks, male and female. As one white woman said in describing her life:

> I'll tell you the truth . . . my husband died in 1960 and I have done just as well having Dorothea come every day and Julius come once every two weeks. I have no illusions about white men, either, you see. One colored woman every day and one colored man working every now and then to do the heavy work makes for more than a replacement for a husband! Of course, I did love him. But he was a child. Like the Negroes in a way. I think most Southern women will admit that . . . if you can get them alone. Certainly ones with young children and old ones like me. What good are men to us?

For white women like this one, employing a black domestic allowed a lifestyle very different from that of her contemporaries in other parts of the country. How did such a lifestyle affect the white women to whom I spoke? Of the forty-eight white women I interviewed, two of the women born before 1940 entered politics and one became a doctor; two born after 1940 became lawyers; many were active in volunteer work. Upper-middle-class for the most part, not one of them expressed an interest in the women's movement. Though by no means a random sample of southern white women, the women interviewed seemed typical in their lack of interest in feminism—educated white women of the South are perhaps more conservative in their views on feminism because any study of feminism would address the full equality of all people, thereby challenging attitudes towards race and class as well. And on a less philosophical but nevertheless important level, in the South educated white women, who in other areas of the country first made up the ranks of the National Organization for Women and other feminist groups, are perhaps less inclined to support change because the traditional roles of women, as mothers or other caretakers within the family, have been easier, more rewarding ones—roles that have not blocked the road outside the domestic sphere, that have not been tinged with exhaustion and underutilization of intellect. The traditional roles of many white southern women, more often than not, have been made easier at the expense of black women.

For example, many white women told me how pleasant young motherhood had been with the help of black women—first a baby nurse who came and stayed for the three weeks following the birth of a child, and later other black nursemaids. Again and again younger white women, mothers today who do not have this help, told me that they remembered their mothers' lives as being very different from their own because of black women:

> The thing I always remember was how close Rachel was to my mother. I mean, I think about it today and almost yearn for that sort of relationship. I can remember Rachel fixing breakfast for Mama and it would just be a poached egg and toast and coffee on a tray, but just the way it looked, I remember. And I remember how she'd take it into Mama's room and sit it on the dressing table.
>
> Today, I feel so . . . tired. I have these two children and I'm pregnant and I'd love someone to bring me breakfast. And Rachel came everyday—well six days a week and did that. I can never remember her going on vacation or anything. She'd go with us on vacation . . . and she came at seven in the morning and left at 6:30 after she'd fed us and had us all cleaned up.

The help of a black domestic also meant the emotional support of a woman who was already symbolically cast as mother in southern culture. A recurrent sentence in the interviews with white women was, "She was closer to me than my own mother." This was probably accurate; in homes that employed full-time help, black women domestics were the more active caregivers. They were the ones who were there in day-to-day emergencies. They were often the ones who told girl children about menstruation, about sex, about relationships with men because they were often with these children at crucial times in their lives. One black woman told me of a young white woman in labor who refused to go into the delivery room without her. It was the maid who cut the newborn's umbilical cord. This was in the 1950's, long before "significant others" were allowed to be present at birthing.

White women in the South generally view black women as stronger, more instinctive mothers than whites.[6] They entrust their children to black domestics, believing them to be more "natural" mothers. Indeed, the most visible role of the black domestic within white southern literature has been that of a mother surrogate. Even in late twentieth-century works, she is most often the mothering character and she is often shown in contrast to an ineffectual white mother.[7]

Black domestics are also seen as emotionally and physically stronger than white women, even though in fact black women have poorer health and a lower life expectancy than do white women. Black people, several women told me, "age slower than white people." And black women in particular, another white woman told me, "stay strong until they die." In describing the care of her dying mother by an older black woman, one white woman said: "Black women are stronger. They can do this more easily than I could ever."

Such a belief in the strength of the black domestic is built upon the mythical quality southern white women ascribe to black domestics. To white women employers, black domestics seemed to have almost magical qualities. They were called healers, therapists, listeners: "They sensed things. If you weren't feeling well, they could just pick up a rag or something and touch you and it felt better."

Such idealization, and the fact that the stories told were often ones handed down through generations of mothers and daughters, suggest that the strength of the black domestic had an important function in the minds of southern white women. Primarily, of course, it "explained" how such a person could labor and continue to give under harsh societal and economic conditions. White women often clearly saw the injustices under which black women lived. But by proclaiming the strength of black women, white women could ignore these injustices. Specifically, they could ignore their own part in the continued exploitation of black women in the workplace. And they could also ignore some of their own guilt for not speaking out against other forms of exploitation, such as the sexual exploitation of black women by white men.

But the strength ascribed to these black domestics in repeated statements by white women seems also to have helped the white women in their own struggles. Particularly, the image of the strong black mother seems to have encouraged white girl children. It may be that this image provided a much-needed vision of woman's strength in a male-dominated society.

How did black domestics view this role assignment? And how, in general, did they view their complex bond with white women employers? Black women, too, saw themselves as the more "instinctive mothers"—both to their own children and to the children of whites. They did not wish to be cast as "mammy" and they did not perceive their child rearing as romantically as whites did, but they saw themselves as warmer and more balanced in their approach to children. They felt white women "didn't know how to love children; white women didn't stay around to know how." And they saw their care of white children as a "decent" or "Christian" response. White women, they felt, did not have the same standards as they—of decency or Christianity: "She couldn't have raised that child. She was too busy with looking out for herself," said one. At the same time, black domestics who did not wish to work with children resented being always cast as experts: "They all think we blacks just love children." Black domestics were also very clear that their care for white children was not the same as their care for their own children. "I loved them," said one black domestic, "like you'd love anyone you knew as a baby—but I wouldn't go help her now, say, like I'd go to my own daughter."

The black domestics I spoke with worked because they had to, because they had children to support alone, or because their husbands' earnings could not support the family. In every interview with black women, there were poignant stories of returning to work shortly after childbirth; of leaving their own children with relatives, neighbors, older children; of seeking jobs near home. As symbolic and surrogate mothers to whites, many of them felt intensely the irony and sadness of their lives—that to support their own children, they had to mother other women's children. They also felt intensely the luxury white women had (and often refused) of being able to choose to care for their own children: "You'd be there just taking good care of their children and yours were probably just somewhere running wild." One woman described the drowning of her own son while she was at work, minding white children.

And yet, black women also expressed a very strong pride that they did provide for their families. Many of the older black women interviewed had migrated from rural areas to southern cities between 1900 and 1950. To agricultural workers in a section of the country that was no longer economically profitable, domestic work in the cities did offer a better standard of living. Today, it is hard to imagine, as one black woman told me, how she worked in the city for $10 a week in 1941 and felt this to be a fortune compared to the $3 a week she could make as a domestic in the country. She left her three-year-old daughter with her family (who were sharecroppers paid not in cash, but from the commissary's stock of food) in order to have actual cash, "to buy a little bit of canned meat, rice, and material. All these meant a lot."

Another rural-born black woman told of an aunt who worked for a wealthy urban family and who, before her death, found jobs with various branches of the white family for six nieces. The aunt's goal was to bring her family out of the poverty of the country. It appears from a reading of scholarly works on domestic workers, and on the history of black women's work, that black women, more than any other ethnic group except the Irish, migrated alone—without men—to better their lives.[8] In the network of aunts, nieces, cousins, mothers, daughters, and finally whole families lay much of the real strength black domestics did have.

From such networks, black women learned to look upon both their jobs and themselves with a great deal of humor and dignity. With laughter, they often spoke of the uniformity with which whites of all social classes seemed to need blacks "to take care of them." They saw clearly their role as signifiers of status within the white community. As one black woman told me, "See, these white people, soon as they got able, they used to get a colored person to wash for them." That is how, she explained, she came to be employed at ten years old in 1904, baby-sitting and washing for a woman who worked in a cotton mill.

Another black woman, born in 1938, told me of her experience with poor whites in this way:

> Now I did get a job sort of as a maid for a poor family once. I mean they were so poor till their house was just so dirty. And they had rabbits in the back yard. And the girls used to roll their hair with paper from the bread. . . . And (the mother) had tons of kids. You know, she worked in a dime store downtown herself! And I think her older daughters were working in the theater. They had the kinds of jobs we couldn't get. . . . And it was a struggle for them to pay me that little $20 a week. . . . And their house was a lot worse than ours. . . . They were poor but they thought they could afford a maid!

This black woman, like many others, maintained her identity outside her work—within her home and her church. As another black woman told me, "My aunt said, 'Never marry yourself to a job, because heh, domestic work, you can find anytime.' " Another recalled, as her reason for "not loving those white folks like they say they love you," a story her mother had told her:

Private collection

> I always had a feeling that people, they like you as long as you're able to do their work. My mother told me that. I told you she worked for a very rich family. And she was up in their house one day helping out with the old grandmother. And this old black man who had worked for them since he was a boy, he passed up there in the house with them. So my mother said, "Oh, I know they're gonna miss him."
>
> And the old lady said, laughing, "I don't know, Margaret, you can always get another darky, just as good or better."

In order to preserve this valued independence, three black domestics explained, they avoided borrowing from whites, even if this meant going without much-needed money. This refusal was considered by older black domestics to be an almost revolutionary concept, for not to borrow from whites "meant you might just be hurting your family for your principles." Although work in cities did mean being paid in cash, black domestics, like their rural counterparts, were still linked to white families in ways that were but one step from the plantation system. Wages were pitifully low and not governed by federal minimum wage laws until the 1970's. Instead, black women's subsistence-level wages were supplemented by cast-off clothing, furniture, food, and loans. Older black women accepted such "gifts" because they had no other choice:

> Of course, at first, I didn't get enough money. . . . At that particular time, it was a certain salary they paid you and that's what they paid unless they gave you extra for being nice.
>
> I got a lot of extra. For doing and being nice and kind to those kids. And they always treated all my kids just like they treated me. Like Old Miz Nevitte, when the kids graduated or something, she'd give me a check.

From 1900 to the present, however, black women have increasingly felt an uneasiness about such "gifts." "I told them I didn't tote,"[9] said one, discussing the "old days" after slavery, when whites did not pay except by giving food in "the service pan." Black women correctly associated these gifts with a system designed to keep them in the service of whites, without the monetary means to achieve a higher standard of living. A domestic who worked in the 1950's described the effect of such offers:

> "Want some watermelon?" she'd say. "Take your mother a slice of watermelon."
>
> That made me detest domestic work. And the more I would work for people and see the books they had, the furnishings, everything in their houses, all nice, I just couldn't understand why we couldn't have this. Why we couldn't get paid more, instead of just being offered a slice of watermelon or whatever?

If they worked for a wealthy enough family, like the aunt who brought her nieces to the city, domestics did often make a slightly better wage, and they tended to remain with the same employer for longer periods of time.[10] They also seemed more inclined to use loans from whites to buy land, homes, automobiles, and educations for their children. Five black women spoke of such loans. They often spoke quite gratefully of these whites, telling me stories of gifts of "good things, not just what they didn't want"; they spoke of gifts that could actually be categorized as gifts between equals, not just the cast-offs offered almost as an apology for low wages.

And yet, even these domestics were painfully aware that their bond with whites rested upon the paternalistic system that served to keep blacks subordinate. The following story pinpoints their knowledge of their unfair position. It is from an interview with a black woman born in 1930, who at the time she describes was working for a white family for $20 a week. Her father became ill, and the hospital in the town refused to operate on him without being paid first.

> I called Miz Jones . . . told her I couldn't come to work 'cause my Daddy was very sick and I had to try and see if I could help my mother to get some money.
> She said, "How much money?"
> I said, "A hundred and forty dollars is what Mama needs before the doctors would touch him."
> Now, you understand I'm only making $20 a week so by the time I'd get a hundred and forty dollars is a long time. But at any rate, she said, "I'll talk to my husband, Mr. Jones."
> So she told him, "Leila's father is sick and has to have an operation and they won't touch him unless somebody else says the money will be paid."
> See, she knew the system.
> So, Mr. Jones called the hospital and told them to operate on the man and start right away and don't make no more much ado about it.
> I never will forget that. . . .
> I was so thankful. But I still knew it wasn't right. The whole system was wrong. Because, of course, Mr. Jones never did have to pay a cent. The fact was that the doctors wouldn't touch my Daddy until somebody white said they'd pay the money.

Black women like this one saw clearly the unfair discrepancies between their own lives and those of the white families for whom they labored. The same white women who idealized domestics were often seen by those domestics as frivolous, dependent, and silly. Idleness encouraged craziness in white women, one black woman told me, explaining alcoholism and depression in her employer. Although the money they earned was very little, black women did recognize that having money of their own gave them an independence white women lacked. Two black women told me humorous stories of white women who had "allowances" from their husbands. Another described the emptiness in the life of her employer, who "shopped for a living."

Black women, also, in most cases, knew that the white women for whom they labored saw them as independent, strong people, worthy of admiration and emulation. Their awareness that they were seen as healers, as professional caretakers, did in many cases enable them to feel a sense of reciprocity and tenderness towards white women employers. One black woman described the death of a white child and her constant support of the white mother during the following months. Between these two women, as between other black and white women who shared important points in each other's lives, a true bond of affection did develop and endure.

But such bonds failed not only to rectify social and economic injustices, but even to end the persistent silence between white and black women about these injustices. The same white employers who saw black women as strong and persevering, who wondered "how they did it," did not even, for example, talk to black domestics about societal troubles.

In recitals of everyday meetings between black domestics and white employers there are many small examples of how this silence prevented change. For example, a white woman who had expressed affection towards her black domestic also explained that, when the domestic's husband was among the first to be laid off a job, the employer was afraid to mention race as a factor in his dismissal. She also told me how she paid the woman during pregnancy leave but made her promise not to speak of this to anyone in the white family—and particularly not to other domestics,[11] lest they also ask for paid pregnancy leave. She did not want her friends to know. Surely, an open stand on the part of this white woman could have ended the silence, at least in her immediate environment. This could have been a beginning, even if a small one.

Instead, southern white women like this one were early taught that it was "impolite" to discuss race and they seem to have fallen back on this as a standard response in their confusion and guilt over social injustices. I was told over and over that race was not mentioned between black domestics and white employers because "you didn't want to hurt their feelings." Recalling how her young daughter had asked, in the presence of a domestic, why Willie Bell could not sit in the little booths at the drugstore, a white woman said, "I just froze. We didn't think it right to bring up unpleasant things. We thought it would hurt their feelings." When I asked if this black domestic's feelings were not hurt by the daily reminders of segregation, she replied, "I suppose now that they were. But then we didn't think of it. We thought it was a rule."

Another white woman described the silence this way:

> Once when Beatrice went home sick, Mother went over to her room to clean it up. There was like a writing paper box and on the top, as you opened the lid, there was a picture of Mother's best friend. It was probably something that Mother had thrown away . . . and underneath that were all these things that Beatrice had cut out of the newspaper about racial matters. We never knew why that was or why. But I know that she really loved Mother. And I know Mother really loved her.

This white interviewee was typical of others in that she brought up the silence and the affection in close proximity. Thus, although the code of silence governed all southerners, white women's choice of words—words such as *feelings, politeness, love*—suggests that they formed their own peculiarly female justifications for the written and unwritten laws of segregation. And although their particular justification took into account their connections to black women, the end result of their silence was that they, too, participated in the entire system designed to keep blacks at a subsistence level.

Private collection

The silence of white women was reinforced by the silence of black women. As has been noted by many black writers, silence as a form of mask-wearing was central to the survival of black people both in slavery and later. Most of the black domestics interviewed mentioned that any discussion of race with white women might get them labeled "uppity" and could mean a loss of vital income. Not only were their wages crucial to their families' survival, but these black domestics seemed also to be go-betweens in finding legal, medical, and other forms of help for neighbors and friends, as well as their own families. Charles S. Johnson, a black sociologist who studied the rural South during the first half of the twentieth century, found that "for those [blacks] still living in the country there is, it would appear, one unfailing rule of life. If they would get along with least difficulty, they should get for themselves a protecting white family."[12] Perhaps because many of the older black women interviewees had migrated from the country to the cities, I found this means of coping still prevalent.

To prepare black children for adulthood in a white-dominated world, black children, then, like white children, were early instructed in the code of silence. Robert Coles, studying black southern children in the 1960's and 1970's, found that black parents thought it necessary that children "grow up scared of whites."[13] As one black woman told me—"You just flat didn't mention anything. You acted—even in the 1960's—like you was pleased [with] *every* thing. *Pleased.*" Said another, "When the Roosevelts were speaking for black people you just went along like you'd never even heard of them."

Such reticence has left a legacy of silence between white and black southern women that is only now fading. Like Meridian, the women we interviewed seem to be still guessing about one another, still extrapolating from the earlier, segregated versions of black or white women they have known or known of. Said one younger white woman, "Sure, I know black women at work to say hello to, to talk with about the weather. But, as far as really knowing them, knowing their home life or even their thoughts, there is a certain restraint, a wall between us. I'm afraid of saying the wrong thing." And said a black woman, "Every white woman reminds me a little bit, underneath—even those I know at work, know well—of the woman my mother worked for. I don't get too close to them. I'm careful what I say." Said another black woman, "They don't put out that back door now,[14] they'll even call you 'Mrs.' if you tell them, but underneath, you scratch them and it's still, you're black and they're white and you got to work up courage to speak up."

The need to end such a legacy of silence is great. As black and white southern women begin to meet one another on more common grounds, we must look honestly at the ways in which our mothers and grandmothers have been known to one another. Particularly, we can then begin to look at the vocabulary we have used, as women, to explain, and even to justify our complicity in the hierarchy of laws and customs that exploit women. In so doing, we can begin to sort out the ways that class, race, and gender have figured in the history of southern women.

And in so doing, we can begin to work for change in areas, such as domestic work, that have been hidden from the public eye. Black domestic workers are, after all, still the lowest paid of all workers. Despite various legislative measures enacted in the 1970's, some do not receive minimum wage. Many will not receive Social Security benefits because they cannot afford now to have money withheld from their paychecks. Almost never do they have any insurance paid by their employers. Their working conditions are determined, still, by a complicated entanglement of race relations and economics. An end to the legacy of silence could signal the beginning of measures to correct such conditions.

It is important, therefore, that we do not lose sight of either the present conditions or the past history of domestic workers.[15] And if we can begin to urge that domestic workers be justly compensated for their work—work that is, more than any other, what has been labeled "women's work"—will we not, then, also begin to fight for a more just compensation of all work?

NOTES

1. Alice Walker, *Meridian* (New York: Harcourt, Brace, Jovanovich, 1976), pp. 103-05.

2. Because the numbers of white household workers and nonwhite employers of household workers were statistically low in this area of the South, I chose to interview only black domestics who labored primarily for whites, white employers of black domestics, and the children of these two groups.

3. See U.S. Bureau of the Census, *Decennial Census* for the years 1950 and 1960 for cities in Alabama. See also the census for Louisiana, Mississippi, South Carolina, Georgia, and Florida.

4. C. Arnold Anderson and Mary Jean Bowman, "The Vanishing Servant and the Contemporary Status of the American South," *American Journal of Sociology*, 54 (November 1953), 215-30, especially p. 223.

5. Katherine Anne Porter, "The Old Order," in *The Leaning Tower and Other Stories* (New York: Harcourt, Brace and Company, 1934), pp. 37-38.

6. The idea of the black woman as the strong, instinctive mother to the white family for whom she worked is discussed by Lillian Smith, *The Killers of the Dream* (New York: Norton, 1961); by Catherine Juanita Starke, *Black Portraiture in American Fiction: Stock Characters, Archetypes and Individuals* (New York: Bantam Books, 1971), pp. 125-35; and by Richard King, *A Southern Renaissance: The Cultural Awakening of the American South, 1930-1955* (New York: Oxford Univ. Press, 1980).

pp. 172-93. Although King and Smith both discuss the view of black woman as seductress, I found no evidence that white women viewed black women in this way. White interviewees, instead, seemed to sometimes categorize black women "as having different morals" and in this way, they seemed to rationalize the rape of black women by white men. In interviewing over 100 black and white women, I did not find any instance where black women were described as being sexually more ardent. Rather, white women—if they spoke at all of the sexuality of black women—saw these black women as "more accepting of their bodies," "looser, but not in a bad way," "just different." The view of black woman as seductress seems to be a stereotype used primarily by southern men to excuse rape: a stereotype popularized by women only in romantic novels.

7. In the nineteenth century, the black domestic was represented by such characters as Nanny in *The Recollections of a Southern Matron* (1836) by Caroline Howard Gilman, Mammy in *Uncle Tom's Cabin* (1851) by Harriet Beecher Stowe, Aunt Phillis in *Aunt Phillis' Cabin* (1852) by Mary H. Eastman, Mammy in *Diddie, Dumps, and Tot* (1883) by Louise Clarke Pyrennelle, Mom Bi in "Mom Bi: Her Friends and Her Enemies" (1884) by Joel Chandler Harris, and Mammy Krenda in *Red Rock* (1898) by Thomas Nelson Page. All these works show the black domestic as a devoted mother surrogate to white children.

Twentieth-century works such as Julia Peterkin's *Green Thursday* (1924), William Faulkner's *The Sound and the Fury* (1929), Margaret Mitchell's *Gone with the Wind* (1936), Lillian Smith's *Strange Fruit* (1944), Ann Petry's *The Street* (1946), Carson McCullers' *The Member of the Wedding* (1958), Harper Lee's *To Kill a Mockingbird* (1960), Shirley Ann Grau's *The Keepers of the House* (1964), Lisa Alther's *Original Sins* (1981), Toni Morrison's *Tar Baby* (1981), and Roy Hoffman's *Almost Family* (1982)—to name a few—continue in the tradition of idealizing black domestics, presenting household workers who mother white families.

8. This is suggested in David Katzman's *Seven Days a Week: Women and Domestic Service in Industrializing America* (New York: Oxford Univ. Press, 1978), which looks at the period 1870 to 1920, and Daniel Sutherland's *Americans and their Servants: Domestic Service in the United States from 1800 to 1920* (Baton Rouge: Louisiana State Univ. Press, 1981). Elizabeth Pleck's "The Two-Parent Household: Black Family Structure in Late Nineteenth-Century Boston," in *The American Family in Social-Historical Perspective*, ed. Michael Gordon (New York: St Martin's Press, 1973), pp. 152-77, also touches upon the migration of single black women. Further study of census and other records is needed to fully assess how often black women migrated alone, with the intent of living with an aunt or older sister once they arrived.

9. "Toting" was the practice of accepting food from the employer's kitchen as a "supplement" to paid wages, or less frequently in place of paid wages. "Toting" was also referred to as "taking home the service pan." To tote means to add up to—in this case to add up to the total payment earned for work.

10. Twelve of the fifty-two black women interviewed had worked for the same family for twenty years or more. Four of the younger black women interviewed had mothers who had worked for the same family for long periods of time. These women, of course, are not a sample representative of all domestic workers. Further studies are needed to determine the average length of employment with one family.

11. "Waiting on" was the term used to describe pregnancy leave. The employer chose whether to leave the position available for the worker, that is, to "wait" on her. This leave seems generally to have been, and

to be still, unpaid. Black women often recalled sending someone else—a sister, a daughter, or other relative—in their place to work "to keep the job going" for two or three months.

12. As quoted by Eugene Genovese in *Roll, Jordan, Roll: The World The Slaves Made* (New York: Pantheon Books, 1974), p. 118.

13. Robert Coles, *Children of Crisis: A study of Courage and Fear* (Boston: Little, Brown and Company, 1964), p. 66.

14. To "put out that back door" means to open the back door of a car, showing the person about to enter that he or she must ride in the back seat, must not be seated in the front seat by the (white) driver.

15. Recent sociological studies include Robert Hamburger's *A Stranger in the House* (New York: Macmillan, 1978), a book of oral histories of northern domestic workers; a chapter in Bettina Aptheker's book, *Woman's Legacy: Essays on Race, Sex, Class in American History* (Amherst: Univ. of Massachusetts Press, 1982), a study of domestic work within a Marxist framework; Elizabeth Clark-Lewis' "This Work Had A' End: The Transition From Live-in to Day Work," (*Southern Women: The Intersection of Race, Class and Gender*, Working Paper 2; Memphis: Center for Research on Women, Memphis State University, 1985), a comparison of live-in versus live-out work among domestic workers in the Washington, D.C. area from 1900 to 1920; Judith Rollins' book *Between Women: Domestics and Their Employers* (Philadelphia: Temple Univ. Press, 1985), a study of the relationship of domestic workers to their employers in the Boston area in the 1980's; Linda Martin and Kerry Segrave's *The Servant Problem: Domestic Workers in North America* (Jefferson, N.C.: McFarland, 1985), a look at the status of domestic workers from 1940 to the present; and scattered publications of the Department of Labor and the National Committee on Household Employment. Historical studies include Katzman's *Seven Days a Week* and Sutherland's *Americans and Their Servants*. Literary criticism includes only one book-length work, Trudier Harris' *From Mammies to Militants: Domestics in Black American Literature* (Philadelphia: Temple Univ. Press, 1982).

The Pocahontas Perplex: the Image of Indian Women in American Culture

by Rayna Green

In one of the best known old Scottish ballads, "Young Beichan" or "Lord Bateman and the Turkish King's Daughter" as it is often known in America, a young English adventurer travels to a strange, foreign land. The natives are of a darker

1. Pocahontas Saving Captain John Smith. Anonymous painting. *Private Collection.*

color than he, and they practice a pagan religion. The man is captured by the King (Pasha, Moor, Sultan) and thrown in a dungeon to await death. Before he is executed, however, the pasha's beautiful daughter—smitten with the elegant and wealthy visitor—rescues him and sends him homeward. But she pines away for love of the now remote stranger who has gone home, apparently forgotten her, and contracted a marriage with a "noble" "lady" of his own kind. In all the versions, she follows him to his own land, and in most, she arrives on his wedding day whereupon he throws over his bride-to-be for the darker but more beautiful Princess. In most versions, she becomes a Christian, and she and Lord Beichan live happily ever after.

In an article called "The Mother of Us All," Philip Young suggests the parallel between the ballad story and the Pocohontas-John Smith rescue tale.[1] With the exception of Pocohontas' marriage to John Rolfe (still, after all, a Christian stranger), the tale should indeed sound familiar to most Americans nurtured on Smith's salvation by the Indian Princess. Actually, Europeans were familiar with the motif before John Smith offered his particular variant in the *Generall Historie of Virginie* (1624).

Francis James Child, the famous ballad collector, tells us in his *English and Scottish Popular Ballads* that "Young Beichan" (Child #40) matches the tale of Gilbert Beket, St. Thomas Aquinas' father, as well as a legend recounted in the *Gesta Romanorum*, one of the oldest collections of popular tales. So the frame story was printed before 1300 and was, no doubt, well distributed in oral tradition before then. Whether or not our rakish adventurer-hero, John Smith, had heard the stories or the ballad, we cannot say, but we must admire how life mirrors art since his story follows the outlines of the traditional tale most admirably. What we do know is that the elements of the tale appealed to Europeans long before Americans had the opportunity to attach their affection for it onto

---

[1] "The Mother of Us All," *Kenyon Review* 24 (Summer, 1962), 391–441.

Pocahontas. Whether or not we believe Smith's tale—and there are many reasons not to—we cannot ignore the impact the story has had on the American imagination.

"The Mother of Us All" became our first aristocrat, and perhaps our first saint, as Young implies. Certainly, the image of her body flung over the endangered head of our hero constitutes a major scene in national myth *(fig. 1)*. Many paintings and drawings of this scene exist, and it appears in popular art on everything from wooden fire engine side panels to calendars. Some renderings betray such ignorance about the Powhatan Indians of Virginia—often portraying them in Plains dress—that one quickly comes to understand that it is the mythical scene, not the accuracy of detail that moved artists. The most famous portrait of Pocahontas, the only one said to be done from life (at John Rolfe's request), shows the Princess in Elizabethan dress, complete with ruff and velvet hat—the Christian, English lady the ballad expects her to become and the lady she indeed became for her English husband and her faithful audience for all time. The earliest literary efforts in America, intended to give us American rather than European topics, featured Pocahontas in plenty. Poems and plays—like James Nelson Barber's *The Indian Princess*; or, *La Belle Sauvage* (1808) and George Washington Custis' *The Settlers of Virginia* (1827), as well as contemporary American novels, discussed by Leslie Fiedler in *The Return of the Vanishing American*—dealt with her presence, or sang her praises from the pages of literary magazines and from the stages of popular playhouses throughout the east.[2] Traditional American ballads like "Jonathan Smith" retold the thrilling story; schoolbook histories included it in the first pages of every text; nineteenth century commercial products like cigars, perfume and even flour used Pocahontas' name as come-on *(fig. 2)*; and she appeared as the figurehead for American warships and clippers. Whether or not she saved John Smith, her actions as recounted by Smith set up one kind of model for Indian-White relations that per-

[2] See Jay B. Hubbell, "The Smith-Pocahontas Story in Literature," *The Virginia Magazine of History and Biography* 65 (July 1957), 275–300.

sists—long after most Indians and Anglos ceased to have face-to-face relationships. Moreover, as a model for the national understanding of Indian women, her significance is undeniable. With her darker, negatively viewed sister, the Squaw—or, the anti-Pocahontas, as Fiedler calls her—the Princess intrudes on the national consciousness, and a potential cult waits to be resurrected when our anxieties about who we are make us recall her from her woodland retreat.[3]

Americans had a Pocahontas Perplex even before the teenage Princess offered us a real figure to hang the iconography on. The powerfully symbolic Indian woman, as Queen and Princess, has been with us since 1575 when she appeared to stand for the New World. Artists, explorers, writers and political leaders found the Indian as they cast about for some symbol with which to identify this earthly, frightening, and beautiful paradise; E. McClung Fleming has given one of the most complete explications of these images.[4] The misnamed Indian was the native dweller, who fit conveniently into the various traditional folkloric, philosophical and literary patterns characteristic of European thought at the time.[5] Europeans easily adopted the Indian as the iconographic representative of the Americas. At first, Caribbean and Brazilian (Tupinamba) Indians, portrayed amidst exotic flora and fauna, stood for the New World's promises and dangers. The famous and much-repro-

---

[3] The many models, stereotypes and images operative for the Indian in Anglo-American vernacular culture are discussed in my dissertation, "The Only Good Indian: The Image of the Indian in Vernacular American Culture," Indiana University, 1973.

[4] E. McClung Fleming, "Symbols of the United States; From Indian Queen to Uncle Sam," in Ray B. Browne *et al.*, eds. *The Frontiers of American Culture* (Lafayette, Indiana: Purdue University Press, 1967), pp. 1–24; "The American Image as Indian Princess, 1765–1783," *Winterthur Portfolio* 2 (1968), pp. 65–81.

[5] For a summary of the philosophical backgrounds of the "Noble Savage" complex of beliefs and ideas, see Roy Harvey Pearce. *Savagism and Civilization: A Study of the Indian and the American Mind* (rpt. 1953, Baltimore: Johns Hopkins University Press, 1967). For references to folk motifs in Indo-European tradition, see Stith Thompson. *The Motif Index of Folk Literature*. 6 vols. (rpt. 1932–36, Bloomington, Indiana: Indiana University Press, 1955–58).

duced "Four Continents" illustrations (circa, early 16th century) executed by artists who had seen Indians and ones who had not, ordinarily pictured a male and female pair in America's place.[6] But the paired symbol apparently did not satisfy the need for a personified figure, and the Indian Queen began to appear as the sole representation for the Americas in 1575. And until 1765 or thereabouts, the bare-breasted, Amazonian Native American Queen reigned *(fig. 3)*. Draped in leaves, feathers, and animal skins as well as in heavy Caribbean jewelry, she appeared aggressive, militant, and armed with spears and arrows. Often, she rode on an armadillo, and stood with her foot on the slain body of an animal or human enemy. She was the familiar Mother-Goddess figure—full-bodied, powerful, nurturing but dangerous—embodying the opulence and peril of the New World. Her environment was rich and colorful, and that, with the allusions to Classical Europe through the Renaissance portrayal of her large, naked body, attached her to Old World History as well as to New World virtue.

Her daughter, the Princess, enters the scene when the colonies begin to move toward independence, and she becomes more "American" and less Latin than her mother. She seems less barbarous than the Queen; the rattlesnake (Jones' "Dont Tread On Me" sign) defends her, and her enemies are defeated by male warriors rather than by her own armed hand. She is Britannia's daughter as well as that of the Carib Queen, and she wears the triangular Phrygian cap and holds the liberty pole of her later, metamorphosed sister, Miss Liberty (the figure on the Statue of Liberty and the Liberty dime). She is young, leaner in the Romanesque rather than Greek mode, and distinctly Caucasian, though her skin remains slightly tinted in some renderings. She wears the loose, flowing gowns of classical statuary rather than animal skins, and Roman sandals grace her feet. She is armed, usually with a spear, but she also carries

---

[6] See Clare de Corbellier, "Miss America and Her Sisters: Personification of the Four Parts of the World." *Bulletin of the Metropolitan Museum of Art* 19 (1961), pp. 209–223; James Hazen Hyde, *L'Iconographie des quatre parties du monde dans les tapisseries de Gazette des Beaux Arts* (Paris: Beaux Arts, 1924).

a peace pipe, a flag, or the starred and striped shield of Colonial America. She often stands with The Sons of Liberty, or later, with George Washington *(fig. 4)*.

Thus, the Indian woman began her symbolic, many-faceted life as a Mother figure—exotic, powerful, dangerous, and beautiful—and as a representative of American liberty and European classical virtue translated into New World terms. She represented, even defended America. But when real Indian women—Pocahontas and her sisters—intruded into the needs bound up in symbols and the desires inherent in daily life, the responses to the symbol became more complex, and the Pocahontas perplex emerged as a controlling metaphor in the American experience. The Indian woman, along with her male counterparts, continued to stand for the New World and for rude native nobility, but the image of the savage remained as well. The dark side of the Mother-Queen figure is the savage Squaw, and even Pocahontas, as John Barth suggests in *The Sotweed Factor*, is motivated by lust.

Both her nobility as a Princess and her savagery as a Squaw are defined in terms of her relationships with male figures. If she wishes to be called a Princess, she must save or give aid to white men. The only good Indian—male or female, Squanto, Pocahontas, Sacagawea, Cochise, the Little Mohee or the Indian Doctor—rescues and helps white men. But the Indian woman is even more burdened by this narrow definition of a "good Indian," for it is she, not the males, whom white men desire sexually. Because her image is so tied up with abstract virtue—indeed, with America—she must remain the Mother Goddess-Queen. But acting as a real female, she must be a partner and lover of Indian men, a mother to Indian children, and an object of lust for white men. To be Mother, Queen and lover is, as Oedipus' mother, Jocasta, discovered, difficult and perhaps impossible. The paradox so often noted in Latin/Catholic countries where men revere their mothers and sisters, but use prostitutes so that their "good" women can stay pure is to the point here. Both race conflict and national identity, however, make this particular Virgin-Whore paradox more complicated than others. The Indian woman finds herself burdened with an image that can only be understood as dysfunctional, even though the Pocahontas perplex affects us all. Some examination of the complicated dimensions of that image might help us move toward change.

In songs like "Jonathan Smith," "Chipeta's Ride" and others sung in oral tradition, the Indian woman saves white men.[7] In "Chipeta's Ride," she even saves a white woman from lust-enraged Indian males. Ordinarily, however, she rescues her white lover or an anonymous male captive. Always called a Princess (or Chieftain's Daughter), she, like Pocahontas, has to violate the wishes and customs of her own "barbarous" people to make good the rescue, saving the man out of love and often out of "Christian sympathy." Nearly all the "good" Princess figures are converts, and they cannot bear to see their fellow Christians slain by "savages." The Princess is "civilized"; to illustrate her native nobility, most pictures portray her as white, darker than the Europeans, but more Caucasian than her fellow natives (see *fig. 1*).

If unable to make the grand gesture of saving her captive lover or if thwarted from marrying him by her cruel father, the Chieftain, the Princess is allowed the even grander gesture of committing suicide when her lover is slain or fails to return to her after she rescues him. In the hundreds of "Lover's Leap" legends which abound throughout the country, and in traditional songs like "The Indian Bride's Lament," our heroine leaps over a precipice, unable to live without her loved one. In this movement from political symbolism (where the Indian woman defends America) to psychosexual symbolism (where she defends or dies for white lovers), we can see part of the Indian woman's dilemma. To be "good," she must defy her own people, exile herself from them, become white, and perhaps suffer death.

---

[7] Austin Fife and Francesca Redden. "The Pseudo-Indian Folksongs of the Anglo-Americans and French-Canadians," *The Journal of American Folklore* 67, no. 266 (1954), 381; Olive Wooley Burt. *American Murder Ballads and Their Stories* (rpt. 1958, New York: Citadel Press, 1964), pp. 146–49.

2. Pocahontas. Tobacco Label. *Library of Congress.*

3. Personification of America. Engraving, ca. 1595, by Adrien Collaert II after Martin de Vos. *Winterthur Museum.*

4. Holland Recognizes American Independence. Engraving, 1782, by G. Brouwer after A. Borghers and P. Wagenaar. *F. D. Roosevelt Library*.

5. Louden & Co.'s Cherokee Liniment. Advertisement. *Library of Congress*.

6. Poster advertisement.
Smithsonian Institution.

7. Tobacco advertisement. *Library of Congress.*

8. Princess. Cigar Store Figure, ca. 1865. *National Gallery of Art.*

9. Squaw. Cigar Store Figure. *Nation Gallery of Art.*

Those who did not leap for love continued to fall in love with white men by the scores, and here the sacrifices are several. The women in songs like "The Little Mohee," "Little Red Wing," and "Juanita, the Sachem's Daughter" fall in love with white travellers, often inviting them to share their blissful, idyllic, woodland paradise. If their lovers leave them, they often pine away, die of grief, or leap off a cliff, but in a number of songs, the white man remains with the maiden, preferring her life to his own, "civilized" way. "The Little Mohee" is a prime example of such a song.

As I went out walking for pleasure one day,
In the sweet recollection, to dwell time away.
As I sat amusing myself on the grass,
Oh, who should I spy but a fair Indian lass.

She walked up behind me, taking hold of my hand,
She said, "You are a stranger and in a strange land,
But if you will follow, you're welcome to come
And dwell in my cottage that I call my home."

My Mohea was gentle, my Mohea was kind.
She took me when a stranger and clothed me when cold.
She learned me the language of the lass of Mohea.

"I'm going to leave you, so farewell my dear.
The ship's sails are spreading and home I must steer."
The last time I saw her she was standing on the strand,
And as my boat passed her she waved me her hand.

Saying "when you have landed and with the one you love,
Think of pretty Mohea in the coconut grove."
I am home but no one comes near me nor none do I see,
That would equal compare with the lass of Mohea.

Oh, the girl that I loved proved untrue to me.
I'll turn my course backward far over the sea.
I'll turn my course backward, from this land I'll go free,
And go spend my days with the little Mohea.

Such songs add to the exotic and sexual, yet maternal and contradictorily virginal image of the Indian Princess, and are reminiscent of the contemporary white soldier's attachments to "submissive," "sacrificial," "exotic" Asian women.

As long as Indian women keep their exotic distance or die (even occasionally for love of Indian men), they are permitted to remain on the positive side of the image. They can help, stand by, sacrifice for, and aid white men. They can, like their native brothers, heal white men, and the Indian reputation as healer dominated the nineteenth century patent medicine business. In the ads for such medicines, the Indian woman appears either as a helpmate to her "doctor" husband or partner or as a healer herself *(fig. 5)*. In several ads (and the little dime novels often accompanying the patent medicine products), she is the mysterious witch-healer. Thus, she shares in the Caucasian or European female's reputation for potential evil. The references here to power, knowledge, and sexuality remain on the good side of the image. In this incarnation, the Princess offers help in the form of medicine rather than love *(fig. 6)*.

The tobacco industry also capitalized on the Princess' image, and the cigar-store figures and ads associated with the tobacco business replicate the Princess figures to sell its products *(fig. 7)*. Cigar-store Princesses smile and beckon men into tobacco shops. They hold a rose, a bundle of cigars, or some tobacco leaves (a sign of welcome in the colonial days), and they smile invitingly with their Caucasian lips. They also sell the product from tobacco packages, and here, like some of the figures in front of the shops, Diana-like or more militant Minerva (Wonder-Woman)-like heroines offer the comforts of the "Indian weed." They have either the rounded, infantile, semi-naked (indicating innocence) bodies of Renaissance angels or the bodies and clothes of classical heroines *(fig. 8)*. The Mother Goddess and Miss Liberty peddle their more abstract wares, as Indian Princesses, along with those of the manufacturer. Once again, the Princess comforts white men, and while she promises much, she remains aloof.

But who becomes the white man's sexual partner? Who

forms liaisons with him? It cannot be the Princess, for she is sacrosanct. Her sexuality can be hinted at but never realized. The Princess' darker twin, the Squaw, must serve this side of the image, and again, relationships with males determine what the image will be. In the case of the Squaw, the presence of overt and realized sexuality converts the image from positive to negative. White men cannot share sex with the Princess, but once they do so with a real Indian woman, she cannot follow the required love-and-rescue pattern. She does what white men want for money or lust. In the traditional songs, stories, obscene jokes, contemporary literary works and popular and pictorializations of the Squaw, no heroines are allowed. Squaws share in the same vices attributed to Indian men—drunkenness, stupidity, thievery, venality of every kind—and they live in shacks on the edge of town rather than in a woodland paradise.

Here, Squaws are shamed for their relationships with white men, and the males who share their beds—the "squaw men"—or "bucks," if they are Indian—share their shame. When they live with Indian males, Squaws work for their lazy bucks and bear large numbers of fat "papooses." In one joke, a white visitor to a reservation sees an overburdened squaw with ten children hanging on her skirts. "Where's your husband?" the visitor demands. "He ought to be hung!" "Ugh," says the squaw, "pretty well-hung!" They too are fat, and unlike their Princess sisters, dark and possessed of cruder, more "Indian" features. When stories and songs describe relationships with white men, Squaws are understood as mere economic and sexual conveniences for the men who—unlike John Smith or a "brave"—are tainted by association with her. Tale after tale describes the Indian whores, their alcoholic and sexual excesses with white trappers and hunters. A parody of the beautiful-maiden song, "Little Red Wing," speaks of her lewd sister who "lays on her back in a cowboy shack, and lets cowboys poke her in the crack." The result of this cowboy-squaw liaison is a "brat in a cowboy hat with his asshole between his eyes." This Squaw is dark, and squat, and even the cigar-store Indians show the changes in conception. No Roman sandals grace their feet, and their features are more "Indian" and "primitive" than even their male counterparts. The cigar-store squaws often had papooses on their backs, and some had corrugated places on their hips to light the store patrons' matches. When realities intrude on mythos, even Princesses can become Squaws as the text of the ragtime song, "On An Indian Reservation," illustrates.

On an Indian reservation, far from home and civilization,
Where the foot of Whiteman seldom trod.
Whiteman went to fish one summer,
Met an Indian maid—a hummer,
Daughter of Big-Chief-Spare-the-rod.
Whiteman threw some loving glances, took this maid to
    Indian dances,
Smoked his pipe of peace, took chances living in a
    teepee made of fur.
Rode with her on Indian ponies, bought her diamond
    rings, all phonies,
And he sang these loving words to her:
Chorus:
  You're my pretty little Indian Napanee.
  Won't you take a chance and marry me.
  Your Daddy Chief, 'tis my belief,
  To a very merry wedding will agree.
  True, you're a dark little Indian maid,
  But I'll sunburn to a darker shade,
  I'll wear feathers on my head,
  Paint my skin an Indian red,
  If you will be my Napanee.
With his contact soon he caught her,
Soon he married this big chief's daughter,
Happiest couple that you ever saw.
But his dreams of love soon faded,
Napanee looked old and jaded,
Just about like any other squaw.
Soon there came papoose in numbers, redskin yells
    disturbed his slumbers,

Whiteman wonders at his blunders—now the feathers
drop upon his head.
Sorry to say it, but he's a-wishing, that he'd
never gone a-fishing,
Or had met this Indian maid and said:
Chorus:

The Indian woman is between a rock and a hard place. Like that of her male counterpart, her image is freighted with such ambivalence that she has little room to move. He, however, has many more modes in which to participate though he is still severely handicapped by the prevailing stereotypes. They are both tied to definition by relationships with white men, but she is especially burdened by the narrowness of that definition. Obviously, her image is one that is troublesome to all women, but, tied as it is to a national mythos, its complexity has a special piquance. As Vine Deloria points out in *Custer Died For Your Sins*, many whites claim kinship with some distant Indian Princess grandmother, and thus try to resolve their "Indian problem" with such sincere affirmations of relationship.[8]

Such claims make it impossible for the Indian woman to be seen as real. She does not have the power to evoke feeling as a real mother figure, like the black woman, even though *that* image has a burdensome negative side. American children play with no red mammy dolls. She cannot even evoke the terror the "castrating (white) bitch" inspires. Only the male, with upraised tomahawk, does that. The many expressions which treat of her image remove her from consideration as more than an image. As some abstract, noble Princess tied to "America" and to sacrificial zeal, she has power as a symbol. As the Squaw, a depersonalized object of scornful convenience, she is powerless. Like her male relatives she may be easily destroyed without reference to her humanity. (When asked why he killed women and children at Sand Creek, the commanding general of the U.S. Cavalry was said to have replied, "nits make lice.")

---

[8] Vine Deloria. *Custer Died For Your Sins* (N.Y.: Avon Books, 1968), p. 11.

As the Squaw, her physical removal or destruction can be understood as necessary to the progress of civilization even though her abstracted sister, the Princess, stands for that very civilization. Perhaps the Princess had to be removed from her powerful symbolic place, and replaced with the male Uncle Sam because she confronted America with too many contradictions. As symbol and reality, the Indian woman suffers from our needs, and by both race and sex stands damned.

Since the Indian so much represents America's attachment to a romantic past and to a far distant nobility, it is predictable but horrible that the Indian woman should symbolize the paradoxical entity once embodied for the European in the Princess in the tower and the old crone in the cave. It is time that the Princess herself is rescued and the Squaw relieved of her obligatory service. The Native American woman, like all women, needs a definition that stands apart from that of males, red or white. Certainly, the Native woman needs to be defined as Indian, in Indian terms. Delightful and interesting as Pocahontas' story may be, she offers an intolerable metaphor for the Indian-White experience. She and the Squaw offer unendurable metaphors for the lives of Indian women. Perhaps if we give up the need for John Smith's fantasy and the trappers' harsher realities, we will find, for each of us, an image that does not haunt and perplex us. Perhaps if we explore the meaning of Native American lives outside the boundaries of the stories, songs, and pictures given us in tradition, we will find a more humane truth.

☆

Mexican Women in San Antonio, 1830-1860: The Assimilation Process

JANE DYSART

During the course of European expansion, social contact between different ethnic, racial, and national groups initiated a process of assimilation. In those instances where widespread intermarriage occurred, cultural, ethnic, and even racial distinctions were blurred as the two groups incorporated in a common culture. Where prevailing attitudes assuming cultural or racial superiority prevented extensive intermarriage, the assimilation process was only partially complete.[1] Such attitudes on the part of Anglo-Americans inhibited large-scale marriage with Mexicans, and the celebrated frontier melting pot failed to absorb the majority of Mexicans in the southwestern United States.[2]

The continuing existence of a culturally and visibly distinct Mexican minority in the Southwest can be partially explained by a historical analysis of the relationship between Mexican women and Anglo men. Following the pattern of settlement and conquest in other frontier regions, Anglo immigration into the southwestern frontier was preponderantly male; consequently, intermarriage as well as informal sexual unions almost exclusively involved Mexican women and Anglo men. Focusing this study

Jane E. Dysart is assistant professor of history at the University of West Florida.

[1] The most comprehensive study of the assimilation process is Milton M. Gordon, *Assimilation in American Life: The Role of Race, Religion and National Origins* (New York, 1964). An excellent anthology on the various aspects of intermarriage is Milton L. Barron, ed., *The Blending American: Patterns of Intermarriage* (Chicago, 1972). In this collection the article by Robert K. Merton, "Intermarriage and the Social Structure: Fact and Theory," 12–35, is especially pertinent.

[2] The term *Anglo* is used in this study to designate all non-Spanish-surnamed individuals, while the term *Mexican* refers to all persons of Hispanic ancestry and/or those with Spanish surnames. This choice is admittedly arbitrary, but it is sanctioned by customary usage in San Antonio during the midnineteenth century. See the explanation of this practice in Carland Elaine Crook, "San Antonio, Texas, 1846–1861" (M.A. thesis, Rice University, 1964), 14.

upon the Mexican women rather than describing male attitudes toward them provides insights into the nature of the assimilation process and delineates more clearly the active role of the women.

To treat the women as active participants rather than passive objects in the historical process, however, requires delving into church and civil records, marriage and baptismal books, census schedules and tax rolls, for most of the traditional sources such as diaries, memoirs, and letters were written by men. Centering the study on San Antonio, a city with rich archival resources and a long history of interaction between Anglos and Mexicans, provides an excellent opportunity to analyze the assimilation process and to establish a basis for comparison with other areas.

Frontier conditions forced limited modifications in traditional sex roles for both Anglo-American and Hispanic societies. When men were absent for extended periods of time — hunting, fighting, or conducting business in distant cities — women had to assume responsibility for managing family and business affairs. The wife of Spanish Governor Antonio Cordero, for example, drilled the troops stationed in San Antonio during her husband's frequent absences.[3] During the 1820s Josefa Becerra Seguín wrangled with city authorities over water rights while her husband attended congressional sessions in Mexico City.[4] Yet women's assumption of such responsibilities was a temporary response to necessity, not a basic alteration in role.

Despite certain liberating tendencies of the frontier, which might have enhanced or modified women's economic and social status, both Anglo and Hispanic cultures remained basically masculine in orientation. They shared a common belief in the subordination of women, and both societies restricted women's political, legal, social, and economic activities. While men dominated business and politics, women's sphere was home and family.[5] In customs and manners the two cultures were markedly

[3] Notes concerning Cassiano-Cordero family, undated and unsigned, Charles P. Smith Family Collection, Archives of the University of Texas, Austin. (AUT.)

[4] María Josefa Agustina Becerra de Seguín to Erasmo Seguín, February 2, 1824, Seguín Papers, AUT.

[5] For a discussion of female role modifications on the Anglo frontier see Mattie Lloyd Wooten, "The Roles of Pioneer Women in the Texas Frontier Community" (M.A. thesis, University of Texas, Austin, 1929) and Rubye Du Terroil, "The Role of Women in Nineteenth Century San Antonio" (M.A. thesis, Saint Mary's University, San Antonio, Texas, 1949). While no comparable study relevant to Mexican women could be found, several works support the conclusions. See especially Crook, "San Antonio"; and Robert Staples, "The Mexican-American Family: Its Modification over Time and Space," *Phylon*, 32 (Summer 1971), 179–92.

different, but an exaggeratedly masculine style of behavior was just as evident among Anglo males as *machismo* among Mexicans. Hero of the Alamo, William Barret Travis, for example, carefully noted in his diary his frequent sexual affairs with young women, both Anglo and Mexican.[6] A double standard of sexual morality enjoined chastity and legal marriage on women but applauded sexual prowess and experience in men. Frontiersmen resolved this dualistic attitude by shielding certain women behind an elaborate code of chivalry while regarding others, especially those with darker skins, as suitable partners in casual sexual relations.[7] Thus, both societies defined appropriate female roles as either wife and mother or mistress. Passive acceptance of such roles was expected, and research to date has not presented evidence that Mexican women in San Antonio deviated from role expectations to any significant degree.

During the 1840s and 1850s American frontiersmen apparently delighted in recounting tales of the passionate and pleasure-loving senoritas of San Antonio. Wishful thinking probably prompted many Anglo males to exaggerate the promiscuity of Mexican women. Different ideas about proper behavior and appropriate dress also accounted for reports of moral laxity. American travelers found the Mexicans' practice of nude public bathing offensive, though judging from their detailed descriptions, few left the scene quickly. Nor did they refrain from attending fandangos, public dances which were held almost nightly in San Antonio, but most expressed shock at the sensuous movements of the Mexican women. (The fandangos, in fact, were taxed by the municipal government and provided the largest single source of public revenue in 1847.) Anglos also regarded the native women's low-cut dresses as provocative and their uncorseted figures immodest. In most instances they did acknowledge that female immorality was largely confined to the lower classes.[8] Fair skin and wealth apparently protected a woman from criticism as well as from unwelcome sexual advances.

[6] Robert E. Davis, ed., *The Diary of William Barret Travis, August 30, 1833–June 26, 1834* (Waco, 1966).

[7] This dualism with racial connotations is discussed fully in Woodrow Borah and Sherburne F. Cook, "Marriage and Legitimacy in Mexican Culture: Mexico and California," *California Law Review*, 54 (May 1966), 960–61.

[8] While almost every Anglo who kept a journal or wrote letters about impressions of San Antonio commented on the behavior and dress of Mexican women, especially graphic accounts can be found in George Wilkins Kendall, *Narrative of the Texan Santa Fe Expedition*, 2 vols. (Austin, 1935), I:46–48; Ferdinand Roemer, *Texas with Particular Reference to German Immigration and the Physical Appearance of the Country*, trans. Oswald Mueller (San Antonio, 1935), 121–25; W. Eugene Hollon

Both Hispanic and Anglo frontier societies espoused marriage as the only respectable status for a woman, but if she were unacceptable as a wife, then an informal alliance could serve a man's physical and domestic needs satisfactorily. Concubinage or *barraganía,* an institution deeply rooted in Hispanic society, was a widespread practice in Spanish-American military outposts like San Antonio. Under such conditions where single men significantly outnumbered women, *barraganía* usually characterized informal unions between higher status men of European ancestry and lower status women of Indian or mixed racial stock.[9] It was ideally suited to the man's mobile life-style, and besides, actual marriage to a darker-skinned woman was a step down in the social scale for Spaniard or Creole. The custom was evidently firmly established in San Antonio when the first Anglo traders, hunters, and adventurers began to enter the city.[10] In readily adopting *barraganía,* these unattached frontiersmen maintained both its social and racial connotations. Evidence for such arrangements is scattered throughout the baptismal records of San Fernando Church, where priests until the 1850s distinguished between "natural" children, whose fathers acknowledged paternity, and bastards, usually the offspring of Negro slaves.[11]

For a time at least, *barraganía* evidently provided a partial substitute for a typical Anglo frontier institution—the bawdy house. A young Alabamian, writing from San Antonio in 1855, reported that there were "no houses of ill fame in this place, but many of these 'greasers' of fine figures and good features, the color of a mulatto, are kept by votaries of sensuability." [12] His racial associations underline prevailing attitudes—in Anglo minds the darker-skinned Mexicans were linked with Negroes, and cohabitative unions with black women were common in the South. Baptismal records confirm his observation in part, for

and Ruth Lapham Butler, eds., *William Bollaert's Texas* (Norman, 1956), 217–19. The city collected $560 from the tax levied on fandangos at the rate of $1 per occasion. This was more than one third of the entire city revenue for the year. San Antonio City Records, Journal A, December 31, 1847, transcribed and translated by the Texas Works Progress Administration, AUT.

[9] Borah and Cook, "Marriage and Legitimacy," 960–61.

[10] Alicia V. Tjarks, "Comparative Demographic Analysis of Texas, 1777–1793," *Southwestern Historical Quarterly,* 77 (January 1974), 310.

[11] Baptismal Books, San Fernando Cathedral, 1793–1898, microfilm roll nos. 35, 36, and 37, Archives of the Roman Catholic Archdiocese of San Antonio, San Antonio, Texas. (Baptisms, CASF.)

[12] Aaron M. Boom, ed., "Texas in the 1850's, As Viewed by a Recent Arrival," *Southwestern Historical Quarterly,* 70 (October 1966), 283–84.

several prominent Anglo men acknowledged paternity of their "natural" children.[13]

While Hispanic folk practices and customs recognized an intermediary position between legitimacy and illegitimacy, Anglo-American society refused to acknowledge degrees.[14] Census records from the Spanish and Mexican periods indicate that concubinage implied living together, for usually both parties were listed as single but sharing the same house, and children born to these couples carried their father's name.[15] Such arrangements encouraged hispanicization of Indian women and their mestizo offspring and probably provided them a limited degree of economic security.[16] Under American rule, however, the manuscript census schedules of 1850 and 1860 reflect that the man and woman generally lived apart, and the children assumed their mother's surname. Moreover, none of these children were listed in the census records as attending school.[17] Concubinage without the sustained contact of sharing the same household was unlikely to promote americanization of the Mexican woman or her children, at least not to the extent that *barragania* had hispanicized many of the Indians.

For the majority of Mexican women formal marriage provided a far more acceptable social status along with a more dependable economic position than concubinage. Civil marriage records dating from 1837 to 1860 list 906 Mexican women who wed Mexican men, while only 88 chose to marry Anglos.[18] But of those Anglo-Mexican unions almost half,

[13] Baptisms, roll nos. 35 and 36, CASF.

[14] See Borah and Cook, "Marriage and Legitimacy," 960–63; and Tjarks, "Demographic Analysis of Texas," 310, for a complete discussion of social attitudes toward concubinage and illegitimacy in Hispanic societies.

[15] Carmela Leal, comp. and trans., "The Negro in Colonial Texas, 1831–1834: Census of Texas," typescript (San Antonio: University of Texas at San Antonio, Institute of Texan Cultures, vol. 7). Leal has compiled and translated all of the census records from the Spanish and Mexican periods originally included in the Bexar Archives. Although the objective was to identify Negroes in the census records, the listing encompasses the entire population.

[16] Tjarks, "Demographic Analysis of Texas," 310–38.

[17] Lauretta Russell, trans., "1850 Census of Bexar County, Texas," mimeographed (San Antonio, 1966). U.S. National Archives, Microfilm Publications, "White and Free Colored Population—1860," microfilm roll no. 1288 (Bastrop, Bell and Bexar counties of Texas). (1860 Census, Bexar County.)

[18] Civil marriages are found in Marriage Book A, B, C, D_1 and D_2 (1837–60), Bexar County Archives, San Antonio, Texas. (BCA.) Prior to 1837 in San Antonio marriages were registered only by the church, and there are large gaps in the San Fernando records. For example, no marriages were recorded between 1833 and 1840.

or 42, involved women from high status families. The significance of these interethnic marriages goes far beyond their number, since at least one daughter from almost every *rico* family in San Antonio married an Anglo.[19] It should be noted that marriage between an Anglo woman and a Spanish-surnamed man was rare; only five unions can be verified in the records between 1830 and 1860.[20]

Before the outbreak of hostilities in the mid-1830s, upper class Tejanos often identified their own political liberalism with Anglo American ideals and welcomed newcomers from the United States into their homes. In this manner James Bowie met and later wed Ursula Veramendi, daughter of the liberal Mexican governor of Texas. After 1836 it was politically advantageous for Texas Mexicans, often indiscriminately regarded as enemies, to establish family connections with the dominant Anglo group. Several marriages, in fact, united Anglo political influence with Mexican landed wealth. For example, one daughter of José Antonio Navarro married the adjutant general of the state, while one of the De la Garzas married the county clerk, and her sister wed the sheriff. The political benefits of such familial alliances, however, were not entirely one-sided; for although the number of Spanish-surnamed office holders declined after 1840, the Mexican vote remained a significant factor in San Antonio elections.[21] Anglo men with family ties in the Mexican community consistently won election to city office during the 1840s and 1850s.[22]

Mexican *ricos* more than likely regarded retention of political influence an economic necessity. Unfamiliar with American legal practices and suspected of disloyalty to the American cause, many of the wealthy

[19] High status families were identified primarily from the genealogical lists found in Frederick C. Chabot, *With the Makers of San Antonio: Genealogies of the Early Latin, Anglo American, and German Families with Occasional Biographies, Each Group Being Prefaced with a Brief Historical Sketch and Illustrations* (San Antonio, 1937). Chabot was a recognized authority on San Antonio history and utilized private family papers, now unavailable, to compile this study. His lists were also compared with others identifying the principal San Antonio Mexican families, especially José Rodriguez, *Memoirs of Early Texas* (San Antonio, 1913).

[20] Marriage Books, San Fernando Cathedral, 1820–83, microfilm roll nos. 37 and 47, Archives of the Roman Catholic Archdiocese of San Antonio, San Antonio, Texas. (Marriages, CASF); Marriage Books A-D_2, BCA.

[21] Terry G. Jordan, "Population Origins in Texas, 1850," *Geographical Review*, 59 (January 1969), 96.

[22] *Historical Facts from the First City Directory of San Antonio for 1877–1878*, reprinted edition of *Mooney and Morrison's General Directory of San Antonio* (n.p.; n.d.), 39–46.

Tejanos undoubtedly viewed an Anglo son-in-law as a protection from the loss of their extensive landholdings. Several of the wealthiest families did indeed marry one or more of their daughters to Anglo men, thereby reinforcing their political as well as economic position. Included among them were the Seguíns, whose family holdings according to the 1840 tax rolls totaled almost twenty thousand acres; the Navarros, who held title to more than twenty thousand acres in addition to fifteen town lots; and the Cassianos with almost twenty-three thousand acres of land and twelve town lots.[23]

The prospect of marrying a Mexican woman from one of the wealthy families was all the more attractive to an enterprising Anglo male, since daughters customarily inherited property, often on an equal basis with sons.[24] Through his marriage to Margarita de la Garza, James Trueheart, a San Antonio politician, acquired a large tract of valuable land, formerly part of the Mission Espada. There he lived in the style of a *patrón* with a number of peon families who maintained his farming operations. Several other Anglo men like Trueheart advanced their own economic position considerably by marrying the daughters of land-rich Tejanos.[25]

Frequent social contacts coupled with a surplus male population promoted intermarriage between Mexican women and Anglo men. During the 1840s and 1850s dances and parties in San Antonio included leading families from both Anglo and Hispanic groups.[26] José María Rodríguez, whose family was counted among the aristocracy, recalled that he was "kept busy acting as an escort" for his sisters, three of whom did marry Anglos.[27] A young soldier stationed in San Antonio during the 1850s reported attending a dance where "two or three of the bloods of Castile were present." Their land-rich parents, he added, were determined that the girls must wed "genuine Americans." [28]

[23] Gifford White, ed., *The 1840 Census of the Republic of Texas* (Austin, 1966), 12–18.

[24] Typescript copies of a number of wills dating from the late 1700s to the 1820s are located in the Bexar County Archives, San Antonio, Texas. In addition, see Probate Minutes, vols. A-H (May 1837–July 1880), also BCA.

[25] *A Twentieth Century History of Southwest Texas*, 2 vols. (Chicago, 1907), II: 418. This work contains a number of biographies of prominent San Antonians. See also Frederick C. Chabot, ed., *The Perote Prisoners: Being the Diary of James L. Trueheart* (San Antonio, 1934), 2–3.

[26] One of the best sources for a history of social life in San Antonio during the midnineteenth century is Rena Maverick Green, ed., *Memoirs of Mary A. Maverick* (San Antonio, 1921), 51–57.

[27] Rodriguez, *Memoirs*, 21, 46.

[28] Boom, "Texas in the 1850's," 283.

For the upper-class Mexican woman, marriage to an Anglo after 1830 initiated a process of assimilation and acculturation which in the vast majority of cases led to the americanization of their children. This pattern represented a divergence from past experiences and differed markedly from the process which occurred in rural areas of Texas even during the midnineteenth century. The paternal ancestors of the Navarros had emigrated from Corsica and those of the Cassianos from Italy, but both of these prominent San Antonio families were thoroughly hispanicized by 1830.[29] Among the isolated ranchos of the lower Rio Grande Valley, descendants of Americans who married Mexican wives in the 1850s attended schools in Mexico and were, in fact, thoroughly mexicanized.[30] After 1840, however, San Antonio became a commercial and military center dominated economically, politically, and socially by Anglos.

The trend toward americanization of Anglo-Mexican families in San Antonio developed in spite of certain factors which seemed to lend greater support to a hispanicization process. The familial ties of the men who married upper-class Mexican women were generally weak and their cultural backgrounds diverse. Few of the men who chose high status Mexican brides between 1830 and 1860 had relatives living in San Antonio. Only seven were born in nearby states of the lower South, and judging by their surnames three of those men were of French extraction. Approximately one-third, however, came from the upper South or the North. Europeans were also well represented in these mixed marriages, including five German husbands, two Irish, two French, and one each from England and Scotland.[31] In contrast to the women who maintained close familial ties and whose cultural background was homogeneous, the men seemingly lacked strong reinforcements for americanization of their families.

[29] Chabot, *With the Makers of San Antonio,* 202–5; 223–24.

[30] Jovita Gonzalez, "Social Life in Cameron, Starr and Zapata Counties" (M.A. thesis, University of Texas, Austin, 1930), 26–27; 69–70.

[31] The husband's place of birth was determined largely from census records. 1850 Census and 1860 Census, Bexar County. Two references are especially valuable for interpretation of these census records: Jordan, "Population Origins in Texas," 83–103; and Barnes F. Lathrop, "History from the Census Returns," *Southwestern Historical Quarterly,* 51 (April 1948), 93–312. Unlike other sections of Texas where families seemed to migrate together and settle in clusters, San Antonio as a military outpost and trading center received a high percentage of unattached males. See also Crook, "San Antonio," 38–47.

To the extent that religion influenced the acculturation process, it was the woman's Hispanic Catholic faith that prevailed. Mexican Catholics in San Antonio continued to observe the feast day of Our Lady of Guadalupe, patron saint of Mexico, with grand processions through the city streets, and they celebrated holidays such as Christmas with traditional Mexican fiestas.[32] Until 1852 all of the priests serving the San Fernando parish were either Mexicans or Spaniards. San Fernando was, in fact, the only Catholic church in San Antonio until the mid-1850s when church officials began to organize separate parishes for the different ethnic groups. There were no permanent Protestant churches established until 1857.[33] Even though the majority of the Anglo husbands claimed to be Catholic at the time of their marriage, they more than likely had little understanding of the customs and practices which distinguished Mexican Catholicism.

The Mexican woman and her family evidently assumed primary responsibility for the rearing of young children. Whether the father was Catholic or not, the children were customarily baptized in the Roman Catholic faith and most were given typically Spanish names.[34] Since the father usually had no relatives living in San Antonio, the children's kinship associations were with their mother's family. In several instances, these families even shared the same household with the Mexican grandparents.[35] In addition to biological kinship ties, the relationship with godparents, or *compadres,* was particularly important in Hispanic societies. Because they were regarded in much the same manner as blood relatives, the selection of *compadres* was an important decision.[36] In San Antonio, choosing *compadres* from among the mother's relatives was the usual practice; an Anglo godparent was rare.[37] Although evidence derived from census schedules and church records can sketch only the bare outlines of family life and experience, the data does suggest the presence of strong Mexican influences during early childhood.

[32] Green, *Maverick Memoirs,* 53; Caroline Remy, "Hispanic-Mexican San Antonio: 1836–1861," *Southwestern Historical Quarterly,* 71 (April 1968), 569.

[33] Crook, "San Antonio," 78–80.

[34] Baptisms, roll nos. 35 and 36, CASF.

[35] 1850 Census; 1860 Census, Bexar County. The 1860 census schedules particularly indicate the presence of Mexican grandparents in the household. By that time, of course, most of them were elderly.

[36] Sidney W. Mintz and Eric R. Wolf, "An Analysis of Ritual Co-Parenthood (*Compadrazgo*)," in *Marriage, Family and Residence,* eds. Paul Bohannan and John Middleton (Garden City, 1968), 327–54.

[37] Baptisms, roll nos. 35 and 36, CASF.

Nevertheless, the vast majority of these upper-class children of mixed marriages established identity with their father's ethnic group rather than that of their mother. Since the well-to-do Tejano and Anglo-Mexican families did not live in separate residential districts, they had frequent contacts with their American neighbors.[38] School attendance also aided the assimilation process, for according to the 1850 census all of these children between the ages of six and fifteen were attending school.[39] A few children from affluent families were sent to boarding schools and colleges in other states—some as far away as New Jersey, Kentucky, and Virginia.[40] By the time they became adults, the majority had anglicized their given names.[41] At least three families even joined Protestant churches, while five others affiliated with the English-speaking Roman Catholic parish.[42] With rare exceptions both sons and daughters married non-Mexicans.[43] In short, the second generation became assimilated into Anglo-American society.

[38] 1850 Census; 1860 Census, Bexar County.

[39] 1850 Census.

[40] Josephine Tobin, whose maiden name was Josefa Agusta Smith y Curbelo, attended a boarding school in Newark, New Jersey. San Antonio *Daily Express,* October 23, 1908. Anita Dwyer, whose parents were Edward Dwyer and Mariana Leal, attended college in Bardstown, Kentucky. Charles Campbell, son of Martin Campbell and Dolores de Concepcion Barrera, received his medical degree from Tulane University. *Twentieth Century History.* I: 319; II: 486.

[41] Substantiating evidence was obtained by comparing a sample of baptismal names with the names used by these individuals as adults in civil records, especially marriage registries. For example, Anton Lockmar and his wife, María Apolinaria Trevino, gave their daughter the baptismal name, María Catalina Lockmar y Trevino. Baptisms, roll no. 35, September 20, 1842. At the time of her marriage in 1859 to James R. Marmion she listed her name in the registry as Catherine Lockmar. Marriage Book D_2, no. 1736. Baptized Josefa Agusta Smith y Curbelo, the prominent San Antonio woman, who married William G. Tobin, was consistently referred to in newspapers and public records as Josephine Tobin.

[42] According to Crook, "San Antonio," 91, the daughters of Antonio Navarro became Methodists. One of the daughters of Erastus "Deaf" Smith and Guadalupe Ruíz Duran joined Saint Mark's Episcopal Church in San Antonio, as did Josephine Tobin. "Family Records from Book I, Saint Mark's Episcopal Church of San Antonio, Texas," copied by Cordelia Greer Williams, 1950, in Genealogical Division, Texas State Archives, Austin, Texas. Anglo-Mexican families who affiliated with the English-speaking Roman Catholic parish included the Hewitts, Crawfords, Girauds, Withers, and Marmions. Confirmation Book, Saint Mary's Catholic Church, San Antonio, Book I (1860–1907), in the Archives, Roman Catholic Archdiocese of San Antonio.

[43] Marriage Books C-K, BCA. Names of children were obtained from baptismal and census records, and whenever possible they were located in the marriage records of Bexar County.

The pressures urging Anglo conformity on upper-class Mexican women and their children were indeed intense. In addition to the nativist movement of the 1850s, which exacerbated hostilities against non-Anglo-Saxon and Catholic groups, Anglo Texans forced upon the Mexicans an onus of guilt for the Alamo and Goliad. At the root of discrimination and violence, however, was the Anglo's sense of racial and cultural superiority. They considered Mexicans as innately inferior and as obstacles to economic and political progress. Even the high-status Tejanos felt the sting of cultural, if not racial, prejudice. Thus, the majority of Mexicans in San Antonio, even if they desired to become americanized, found that Anglos had erected almost insurmountable obstacles to assimilation.[44] Only the women and children with Anglo surnames, light skins, and wealth had a reasonable chance to escape the stigma attached to their Mexican ancestry. Judging from their actions, many of them considered it important, perhaps even necessary to do so.

Mexican women were not in a position to direct the course of social change that occurred in San Antonio during the midnineteenth century. The male-oriented frontier society limited female role alternatives to either wife and mother or mistress and at the same time determined the racial and class criteria which shaped the nature of relationships between Anglo men and Mexican women. Given the patriarchal family structure of both ethnic groups, the wife's function was child care and home management, while the husband assumed primary responsibility for making decisions affecting the family's relationship to the society. Because the assimilation process in San Antonio demanded conformity to Anglo social and cultural patterns, those few Mexican women whom Anglo men found acceptable as wives lost their own distinctive ethnic identity, and in many cases their children rejected the rich cultural legacy of their Mexican ancestry.[45]

[44] A number of sources will substantiate these conclusions, but see especially Félix D. Almaráz, Jr., "The Historical Heritage of the Mexican American in 19th Century Texas, An Interpretation," 12–23, in *The Role of the Mexican American in the History of the Southwest*, conference sponsored by the Inter-American Institute, Pan American College, Edinburg, Texas, November 17, 18, 1969; and Crook, "San Antonio," 14–15.

[45] While conducting research in San Antonio, sociologist Frances Jerome Woods observed that descendants of old Mexican families who had acquired non-Spanish surnames through intermarriage often ignored or forgot their Mexican ancestry. Frances Jerome Woods, *Mexican Ethnic Leadership in San Antonio, Texas* (Washington, D.C., 1949), 96.

BLACK WOMEN AND THEIR COMMUNITIES IN COLORADO

Sue Armitage, Theresa Banfield, and Sarah Jacobus

In conventional histories of the American West, black men are seldom mentioned, black women even more rarely, and black communities, never. When we think about blacks in the West at all, our image is of the black individual: trapper, cowboy, or--less frequently mentioned, but surely very prevalent--army cook. We have one poignant glimpse of a lonely black woman, recorded by Elizabeth Custer in conversation with Eliza, her army cook:

> Miss Libbie, you's always got the ginnel, but I hain't got nobody, and there ain't no picnics nor church sociables nor no buryings out here.[1]

Yet, in fact, this image of the isolated black individual is incorrect. The most remarkable thing about black westward migration was its communal character. This characteristic first captured national attention in 1880 when a mass migration of six to ten thousand black people left the South for Kansas. The Exodusters, as they were called, fled the terror of nightriding and killing which marked the end of the Reconstruction era and the creation of the "Redeemed" (i.e., white supremacist) South. The Exodusters' migration into Kansas had a deeper purpose than simple flight: they shared a vision. Wherever they could, the Exodusters and subsequent black migrants formed their own all-black communities, and there they did have the picnics, church socials, and buryings that Eliza missed so much. Most of the all-black communities failed for lack of capital, and their inhabitants returned to the larger society on white terms. For women, this meant work as domestic servants, and for the men, construction or railroad work. Or, like the white folks, they tried their luck farther west.[2]

Among the Rocky Mountain states, Colorado was the most promising destination for blacks. From 1880 onward, Colorado's black population, largely fed by migrants from Kansas, grew at approximately the same rate as the white population. Although proportionately small (never more than 1.5 percent of the total population), by 1910 black people in Colorado numbered 11,453--most of them gathered together in urban centers.[3] These black communities were rigidly segregated enclaves inside white cities and towns. Our oral histories show that enforced isolation from white social activities forced these small black communities to depend upon their own internal social networks, which were created and maintained by women.

The following oral history excerpts about black communities in Colorado were obtained through interviews with six black women. They provide insight into the support networks of several different black communities, and they also show why the Exodusters' vision of autonomous, self-sufficient black communities remained alive.

Sue Armitage is a Visiting Assistant Professor of History at the University of Colorado, Boulder. She is one of fifteen participants in the national Modern Language Association grant, "Teaching Women's Literature From a Regional Perspective." During 1977-78, she intends to focus her research and teaching on the history of women in Boulder County. Theresa Banfield majored in anthropology at the University of Colorado, and is now a writer doing independent research into little-known aspects of Western history. Her last project was a photographic exhibit about women in Boulder. Currently she is researching the Southern Arapahoe Indians for the Boulder County Parks and Open Space Council. Ms. Banfield is a Colorado native. Sarah Jacobus is Historical Coordinator of "Women in Colorado: Hidden Faces" (see Resource Section at the back of this issue for a full project description). She has traveled extensively in Colorado, gathering research materials, photographs, and oral histories about Colorado women.

FRONTIERS Vol. II, No. 2. © 1977 Women Studies Program, University of Colorado

Boulder: The Small Town Experience

Dr. Ruth Flowers,[4] today a distinguished educator was born into a poor black family in 1902. She moved to Boulder--a health resort, supply center, and university town of about 10,000 people--in 1917. At that time, sixty black families lived in Boulder. Housing was strictly segregated. Blacks either lived on the "wrong side of the tracks" in the poorest part of town, or in a four-block area on a nearby street. The rest of the town was closed to them.

> Now of these sixty families, I counted, there were only twenty men--fathers--who were here when we got here. There was no work; no work for Negro men at all . . . the only men who remained here were the older men . . . the younger men who could get out . . . they all left Boulder . . . to get work in Denver. They would go back and forth, you see. The rest of them, of course, worked on the railroad--dining car porters, and sleeping car porters, and so forth. When they had any time off, they would come back home. . . . So it left the women to support their families and to look after their families and to raise their families and to work . . . the Negro women, of course, were the backbone of the church, the backbone of the family, they were the backbone of the social life, everything.

Dr. Flowers painfully recalled her first encounter with discrimination in Boulder:

> The first day that we came down, on Saturday, we had a couple or three nickels, and we went to get an ice cream cone. We were refused service. You couldn't go in any restaurant, any hot dog stand, any ice cream parlor, any movies--you could go no place, absolutely no place.

The black community in response had its own resources:

> Everybody supported both churches. Now I won't say that the old people went from the Baptist to the Methodist and from the Methodist to the Baptist, because that wasn't true. It was the young people that went!
>
> . . . [Since] you couldn't get an ice cream cone or anything like that . . . various people would have ice cream socials. And they would put their tables outdoors, you know, and the whole neighborhood would come . . . Mrs. Harris, she had a jersey cow . . . and she always had plenty of milk and plenty of cream. . . . So she would have ice cream socials quite often.
>
> We couldn't go to the movies, so what we did was to go to the various homes . . . the first thing they would put in their house was a piano in the front room. So, you see, we would gather together there. . . . My sister could play the piano a little bit. I couldn't and neither one of us could sing. That didn't make any difference, you know. Off a key and off a tune, but still we sang!
>
> Then the other thing that we did, since we couldn't go anywhere, was to go hiking. We hiked in, I think, every canyon, and every part of the hills. . . . The mountains were free and we loved them.

Why did blacks remain in Boulder? Because Boulder's affluence and the presence of university students meant more work opportunities for black women as cooks, maids, and laundresses than in other small cities and towns. And because conditions for blacks, both economically and socially, were not significantly better anywhere else.

When economic conditions changed, and jobs opened up in California at the beginning of World War II, Dr. Flowers' black community all but disappeared:

> The people just left in droves. . . . Those people made more money in one month than they had seen in a year. And they found out they could do something else beside washing and ironing.

Denver: The Big City

Denver--Colorado's largest city--was a thriving railroad center of 213,381 people in 1910. It offered employment opportunities for black men which Boulder lacked, particularly in railroad and construction work. Sarah Sims,[5] born in 1907, came with her parents to Denver in 1909 for just that reason. Her father, a foundry worker, "had decided he would progress more" in Denver than in his hometown of Atchison, Kansas.

Although Sarah Sims recalled that "in those days there weren't many Negroes in Denver at all," in fact 5,426 blacks (almost half of Colorado's black population) lived in Denver in 1910.[6] Their concentration created a more institutionalized support network than existed in the Boulder black community.

For although economic conditions were better for blacks in Denver than in Boulder, social conditions produced the same need for internal support networks. Sarah Sims, like Dr. Flowers, experienced persistent segregation and discrimination in both housing and employment.

As a child, Sarah Sims was supported by the community of the black church:

> And I can see it right now--when we came out of Sunday School, we always marched out two-by-two, and they played, "Onward Christian Soldiers" as you marched out . . . and we just really believed we were Christian soldiers.

She had special words to say about an organization totally unmentioned in the Boulder account--the YWCA. The Denver YWCA, basically a white philanthropic association,[7] "helped to mold many a [black] child's life," according to Mrs. Sims. Although a black woman, Mrs. Fairfax Homes, was appointed YWCA secretary in 1923, de facto segregation continued the YWCA branch that Mrs. Sims attended, for instance, was totally black. Nevertheless, citywide YWCA activities, like summer camp, which Mrs. Sims remembers with great fondness, were always integrated, and at a later date (see below) the Y was active in anti-discrimination protests.

The YWCA and the YMCA sponsored picnics, summer camp in the mountains, and sports days, which compensated to some degree for the athletic discrimination black children encountered in Denver's integrated schools.

The YWCA also encouraged young black women to join the female network of women's clubs:

> There was a group of us that used to go there [to the Y]. We wanted to have kind of a club. So they said that we could. And we named it the Yakawana Club. This club--we were supposed to help the Y any way we could. And we were also supposed to do any community work we could do.
>
> I never will forget. We didn't have what you call the Welfare then. Just people and groups donated and helped the poor people. And our club, the Yakawana, every Christmas we would try to give things to the families--and at Thanksgiving time, we gave baskets. There was a family over on Emerson Street that was quite poor. They had a lot of children. And we bought coal the whole winter. We were in high school then. . . . We would have bake sales and things like that, which our parents would do the baking. We'd get the orders and then we'd go deliver them. And then we would also have like a carnival and little dances over at the Parish House and at the Y. We'd have teas . . . we'd make money and then our dues we used, and we helped.

Throughout her life, Sarah Sims has helped. She has been an active member of many black women's clubs, all of which, whatever their cultural goals, were deeply committed to welfare activity within the black community. She was not alone:

> We've had a lot of people who started in when they were young, and they have still never given up.

At the beginning of World War II, Denver was still a segregated city. In downtown movie theaters, blacks were restricted to the balcony. The "better" restaurants refused service to blacks. In 1942, a sit-in campaign was begun by black members of the Denver

YWCA, with white support. Mrs. Sims and many of her friends from the black women's groups were among the demonstrators:

> A couple of people from the Y, Katherine Corin and Mrs. Lightner . . . would pick [us] up. I think a lot of us, after we'd had one or two experiences . . . maybe would have dropped out. But they wouldn't let us. And they certainly deserve a lot of credit. A lot of people, right now, don't realize it . . . it wasn't anything that was pleasant. But it was a thing that you did to make our community a better community. . . . And I feel very proud that I was a part.

Today, Sarah Sims enjoys the results of the changes which the Denver black community fought for:

> Now we feel we can go anywhere that we want to, and enjoy ourselves, just like the other people can. We are part of the community.

Dearfield: The Vision

We have seen that Colorado blacks, whether they lived in small towns or large cities, endured constant and enforced discrimination and segregation. Quite naturally, the Exodusters' vision of an autonomous black community remained alive--and because homestead land still existed in Colorado, some blacks were able to act upon their vision. Dearfield,[8] an all-black farming community founded in 1910, is an outstanding example of black autonomy--and of white oversight. Few people in Colorado today have ever heard of Dearfield.

Dearfield, thirty miles east of Greeley, Colorado, was so named because the black homesteaders there considered the property so "dear to us." The founder and unofficial head of Dearfield was Oliver T. Jackson, an enterprising and successful black Colorado businessman. In the early 1900's, Jackson served as a messenger to Governor John Shafroth, a western Progressive, who encouraged him in his land-buying venture. O. T. Jackson's dream was to give blacks vocational training on the land, to enable them to be self-sufficient farmers and merchants. He and his wife, Minerva Matlock Jackson, invested their lives in that dream. Irma Ingram remembered from her childhood:

> We always saw the Jacksons in town, they had the restaurant there, and we liked to eat there. Mrs. O. T. Jackson was a warm, outgoing person. He [Mr. Jackson] was mostly in town and she was left to keep the home fires burning--she was the cook, the overseer, everything.

Mrs. Jackson's strong role was not unusual in Dearfield. In the hard early years, and again during the drought of the 1930's, many women farmed while their husbands worked out of town for cash income. Irma Ingram said:

> My father was a foreman on the railroad, and he farmed too. My older brother and mother did a lot of the farming because that was the only way we could make it. . . . I don't remember any of the women ever working out, only at potato harvest time. . . .

Sarah Fountain explained:

> There was too much for women to do in their homes and fields to hire out--those dry fields--took all their effort. Money came from crops and men working outside. You know, Negroes were always at the "poverty level" but they did not consider themselves poor, they always had food, and necessities.
>
> Every household expected the woman in the home to do the work. A woman works everywhere, she worked in the home, would put her cooking on before she went to the field, and then came back and tended to it, serve it, and if necessary go back out to the fields, or milk the cows, she would do that. A woman can adapt herself to every place and they were that kind of women. To make a life you endure most anything, women do. . . . That was a hardship area, you had to irrigate from windmills, with all that blowing sand. They'd

come from fertile lands, better farms, but they went there to stick it out.

At least eight single women are listed in the Bureau of Land Management Homestead entries for Dearfield. Olietta Moore described two of them:

> Mother was widowed and went to work in Denver to support her family. She homesteaded 160 acres in Dearfield so that Grandpa would have a place to garden and putter around on. They worked in the fields, raised corn; they would bring it to Denver and give it away to friends.
>
> My aunt owned property there too. . . . My aunt was highly educated, many black people were, but they weren't hiring Negro teachers; mostly they worked as domestics, because it was better in Colorado than in the South.

The key to the success of Dearfield was cooperation and "sharing with each other." As Eunice Norris recalled:

> People got along well. It was a peaceful sort of situation: struggling people working hard; they didn't have time for trouble. There was a spirit of helpfulness. . . .

The other women had similar memories:

> I remember places in Dearfield where they had dances, a dancehall. There were moonlight picnics, with lanterns, and big chicken fries. The people were friendly, neighborly.
>
> For recreation [there] was dancing, and church socials, and the women would get these together, there were picnics, and the younger folks had card parties. Denver was just about seventy miles away and the people of Denver liked to come up for social weekends. People didn't mix racially, but white folks would come up to hunt and fish.
>
> All holidays were celebrated by the whole community. On Labor Day there was a white family, the McPhersons, they always gave a barbecue for the whole community, before school started. That's one time black and white and all got together and had a real good time.
>
> Parents went to the school, to hear the children's recitations, and the picnics, the families all got together and worked at that, the ladies did the cooking and things.
>
> Everyone had large families and they took care of each other. And I remember we always left a light on at night so if someone was lost they could find their way.

Sarah Fountain came to Dearfield in 1918 to teach at the school. She was welcomed by the community both personally and professionally:

> I was staying with the Clarks, friends of my family, and they accepted me as family. I'd wash and dry after dinner, wash my clothes in a tub and washboard. I made my own clothes and cooked. . . . You just assume certain duties if you're a girl. . . . Mother Clark protected me. She'd say to these young fellows who'd take me off on the ponies, "You be back home before dark," just like my mother would say, and I always was.
>
> People were friendly, you know there's a deep respect for teachers. They liked me and I liked them and they accepted me as their teacher. I had to use a little whip once in a while--for discipline--[on] the younger ones. It was all right with the parents that I did, make 'em mind. They were plain folks, they wanted their children educated, some of them were educated themselves.

Sarah Fountain also provided important information about the role women--including herself--played in social welfare:

> The church was just up the hill from the school and we praticed singing there. I organized the students into a church choir. They permitted us to do that, practice, because it was the community church; everything belonged to everybody. I do believe women are more responsible for getting the church going; they're behind it. [For example,] I knew some women in Denver who could get money from the wealthy people they worked for--they went all out to get money for their churches. They [were] the backbone of the church. It was women who kept that [Dearfield] church clean, went out and kept it in order. There were the women's church organizations, you know, the sewing circle and missionary group; it was well-organized. The children worked into the church programs; they would sing and I played piano. At school we played games; I was a YWCA person, had conducted a Y camp in the mountains, all kinds of games, volleyball and football. I taught them everything in the books and everything I knew. The girls taught me to knit and embroider. I had membership in the YWCA Girl Reserves since its inception in Denver--it emphasized community activities--helped me to help these children.

On the land that Jackson had purchased, a handful of beleaguered settlers grew to a prosperous, dryland farming community of some 700 people. Unfortunately, however, this achievement was short-lived. Deflated market prices after World War I signaled the decline of Dearfield, and severe drought in the 1930's sealed its fate:

> Most people went out there with high hopes and left with bitter disappointment. It all dried up and blew away.

By the 1950's, Dearfield had dwindled to one inhabitant, a woman who remained in the settlement hoping that others would return and again "share with each other." When she died, Dearfield vanished--except, of course, in the memories of the former inhabitants.

These oral histories with black women uncover a new aspect of the black westward migration. Although the public institutions of Western black communities have attracted some notice, their internal support networks, for which women were primarily responsible, have been overlooked. We have the strong suspicion that previous researchers did not consider the role of women, and because they did not think to ask, nobody told them. The result is that the published accounts rarely mention women.[9] Yet our interviews show clearly that black women played an indispensable role in the organization and survival of their communities. We hope that our research on black communities in the West will be continued by researchers attuned to the vital role of black women. We believe, also, that oral history is essential in the recovery of these hidden realities.

NOTES

[1]Elizabeth B. Custer, Following the Guidon (New York: Harper and Brother, 1890), p. 238.

[2]Nell Irvin Painter, Exodusters: Black Migration to Kansas After Reconstruction (New York: Knopf, 1977).

[3]W. Sherman Savage, Blacks in the West (Westport, Conn.: Greenwood Press, 1976), p. 200. By 1900, the total number of blacks settled west of the Mississippi (excluding Missouri and Texas) was 165,432. Of this number, more than 100,000 were concentrated in two states--Kansas and Oklahoma.

See also Kathleen Bruyn, 'Aunt' Clara Brown (Boulder, Colo.: Pruett Publishing Company, 1970) for an account of early black settlers in Colorado, and their efforts to aid the Exodusters of 1880.

[4]Dr. Flowers was interviewed by Theresa Banfield for the Boulder Women's Oral History Project.

[5]Sarah Sims was interviewed by Sarah Jacobus as a part of the oral history research for "Women in Colorado: Hidden Faces."

[6]Census figures. Sarah Sims was correct about the black/white proportion: blacks were less than 2 percent of Denver's total population in 1910. Present black population of Denver is 50,164 or 4 percent of the total of 1,227,529 (1970 figures).

[7]See Gerda Lerner, ed., Black Women in White America (New York: Vintage, 1973), pp. 477-97 for an account of the integration of the YWCA on the national level. See also her, "Black and White Women in Interaction and Confrontation" in Prospects: An Annual of American Cultural Studies, Vol. II, ed. Jack Salzman (New York: Burt Franklin, 1976), pp. 193-208.

[8]Theresa Banfield first heard of Dearfield when she interviewed Dr. Flowers. Her subsequent search for archival information was disappointing, and she decided to try oral history. The founding generation is dead, but their children still carry vivid memories of Dearfield. Dr. Flowers and a neighbor gave her the name of a Denver woman, who told of someone else. Eventually, she interviewed four women--Sarah Fountain, Irma Ingram, Eunice Morris, Olietta Moore--parts of whose interviews are presented here.

[9]The best general study, because of its emphasis on black hopes and motivations, remains William Loren Katz, The Black West (New York: Doubleday, 1971). More detailed studies are: Glen Schwendermann, "Nicodemus: Negro Haven on the Solomon," Kansas Historical Quarterly, XXXIV, No. 1 (Spring 1968), 10-31; Mozell C. Hill, "The All-Negro Communities of Oklahoma: The Natural History of a Social Movement," Journal of Negro History, XXXI, No. 3 (July 1946), 254-68; and George H. Wayne, "Negro Migration and Colonization in Colorado 1870-1930," Journal of the West, XV, No. 1 (January 1976), 102-20.

Black and White Women in Interaction and Confrontation

Gerda Lerner

The parallels in the status of women and of Blacks have been noted by social scientists and historians, and recently, by theoreticians of the women's liberation movement. It is obvious that there are similarities in the status and history of the two groups, but these are offset by important differences. The analogy between Blacks in general and women is valid and useful as long as it is confined to the psychological effect of inferior status, but not when it is extended to a general comparison between the two groups.

It may be more appropriate to compare the history and status of white and black women in this country, but to do so adequately would go beyond the scope of this article. What will be attempted here is to view the contacts between black and white women, especially as expressed through their organizations, in historical perspective, and to examine the nature of this contact more closely. One will find that a similarity of interests did not always express itself in cooperation, and that the relationship between the two groups was and is quite complicated, and frequently ambivalent, if not actually hostile.

Black and white women throughout U.S. history have shared a certain common experience. As women, they were members of the one group in society holding the lowest economic position, longest denied access to equal education, faced with discriminatory practices in every aspect of life, and kept marginal to the institutional power structure. But black women were at all times discriminated against more severely than any other group in our society: as Blacks, as women, and frequently as low-paid workers. Most white women were unaware of their own inferior status in society, were treated with chivalry and with deference, and shared indirectly in the status privileges of their men. They also shared in the racist attitudes of white men. Quite frequently, many of the privileges white women enjoyed were held at the expense of black

Copyright © 1976 by Gerda Lerner.

women or of lower-class white women, especially in their function as domestic workers. The vast majority of black and white women lived their separate lives in segregated spheres, and despite their common status as women, had little awareness of and little contact with each other. And yet they were in many ways interdependent.

The ambivalent interdependence of black and white women was nowhere better symbolized than in the complex relationship of the white mistress and her black slave. The very existence of the white woman and of her family was founded on the economic and physical exploitation and ownership of her black chattel. Yet, in the daily life of the plantation household, black and white women were put into close daily contact, companionship, and intimate interdependency. What bound them together was, not infrequently, their relationship to the master of the house. A white southern woman, mistress of a large plantation and later a stanch defender of the Confederacy, described this ambivalent situation astutely:

> Under slavery we live surrounded by prostitutes. . . . God forgive us, but ours is a monstrous system. . . . Like the patriarchs of old, our men live all in one house with their wives and their concubines; and the mulattoes one sees in every family partly resemble the white children. Any lady is ready to tell you who is the father of all the mulatto children in everybody's household but her own. Those, she seems to think, drop from the clouds.[1]

On the side of the black woman there was ambivalence as well; the licentious relationship with the master was often hated, fought against, and always degrading. It weakened the black family, poisoned motherhood, and served to separate sex from affection. On the other hand, it was for many slave women the one and only avenue toward some precarious improvement in their lot and that of their offspring. And there are sufficient cases on record of genuine human attachment between master and slave concubine to make all facile generalizations invalid. In such cases it was the black woman who held the respect and affection of the man, while the white lady, the "chief slave in the harem," had the empty shell of respectability and fancied superiority as a substitute for a genuine marriage. There is ambivalence, too, in the role of the legendary "Mammy" of the plantation household—substitute mother of the white children while deprived of the care of her own, respected domestic tyrant, often sole confidante of her mistress. A curious psychological revenge of the black oppressed class over their white oppressors occurred within the house of the maters; the white lady, sexually deprived of her husband by his slave women, *allowed* herself to be deprived of her children by their black Mammy. For the white boy, mother love was *black* love and sexual satisfaction was found with the black women, while the white girl learned from early childhood that the price of respectability and wealth was submission and acceptance of total powerlessness to affect one's fate.[2]

In regard to law, economics, education, and political life, black and white women were equally powerless in a society dominated by white men. But the degree of their powerlessness was greatly different, for the slave was considered a chattel, while the white woman was considered free. The white woman had, at all times, sufficient power to exploit and mistreat her slaves, but she seldom had enough power to protect them from abuse, should she so desire. The experiences of the British-born actress Frances Kemble, who wrecked her marriage through her efforts to ameliorate the lot of her husband's female slaves, is a case in point.[3] The South Carolina-born Grimké sisters, daughters of a planter, also tried and failed in their efforts at improving the lot of their family's slaves, and concluded that slave society would permit the elevation of neither slaves nor white women. They took the unique step, for southern women of their station, of leaving the south and becoming abolitionists. They were radical, even among abolitionists, in their total acceptance of black women and in their emphasis on combating racism.

"They are our countrywomen," Angelina Grimké wrote of the slaves, "they are our sisters; and to us as women, they have a right to look for sympathy with their sorrows, and effort and prayer for their rescue."[4]

For roughly two decades prior to the Civil War the movements for the emancipation of Negroes and of women coincided and frequently overlapped. The close collaboration then existing between these two reform movements has obscured the much more complex and problematical relationship existing between the members of these two groups over the longer span of history.

It was not so much that black women were helped and sustained through the sympathies and organizational efforts of white women. Even from the outset, things worked in the opposite way. It was through the struggle for the rights of black people that many northern white women first became aware of their own oppression. It is only in this sense that we can say that the antislavery movement gave birth to the woman's rights movement. In 1837, when the Grimké sisters, as agents of the American Anti-Slavery Society, toured New England, they met much opposition as the first American-born white women to lecture in public.*

*The first American woman ever to lecture in public was a Black, Maria Stewart.

The sisters defended their right to speak and organize, and linked the cause of Blacks and of white women. "If we have no right to act, then may we well be termed 'the white slaves of the North.' "[5]

Like them, most of the early feminists came to their convictions because of their interest in abolition. Elizabeth Cady Stanton, Susan B. Anthony, Lucy Stone, Abby Kelley, and scores of others found that if they wished to work for reforms in general, they would first have to fight for their right as women to engage in public political activity.

By and large, the antislavery women showed a greater awareness of the implications of prejudice than their contemporaries; their meetings were integrated; they gave their Negro members a chance to take leadership positions in their organizations. Year after year they passed resolutions against race prejudice, such as this one:

> Resolved . . . that it is . . . the duty of abolitionists to identify themselves with these oppressed Americans by sitting with them in places of worship, by appearing with them in our streets, by giving them our countenance in steam-boats and stages, by visiting them in their homes and encouraging them to visit us, receiving them as we do our white fellow citizens.[6]

Both the Boston and the Philadelphia Female Anti-Slavery Society were faced with mob actions because of their insistence on holding interracial public meetings; both societies met the challenge by an absolute refusal to back down from this policy. In Boston, Negro and white women linked arms as they marched out in pairs through a furious mob; similar so-called amalgamation incidents so incited public prejudice in Philadelphia that in 1838 the newly built Pennsylvania Hall was attacked by a mob while the antislavery women were meeting there and, a few hours later, was burned to the ground.

Frederick Douglass played a leading role at the first woman's rights convention in Seneca Falls, New York. Three years later, that remarkable black leader, Sojourner Truth, illuminated the connection between the two causes in her unique, dramatic way when she rose during a woman's rights convention to point to one of the clergymen who had lectured the women on the impropriety of their demands. "That man over there says dat women needs to be helped into carriages and lifted over ditches and to have the best place everywhere. Nobody ever help me into carriages or over mud puddles or gives me any best place—and aren't I a woman? I have plowed and planted and gathered into barns, and no man could head me—and aren't I a woman?" and pointing to another who had blamed the trouble of mankind on mother Eve, she declared: "If the first woman God ever made was strong enough to turn the world upside down all alone, these together ought to be able to get it right side up again, and now they're asking to do it, the men better let em."[7]

In the person of Sojourner Truth, the fusion of the abolition and woman's rights movements seemed personified.

In the abolitionist movement black and white people experienced regular personal contact and close collaboration for a common cause. It was inevitable that this should lead to an awareness of racial differences, racial tensions, at times friction, at times a friendly adjustment.

Intimate friendships between black and white women in the nineteenth century are rare. One example of such a relationship was the life-long friendship between Sarah and Angelina Grimké and Sarah Douglass, the Philadelphia school teacher. The Grimké sisters had met Sarah Douglass and her mother at Quaker meetings and had noticed that the two black women were made to sit on a separate, "colored" bench at Meeting. In protest, the sisters demonstratively seated themselves with the black women. Later, the three young women collaborated in exposing other discriminatory practices among Philadelphia Quakers. Sarah Douglass furnished factual data from her own and her mother's experience, the Grimké sisters, failing to find a publisher in the United States, transmitted the information to British Quakers, who published it in a pamphlet, in the hope of influencing American Friends. The three women worked together for years in the Philadelphia Female Anti-Slavery Society. The basis for the friendship was the white women's proven service to the antislavery cause, their willingness to identify themselves with their black sisters in action, not only in words, and their understanding that in racial matters they must and should accept the guidance of their black friends. On the other hand, there was a mutual willingness to face up to the complexities of interracial friendships. The Grimké sisters had frequently visited and been houseguests of Mrs. Douglass and her mother. When Angelina married Theodore Weld, she, her husband, and Sarah extended invitations to all their friends for visits in their new home. Sarah Douglass came, insisted on staying only for one day, and wrote a polite "Thank You" note commending them for their hospitality and "Christian conduct."

> But the sisters were not pleased with this polite gesture. "It seemed to me thy proposal 'to spend a day' with us," wrote Sarah, "was made under a little feeling something like this: 'Well, after all, I am not quite certain I shall be an acceptable visitor.' " She could well understand that her friend might feel that kind of apprehension,

> but hoped she could "rise above thy suspicions." Angelina put the matter more bluntly.... Sarah's gratitude for their "Christian conduct" had caused them pain. "In what did it consist? In receiving and treating thee as an equal.... Oh, how humbling to receive such thanks!"[8]

This frank exchange obviously cleared the air. Sarah Douglass' next visits to the Weld home lasted several weeks. She and Sarah Grimké remained close friends for the rest of their lives. Such intimate interracial friendships were rare.

The frictions and tensions between black and white abolitionists have received a good deal of attention from modern scholars. Best known are the bitter exchanges between Frederick Douglass and William L. Garrison, who insisted on guiding and directing the great Negro leader, as though he needed such tutelage. Douglass' letters to the abolitionist Maria Chapman, in which he complained, with justification, against the patronizing treatment he was receiving at the hand of white abolitionists, are also well known.

Another example of interracial confrontation among antislavery people in the pre-Civil War period appeared in the pages of the *Provincial Freeman*, a Canadian newspaper, then edited by a black woman, Mary Ann Shadd. On December 16, 1854, there is a column discussing the case of Mrs. Margaret Douglass of Virginia, a white woman who had kept a school for slave children. She had been indicted and tried by the state of Virginia for violating the slave code, had been found guilty and imprisoned for one month. The case commanded a good deal of attention because of the fact that the violator of the law was a white southern woman, a species rarely found on the side of the slaves. The abolitionist press had praised Mrs. Douglass and featured her story prominently.

Mary Ann Shadd, however, found something else worth featuring. She reprinted parts of Mrs. Douglass' speech in court. Acting without counsel in her own defense, Mrs. Douglass had said that she considered amalgamation [a genteel nineteenth-century word for miscegenation] the cause "of the opposition to the instruction of the colored race."

> It is impossible to deny that this unnatural custom prevails to a fearful extend throughout the South.... It pervades the entire society... The white mothers and daughters of the South have suffered under it for years—have seen their dearest affections trampled upon—their hopes of domestic happiness destroyed... The female slave... knows that she is powerless beneath the whims and fancies of her master.... She knows that she must submit. There is no way of escape.... Still, she feels her degradation, and so do

> others with whom she is connected. . . .[9]

In these words Mrs. Douglass had described quite accurately the ambivalent bonds that tied black and white women in a common oppression under slavery. But to her, the cause lay not in the system of slavery, but in the lack of religious instruction offered the slaves. These were needed, she stated, especially in view of the sinfulness of the masters, to "instruct the negroes in their obligations to

> their masters and their God. Were these instructions exemplified by the consistent lives of their masters . . . the South would become the very garden of the Lord. There would be no fear of insurrections, for there would be no inducement. But when a man, black though he be, knows that at any moment he is compelled to hand over his wife, his sister, or his daughter to the loathsome embraces of the man whose chain he wears, how can it be expected that he will submit without the feelings of hatred and revenge taking possession of his heart? . . . [10]

Obviously, these words were spoken in self-defense and designed to reassure the court that she had acted from the highest of motives. None of the abolitionists had found anything but admiration for this southern white woman. But Mary Ann Shadd, while admitting that she had previously regarded the lady as a friend of the race, now found that she had to view her as a friend of the slaveholder. Mary Ann Shadd had a keen ear for the racism hidden beneath this defense of the slave's humanity. She pointed out that Mrs. Douglass regarded amalgamation

> as the cause of the ignorance, degradation and crime which hang over the sunny South; if it were not for it, the slave, having no natural aspirations to liberty, would it is presumed be quiet, submissive, enjoy his corn, bacon, dirt and rags through untold generations. . . . What a libel upon humanity!

She quoted Mrs. Douglass as saying that "the fathers, sons

> and husbands of her southern sisters have not even the paltry excuse . . . that their love [for their tawny mistresses] is real, though illicit; the whole practice is plainly, unequivocally shamelessly beastly."

"They cannot love those tawny mistresses," commented Mary Ann Shadd,

> because they are tawny or colored, if you please; therefore if they are colored they must be a lower grade of animal than are the southern gentlemen.... Mrs. Douglass then—as do all pro-slavery people—is endeavoring to fan the flames of prejudice... at the same time that she would rivet the chains on the slave. Note the process by which they are to be riveted and the remedy for the evils, which is in the hands of the southern woman. That remedy is the instruction of the negroes in their duty to their *masters*. ... "One good preacher among my negroes is more efficacious than a wagonload of cowhides," said a planter, and this is Mrs. Douglass' sentiment which she had plainly, unequivocally and shamefully set forth.... We cannot sufficiently express out abhorrence of such hollow-heartedness as this.[11]

The exchange illustrates what is obviously a recurring pattern in black and white relationships: Blacks, allied with whites in radical causes, constantly have to educate their white allies as to the realities and implications of racism. Evidently, even in 1854, such education often took the form of confrontation and sharp debate.

Another such debate occurred shortly after the Civil War. The advocates of woman's rights had worked hard for passage of the Fourteenth Amendment, fully expecting it to provide voting rights both for Negroes and for women. To their bitter disappointment, the amendment not only failed to grant suffrage to women, but actually limited suffrage to male citizens. The addition of the word "male" as a qualification for suffrage in the federal Constitution seemed to the feminists actually to worsen the legal disabilities of women, who had previously been excluded from voting by state law only. Even stanch abolitionists such as Elizabeth C. Stanton and Susan B. Anthony now wavered in their support of the Negro's cause. Frederick Douglass reproached these wavering allies by pointing to the greater urgency of his people's cause.

> When women, because they are women, are dragged from their homes and hung upon lamp-posts; when their children are torn from their arms and their brains dashed upon the pavement; when they are objects of insult and outrage at every turn; when they are in danger of having their homes burnt down over their heads; when their children are not allowed to enter school; then they will have an urgency to obtain the ballot [similar to that of the Negro].... Yes, it is true of the black woman, but not because she is a woman but because she is black.[12]

In retrospect, it is clear that in 1868 woman's suffrage had no chance of passage even with abolitionist support. It took the woman's rights movement several decades to recover from the shattering of the old abolitionist-feminist alliance. Organized feminists, under the leadership of a new generation of middle- and upper-class women, who shared the nativist and racist ideas of men of their class, concentrated on winning wide support for the woman's suffrage amendment. They followed the spirit of the times in turning away from the race issues, yet the consequence of this ideological shift and of the tactical turn to "expediency" and pragmatism was to push the suffrage movement into an acceptance of the status quo in race relations.

In the twentieth century, southern suffragists made frequent use of the argument first developed by Henry Blackwell in *The Woman's Journal* that granting the vote to southern white women would result in strengthening white rule in the South, since there were more white women in the South than there were black men and women combined.[13] The same argument was used in the North in reference to the "ignorant vote" of the immigrants. An extremist such as Kate Gordon of New Orleans, a member of the board of the National American Woman's Suffrage Association in 1901, who later resigned to build a states' rights southern women's organization dedicated to winning suffrage for white women only, was not typical of the national leadership. Yet the constant compromise of suffrage leaders with the southern viewpoint on the race issue inevitably led to discriminatory practices and racist incidents.[14] The few black women's suffrage clubs participated in conventions and national suffrage parades on a segregated basis. Leadership by black women was discouraged.[15] Ironically, such tactics, supposedly designed to strengthen the movement, did not serve to bring the southern states into the pro-suffrage lineup. In fact, all the deep South states held out against the Nineteenth Amendment to the end, refusing even to ratify it. A number of racist incidents involving the Woman's Party after the winning of suffrage indicate that "expediency" had frequently served as an excuse for bigotry.

While the organized suffrage movement and the movement for Negro rights ran in separate and at times opposed directions, black and white women cooperated on other levels. Josephine Griffing, a white abolitionist, devoted herself wholeheartedly to relief and welfare work for the freedmen in Washington, D.C. and was later active in the drive for their resettlement in Kansas. Similarly, other abolitionist women expressed their support of blacks through freedmen relief and welfare activities, supporting and adding to the work of such black women as Harriet Tubman and Sojourner Truth.* After the Civil War, many of the northern female anti-slavery societies devoted themselves to relieving the wants of the freedmen and raising funds in support of their schools. Northern abolitionist women had begun the enormous task of educating the millions of freedmen, even while the war was still raging, by sending teachers to the Union-held areas of the South. After the war their ranks were increased by southern women in need of employment and, gradually, by male and female black teachers. The white southern community generally shunned these northern teachers, refused them housing and food and treated them as outcasts. Of necessity and often by choice they lived in the black community and shared the lives of their students. Yet the relationship of these educated white women and the illiterate poverty-stricken freedmen was not one of equals. It was of necessity tinged with paternalistic—or in this case maternalistic—attitudes and racial prejudice. A sincere dedication to social and moral uplift and a missionary approach characterized these teachers. It should be added that the few northern black women who went south as teachers displayed a similar somewhat patronizing attitude toward the freedmen.[16]

The pattern of paternalism continued into the postwar decades. White northern women were instrumental in supporting the self-help efforts of black women, who founded schools and training institutes for black girls in the South. Lucy Lainey could not have succeeded without Mrs. F. E. Haines in founding and maintaining Haines School in Georgia; Charlotte Hawkins Brown was able to start her girls' school in Sedalia, North Carolina, through the help of Alice Freeman Palmer; Emma J. Wilson depended on funds raised in the North, mostly by women, to maintain Mayesville Industrial Institute in South Carolina. Later Mary McLeod Bethune and Nannie Burroughs enlisted the cooperation of wealthy whites in support of the schools they had founded and built.

Southern blacks, living in poverty and under the most repressive political conditions, were obliged, for the time being, to accept the help of liberal-minded northern whites, but they never stopped protesting against white paternalism in its various manifestations. White boards of trustees for black schools, incessant investigation of school management by well-meaning white donors, innumerable indignities and snubs, not to speak of indifference or often hostility on the part of local whites, were the price paid by the dedicated black women who raised the educational and cultural level of their communities by founding schools. Charlotte Hawkins Brown bore the load patiently for years, making her Palmer Memorial Institute grow from a log cabin school into a finishing school

*Sojourner Truth and Josephine Griffing had earlier braved hostile crowds during their 1862 speaking tour in Kansas.

for girls worth half a million dollars in plant and equipment. Yet even her patience had limits. "Now that things are turning and many are opening their eyes to what I've tried to do," she wrote, "and desiring to have a share in the same, the question in my heart and mind, and God only knows how it hurts, is just what are they going to ask me to submit to as a negro woman to get their interest. . . . My only point is in my efforts to get money now, I don't want my friends in the North to tie my hands so I can't speak out when I'm being crushed."[17]

Frequently, black women had to prod their white friends on the racial issue and insist on raising their level of understanding. This was done very politely, and with excessive caution, but it was done. An example is to be found in Mrs. Booker T. Washington's correspondence with Mrs. Edna Dow Cheney, a wealthy Bostonian, who cooperated with black club women in Boston and supported the Tuskegee Institute Mother's Club.

In 1896, Margaret M. Washington wrote to Mrs. Cheney:

> I am writing you now of a matter which concerns me and the rest of women of my race. I want your advice. You know as much about this separate car business in the South as I can tell you. [The reference is to segregated and inferior Jim Crow railroad facilities.] The Southern people of course make these laws. . . . The Southern women keep up this thing. They are behind the men because their education is more limited. They have little to do except nurse their prejudices. . . . I hear that the Executive Board of the National Council of Women meet in Boston this winter to prepare for their meeting next year. I thought our cause in this matter might be helped by having a colored woman to appear in this Council, to present not only this question but she might represent us in a general way. I understand that organizations of Southern white women will not enter the Federation. . . . because they are opposed to Colored organizations entering these clubs. . . . I do believe if such women as Miss Willard, Mrs. Henrotin, Mrs. Dickinson and others were to show a little less fear of their southern sisters, these conditions of which I speak would be altered.[18]

Mrs. Washington was not alone in advancing the issue of black representation in the National Women's Club movement. White women had begun to organize clubs on a national level after the Civil War. Black women launched their national club movement in 1892. Like the white clubwomen they emphasized community betterment, education, uplift, and self-improvement. Additionally, the Negro women's clubs were dedicated to racial improvement, defense of the home, raising of the standards of education, and an end to the various discriminatory restrictions that hedged and impeded every aspect of Negro life. The establishment of social welfare agencies for black children, orphans, the aged, and the delinquent was largely the work of these women's clubs. In state after state the first welfare services available to black people were initiated by black women and only later taken over by local government.[19] It is perhaps significant of the spirit of interracial cooperation that in 1896 the National Association of Colored Women appealed to all of its member clubs to donate $5 per club to support the aged and now destitute daughter of old John Brown of Harpers Ferry.

Cooperation with white women was first established locally. Individual black women were sometimes admitted to white clubs.* Negro women's clubs were gradually admitted to state federations, but the issue of national representation remained controversial. As late as 1900 the General Federation of Women's Clubs, at its Milwaukee Convention, refused the credentials of Mrs. Josephine Ruffin, who represented the New Era Club, the oldest of the Negro women's clubs. She also had been elected a delegate of the New England Federation of Women's Clubs. The national organization was willing to accept her credentials from the white organization, but refused those from the black women's club. Mrs. Ruffin refused this "compromise." The incident led to discussion of the race issue in many clubs and in the nation's newspapers, but the color bar in national women's organizations did not drop until several decades later.[20]

In the South, it was in temperance societies that black and white women took their first faltering steps toward cooperation. From the first timid contact among leaders of color-separated locals, came county and state meetings which at times even discussed such formerly taboo subjects as the sexual exploitation of Negro women by white men. Since the greatest impediment to black and white cooperation was the slanderous myth that black women were morally degraded, this issue was of considerable importance. Mere contact with black clubwomen dissolved the stereotyped notions of prejudiced isolation. The white women had to learn to see a connection between the protection of their own homes and the protection of the honor and rights of black women. The issue around which this education and politicalization was effected was lynching.

In the 1890s, under the leadership if Ida Wells Barnett, who initiated an international crusade against lynching, Negro women's clubs launched a national campaign against this evil, and challenged white

*Josephine St. Pierre Ruffin was a member of the New England Women's Club. Fannie B. Williams was admitted to membership in the Chicago Club in 1894.

clubwomen to support them. An early example of the now familiar pattern of the white liberal, accused of racism by black friends, grew out of this antilynching campaign and involved Frances Willard, the president of the Women's Christian Temperance Union, whose earlier abolitionist convictions and interracial work were a matter of record. Mrs. Willard was hesitant and equivocal on the issue of lynching and defended the southern record against accusations made by Ida Wells Barnett on her English speaking-tour. Severe attacks on her in the women's press and a protracted public controversy helped to move Mrs. Willard to a cautious stand in opposition to lynching. Black women continued to agitate this issue and to confront white women with a moral challenge to their professed Christianity.[21]

Black women early perceived that lynchings could be tolerated by white communities because of the rape charge against black men and the general white belief in the inherent immorality of black women. They therefore attacked lynching by exposing the falsity of the rape charge, case by case, and by trying to maximize the cooperative and friendly contacts between women of both races. Custom, tradition, institutional and legal practices made this difficult, but they persisted.

As a result of the democratic hopes raised by World War I and the shocking polarization at the end of the war, which found expression in race riots and lynchings, women of both races felt impelled to make stronger efforts than ever before to bridge the gap between the races. Eva Bowles, the first YWCA secretary in charge of "colored work," Mrs. Lugenia Hope, an Atlanta community leader, Charlotte Hawkins Brown, and Mary McLeod Bethune led black women in this effort. White church women were the first to respond. In 1919, the Women's Missionary Council Committee on Race Relations sent two white observers to a Tuskegee conference of black clubwomen. Frank discussion and position papers were exchanged. In 1920, through the efforts of the Commission on Inter-Racial Cooperation (CIC), four black women were invited to a conference of southern church women. This tradition-shattering meeting ended with 105 representatives of white church and women's organizations constituting themselves the Women's Council of the CIC and pledging themselves to grassroots interracial work. Patient work on a local level and the slow integration of state and national organizations continued for several decades. By 1929, 805 interracial county committees were functioning in the southern states.

In 1930, the all-white Association of Southern Women for the Prevention of Lynching was formed. Its major contribution was the repudiation of the myth that lynchings were done to protect white womanhood. Over 40,000 signatures of white women leaders to a statement condemning lynchings were collected throughout the South. The organization also acted effectively on the local level to stop actual lynchings.[22] The ensuing decline of lynchings is so dramatic, that one can be justified in crediting black and white women with a major victory in this long campaign.

The winning of full equality for black women in the civic and community organizations of the South proceeded with painful slowness. As late as World War II it was considered a remarkable breakthrough for a black woman, Septima Clark, to sit on the board of the Community Chest of Charleston, South Carolina. A similarly long process of organizing, prodding, and educating on the part of a few black pioneers led to the eventual integration of the national YWCA, but this was not achieved until the 1950s. Still, the positive role of white women in combating discrimination, in helping to support black schools and welfare institutions, and in laying the groundwork in the southern communities for an acceptance of later civil rights legislation should not be understated. Black and white women were, in regard to interracial cooperation, ahead of their communities and their men, possibly because the common concerns of women for their homes and their children prevailed over prejudice and vested interests.

All women, black and white, experienced sex discrimination in education, employment, and politics. But to most black women, the race discrimination they experienced was much more pervasive, devastating, and threatening. Black women usually put their needs as Blacks before their needs as women. Many white women, on the other hand, were made more politically sophisticated by the very process of working for their own emancipation. Inevitably, those demanding an extension of the ballot to women, attacking the low economic status of women, and even questioning the fundamental assumptions of society in regard to matrimony, divorce, and sexual mores began to challenge the established institutions of society. White women in their quest for emancipation came into conflict with the churches, the law, the political and economic establishment, and with the men in power on the local scene, inevitably white men. These were the same forces traditionally arrayed against black people. In the labor movement, too, those seeking to abolish child labor and advance the conditions of working women came up against the same forces that had so long kept black people oppressed. Thus white women were radicalized through their contacts with black women.

Despite the close linkage of the movements for Negro rights and women's emancipation in the early nineteenth century, which might make it appear as though white women were just "naturally" advocates of and sympathetic to the cause of Blacks, interaction between black and white women was much more ambivalent and problematical. Not infrequently there was confrontation, competition and conflict. Black and white cooperation, wherever it was effective, was based on the healthy self-interest of each of the groups involved, rather than on altruistic motives and paternalism. Although they have their womanhood in common, black and white women could not escape the confines and limitations of a society in which a person's status and power are defined not only by sex, but—more importantly—by race.

Notes

The findings in this article are based on extensive research in primary sources, including letters and manuscripts of feminists, antislavery women, and leaders of Negro women's clubs. Among the organizational records consulted were those of the various Female Anti-Slavery Societies, Anti-Slavery Conventions of American Women, all the Women's Rights Conventions, New Era Club, Tuskegee Mothers' Club, YWCA, National Association of Colored Women, and others. Among the newspapers consulted were all the antislavery papers; *Frederick Douglass' Paper; Woman's Journal; Revolution; Woman's Era; Afro-American Woman; National Notes; Provincial Freeman*.

1. Mary Boykin Chesnut, *A Diary from Dixie*, ed. Ben A. Williams (Boston: Houghton Mifflin, 1961), pp. 21–22.
2. For a fuller discussion of this theme, see Lillian Smith, *The Killers of the Dream* (New York: W. W. Norton, 1949) I, 1, 2; II, 1–4; III, 1–4; W. J. Cash, *The Mind of the South* (New York: Alfred Knopf, 1941), pp. 87–89; Winthrop D. Jordan, *White over Black: American Attitudes toward the Negro, 1550–1812* (Chapel Hill, N.C.: Univ. of North Carolina Press, 1968), chap. 4.
3. Frances Ann Kemble, *Journal of a Residence on a Georgia Plantation in 1838–1839*, ed. John A. Scott (New York: Alfred A. Knopf, 1961), pp. 224–41.
4. For childhood and youth of the Grimké sisters see Gerda Lerner, *The Grimké Sisters from South Carolina: Rebels against Slavery* (Boston: Houghton Mifflin, 1967), chaps. 1–5; citation from Angelina E. Grinké, *An Appeal to the Women of the Nominally Free States* . . . (New York: W. S. Dorr, 1837), p. 62.
5. Ibid., p. 63.
6. Proceedings, Anti-Slavery Convention of American Women . . . 1837 (New York: W. S. Dorr, 1837).
7. *Narrative of Sojourner Truth* (Battle Creek: Review and Herald Office, 1884), p. 135.
8. Sarah and Angelina Grimké to Sarah Douglass (undated), Mss, Weld-Grimké Papers, Wm. L. Clements Library, the University of Michigan.
9. *Provincial Freeman*, I, No. 39, December 16, 1854.
10. Ibid.
11. Ibid.
12. Frederick Douglass, speech before Equal Rights Association, New York City, May 1869, as cited in *The Revolution*, May 20, 1869.
13. *Woman's Journal*, September 27, 1890.
14. Aileen Kraditer, *The Ideas of the Woman Suffrage Movement: 1890–1920* (New York: Columbia Univ. Press, 1965), chap. 7.
15. Letters by Daisy Lampkin to Heywood Broun (August 28, 1924) and to Walter White (August 18, 1924) describe several incidents of discrimina-

tion in the years 1913–24. NAACP Mss., Library of Congress.

16. The generalizations concerning the teachers of the freedmen are based on the study of manuscript sources, particularly those of the American Missionary Association; Amistad Research Center, Dillard University; Freedmen's Aid Commission, Papers, Cornell University; and the *Freedmen's Record*. Also, diaries and letters of Charlotte Forten, Lucy Chase, Susie King Taylor, Frances E. W. Harper, Virginia Randolph, Laura Mobley, and others.
17. Undated letter fragment, Charlotte Hawkins Brown Mss., Schlesinger Library, Radcliffe College. Also letters by Mary McLeod Bethune in the Rosenwald Fund Papers, Fisk University.
18. Margaret M. Washington to Edna D. Cheney, November 23, 1896, Cheney Papers, Boston Public Library.
19. Information on Negro women's clubs comes from a study of the organizational records of the National Association of Colored Women, the Atlanta Neighborhood Union, the Tuskegee Woman's Club, the Boston New Era Club, and others.
20. Mrs. Booker T. Washington, "Club Movement among Negro Women," in J. L. Nichols and W. H. Crogman, eds., *Progress of the Race* (Naperville, Ga.: J. L. Nichols Co., 1929), pp. 220–26.
21. The Willard incident is described in several issues of the *Woman's Era* (February 1895–July 1895).
22. The foregoing is based on manuscript materials, chiefly: YWCA organizational files, Sophia Smith Collection, Smith College; Neighborhood Union papers, Commission on Interracial Cooperation papers and the files of the Association of Southern Women for the Prevention of Lynching, all at Atlanta University.

Sharing Bed and Board: Cohabitation and Cultural Difference in Central Arizona Mining Towns, 1863–1873

SUSAN L. JOHNSON

This article compares two very different cultural patterns, the Mexican informal union and the Anglo double standard of morality, which co-existed in the Arizona goldfields of the 1860s. Both are examples of the persistence of earlier social forms, yet they became particular adaptations to boom town society, and their conjunction briefly produced something new.

Working from census records, Susan Johnson carefully reconstructs the lives of the Mexican women who lived in informal unions with Anglo or Mexican men. She effectively uses local folklore about two unusual Anglo women to explore Anglo attitudes toward race and sexuality. By tracing the two cultural patterns and analyzing their interaction, she widens our notion of culture contact as well as that of cultural persistence.

By the spring of 1864, nineteen-year-old Juanita Bachichia was well situated in a large, sturdy cabin on Lynx Creek, at the heart of central Arizona's burgeoning gold-mining districts. She had arrived only five months before, following close on the heels of the first prospectors. A native New Mexican, Bachichia cast her lot with George Clinton, a twenty-four-year-old miner and hotelkeeper from New York; their cabin soon became a boardinghouse where miners ate for two dollars a day. They were making final preparations for the new enterprise when the Reverend Hiram Walter Read approached the camp at Lynx Creek.

Like many of the first settlers, Reverend Read did double duty during the early months of the gold excitement. In addition to his religious role, as postmaster of the newly organized Territory of Arizona, he assumed responsibility for the census returns in the Third Judicial District. But Read, formerly a missionary in New Mexico, had more than census taking on his mind: "At Lynx Creek he fell in with George Clinton and Juanita Bachichia and a wedding was the consequence. The miners were quickly summoned, and the affair was conducted in an off-hand and truly Western manner. George was in his shirt sleeves and Juanita in her morning gown." Territorial Secretary Richard McCormick witnessed the bilingual ceremony, and remarked to the groom afterward that he "had as soon expected an earthquake as a wedding in the gulch."[1]

No clues are left to explain how the newlyweds met; why they decided to live together and, later, to consent to Read's makeshift marriage ceremony; how they shared the responsibilities and rewards of the boardinghouse. We know, however, that Juanita Bachichia was on her own again by the end of the decade. Clinton was killed in the spring of 1869, and the *Arizona Miner* concluded his obituary with the simple statement, "He leaves a Mexican woman."[2]

During her young adulthood Juanita Bachichia left her imprint on the historical record only three times—in the newspaper account of her wedding, in the 1864 territorial census, and in her husband's obituary. This stark outline of her existence suggests something of the character of life for most of the women who first responded to central Arizona's mining boom in the mid-1860s. Indeed, the largest group of women whom census taker Read identified in the spring of 1864 (almost half of the total number) were those sharing households in the Walker-Weaver mining area with men to whom they were not married. This essay, using census records and the few available accounts of individual lives, focuses on that subgroup of central Arizona women: those who, particularly during the heyday of the initial gold rush, lived informally with male companions.

By far the greatest number of these women were young and of Mexican descent, though a handful of Anglo women also cohabited with men. The experience of cohabitation, however, varied with the ethnicities of a woman and her companion. While Mexican working-class culture maintained a system of informal union which paralleled that of formal marriage, the dominant Anglo-American culture perpetuated a double standard of sexual morality that discouraged sex outside of marriage for women, but not, or at least not to the same extent, for men. As a result of this cultural difference, together with negative Anglo attitudes toward Mexicans in general, and with the imposition of Anglo dominance throughout the Southwest,[3] most Anglos condemned Mexican women who lived with men, while ignoring or rationalizing the behavior of the few Anglo women who cohabited. Finally, the incidence of Mexican women's cohabitation declined after the first turbulent year or two of the mining boom. This decline suggests that its earlier occurrence was not a simple reconstruction of Mexican culture in the gold fields, but rather an adaptation of cultural patterns to new circumstances where such patterns proved particularly appropriate.

MEXICAN WOMEN AND INFORMAL UNION

Census records gathered just months after a series of placer strikes are a valuable and uncommon primary source. When census taker Read made his rounds in central Arizona in 1864, however, he identified only forty women living in the area. Meanwhile, literary sources indicate that the actual female population far exceeded the numbers reported in the census. When one miner arrived at Weaver in September of 1863, for example, he found a population of about twenty Anglos (one of them a woman) and more than three hundred Mexican inhabitants, including "scores of Mexican women."[4] Despite this discrepancy in the sources, there is no reason to believe that the lives and circumstances of the women enumerated in the census differed significantly from those not counted. Thus, the reported female population can be taken as representative of the entire female population.

Seventeen (55 percent) of the thirty-one Mexican women enumerated by Reverend Read in 1864 lived with male companions.[5] Several probably came to Arizona from earlier territorial gold camps like La Paz and Pinos Altos, while others emigrated from various locations in New Mexico, southern Arizona, California, and the Mexican state of Sonora. Neither the census nor literary sources, however, reveal whether the women had accompanied their male companions to the diggings or became acquainted with them after arrival. Indeed, in many cases it is difficult to determine which woman lived with which man, as the 1864 census did not list residents by household. But Read saw fit to identify the occupation of almost all of the unmarried, Spanish-surnamed women as "mistress." Read's use of the term "mistress" may reflect his misconceptions of Mexican women's relational styles. First, if it is regarded as a sexual, and not an economic, term, then it reduces the phenomenon of informal union to its erotic component and, by selectively casting aspersions on the moral character of only the female partner, it lays full responsibility for cohabitation at the feet of the Mexican woman.[6] Second, the term suggests Read's ignorance of class differences in Mexican intimate relationships; while the Mexican middle and upper classes maintained a sexual double standard that permitted men to "take mistresses" (not unlike the one that characterized Anglo society), Mexican working-class culture tended to uphold, practically if not ideologically, a single standard in which the concept of a "mistress" had less prominence.[7]

The best documented of these informal heterosexual unions are those that existed between Mexican women and Anglo men. Juanita Bachichia's relationship with George Clinton is one case in point. The newspaper report of their marriage in April sheds no light on what Bachichia may have expected of the cohabitation. But her new husband seems to have been as much taken aback by the wedding as were the onlookers; the *Miner* insists that "he knew nothing of it himself two hours before." Invoking thinly veiled ethnocentrism, the editors then quip, "Despite his haste George has obeyed the Spanish maxim: 'Before you marry be sure of a house wherein you tarry.'"[8] The relationship between Pancha Acuña and Calvin Jackson is another documented case. Acuña was twenty-five when she came to central Arizona, though she had lived elsewhere in the territory for three years. She is listed along with her one-year-old daughter Faustina, in the 1864 census. Read recorded the young mother's occupation as "mistress."[9] By 1866 a county census taker in Prescott took down the name "Pancha Jackson," though it is unlikely that she and Calvin Jackson ever actually wed; neither the *Miner* nor the county legal records note any such marriage.[10] In fact, when Calvin Jackson died in the late

1870s, Pancha's name failed to appear in his obituary. The newspaper reports state only that Jackson had lost a wife in California in 1859 and that Faustina, his sixteen-year-old daughter, had "been his constant companion and nurse during his sickness."[11]

What became of Pancha Acuña is unclear. What *is* clear in this absence of records is the prevalent Anglo attitude toward informal unions between Mexican women and Anglo men. When an Anglo husband died and left an Anglo wife, obituaries never specified the woman's ethnicity, almost always gave her name, and generally ended with a laudatory statement about her actions or her character.[12] But Clinton's obituary, even though he eventually married Bachichia, concluded with the begrudging comment, "He leaves a Mexican woman." Pancha Acuña, perhaps because she did not marry her companion, fared even worse. When Jackson died, only the daughter of their union and a wife long since deceased were publicly recognized.

It did not take an event as solemn as a man's death to expose Anglo disdain for Mexican women and Anglo men who lived together. An Anglo woman vividly recalled a dinner she prepared for a dance sponsored by the Masons in Prescott in 1866. "One man living with a Mexican woman," she wrote, "was not invited to the dance. He supposed we had the inviting to do and he was very angry"—so angry, in fact, that he threatened to kill the Anglo woman's husband.[13] There is no record of the Mexican woman's response to the snub, but her companion, accustomed to the privilege inherent in being both Anglo and male, was outraged.[14]

While Mexican women's relationships with Anglo men are the most thoroughly documented in the literary sources (which were generated by Anglos), it was actually far more common for an unmarried Mexican woman who came to the gold fields to set up housekeeping with a Mexican man. But detailed accounts of these relationships are unavailable, due to both the paucity of Spanish-language source materials (there were, for example, no Spanish-language newspapers in the area) and the Anglo indifference to anything that occurred outside the boundaries of the Anglo community. Only the 1864 census reveals the preponderance of Mexican-Mexican informal unions. Although Reverend Read did not list residents by household, internal evidence in the census verifies that he did move from household to household, from neighborhood to neighborhood, and from camp to camp in an orderly fashion. Almost all of the Mexican women identified as "mistresses" in the census are listed within large blocks of Spanish-surnamed individuals, indicating that they lived with Mexican men in Mexican communities. Nineteen, or 61 percent, of the Mexican women enumerated lived with Mexican companions; this includes both the informal unions and five marriages.[15]

The recent focus on cross-cultural marriage in the Southwest,[16] then, may prove an inappropriate approach to the study of mining communities in their boom years. In central Arizona, at least, 55 percent of the Mexican women who followed the first prospectors cohabited informally with men; and 61 percent of those early female arrivals (including those few who were married) lived with Mexican men. If the more appropriate focus is on nonmarital relationships, particularly between Mexican women and Mexican men, it is important to investigate the meanings of such relationships to the participants. In the absence of self-reflective accounts by women who lived with men in the early years of central Arizona's gold excitement, secondary accounts detailing the significance of informal unions in Mexican culture are useful.

Scholars trace the Hispanic "folk custom" of informal union to its origins in European practices that were recognized by late Roman law; Spanish law on marriage essentially restated late Roman law.[17] In medieval Spain, the practice was called *barrangía*. Transported to Mexico with the sixteenth-century conquest, the Spanish custom rivaled the more official system of morality that required formal marriage. This was particularly true among those who could not afford the fees necessary to formalize a union and who, lacking wealth or access to public office, had little reason to concern themselves with issues of legitimacy and inheritance. Mexican Indians constituted an exception to this practice for a time; Christian missionary zeal and Spanish fiscal policy (the Spanish authorities exacted tribute from the Indians with the married couple as the fiscal unit) coalesced to encourage (that is, enforce) early marriage among the native peoples. But Mexican independence from Spain and, in particular, the reform movements of the 1850s and 1860s, led native Mexicans increasingly to adopt the practice of informal union that characterized the lower classes among Hispanicized Mexicans. These reforms, engendered in large part by conflict between church and state, included an 1859 law issued by Benito Juarez which declared marriage a civil contract that was valid only if made before and registered with civil authorities. The diminished influence of the church among Indians was accompanied by a sharp increase in the proportion of Indian births outside of civil marriage. Among Hispanicized Mexicans, the church-state conflict served to reinforce the already common practice of informal union. The legal reform, which occurred just four or five years before the central Arizona gold rush, seems neither to have reflected nor induced a change in Mexican couples' propensity to wed: women and men continued to live with one another, and those inclined to marry still tended to equate marriage with a religious, rather than a civil, ceremony.

These, then, were the antecedents of Mexican women's intimate relationships in the Arizona gold fields, where the absence of Catholic clergy must have augmented the trend. While this absence of clergy, and other factors, may have contributed to the substantial proportion of unmarried Mexican women cohabiting with men in the early years of the gold rush, it seems most reasonable—given the prevalence of informal union in Mexico, particularly among working-class and, later, native Mexicans—to view such unions not only as a response to specific mining frontier conditions, but also as a reconstruction of traditional Mexican culture in Arizona.

When a Mexican woman lived with a Mexican man in Arizona, it is likely that she and her partner came to the relationship with some like understandings of this tradition. But when a Mexican woman and an Anglo man shared a household, they may have approached the cohabitation with dissimilar notions about appropriate contexts for sexual intimacy and economic partnership. Unlike Mexicans, Anglo Americans did not maintain a system of informal union that paralleled the conditions of formal marriage. Anglos did maintain a sexual double standard that encouraged single women to be chaste and married women monogamous, while allowing men, married or single, considerably more latitude.[18] Anglos repeatedly ignored, discounted, and otherwise stigmatized relationships between unmarried Anglo men and Mexican women. In keeping with the prevalent double standard and the Anglo tendency to project unrestrained sexual expression upon those of other cultures and races, such censure fell disproportionately on Mexican women.

In Mexican-Anglo informal unions, then, intimacy occurred in the context of conflicting cultural conceptions of sexual morality. However, since all accounts of such unions originated with observers, rather than participants, one cannot determine the particular meanings that individual Mexican women and Anglo men attached to their relationships. One can only speculate that they brought their respective cultural beliefs to bear upon their actions. Thus, where both Mexican women and Anglo men must have seen potential for intimacy and economic partnership, the Anglo man may also have seen opportunity for sexual relations outside of marriage—opportunity less openly available in Anglo society, save with prostitutes. As for the Mexican woman, cohabitation with an Anglo man provided access to a standard of living otherwise closed to her; the 1864 and 1870 censuses reveal that Anglo household companions were far more apt than their Mexican counterparts to work in occupations of medium-to-high socioeconomic standing, and that male Anglo property values greatly exceeded those of Mexican men.[19] Still, a reductive analysis that imputes primarily sexual motivation to Anglo men and primarily economic motivation to Mexican women is inadequate. Anglo men must have benefited from the domestic labor performed by their companions, and there is no reason to believe that Mexican women did not also obtain erotic satisfaction in these informal unions. Certainly, both partners gained companionship in an otherwise unfamiliar, harsh, and chaotic environment.

ANGLO WOMEN AND INFORMAL UNION

Only a few Anglo-American women cohabited with men during the central Arizona boom; the households they maintained serve to delineate for us the boundaries of acceptable female behavior in the mining area.

One Anglo woman who seems to have moved with relative ease across those behavioral boundaries has captured the imagination of several writers concerned with the central Arizona gold rush; she was known variously as Mary DeCrow, Mary Brown, Mary Ramos, and Virgin Mary. She may have come to Arizona with a black Texan whom Anglos called "Negro Brown."[20] One source indicated that while a slave in Texas, Brown killed his master and fled to Arizona with the master's widow—and Mary DeCrow may well have been that widow.[21] But the partnership ended soon after Brown and DeCrow arrived in central Arizona in 1864. That year census taker Read identified seventeen-year-old Santa Lopez as the "mistress of Negro Brown" and found Mary "Brown" at Weaver with Cornelius Ramos, a twenty-nine-year-old, Mexican-born blacksmith.[22] At Weaver, DeCrow ran a tiny restaurant. By 1865, she and Ramos married, and she then kept a boardinghouse in Prescott before moving to Lynx Creek, where together she and her husband managed their goat ranch and looked after their placer claims.[23] One might expect, then, that if DeCrow would be remembered at all she would be remembered primarily as a woman of the dominant Anglo culture who flouted social boundaries, not only by entering into intimate relationships with men outside of marriage, but by establishing those relationships with men of color.

On the contrary, however, history and local lore have whitewashed the memory of Mary DeCrow to such a degree that it bears little resemblance to reality. Secondary accounts focus, first, on the origin of the name "Virgin Mary" and, second, on the competition between DeCrow's Prescott boardinghouse and that of another early entrepreneur. Storytellers generally agree that DeCrow's nickname came as a consequence of her kindness and generosity. Their explanations range from the simple "She received her nickname because of her benevolence," to the florid "None knew her name and none cared to. She was christened 'Virgin Mary' and when she passed away it was 'Virgin Mary has gone.' Her life was a beautiful exemplification of the Bible, . . . devoted to the wounded and distressed, and her purse and every farthing she could procure went in the same way."[24] Stories about the competing Prescott boardinghouse vary. All hold that Virgin Mary's establishment held the advantage of providing goat's milk for the miners' coffee. The proprietor of the other boardinghouse, however, is identified sometimes as a man named Jackson and sometimes as Negro Brown himself. One account maintains that Virgin Mary's competitor (in this case, Jackson) offered only stewed prunes to offset the coveted goat's milk,[25] while two other accounts focus on a female relative in the employ of the competitor. It was Brown's "buxom sixteen-year-old daughter" that lured miners away from Virgin Mary's establishment, according to a second chronicler.[26] A third explains how Jackson's boardinghouse, which featured chili at every meal, drew customers: "Jackson's step-daughter," the storyteller suggests, "was not so completely chilly as the menu."[27]

These local legends are curious for two reasons. First, they ignore Mary DeCrow's relational history, which more clearly sets her apart from the vast majority of central Arizona Anglo women than any other aspect of her life; that is, while it was not uncommon for Anglo women to gain reputations for generosity or to run boardinghouses, it was extremely unusual for them to enter into intimate unions with black or Mexican men. Second, the accounts oppose an image of womanhood that is white, Christian, and asexual to one that is primarily sexual. Thus, although the name

"Virgin Mary" could be seen as an ironic suggestion of actual misconduct (according to Anglo standards), the storytellers dissociate DeCrow from the erotic and identify her instead with a Christian image of the benevolent Virgin. In the origin-of-the-name stories, the sexual conception of womanhood is suggested mainly by its conspicuous absence and by the storytellers' obvious rhetorical attempts to steer readers away from such a conception. In the stories of the competing boardinghouses, furthermore, the opposing image of sexualized womanhood actually is embodied in the daughter (or stepdaughter) of the other proprietor. Given the Anglo propensity to associate unbounded passion with people of other cultures, and particularly with people of color, it is not surprising that in at least one version the erotic counterimage is a young black woman.

Virgin Mary shares the spotlight in central Arizona's local lore with another female figure whose cohabitation is documented in primary source materials. Mary Sawyer, otherwise known as Mollie Monroe, seems to have arrived in the area during the late 1860s, when she was scarcely twenty years old. She may have married one or more times as a young woman,[28] but the historical record links her most closely with an Anglo prospector named George Monroe. While Monroe and Sawyer probably never wed, in 1870 the census taker found them living together in Wickenburg.[29] Whatever the nature of their relationship, it is clear that Sawyer did not confine herself to a traditional wifely role. Early in the spring of 1872, for example, a newspaper correspondent from Wickenburg sent the following report to the *Miner* in Prescott: "The 'boys' were out last week prospecting. George Monroe, Joe Fuggit, Wm. Gellaspie, Tom Graves and Molly struck a galena lode, and styled it the 'Knock Down.'"[30]

Her name does not appear again in the historical record until 1877. On May 9 of that year the Yavapai County probate judge declared Sawyer insane and ordered her temporarily confined in the county jail. Arizona Territory did not yet have its own insane asylum, so the county board of supervisors decided to send her to the asylum in Stockton, California. Eventually, she was transferred to the insane asylum that was built in Phoenix, and it was there that she died in 1902.[31]

What remains unexplored in all accounts of Mary Sawyer's life is the nature of her "insanity"; not even the county probate records reveal anything about the behavior that led an acquaintance in 1877 to bring her into Prescott from a neighboring community, charging her with lunacy. Once she had been declared insane and sent off to Stockton, Mollie Monroe acquired notoriety in central Arizona. Local newspapers, which only casually noted her activities before 1877, began both to follow her condition closely and to recall in greater detail her early years in Arizona. Just months after her departure for California, the *Miner* reported that Sawyer had been transferred from Stockton to San Quentin Prison because she had become violent and "intent on burning the Asylum."[32] But within a year a California correspondent for the Yuma newspaper found her back at the asylum, "greatly improved mentally": she showed interest in old friends and in Arizona politics, and she stated firmly "that she had no longer any desire to drink."[33] In 1880, however, another correspondent held that Sawyer was "entirely devoid of any higher aspirations than to go back and resume the wild and dissolute life she led in the mountains of Arizona." She told her Arizona visitor that, although the doctors would tell him she was "crazier than ever," it was actually "only meanness in her. She said that she was the meanest thing on earth, and intended to be so until she was turned out and allowed to do as she pleased."[34]

Eventually Sawyer tired of waiting to be "turned out." By the late 1880s she had been transferred back to Phoenix, and in 1895, after almost twenty years of asylum life, she bolted the institution and set out across the desert on foot. For several days area newspapers reported on the sheriff's attempts to trail her through the hot sand and mountain rocks, reminding readers of her younger days in central Arizona when she "would invariably dress in male attire"[35] and "could ride anything with four feet, chew more tobacco and swear harder than any man" in the territory.[36] But it was not long before Indian men from the Maricopa-Pima reservation on the Gila River overtook her and turned her over to the sheriff, who in turn took her back to the asylum. A Phoenix newspaper reported that Sawyer was quite pleased with her adventure—that she "described it with eloquence and profanity," stating, "'If I'd a' only had my breeches and my gun I'd a' been all right.'"[37]

By the time of Sawyer's death in 1902, Arizonans already had adopted a formulaic story that explained her behavior. Mollie Monroe, they claimed, was a New Englander who became engaged to a prosperous young man in the 1860s. Parental disapproval prevented the marriage, and the young man departed for the far West with plans for Mollie to follow soon thereafter. Follow she did, the story goes, but always clad in male apparel to elude pursuers. Yet when Mollie reached her destination, she found that her fiancé had been murdered. She searched in vain for the killer throughout the Southwest until finally, her hope for vengeance thwarted, she remained in central Arizona, becoming "addicted to liquor and finally to morals that are dissolute." Those who recounted Mollie Monroe's life story, however, also maintained that she invariably "assisted the needy," that "she was, with all of these faults, a noble and charitable woman."[38]

Questions about Sawyer's insanity, then, reflect a twentieth-century—and, in this case, feminist—concern with the nature and etiology of madness. The nineteenth-century Arizonan who followed Sawyer's story over the years and read the early reports of her activities did not ask, "What in this behavior makes officials conclude that Mollie Monroe is crazy?" but rather asked, "What drove Mollie Monroe crazy?" At least it is this second question that is answered in accounts of her life popular at the turn of the century. Sawyer's life during the boom years did indeed include participation in various mining ventures, dressing in male attire, heavy drinking (perhaps alcoholism), and informal unions with men. On the basis of this set of facts and perhaps others not disclosed in the primary sources, her contemporaries assumed her insanity and sought to explain its origins. And what better explanation for a woman's appropriation of the trappings of male privilege—masculine clothing, multiple sexual partners, men's work—than disappointment in heterosexual romance? This explanation also accounted for Sawyer's oft-mentioned generosity: she was, by Anglo sexual standards, a "good" woman who, through no fault of her own, had bad luck in romance. That failure, according to the story, quite literally drove her insane.

Mary Sawyer and Mary DeCrow are the only women from central Arizona's gold and silver boom years whose life stories have become local legends. They are also the only Anglo women whose nonmarital relationships with men can be thoroughly documented. These facts are not unrelated. The dominant Anglo culture was unlikely to move beyond its ethnic boundaries in recognizing and cultivating legendary figures—that is, Sawyer and DeCrow were much more likely candidates than Juanita Bachichia and Pancha Acuña. But what explains local lore's inclusion of two female figures—ethnicity aside—in the first place? The answer lies in the ways in which Sawyer and DeCrow defied the dominant culture's prescriptions of behavior for women.

DeCrow challenged Anglo notions of womanhood solely in her intimate relationships. She lived with two men to whom she was not married, one a black Texan and the other a Mexican immigrant. But, once the initial tumult of the gold rush subsided, she only partially persisted in her challenge; although throughout her years in Arizona she was involved with men of color, by 1865 she and Cornelius Ramos had wed. Still, the stories about Mary DeCrow represent Anglo attempts to take up the problem presented by her intimate life. Perhaps because of her apparent, if incomplete, bow to convention (her eventual marriage), and because of needed services she provided in the community as one of the first boardinghouse keepers, Anglo legend dealt with DeCrow's relationships by forgetting them and, what is more, by supplanting them with exaggerated accounts of her benevolence.

Mary Sawyer's "transgressions" were not so easily forgotten. In almost every aspect of her life she was the antithesis of Anglo womanhood—in her work, in her dress and other personal habits, in her relationships. True, her intimate attachments appear to have been heterosexual, and all of the men she chose may well have been Anglos. But her compliance with societal expectations stopped there. Furthermore, Sawyer never gave up her whiskey, her prospecting, or her men's apparel. Nor did she consent to a lasting marriage, not even when the boom years in central Arizona gave way to less turbulent times. The Anglo community, then, needed not only to control Sawyer's actions but also to explain them, and a charge of insanity served both purposes. In a single stroke the charge enabled officials, first, to restrain her and remove her from the area and, second, to account for her most unladylike conduct. As the years passed, storytellers delved deeper into their own powers of explanation and found as well a *cause* for Sawyer's lunacy. Thus, where the early story claimed simply that "she lived a man's life because she was crazy," later developments took the argument a step further: "she was crazy because she lost a male lover."

Mary Sawyer and Mary DeCrow, then, diverged in their attempts to resist their culture's behavioral prescriptions for women. DeCrow defied convention by acting more like the Mexican women in the community than like her Anglo neighbors. In contrast, Sawyer behaved primarily like an Anglo man. Both must have provoked incredulity in their contemporaries. But DeCrow was emulating individuals who were, structurally, members of the least powerful group in Arizona mining town society, and the dominant culture could afford to deal with her behavior by ignoring it. Sawyer, on the other hand, aspired to a higher position in that power structure. For that offense alone she could have received her just deserts—a lifetime in an asylum and a local legend that continues to discount her actions as those of a mad woman—though the historical record does not reveal the precise reasons for her asylum commitment. The lives of DeCrow and Sawyer indicate the struggle women faced in challenging the dominant culture's notion of Anglo womanhood. The legends of Virgin Mary and Mollie Monroe poignantly reveal the nature and extent of the ideological obstacles they encountered in that struggle.

CONCLUSIONS

Mary DeCrow's marriage to Cornelius Ramos in 1865, after a year or so of cohabitation, coincided with, and perhaps can be explained by, the start of a major shift in the ways central Arizona mining-town women conducted their intimate relationships and organized their households. That same shift helps to account for Sawyer's expulsion from the community in the 1870s. In 1864, just a year after the initial gold strikes, 45 percent of the forty women enumerated by the census taker lived with men, while another 18 percent lived without male companionship. Only 37 percent were married and living with their husbands.[39] By 1870 the female population had more than quadrupled to 170 women, and the percentage cohabiting with men had dropped to 4 percent. A full 43 percent were not economically bound to a husband or male lover. But in 1870 the majority, 53 percent, were married women who dwelled with their husbands. Among Mexican women the percentages differed: half were not living with husbands or male companions, while 42 percent were married and 8 percent still cohabited with men.[40] This shift did not reflect a wholesale movement toward marriage among those who formerly had cohabited with their companions, notwithstanding the case of Mary DeCrow. It reflected the exodus of early immigrants to the gold fields and the constant influx of new settlers.[41] The later immigrants created a new ethnic balance in central Arizona as well; the Mexican female population doubled between 1864 and 1870, while twelves times as many Anglo women appeared on the census rolls as were counted just six years earlier. By 1870, then, not only did the female population comprise a virtually new set of individuals; it was also now predominantly Anglo rather than predominantly Mexican.

What do these facts indicate about the women who lived with men in central Arizona between 1863 and 1873? First, the nature, meaning, and consequences of cohabitation differed according to a woman's ethnicity and that of her companion. For Mexican women, informal union existed as a cultural category in a way that it did not for Anglo women. Despite changes over time, then, Mexican women were always more apt than Anglos to set up households with men. When a Mexican woman moved in with a Mexican man, she could expect, first, to share with him a similar understanding of their partnership and, second, to move through her own ethnic community relatively free from public censure. When she lived with an Anglo man, however, in addition to intimacy and economic security, she may have encountered miscommunications (with her companion), hostility (from her Anglo neighbors), and resultant isolation, at least to the extent that her companion and neighbors perpetuated the dominant culture's racism and double standard of sexual morality. The tiny handful of Anglo women who cohabited with men flew in the face of that same double standard. Because there were so few such women and because their numbers did not change significantly over time, their relationships represent anomalous cases that probe the boundaries of Anglo prescriptions for female behavior.

Second, the decrease in the percentage of Mexican women who lived with men (from 55 percent in 1864 to 8 percent in 1870) indicates that the phenomenon of informal union was more than a simple reconstruction of traditional Mexican culture in central Arizona. By comparison, in Los Angeles between 1850 and 1880, the proportion of unmarried couples, taken as a percentage of all couples who lived together, held quite constant between 7 and 8 percent.[42] (If the central Arizona data are considered in this manner, one finds that in 1864, 65 percent of all unions involving a Mexican woman were informal, whereas in 1870, only 16 percent of them were.) The comparative data suggest that these nonmarital relationships, while grounded in Mexican cultural patterns, were especially well suited to the vagaries of mining-town life, particularly in the tumultuous months of the initial boom. The subsequent decline in the proportion of women who lived with men, and the accompanying increase in the proportion who married or lived without male companionship, came as a consequence of stabilizing conditions in the mining area and perhaps also as a response to the consolidation of Anglo dominance in the area. But the gold-rush phenomenon of widespread informal union among Mexican women represents their creative adaptation of a cultural tradition to circumstances where intimacy, economic security, and an ease of coming together were at a premium.

Notes

I would like to thank Estelle Freedman, David Gutierrez, Elizabeth Jameson, Mary Rothschild, and members of the women's history dissertation reading group at Stanford University—Sue Cobble, Gary Sue Goodman, Yukiko Hanawa, Sue Lynn, Valerie Matsumoto, Peggy Pascoe, and Linda Schott—for helpful comments on earlier versions of this paper.

1. *Arizona Miner* (Fort Whipple), 9 Apr. 1864. See also *Arizona Miner*, 20 Apr., 11 May, 6 July, 7 Sept. 1864; and *1864 Census of the Arizona Territory* (Territorial Copy), Department of Library and Archives, Arizona State Capitol, Phoenix (hereafter cited as *1864 Census*).

2. *Weekly Arizona Miner* (Prescott), 13 Mar. 1869.

3. On Anglo racism and the imposition of Anglo dominance in the Southwest, see David J. Weber, "'Scarce More Than Apes': Historical Roots of Anglo American Stereotypes of Mexicans in the Border Regions," in David J. Weber, ed., *New Spain's Far Northern Frontier* (Albuquerque: University of New Mexico Press, 1979); S. Dale McLemore, "The Origins of Mexican American Subordination in Texas," *Social Science Quarterly* 53, no. 4 (1973): 656–70; Mario Barrera, *Race and Class in the Southwest: A Theory of Racial Inequality* (Notre Dame, Ind.: University of Notre Dame Press, 1979), esp. pp. 7–57; Rudolfo Acuña, "Sonora Invaded: The Occupation of Arizona," in *Occupied America: A History of Chicanos*, 2d ed. (New York: Harper & Row, 1981), esp. pp. 73–94; Richard Griswold del Castillo, *The Los Angeles Barrio, 1850–1890: A Social History* (Berkeley: University of California Press, 1979), esp. pp. 30–61; Albert Camarillo, *Chicanos in a Changing Society: From Mexican Pueblos to American Barrios in Santa Barbara and Southern California, 1848–1930* (Cambridge, Mass.: Harvard University Press, 1979), esp. pp. 33–78. On the exclusion of Mexican workers from California mining towns, see Leonard Pitt, "'Greasers' in the Diggings: Californians and Sonorans under Attack," in *The Decline of the Californios: A Social History of the Spanish-Speaking Californians, 1846–1890* (Berkeley: University of California Press, 1966), pp. 48–68. On discriminatory laws against Mexican miners in central Arizona, see Robert L. Spude, "The Walker-Weaver Diggings and the Mexican Placero, 1863–1864," *Journal of the West* 14 (October, 1975): 64–74.

4. Hayden Biographical Files ("Henry Augustus Bigelow"), Arizona Collection, Hayden Library, Arizona State University, Tempe (hereafter cited as Arizona Collection, Tempe).

5. *1864 Census*.

6. For a more thorough analysis of Anglo racist and sexist conceptions of Mexican women, see Beverly Trulio, "Anglo-American Attitudes Toward New Mexican Women," *Journal of the West* 12 (1973): 229–39.

7. See Woodrow Borah and Sherburne F. Cook, "Marriage and Legitimacy in Mexican Culture: Mexico and California," *California Law Review* 54 (May, 1966): 946–1008, esp. pp. 960–61; Ramon Arturo Gutierrez, "Marriage, Sex and the Family: Social Change in Colonial New Mexico, 1690–1846" (Ph.D. diss., University of Wisconsin—Madison, 1980), pp. 115–40.

8. *Arizona Miner* (Fort Whipple), 9 Apr. 1864.

9. *1864 Census*.

10. *Census of the Inhabitants of Yavapai County, Arizona* (April, 1866), Arizona Collection, Tempe (hereafter cited as *1866 County Census*).

11. Unidentified clipping (ca. 1879), Obituary Books, vol. 3, Sharlot Hall Museum Library and Archives, Prescott, Ariz. (hereafter cited as Sharlot Hall Museum, Prescott).

12. See, e.g., the obituary for Dr. Charles Leib, *Arizona Miner* (Prescott), 15 Feb. 1865.

13. Lois A. [Whitcomb] Boblett Reminiscences, Sharlot Hall Museum, Prescott, p. 25.

14. That there is no record of the woman's response does not necessarily indicate that she had none. If she did not respond, perhaps her experience with Anglo dominance, which included the imposition of Anglo social and sexual ideals, had taught her the futility of such violent reaction. At the same time, her connection with the Mexican community in Prescott may have minimized any importance she may have attached to the Anglo community's exclusive gatherings.

15. *1864 Census*.

16. See, e.g., Jane Dysart, "Mexican Women in San Antonio, 1830–1860: The Assimilation Process," *Western Historical Quarterly* 7, no. 4 (October, 1976): 365–75; Darlis A. Miller, "Cross-Cultural Marriages in the Southwest: The New Mexico Experience, 1846–1900," *New Mexico Historical Review* 57, no. 4 (October, 1982): 335–59.

17. Borah and Cook, "Marriage and Legitimacy"; see also Gutierrez, "Marriage, Sex and the Family." The summary of Spanish and Mexican informal union is based on these studies.

18. Borah and Cook note that a similar double standard operated among the middle and upper classes in Mexico at least through the nineteenth century; pp. 960–62; see also Gutierrez. For a review of the literature dealing with the American double standard, see Estelle B. Freedman, "Sexuality in Nineteenth-Century America: Behavior, Ideology and Politics," *Reviews in American History* 10, no. 4 (December, 1982): 196–216.

19. *1864 Census; 1870 Census Population Schedules of Arizona* (Washington, D.C.: National Archives Microfilm Publications, 1965); hereafter cited as *1870 Census*.

20. What other blacks called Brown is unknown. The name "Negro Brown" appears in sources generated by Anglos, as does the name "Nigger Brown." Unidentified newspaper clippings in Biographical File and in "Tales of Prescott" Notebook, and Sharlot Hall's notes in Biographical File, Sharlot Hall Museum, Prescott; Biographical File, Benjamin Sacks Collection, Arizona Historical Foundation, Hayden Library, Arizona State University, Tempe (hereafter cited as Arizona Historical Foundation, Tempe).

21. An unidentified clipping from the *Tucson Star* in Scrapbook No. 1, Sharlot Hall Museum, Prescott, states that Brown slew his master in Texas and that "throughout all his wanderings . . . he was accompanied by his slain master's wife, . . . who is said to be yet living in the northern part of the Territory." DeCrow was indeed known as Mary Brown at one time, and she did hail from Texas; this evidence suggests, but is not sufficient to prove, that she was the wife of Brown's deceased owner. The *1864 Census* lists "Mary Brown" as a forty-two-year-old laundress from Texas. Her obituary (Biographical File, Sharlot Hall Museum, Prescott) states that she was born in 1819 and that her parents belonged to the Austin Colony.

22. *1864 Census*. The relationship between Santa Lopez and Negro Brown is the only documented union of a Mexican woman and a black man during this period. Directly below Santa Lopez's name Read listed an infant named "Mariana Bran"—perhaps a misspelling or mistranscription of Mariana Brown.

23. Sharlot Hall's notes and unidentified newspaper clipping in Biographical File, Sharlot Hall Museum, Prescott; *1866 County Census*. The name "Ramos" also appears as "Ramez" and "Reamis" in various sources. The historical record reveals little else about Mary Ramos, save a newspaper report that Indians had attempted to ambush her on the road, and another item detailing the Ramoses' sale of their ranch and mining property and their subsequent move to a spot farther up Lynx Creek. See *Weekly Arizona Miner* (Prescott), 13 Mar. 1869 and 4 June 1870.

24. See "Tales of Prescott" clipping; Charles H. Dunning and Edward Peplow, *Rocks to Riches: The Story of American Mining . . . Past, Present and Future . . . As Reflected in the Colorful History of Mining in Arizona, the Nation's Greatest Bonanza* (Phoenix: Southwest Publishing Co., 1959), p. 69; Orick Jackson, *The White Conquest of Arizona: History of the Pioneers* (Los Angeles: West Coast Magazine, 1908), p. 32.

25. "Tales of Prescott" clipping.

26. Glenn Chesney Quiett, *Pay Dirt: A Panorama of American Gold-Rushes* (Lincoln, Nebr.: Johnsen Publishing Co., 1971), p. 400.

27. Dunning and Peplow, *Rocks to Riches*, p. 69.

28. E.g., the *Arizona Miner* (Prescott), 10 Aug. 1867, notes that "Joe and Molly went to La Paz, got married, and are back in Wickenburg enjoying the honeymoon."

29. *1870 Census*.

30. *Weekly Arizona Miner* (Prescott), 23 Mar. 1872. Besides her prospecting work Mary Sawyer was also involved in financial aspects of mining in central Arizona. In 1871, for example, she sold two hundred feet in the Tiger Lode to two Anglo businessmen (*Weekly Arizona Miner*, 24 June 1871).

31. *Territory of Arizona* v. *Mary E. Sawyer or Mollie Monroe*, Probate Records Book 1a, pp. 378–79, Yavapai County, Prescott, Ariz. (1877); *Weekly Arizona Miner* (Prescott), 11 May and 18 May 1877; *Prescott Courier*, 27 Nov. 1902.

32. *Weekly Arizona Miner* (Prescott), 16 Nov. 1877.

33. *Arizona Sentinel* (Yuma), 2 Nov. 1878.
34. *Weekly Arizona Miner* (Prescott), 30 Jan. 1880.
35. *Arizona Gazette* (Phoenix), 28 Apr. 1895.
36. *Arizona Daily Star* (Tucson), 28 Apr. 1895.
37. *Arizona Republican* (Phoenix), 30 Apr. 1895. See also *Arizona Gazette* (Phoenix), 30 Apr. 1895; and *Arizona Daily Star* (Tucson), 1 May 1895. On cross-dressing women in the West, see San Francisco Lesbian and Gay History Project, *"She Even Chewed Tobacco": Passing Women in Nineteenth-Century America* (Berkeley, Calif.: Iris Films, 1983), slide-tape.
38. *Arizona Journal-Miner* (Prescott), 30 Dec. 1897, 24 Nov. 1902. An early version of this story appeared in the *San Francisco Mail* in 1877, just after Sawyer had been transferred to San Quentin. The *Mail* account (apparently written by a former Arizonan who knew Sawyer) states that Sawyer was from California and that "unrequited love drove [her] from her home . . . to seek refuge in the wilds of Arizona. In company with a party of prospectors she started for the Territory on horseback, dressed in male attire, and [from then on she] led a gypsy life." No copies of the *San Francisco Mail* for this date are extant. See clipping in Scrapbook no. 1, and Sharlot Hall's notes from that article in Notebook no. 2, both at Sharlot Hall Museum, Prescott. Comparison of the 1877 story with the 1897 and 1902 versions reveals the elaborate "Mollie Monroe" legend that Arizonans constructed between the time of her asylum commitment and her death.
39. *1864 Census.*
40. *1870 Census.*
41. In 1870, only ten of the fifty women and girls who had immigrated to central Arizona by 1864 (or eight of the original forty adult women) remained.
42. Richard Griswold del Castillo, *The Los Angeles Barrio, 1860–1890: A Social History* (Berkeley: University of California Press, 1979), pp. 67–68. Griswold del Castillo studies informal unions "as a percentage of the married couples in Los Angeles," while I focus on the proportion of women involved in informal unions as a percentage of all adult women. Thus, our statistics cannot be compared directly.

"Hardly a Farm House--A Kitchen without Them": Indian and White Households on the California Borderland Frontier in 1860

ALBERT L. HURTADO

In 1851 Major John Bidwell, a prominent Butte County farmer, commented on Indian affairs in gold rush California. In comparison with conditions in eastern states, he emphasized, California's settlers had not only to contend with Indians on the frontier, but they were "all *among* us, *around* us, *with* us—hardly a farm house—a kitchen without them." According to Bidwell, when a farmer needed laborers he told the Indians to "go into his fields," and in return he fed and clothed them. He thought the Indian farm workers looked up to an employer with "a kind of filial obedience to his commands" and expected from him "a kind of parental protection." The earnest farmer contrasted his description of agrarian paternalism with the activities of "malicious and brutal vagabonds" who roamed the country murdering Indians. Such depredations caused native people to retaliate in kind, "thereby exposing the industrious and well disposed miner to dangers and death." In these desperate times, Bidwell believed, Indians were "sure to cling around and shelter themselves under the protection of him who trats them best."[1]

Bidwell's remarks evoke a strikingly different picture of Indian and white relations than the one conveyed by the usual Anglo-American frontier stereotypes. Instead of resisting the whites, restricting settlement, and impeding development, California's Indians worked obediently in the whites' fields and houses in return for food and shelter. The relationship that Bid-

Albert L. Hurtado is an instructor of history and social science at Sierra College and is a consulting historian for Public History Services Associates, Sacramento, California. An earlier version of this paper was read at the annual meeting of the American Society for Ethnohistory in October 1980.

[1] John Bidwell to J. W. McCorkle, December 20, 1851, enclosed in McCorkle to Luke Lea, February 6, 1852, Office of Indian Affairs, Letters Received, 1824–1881, California Superintendency, RG 75, National Archives (Microfilm Publication M234, roll 32:761–67). For John Bidwell's life see Rockwell D. Hunt, *John Bidwell: Prince of California Pioneers* (Caldwell, Idaho, 1942).

well described was in part the product of nearly a century of Hispanic colonization, with traditions of Indian and white relations far different from Anglo-American practices. Herbert E. Bolton compared these different customs and noted that in Anglo-America "the only good Indians were dead Indians," while in Hispanic America Indians were assimilated and exploited.[2] Moreover, Bolton believed that California and other parts of the Spanish Borderlands were "the meeting place and fusing place of two streams of European civilization," each with substantially different histories with regard to the Indian.[3]

The fusing of Anglo and Hispanic traditions was not a smooth process in gold rush California, especially for Indians. Some Anglos adopted Hispanic labor practices as a convenient expedient, while others sought to drive Native Americans out of the work force where Indians could expect to find little protection. The federal government established a stopgap, temporary reservation system that ministered to only a fraction of the Indian population.[4] Ineffectual federal administration enabled the state government to take a powerful role in Indian affairs. Although the state constitution outlawed slavery, the legislature passed chapter 133, "an act for the government and protection of the Indians," that provided for the indenture of loitering and orphaned Indians, regulated their employment, and defined a special class of crimes and punishment for them.[5] Some students of California history have referred to this law as a form of legalized slavery. Certainly it resembled the "black codes" adopted by

[2] "The Mission as a Frontier Institution in the Spanish American Colonies," John Francis Bannon, ed., *Bolton and the Spanish Borderlands* (Norman, 1964), 190–91, 211.

[3] "Defensive Spanish Expansion and the Significance of the Borderlands," Bannon, ed., *Bolton and the Borderlands*, 59.

[4] James J. Rawls, "Gold Diggers: Indian Miners in the California Gold Rush," *California Historical Quarterly*, LV (Spring 1976), 28–45; wages for Indians are discussed in Stephen Powers, *Tribes of California* (Berkeley, 1976), 401–2; for federal policy see William H. Ellison, "The Federal Indian Policy in California, 1846–1860," *Mississippi Valley Historical Review*, IX (June 1922), 37–67; Alban W. Hoopes, *Indian Affairs and Their Administration with Special Reference to the Far West, 1849–1860* (Philadelphia, 1932), 35–68; Harry Kelsey, "The California Indian Treaty Myth," *Southern California Quarterly*, LV (Fall 1973), 225–38; Michael A. Sievers, "Malfeasance or Indirection? Administration of the California Indian Superintendency's Business Affairs," *Southern California Quarterly*, LVI (Fall 1974), 273–94; Albert L. Hurtado, "Controlling California's Indian Labor Force: Federal Administration of California Indian Affairs during the Mexican War," *Southern California Quarterly*, LXI (Fall 1979), 217–38; and Albert L. Hurtado, "Ranchos, Gold Mines and Rancherías: A Socioeconomic History of Indians and Whites in Northern California, 1821–1860" (doctoral dissertation, University of California, Santa Barbara, 1981), 225–69.

[5] *Statutes of California.*

slave states as a means to control free blacks and bondsmen alike.[6] Simultaneously, the state government subsidized scores of military campaigns aimed at Indian communities considered threatening to white settlement. In fact, these expeditions often killed Indians indiscriminately.[7]

To describe this situation as chaotic hardly does it justice. The gold rush proved to be a catastrophe for the Indians. By 1860 the native population had fallen from perhaps 150,000 to about 32,000. According to Sherburne F. Cook, the preeminent demographer of California Indians, native numbers continued to fall until about 1900, when they reached a population nadir of between 20,000 and 25,000.[8] Cook postulated that Indian demographic decline was due to starvation, homicide, and a "palpable fall in the birth rate concerning which we have little factual knowledge."[9]

Cook's lack of knowledge about the declining birthrate is not surprising. Like other poor working people, the California Indians left no well-documented record of their daily lives. But using techniques derived from social history and demography, it is possible to find evidence that gives a fuller understanding of the gold rush's effect upon native survival. This evidence shows how Indians were useful to white society in the 1850s and provides insights into the ways that Anglo and Hispanic traditions merged on the Spanish Borderland frontier. At the same time, it furnishes a fresh perspective for Native American history, for the California experience is a case study of the process of Indian integration with white society in the mid-nineteenth century. Amidst the turbulent disorders of a unique age, native Californians became the mudsills of Victorian society in the American West.

The 1860 federal census offers a starting point for this reexamination, since it contains a wealth of information on Indian people at the household level. The Constitution and the census law of 1850 empowered United States marshals to enumerate the population in 1860. Under this

6 Owen Coy, "Evidences of Slavery in California," *Grizzly Bear*, 19 (No. 6, 1916), 1–2; and Robert F. Heizer and Alan J. Almquist, *The Other Californians: Prejudice and Discrimination under Spain, Mexico, and the United States to 1920* (Berkeley, 1971), 39–58. On "black codes" see Peter H. Wood, *Black Majority: Negroes in Colonial South Carolina from 1670 through the Stono Rebellion* (New York, 1975), 271–84; and Eugene D. Genovese, *Roll Jordan, Roll: The World the Slaves Made* (New York, 1974), 25–49.

7 For documentary examples see Robert F. Heizer, ed., *Destruction of the California Indians* (Santa Barbara, California, 1974), 243–65.

8 Sherburne F Cook, *The Population of the California Indians, 1769–1970* (Berkeley, 1976), 44–73.

9 Sherburne F. Cook, "The Destruction of the California Indians," *California Monthly* (December 1968), 14–19.

authorization federal officers enumerated Indians to determine political apportionment and taxation. The census takers received two cents for each person they counted, thus giving them an incentive to do a thorough job.[10]

In 1860 the census takers enumerated 17,798 Indians in California, by far the highest state Indian population.[11] Excluded were reservation Indians, those in flight or rebellion, and those "retaining their tribal character," who were estimated to number 13,540.[12] The manuscript census includes such demographic data as name, age, sex, and usually occupation for nearly 18,000 Indians. Often marital status is indicated or can be inferred from circumstantial evidence. In addition, all this data was organized on the basis of each dwelling visited by the census officer, thus making possible an analysis of the household.[13] Moreover, since the enumerated Indians frequently lived in close association with whites, the

[10] George Minot, ed., *The Statutes at Large and Treaties of the United States of America from December 1, 1845 to March 3, 1851* (Boston, 1862), IX, 428–36.

[11] Table VI, "Chinese, Japanese, and Civilized Indian Population at Each Census," *A Compendium of the Ninth Census (June 1, 1870)* (Washington, D.C., 1872), 18.

[12] Table I, "Population by Age and Sex," *Population of the United States in 1860, Compiled from the Original Returns of the Eighth Census* (Washington, D.C., 1864), 22–27, 605 (hereafter cited as *1860 Census*). Sherburne F. Cook found the *1860 Census* a "very poor enumeration" that could be "discarded completely" for his purposes of establishing the total number of Indians in the state. Cook, *Population of the California Indians,* 53. Apparently he did not examine the census carefully. Cook erroneously criticized C. Hart Merriam, "The Indian Population of California," *American Anthropologist,* n.s. 7 (No. 4, 1905), 594–606, because Merriam correctly stated that the 1860 census indicated there were 31,338 Indians in the state. Cook failed to find that the census takers estimated there were 13,540 Indians not enumerated in the *1860 Census,* 605. Cook did not examine the manuscript census returns. Another critic of the *1860 Census,* Francis A. Walker, superintendent of the 1870 census, incorrectly stated that most of the 17,798 California Indians enumerated in 1860 were on reservations and should not have been included in the computation of the representative population. *Compendium of the Ninth Census,* 19. Actually, there were no reservations in many counties that reported substantial Indian populations. In 1859 Indian agents estimated that there were 10,500 Indians on reserves, but the estimates far exceeded the 1860 census totals for the counties in which the reservations were located. In 1861 the Indian department reported there were 6,397 Indians on the reservations, but even this figure was criticized as an inflated number. See "Annual Report, Commissioner of Indian Affairs, 1859," *Report of the Secretary of the Interior [1859]* (Washington, D.C., 1859), 805–8; and "Annual Report, Commissioner of Indian Affairs, 1861," *Report of the Secretary of the Interior [1861]* (Washington, D.C., 1861), 757, 828–29.

[13] Much of the information about Indians in households is inferred from the order in which the census takers listed the inhabitants. The household head was named first, followed by his spouse and children, if any. Other residents were listed after the family unit. For an example of how such inferences can be used see Barbara Laslett, "Household Structure on an American Frontier: Los Angeles, California, in 1850," *American Journal of Sociology,* 81 (July 1975), 109–28.

manuscript census provides a close-up view of their relations with one another.

The census indicated several general demographic characteristics of the California population that must be taken into account in any study of Indian people in 1860. The state contained 379,994 persons, 70 percent of whom were males and 60 percent of whom were white males. Overall, the population was young—nearly 60 percent were under thirty. Of the four racial categories identified in the census—white, colored, Indian, and Asian—all showed exceedingly low female-to-male ratios.[14] Such ratios usually mean that a population will not be able to reproduce itself unless new females of child-bearing age can be acquired elsewhere by migration or by intermarriage with other groups.

Like the white population, the enumerated Indians were mostly young males (see Table 1). Theoretically, this Indian population was the soundest reproductive group because it had the highest female-to-male ratio. Statistically, however, Indian women bore fewer live children and raised fewer of them to maturity than their white counterparts.[15] The published census reveals that the Indian population was not distributed uniformly throughout the state. Fresno County had the highest reported population with 3,294, while Sierra and Yolo counties reported no Indian residents. Likewise, sex and age ratios varied from county to county. The differing regional population patterns displayed in Table 1 assume a larger significance when viewed through the microscope of household analysis.

For comparative purposes this study subdivides California into five areas with differing settlement histories: the Southern, Central Coast, Sacramento Valley, San Joaquin Valley, and Northern regions.[16] To analyze Indian households I reviewed the unpublished manuscript cen-

[14] The female-to-male ratios were: for whites, .42; colored, .44; Asian, .05; and Indians, .68. *1860 Census*, 28. See also Michael S. Teitelbaum, "Factors Associated with the Sex Ratio in Human Populations," G. A. Harrison and A. J. Boyce, ed., *The Structure of Human Populations* (Oxford, England, 1972), 90–109; Jack E. Eblen, "An Analysis of Nineteenth-Century Frontier Populations," *Demography*, 2 (No. 2, 1965), 399–413.

[15] *1860 Census*, 22–28.

[16] The Southern region includes Los Angeles, Santa Barbara, San Bernardino, and San Diego counties. The Central Coast region includes Alameda, Contra Costa, Marin, Mendocino, Monterey, Napa, Santa Clara, Santa Cruz, San Francisco, San Mateo, and Sonoma counties. The Sacramento Valley region includes Butte, Colusa, El Dorado, Nevada, Placer, Plumas, Sacramento, Sierra, Solano, Sutter, Tehama, Yolo, and Yuba counties. The San Joaquin Valley region includes Amador, Calaveras, Fresno, Mariposa, Merced, San Joaquin, Stanislaus, Tulare, and Tuolumne counties. The Northern region includes Del Norte, Humboldt, Klamath, Shasta, Siskiyou and Trinity counties. Note that these were the counties as the boundaries were drawn in 1860.

Table 1: Regional Indian Population by Age and Sex

Region	Age and Sex														
	0–14			15–39			40–59			60+			Totals		
	% M	% F	F/M	% M	% F	F/M	% M	% F	F/M	% M	% F	F/M	N M	N F	Total
1	16.92	14.27	.84	26.58	23.41	.88	7.86	5.23	.67	3.40	2.34	.69	4640	3834	8474
2	19.84	13.94	.70	31.10	17.04	.55	7.42	3.39	.46	4.66	2.61	.56	1690	992	2682
3	13.04	7.42	.57	47.68	25.11	.53	4.72	1.20	.25	0.82			884	450	1334
4	14.01	14.26	1.02	39.58	17.08	.43	8.60	2.37	.28	3.12	0.98	0.31	3059	1625	4684
5	24.36	19.39	.80	22.28	28.37	1.27	3.37	1.92	.57	0.32			314	310	624

Regions 1–5 are the Southern, Central Coast, Sacramento Valley, San Joaquin Valley, and Northern regions respectively.

% M = the percentage of males in the regional population.

% F = the percentage of females in the regional population.

F / M = the ratio of females to males.

suses for precincts that illustrate demographic patterns consistent with those in the published census. I have categorized households in which Indians are found according to five types: No Family, Simple Family, Simple Family Plus Others, Extended Family, and Multiple Family.[17] Household types are compared with data about ethnicity of the household head, as identified by the census takers. For the purposes of this study there are only three kinds of ethnic households: Indian, Non-Indian, and Mixed. Indian households were headed by Indians, although people of other backgrounds may have lived there. Conversely, Non-Indian households were headed by non-Indians and may have included other ethnic representatives. A Mixed household was headed by a conjugal couple, one of whom was an Indian. The correlation of ethnicity and family structure shows wide variations in patterns of Indian household life by their historical origins.

The Southern region was originally the home of Indians whom anthropologists associate with the southern California culture area near the coast and the Great Basin culture area further inland.[18] These people, like other California Indians, divided their labor between the sexes, with men hunting and fishing and women gathering plant foods. Parents often arranged the marriage of their children, a practice that reflected the economic and social utility of the unions. Most couples lived in single family households near the husband's parents. Generally speaking, only chiefs, shamans, or other powerful men had more than one wife.[19]

The Indians in the Southern region were the first California native people to experience Hispanic colonization. Beginning in 1769 Spanish soldiers and missionaries founded a series of twenty-three missions, four military presidios, and three pueblos. With two centuries of frontier ex-

[17] A No Family does not contain an identifiable conjugal couple, while a Simple Family includes a couple and their offspring, if any. The Simple Family Plus Others contains a family unit as well as other unrelated residents. An Extended Family includes blood-related kin in addition to the nuclear group. A Multiple Family household has two or more conjugal couples and their offspring in it. Peter Laslett's definition of family structure is relied on here, except that the term *simple family* rather than *nuclear family* is used, and single parents with children are included in the No Family category so that a clear idea of Indian families capable of reproduction can be obtained. Peter Laslett, ed., *Household and Family in Past Time* (Cambridge, England, 1972), 31.

[18] Robert F. Heizer and Albert B. Elsasser, *The Natural World of the California Indians* (Berkeley, 1980), 45–52. The tribes in the southern California culture area are Chumash, Alliklik, Kitanemuk, Fernandeño, Gabrieleño, Juaneño, Luiseño, Cupeño, Diegueño, Serrano, Cahuilla, and Kamia. The Great Basin groups in the Southern region are Kawaiisu, Vanyume, and Chemehuevi. The Colorado River tribes—Mohave, Halchidoma, and Yuma—were not considered during this study because they were in areas peripheral to southern California settlement. Ibid., 29.

[19] Robert F. Heizer, ed., *Handbook of North American Indians: California* (Washington, D.C., 1978), 511, 523, 544–45, 556, 572, 581–82, 589, 602.

perience, Franciscan missionaries sought to convert the native people to Catholicism and place them on the lowest rungs of the Spanish social ladder as farmers and laborers. The neophytes, as the native converts were called, formed the labor pool for the mission system, the primary economic institution of the colony. The mission profoundly affected the neophyte and adjacent Indian populations; they died at a rapid rate, thus requiring the recruitment of new converts from the interior valleys. Still the demographic decline continued, undercutting the missions' source of labor and causing their decay as the economic mainstay for Spanish California. After 1821 the success of the Mexican Revolution led to the secularization of the missions, the distribution of their vast property holdings, and the dispersal of the neophytes. Some of the Franciscan-trained natives returned to their homes in the interior, while others found work in the Mexican settlements or on large land-grant ranchos that replaced the missions as the dominant institution in the province. Under Mexico, Indians remained California's basic labor force.[20] For Indians, eighty years of relations with Hispanic people led to a statewide demographic decline from an estimated 300,000 to about 150,000, due principally to disease.[21]

After the United States acquired California, the native population decline was exacerbated by the gold rush, even outside the mining regions. The discovery of gold led to a great influx of non-Indian people who soon outnumbered the native people. In the Southern region, Los Angeles grew rapidly and became an important, albeit a slow-moving, regional trading center. The new immigrants displaced many of the old Mexican landholders, but Indians remained as house servants and field hands.[22] Their subservient position was institutionalized to a certain extent by the enforcement of chapter 133, which provided for the arrest and indenture of loitering and intoxicated Indians. Local authorities added another legal feature—every week in Los Angeles Indian prisoners were "auc-

[20] Sherburne F. Cook, "The Indian versus the Spanish Mission," *Ibero-Americana*, 21 (1943), 1–194; Sherburne F. Cook, "The Physical and Demographic Reaction of the Nonmission Indians in Colonial and Provincial California," *Ibero-Americana*, 22 (1943), 1–55; Robert Archibald, *The Economic Aspects of the California Missions* (Washington, D.C., 1978), 142–58; Francis F. Guest, "An Examination of the Thesis of S. F. Cook on the Forced Conversion of Indians in the California Missions," *Southern California Quarterly*, LXI (Spring 1979), 1–77; Hurtado, "Controlling California's Indian Labor Force," 217–38; and George Harwood Phillips, "Indians in Los Angeles, 1781–1875: Economic Integration, Social Disintegration," *Pacific Historical Review*, LXIX (August 1980), 427–51; and George Harwood Phillips, *Chiefs and Challengers: Indian Resistance and Cooperation in Southern California* (Berkeley, 1975).

[21] Cook, *Population of the California Indians*, 43.

[22] Leonard Pitt, *Decline of the Californios: A Social History of the Spanish Speaking Californians, 1846–1890* (Berkeley, 1966), 121; and Phillips, "Indians in Los Angeles," 440–41.

tioned off to the highest bidder for private service."[23] At week's end the rancheros paid these coerced Indian workers partly with liquor, helping to assure enough intoxicated Indians for the next auction and a steady supply of labor. Under the threat of arrest and auction, Indians competed fiercely for a limited number of steady jobs as house servants at wages reportedly from fifty cents to one dollar per day.[24]

The sample household analysis of Los Angeles Indians illustrates the results of these local social and economic conditions (see Table 2). More than half of the Indians lived in Non-Indian households, and most of them lived in No-Family quarters on nearby ranchos with other male workers. Nearly 20 percent of the Indians were household servants in Non-Indian homes. About 30 percent of the sample Indian population lived in Indian-headed households, but less than half of them lived in dwellings with identifiable conjugal couples. There were almost as many Indians living in Mixed households as there were in Indian-headed families.

Examples from the manuscript census provide additional insights into the nature of Los Angeles Indians' town and country life. Typically, Indian household servants lived in the homes of people who were at least moderately well to do. Twenty-five-year-old Indian servant Maria, for example, lived in the house of Polish merchant David Solomon, his wife, and their three children. Solomon owned $1,000 in real and $4,000 in personal property.[25] Maria, no doubt, assisted Mrs. Solomon with domestic chores and the many tasks associated with raising three children, all of whom were less than five years old. Indian men as well as women worked as domestics, and occasionally an Indian couple served in a household, but this was rare.[26]

Some of the large landholders on the town's outskirts kept large houses filled with family, friends, and employees. Abel Stearns, a Massachusetts man who became one of the wealthiest southern Californians, lived with his wife and nineteen unrelated people, including Juan and Antonio, Indian laborers.[27] One of Stearns's neighbors, Mexican Californian Julian Chaves, was a person of more modest means, but he kept eight Indian servants, including six males in their twenties. The former

[23] Los Angeles Common Council minutes (August 16, 1850), quoted in Phillips, "Indians in Los Angeles," 444.

[24] Phillips, "Indians in Los Angeles," 443, 451.

[25] Federal Manuscript Census, Los Angeles County, Schedule A, 30 (hereafter cited as Los Angeles MS Census).

[26] Ibid., 32, 35, for examples of Indian servants.

[27] Ibid., 57; and Doris Marion Wright, *A Yankee in Mexican California: Abel Stearns, 1798–1848* (Santa Barbara, California, 1977).

Table 2: Los Angeles County Indian and White Sample Households

Household Type	*Ethnicity*											
	Non-Indian			*Indian*			*Mixed*			*Total*		
	C	*N*	*%*	*C*	*N*	*%*	*C*	*N*	*%*	*C*	*N*	*%*
No Family	52	125	26.77	16	75	16.06				68	200	42.83
Simple Family				4	15	3.21	6	15	3.21	10	30	6.42
Simple Family Plus Others	51	93	19.91	2	8	1.71	13	42	8.99	66	143	30.62
Extended Family	1	7	1.50							1	7	1.50
Multiple Family	6	35	7.49	2	45	9.64	3	7	1.50	11	87	18.63
Total	110	260	55.67	24	143	30.62	22	64	13.70	156	467	100.00

C = the number of households with Indian members.
N = the number of Indians in each category.
% = the percentage of the sample Indian population in each category.

American fur trapper, William Wolfskill, according to the manuscript census, kept more Indians on his rancho than any of his Los Angeles counterparts. Altogether there were thirty-seven Indians living on Wolfskill's property, including eleven male farm workers, eight washerwomen, a servant, and their children.[28] Wolfskill's rancho was an exception; most ranchos kept only a few workers, except during peak seasons of the year.

Compared with other regions, Los Angeles Indians married non-Indians fairly often (see Tables 2–6). There were twenty-two households with Mixed couples—about 14 percent of the households sampled. Los Angeles Indian women had spouses from Mexico, Kentucky, and elsewhere. The estates of their non-Indian spouses varied greatly, from moderate wealth to apparent pauperism.[29]

George Harwood Phillips has recently described the history of Los Angeles Indians as a dual process of "economic integration" and "social disintegration." Phillips writes that Indian society disintegrated as a result of a limited and essentially exploitative economic role and that the disintegrative process was indicated by Indian drunkenness, vice, and violence, "which in turn led to a drastic population reduction."[30] A main contributor to the decrease in Indian numbers was disease that, in Phillips's view, took its toll among the weakened natives. Beyond the immediate impact of disease, as the analysis of Los Angeles households shows, comparatively few Indians lived in situations in which reproduction and child rearing were feasible. In short, the Los Angeles social order that integrated most Indians into Non-Indian and No Family households substantially contributed to the overall demographic decline. Social disorder, at least as contemporary whites defined it, may have been an ancillary symptom of Los Angeles' socioeconomic conditions.

The 1860 household patterns of Los Angeles Indians were extreme by comparison with households in other parts of Hispanic California. The divergency of living conditions is illustrated in the Central Coast region. In anthropological terminology, the Central Coast Indians belonged to the Central California culture area.[31] Like their southern neigh-

28 Los Angeles MS Census, 113–14; Iris Higbie Wilson, "William Wolfskill," LeRoy R. Hafen, ed., *The Mountain Men and the Fur Trade of the Far West* (10 vols., Glendale, California, 1965), II, 351–62; and for Julian Chaves see "Pioneer Register," Hubert Howe Bancroft, *History of California* (7 vols., San Francisco, 1884–1890), III, 758.

29 Los Angeles MS Census, 6, 13.

30 Phillips, "Indians in Los Angeles," 427–28, 451.

31 The tribes residing in the Central Coast region were: Pomo, Wappo, Coast Miwok, Costanoan, Esselen, and Salinan. Heizer and Elsasser, *Natural World of the California Indians*, 29.

bors, these people were basically monogamous and patrilocal, although anthropologists have reported occasional polygyny.[32] With Spanish settlement in the eighteenth century, Central Coast Indians entered the Franciscan missions, where they suffered the usual consequences of disease and demographic reduction. During the 1820s and 1830s, mission secularization dispersed the Indians to the surrounding ranchos and urban settlements, where they worked as herdsmen and servants. By the time of the gold rush, the Central Coast Indians were gaining social acceptance in the Mexican community. Increasingly, people of undiluted Indian ancestry were recorded in local records as *vecinos* and *vecinas* (citizens) rather than *indigenas* (Indians).[33]

In 1860 the Indian population of the Central Coast region was only about one-third as large as that in the Southern region (see Table 1). The Central Coast Indians were mostly young males, although the age and sex ratios were not so radically deformed as those in other parts of California. The ratio of females of child-bearing age to males shows there was an important deficit of potentially fertile women in the Indian population.

The town of Monterey and its surrounding ranchos provide a household population sample that sheds additional light on the historical demography of the region. The correlation of household types and ethnicity indicates that a majority of Monterey's Indians lived in Indian households (see Table 3). Most of the remainder lived in Non-Indian households, while a small segment of the sample were residents of Mixed households. By household type, Indians were distributed about equally among No Family, Simple Family, and Simple Family Plus Others households. The largest correlative Indian group was living in Simple Families, while the next largest number of Indians lived in Non-Indian Simple Families Plus Others. About 32 percent of the population sample lived in Indian and Non-Indian No Families.[34]

The Monterey census indicates that Indians played economic roles similar to those in southern California. Most of the men were unskilled laborers working on white ranchos, while women labored as domestics in the homes of affluent whites. The Indian women in these homes were usually between the ages of fifteen and forty, although servants as young

[32] Heizer, ed., *Handbook of Indians: California*, 259, 296, 488, 490, 502; and Malcolm Margolin, *The Ohlohne Way: Indian Life in the San Francisco-Monterey Bay Area* (Berkeley, 1978), 83–84.

[33] Sherburne F. Cook and Woodrow Borah, *Essays in Population History: Mexico and California* (Berkeley, 1979), 310.

[34] *1860 Census*, 26–27; and Federal Manuscript Census, Monterey County, Schedule A (hereafter cited as Monterey MS Census).

Table 3: Monterey County Indian and White Sample Households

Household Type	*Ethnicity*											
	Non-Indian			*Indian*			*Mixed*			*Total*		
	C	*N*	*%*	*C*	*N*	*%*	*C*	*N*	*%*	*C*	*N*	*%*
No Family	14	16	11.94	8	27	20.15				22	43	32.09
Simple Family				8	37	27.61	3	6	4.48	11	43	32.09
Simple Family Plus Others	18	36	26.87	1	5	3.73	1	4	2.99	20	45	33.58
Extended Family	1	3	2.24							1	3	2.24
Multiple Family												
Total	33	55	41.04	17	69	51.49	4	10	7.46	54	134	100.00

C = the number of households with Indian members.
N = the number of Indians in each category.
% = the percentage of the sample Indian population in each category.

as eight were recorded. The Indian domestic staff in the David Spence home offers an example.[35] Spence, a wealthy merchant and landowner, lived with his wife, their son and daughter-in-law, and two grandchildren. The Spences kept three female Indians to serve them, aged twenty-five, twelve, and eight.[36] The Spence home was not unlike those of Spence's landed Mexican contemporaries—the Garcias, the Sepulvedas, and the de la Torres.[37] In Monterey's genteel Anglo and Mexican society, for those households classified as Simple Family Plus Others, Indian servants were the others.

Monterey Indian Simple Family and No Family households differed in their social composition, but they were similar in other respects. Both households were composed of working people variously identified as laborers and servants. In some cases the census takers even identified children as servants. For example, in the Indian Simple Family household apparently associated with the rancho of County Treasurer Thomas Day, the Indian parents as well as their children, ages eleven, four, and one, were identified as farm servants.[38] In the mind of the census taker, as this classification implies, Indian occupational status was to some extent hereditary.

The Indian and white household structure in Monterey was the result of several generations of Hispanic colonization and tradition. Like Los Angeles, Monterey's Indians were integrated into the social and economic structure, but they had an additional measure of control over their lives because they headed most of their own households. Still, the deficit of potential Indian mothers and the relative lack of identifiable conjugal couples meant that the Monterey population could not easily sustain itself. Moreover, while Monterey Indians lived in relative peace, they also lived in poverty. None of them reported any real or personal property to the enumerators. As in Los Angeles, Indians in Monterey comprised a part of the working class whose reproductive future was in doubt.

Until the 1840s, permanent settlement in California was confined to a fairly narrow strip of land near the coast. The great interior spaces—the central valleys and the sierras—remained in the hands of native people who were troubled only by the incursions of a few Hispanic exploring expeditions. The natives of this region have also been classified within the Central California culture area, and like their western neighbors, they were

[35] For David Spence's career see Bancroft, "Pioneer Register," *California*, V, 730–31.

[36] Monterey MS Census, 15.

[37] Ibid., 9, 10, 12.

[38] Ibid., 33.

principally monogamous and patrilocal, with polygyny reserved for the privileged few.[39]

The first important intrusions in the Sacramento Valley region began in 1827 when American, and subsequently Hudson's Bay Company, fur trappers began to exploit this territory.[40] In 1833 the Hudson's Bay brigade brought a virulent form of malaria to the region, already the habitat of the anopheles mosquito. The insect quickly spread the malaria among the Indians, and it is estimated that twenty thousand native people died in the lowlands of the Great Central Valley in a few summer months.[41] Severely weakened by this epidemic, the valley Indians could not successfully resist the first permanent non-Indian settler, John A. Sutter, who used Indian workers after 1839 to build New Helvetia, a fortified frontier enterprise near the confluence of the American and Sacramento rivers.[42]

By the time of the Mexican War, Sutter and other newcomers controlled most of the Sacramento Valley and the Indians in it. But for native people the worst was yet to come. Sutter's Indian and white workers discovered gold on the American River in January of 1848. During the first season of gold mining, the experienced California settlers maintained the usual white employer-Indian employee relationship, with native workers digging and panning gold for non-Indians. By the end of 1848 there arrived a huge influx of miners who were unfamiliar with the established place of Indian laborers in California. These latecomers drove most Indian people out of the mines, attacking and murdering the native work force, leaving only a remnant population in the mining districts.[43]

In the 1860 census only a handful of Indians were enumerated in the mining counties of the Sierra foothills, but modest populations were recorded in the bordering Sacramento Valley agricultural counties. More than 60 percent of the male Indians were under forty, about twice the number of their female cohorts. Proportionately, there were more Indian women of child-bearing age in the Sacramento Valley than in any other region except the Northern, but they produced fewer children. Indians over forty were downright rare, accounting for less than 7 percent of the population (see Table 1).

[39] The tribes living in the Sacramento Valley region included the Wintu, Nomlaki, Patwin, Yana, Maidu, Konkow, and Nisenan. See Heizer, ed., *Handbook of Indians: California,* ix. For marriage practices see ibid., 329, 346, 357, 366–67, 380, 392.

[40] John S. Galbraith, "A Note on the British Fur Trade in California, 1821–1846," *Pacific Historical Review,* XXIV (August 1955), 253–60.

[41] Sherburne F. Cook, "The Epidemic of 1830–1833 in California and Oregon," *University of California Publications in American Archaeology and Ethnology,* 43 (No. 3, 1955), 303–26.

[42] James Peter Zollinger, *Sutter: The Man and His Empire* (New York, 1939).

[43] Rawls, "Gold Diggers," 28–45.

Reasons for these disparities are found in the household structure of Indians in Butte County (see Table 4). More than 70 percent of the Butte Indians lived in Indian No Family households, and most of them were male workers. The remaining Indians were about equally divided between Non-Indian No Family and Simple Family Plus Others households as workers and servants. Three Indians lived in Mixed households. Most remarkably, in the 1860 Butte census there were no identifiable Indian conjugal couples.

The Indian living arrangements on Bidwell's Rancho Chico illustrate the kind of household that dominated Indian life in Butte County. Bidwell kept fifty-two Indians on his rancho, and fifty-one of them lived in Indian No Family households. They lived in four dwellings and were segregated by sex. Thirty-nine male herders, gardeners, and farm laborers lived in three households. Eleven women day laborers lived in a separate dwelling headed by a male named Yummarine, who was designated chief. Ten of the women were in their prime child-bearing years, between the ages of sixteen and thirty-one, yet there were no children listed in the census. Given the segregated living conditions, the absence of children was not surprising. In 1860 the Indians at Rancho Chico were there to work, not to raise families or sustain tribal population.[44]

The Butte County ranchos with Indian households like those on Rancho Chico were all large operations. Bidwell owned $52,000 in real estate and $56,640 in personal property. Former Pennsylvanian J. A. Keefer employed twelve young Indian men and four young women. He owned $3,800 worth of land and had personal property valued at $10,000. Similarly, R. W. Durham claimed $8,000 in real estate and personal property worth $2,000 and employed twenty-one male Indians, all except one in their twenties.[45]

As in Monterey, most of the Butte County Indians who lived in Non-Indian Simple Family Plus Others were servants, but unlike their coastal counterparts, most were young males. On the whole, Butte servants lived

[44] Federal Manuscript Census, Butte County, Schedule A, 37–39 (hereafter cited as Butte MS Census). Dorothy Hill reviewed the Butte Census and claimed that Indian children were "unlisted," but she does not cite evidence to support her assertion that Indians were permitted to retain their "customary dwelling structures, food, and religious customs," even though Bidwell "forced" them to accept "new occupations." Dorothy Hill, *The Indians of Chico Rancheria* (Sacramento, 1978), 27–29. Paul Wallace Gates also reviewed the manuscript census and found in it the importance of Indian labor to Bidwell's grain farming. Paul W. Gates, ed., *California Ranchos and Farms, 1846–1862* (Madison, Wisconsin, 1967), 45–46, n. 7. See also Anne H. Currie, "Bidwell Rancheria," *California Historical Society Quarterly*, 36 (December 1957), 313–25.

[45] Butte MS Census, 46, 54.

Table 4: Butte County Indian and White Sample Households

Household Type	*Ethnicity*											
	Non-Indian			*Indian*			*Mixed*			*Total*		
	C	*N*	*%*	*C*	*N*	*%*	*C*	*N*	*%*	*C*	*N*	*%*
No Family	11	15	12.61	6	85	71.43				17	100	84.03
Simple Family							2	3	2.52	2	3	2.52
Simple Family Plus Others	10	16	13.45							10	16	13.45
Extended Family												
Multiple Family												
Total	21	31	26.05	6	85	71.43	2	3	2.52	29	119	100.00

C = the number of households with Indian members.
N = the number of Indians in each category.
% = the percentage of tho sample Indian population in each category.

in modest homes of white couples with some money, although there were occasional servants in impoverished households.[46]

On the whole, Butte County contrasted sharply with Monterey and Los Angeles in its demographic composition. The Sacramento Valley Indian population seemed precariously based on one generation, with a sharp deficit of women of child-bearing age, although the whole Butte native population may have been more broadly based than the census shows. In the margin of the manuscript census an officer wrote, "16 Indians in Rancheria unemployed," implying that Indians who did not work were not enumerated.[47] If there were other unenumerated Indian communities in the county, they cannot be identified. To have stable family lives, Indian people would have to establish them outside the social and economic realm of 1860 Butte County ranchos, where the sexes were segregated and marriage and child rearing were discouraged.

In 1860 living conditions for Indians in California's Great Central Valley were by no means uniform. At the southern end of the valley, in the San Joaquin region, Indian household structure contrasted sharply with the Butte County sample. The San Joaquin region Indians were also associated with the Central California culture area with mainly monogamous marriage customs, but their historical experience was markedly different. While no permanent non-Indian settlers reached their area until the late 1840s, the Franciscan missionaries had progressively recruited neophytes from the San Joaquin Valley as the coastal population died out. Some of the interior Indian neophytes fled the missions to return to their old homes, and frequently they took mission and rancho horses with them. By 1819 Indians from the valley were raiding the mission herds regularly. It was said that even the San Joaquin women and children rode horseback. One observer claimed that the Indians of that region held regular horse fairs. Periodically, the Spanish and Mexican authorities sent armed expeditions to the San Joaquin Valley to capture runaway neophytes and reclaim stolen horses, but they were never able to quell Indian livestock raiding.[48] While Mexicans and Indians rode east and west, American and Hudson's Bay trappers marched north and south, trapping and trading for furs. Indians continued to hold sway even after the 1833 malaria epidemic swept thousands of them away. Sutter occasionally sent his Indian troops south to suppress livestock raiding, but there were no permanent non-

[46] For example, ibid., 21, 27, 35, 59.

[47] Ibid., 46.

[48] For ethnography see Heizer and Elsasser, *Natural World of the California Indians*, 29; Heizer, ed., *Handbook of Indians: California*, 411, 421, 432. For history see Jack Holterman, "The Revolt of Estanislao," *Indian Historian*, 3 (Winter 1970), 43–54.

Indian settlements in this region until after the gold rush brought thousands of whites into the area.[49]

The gold rush had an uneven impact upon the San Joaquin region's Indian population. San Joaquin, Mariposa, Merced, and Stanislaus counties were virtually depopulated, but according to the 1860 census, Fresno County had 3,294 Indian people, the largest Indian population in the state, and adjacent Tulare County had 1,340 Indians. In Fresno County the Indians remained a substantial majority, since there were only 999 whites and 312 other non-Indians in the county.[50]

The concentration of Indians in Fresno County was due in some measure to the presence of the Fresno River Farm, an Office of Indian Affairs subagency that operated until 1861. The farm was the home of several Indian groups who tilled the soil under white supervision.[51] To augment the farm's produce, some of the agency Indians worked on local ranchos. Even Indians who lived in the mountains relied to some extent on the Fresno River Farm. For example, the Mono Indians worked for white settlers during planting and harvest times, mined gold in the winter and spring, and gathered "the natural products of the mountains," a federal subagent reported.[52] In addition, the Mono Indians received some food and clothing from the subagency. With all these sources of supply, the federal official believed, the Monos had "been able to provide themselves with a comfortable living for Indians."[53] The Fresno River farm was also a refuge for Indians who were driven off their land by whites.[54]

The Fresno County household sample reveals another distinctive pattern. Almost 90 percent of the Fresno Indians lived in Indian households; more than 50 percent of the sample population lived in dwellings containing identifiable conjugal couples. Fewer Indians lived in all kinds of Non-Indian homes than in any other region, and less than 1 percent lived in Mixed households (see Table 5.)

[49] Jack Holterman, "The Revolt of Yozcolo: Indian Warrior in the Fight for Freedom," *Indian Historian*, 3 (Spring 1970), 19–23; Sylvia M. Broadbent, "Conflict at Monterey: Indian Horse Raiding, 1820–1850," *Journal of California Anthropology*, 1 (Spring 1974), 86–101; Bancroft, *California*, II, 335, n. 30; and A. H. Gayton, "Estudillo among the Yokuts," Robert H. Lowie, ed., *Essays in Anthropology: Presented to A. L. Kroeber in Honor of His Sixtieth Birthday* (Freeport, New York, 1968), 67–85; Zollinger, *Sutter*.

[50] *1860 Census*, 28.

[51] Edward E. Hill, *The Office of Indian Affairs, 1824–1880: Historical Sketches* (New York, 1974), 19–27; and Edward F. Beale to Lea, December 14, 1852, Office of Indian Affairs, Letters Received, California Superintendency, RG 75 (M234, roll 33: 851–53).

[52] "Annual Report, Commissioner of Indian Affairs, 1859," 809-10.

[53] Ibid.

[54] Ibid.

Table 5: Fresno County Indian and White Sample Households

Household Type	*Ethnicity*											
	Non-Indian			*Indian*			*Mixed*			*Total*		
	C	*N*	*%*	*C*	*N*	*%*	*C*	*N*	*%*	*C*	*N*	*%*
No Family	15	43	8.88	28	169	34.92				43	212	43.80
Simple Family				11	58	11.98	2	2	0.41	13	60	12.40
Simple Family Plus Others	9	10	2.07	20	147	30.37	1	2	0.41	30	159	32.85
Extended Family												
Multiple Family				5	53	10.95				5	10	10.95
Total	24	53	10.95	64	427	88.22	3	4	0.82	91	484	100.00

C = the number of households with Indian members.
N = the number of Indians in each category.
% = the percentage of the sample Indian population in each category.

Not only did Fresno's native people live in Indian households, they lived in their own communities. One of these communities contained 286 Indians in thirty-seven households. The census officer recorded a forty-year-old man named Wuemekana as chief of the community. Wuemekana lived with his wife and three children, a sixty-year-old servant, the servant's wife, and their four children, plus a forty-year-old woman. No other household listed a servant in this entire large community. Except for Wuemekana's servant, the census taker indicated no non-Indian occupations but occasionally noted that a man was a "brave," which apparently indicated a different status, at least in the mind of the white officer.[55] In other communities the census taker found a "Great War Chief," a woman "fortune-teller," and several Indian "doctors."[56]

Native people defined their own household and social relationships within Fresno County's Indian communities, even though they worked periodically for white ranchers. Outside the Indian communities the patterns in Non-Indian No Families were similar to those found in Butte. Young Indian men lived with whites as servants. Most of the Non-Indian household heads appeared to be men of moderate means or better, with sufficient capital to afford a servant.[57]

Although, as previously stated, Fresno County Indians remained the local majority population and many of them retained some control over their community and household lives, they were somewhat reliant on the white economy and federal assistance for survival. Far from being autonomous native societies in Indian country, the Fresno Indians were a dependent and declining refugee population with a deficiency of women of child-bearing age.

The last example of Indian household life comes from the Northern region, formerly the territory of the northwestern, northeastern, and a small part of the central California culture areas.[58] Polygyny seems to have been more frequent in the two northern culture areas than it was in other parts of California, but like the others, most societies were patrilocal. As in other California native societies, marriage served economic and social

[55] Federal Manuscript Census, Fresno County, Schedule A, 41–48 (hereafter cited as Fresno MS Census).

[56] Ibid., 52.

[57] Ibid., I.

[58] The northwestern culture area tribes are the Tolowa, Karok, Shasta, Yurok, Whilkut, Hupa, Chimariko, Chilula, and Whilkut. The northeastern culture area tribes include the Modoc, Achomawi, and Atsugewi. The remaining central California culture area tribes are the Wintu, Nongatl, Mattole, Sinkyone, Lassik, Wailaki, Cahto, and Yuki. Heizer and Elsasser, *Natural World of the California Indians*, 29.

functions that extended beyond the conjugal family and affected their larger kin groups.[59]

Hispanic colonization had no direct effect on these people; they first encountered whites when the fur trade began in the late 1820s. Th Hudson's Bay Company established friendly relations with the northern Indians, who insured safe passage from Oregon to California, but the fur trade caused hostility between some tribes. The Modoc Indians, for example, raided neighboring tribes for slaves they traded in Oregon for horses and other goods. These raids continued until the gold rush, when as elsewhere in northern California, the first permanent non-Indian settlers arrived. Only poor mines, located in rugged country, were found in the Northern region, so the area attracted comparatively few miners. Furthermore, some Indian groups strove to keep the whites out of their territory. There was armed conflict in mining districts everywhere in the state, but in the northern mines there was almost uninterrupted warfare between 1850 and 1865. State volunteers and federal troops frequently killed Indians indiscriminately, drove off the survivors, or took them to reservations and indentured them under the provisions of chapter 133. In short, worse conditions for Indians can hardly be imagined than those found in this country in 1860.[60]

As might be anticipated, federal census takers enumerated fewer Indians in the Northern region than in any other area in the state. But the small Indian population in the 1860 census presents a unique demographic picture (see Table 1). There were nearly as many Indian women as men in the total population, and there were more women of child-bearing age than their male cohorts. Children under fourteen formed more than 40 percent of the Indian population; nearly 95 percent of the enumerated native people were under forty.

The Trinity County household sample is likewise unique (see Table 6). Nearly three quarters of the enumerated people lived in Mixed Simple Family and Multiple Family households. All of the conjugal couples consisted of white males and Indian females. Their racially mixed offspring—sometimes recorded as half-breeds by the census takers—were counted as Indians. Typically, the husbands of these unions were landless farmers and miners with little or no personal property. Most of the males were be-

[59] Heizer, ed., *Handbook of Indians: California*, 132, 146, 159, 173, 186, 196, 208, 215, 240.

[60] Jack Norton, *When Our Worlds Cried: Genocide in Northwestern California* (San Francisco, 1979); Theodora Kroeber, *Ishi in Two Worlds: A Biography of the Last Wild Indian in California* (Berkeley, 1961); and Keith A. Murray, *The Modocs and Their War* (Norman, 1959), 7–42, present a good overview of conditions in the northern end of the state.

Table 6: Trinity County Indian and White Sample Households

Household Type	*Ethnicity*											
	Non-Indian			*Indian*			*Mixed*			*Total*		
	C	*N*	*%*	*C*	*N*	*%*	*C*	*N*	*%*	*C*	*N*	*%*
No Family	9	12	15.19	1	1	1.27				10	13	16.46
Simple Family							18	35	44.30	18	35	44.30
Simple Family Plus Others	8	9	11.39				8	16	20.25	16	25	31.65
Extended Family												
Multiple Family							2	6	7.59	2	6	7.59
Total	17	21	26.85	1	1	1.27	28	57	72.15	46	79	100.00

C = the number of households with Indian members.
N = the number of Indians in each category.
% = the percentage of the sample Indian population in each category.

tween twenty and forty years of age, but their spouses were very young, usually between the ages of thirteen and twenty.[61]

The emotional depth of these unions is difficult to judge, and it is not unreasonable to suspect that many of them were alliances of male convenience. Still, the manuscript census indicates that about half of the white partners conferred their last names on their spouses and children. Two families from the manuscript census offer illustrations of this point. David Peters, a landless Pennsylvania blacksmith with $190 worth of personal property, headed a Trinity Mixed household. Peters was thirty, and his Indian wife, Ellen Peters, was eighteen. They had a two-month-old infant son named Samuel Peters. On the other hand, J. Stewart, a propertyless miner from Maine, lived with an Indian woman, Mary Jane, and her two-year-old daughter, Mary Ann. Peters seems to have married Ellen and legitimized—at least for the census taker—his young son. Stewart apparently did not seek to formalize his relationship with Mary Jane or her daughter.[62]

Conjugal coupling did not necessarily indicate conjugal bliss nor a humane attitude on the part of the white men who lived with Indian women. A white army officer remarked upon the casual brutality that erupted in one Mixed household in 1862. A frontiersman had lived in the Northern region with an Indian woman for years when without warning the man beat "his own child's brains out against a tree and kill[ed] the squaw, its mother" because he had no other way of getting rid of them, and "to keep them from falling into another person's hands."[63] These intimate murders convey the terrible possibilities of a Mixed household in the war-torn and remote Northern region.

The Trinity County Indian and white social arrangements were distinct from those in other regions in the state. There was no place for Indian households within the compass of white society. Indian labor was important specifically in the context of the family, where women performed the wifely duties of housework and child rearing. The Trinity Indians who lived in Non-Indian households had a place in arrangements that resembled those in Butte and Fresno counties. Young Indian men lived in white households as servants, acting, in a sense, as surrogate wives—cooking, cleaning, and serving for white men.[64]

[61] Federal Manuscript Census, Trinity County, Schedule A, 31, 33–35 (hereafter cited as Trinity MS Census), provides examples of such households.

[62] Ibid., 31, 40.

[63] U.S. Department of War, *War of the Rebellion Records: A Compilation of the Official Records of the Union and Confederate Armies* (70 vols., Washington, D.C., 1880–1901), L, part 1, pp. 73–75.

[64] Trinity MS Census, 27, 31, 71, and 91.

The regional patterns of Indian and white household life found in the 1860 census illustrate the variety of the native experience in the decade following the gold rush. In regions with Hispanic traditions, individual Indians and families were integrated into the larger society as rancho workers and servants in middle- and upper-class homes. Out of the direct path of the gold rush and in areas with substantial Hispanic populations, Anglos in Los Angeles and Monterey counties seemed to conform to the social patterns that were evident among their Hispanic neighbors. In contrast, Butte County ranchers used Indians as workers but rigidly segregated Indian households by sex. In this Anglo-dominated region, white settlers valued Indian labor, but the Indian family had no role to play in Butte society. To the south in Fresno County, Indians were the majority and maintained their own communities with households that they defined. Nevertheless, Indians in Fresno County relied on whites for seasonal work on farms and livestock ranchos. In Trinity County, Indians filled the usual servant's role in Non-Indian households, but more of them lived in Mixed homes as the spouses and children of white men. These different patterns mark the range of household life for Indians who were permitted to live in white society.

Despite the regional variations in households, two trends can be seen throughout California. Except for the Northern region, there were fewer women of child-bearing age than their male cohorts. Even in the north, a significant number of potentially fertile Indian women lived with white men, thus creating a shortage of women available to Indian men. The scarcity of potential mothers was a severe problem for California's Indian population, already under stress and in rapid, prolonged decline. The second trend apparent in the manuscript census was the movement of a large proportion of Indians into living situations that were not conducive to reproduction. This movement explains in part the fall in the birthrate noted by Cook some years ago. To our understanding of Indian death and survival we may now add the limiting effects of household arrangements that discouraged Indian marriage and child rearing. Economic and social integration created conditions that permitted individual Indians to survive but also contributed to an overall decline in native numbers.

A better knowledge of Indian and white household arrangements raises an old and troubling problem that extends beyond California's borders. Given the economic and social possibilities of nineteenth-century America, was integration into white society a better alternative for Indians than segregation or even armed resistance? In Anglo and Hispanic California, the transformation of native Californians from a racial and cultural majority into a working-class minority contributed to their drastic, tragic population decline. Bolton's two streams of European civilization rushed together in California and nearly obliterated native people on the northwestern flank of the Spanish Borderlands frontier. More research is needed to understand the broad range of social and demographic questions implicit in this study. We are fortunate that such questions are only academic for us. California Indians faced them directly. Somehow they quietly persisted, living in a land radically transformed during the course of a single lifetime. For them, the 1860 census charts the landscape of survival and demographic decline.

Women's Work Among the Plains Indians

by Susan M. Hartmann

"War, killing meat, and bringing it into camp, horse-stealing, and taking care of horses, gave our men plenty of hard work; and they had to be in shape to fight at any time, day or night. We women had our children to care for, meat to cook, and to dry, robes to dress, skins to tan, clothes, lodges, and moccasins to make. Besides these things we not only pitched the lodges, but took them down and packed the horses and the travois, when we moved camp; yes, and we gathered the wood for our fires, too. We were busy, especially when we were going to move."

Pretty-Shield a Crow woman, used the words above to describe the division of labor among her tribe.

The Crow's assignment of work according to gender had much in common with the division of labor in the oldest, prehistoric societies where men assumed responsibility for hunting and defense, and women for gathering and child care. As human beings developed more complex economic systems, labor became increasingly varied, yet work continued to be labeled male or female. Even though the division differed from culture to culture—among the Hopi Indians, for example, men did most of the weaving, while the Navajos considered it women's work—within each economic system one's gender largely determined one's occupation.

Pretty-Shield's account of work among the Crows coincides in many respects with our popular image of the Plains Indians. At the center of this image is this mounted brave whose major occupation consisted of warfare and killing the buffalo to provide the economic base of Plains existence. Women appear peripherally, at work caring for children, maintaining the household, and converting the buffalo and other game into food, clothing, and implements.

Pretty-Shield's description indicates the importance and the variety of women's work. Although the activities she lists formed a common experience for native women across the Plains, they do not fully encompass the range or diversity of women's work. In a number of tribes women performed tasks which were considered men's work by their white contemporaries. Moreover, although they did not encourage it, most tribes allowed some women to cross over the sexual division of labor and to perform activities that usually were the province of men. And, even when they specialized in women's work, in many groups women derived significant prestige and some power from their economic roles.

In all Plains tribes, women contributed to the food supply by gathering wild plants. Picking berries, digging roots of onions, turnips and carrots, and gathering nuts and seeds consumed a good bit of women's time. Although not considered as valuable or as tasty as the meat brought home by their husbands and fathers, these plant foods balanced their diets and sometimes kept their people from starvation.

Indian woman dressing a buffalo skin. Engraving by C. E. Wagstaff and J. Andrews from a drawing by Seth Eastman. From Henry R. Schoolcraft, Information Respecting the History Condition and Prospects of the Indian Tribes of the United States (1852).

***At right,** Indian woman gathers wood for fuel, a common task.*

In addition to gathering what nature provided, women in a dozen or more tribes—including the Mandans, Arikaras, Hidatsas, Omahas, Pawnees and Caddos—also cultivated crops. These horticultural tribes occupied semi-permanent villages along river bottoms in the eastern and central Plains and depended heavily on the corn, squash, pumpkins and beans planted and harvested by women. They produced yields bountiful enough to allow trade with the Sioux, Cheyennes and other nomadic tribes and to provision white explorers. Lewis and Clark, for example, recorded eating a meal prepared by a Mandan woman. Consisting of pumpkins, beans, corn and choke cherries, they found it "by no means unpalatable." It is unlikely that white explorers and traders could have carried on their operations without the food provided by Indian women. The Lewis and Clark expedition ran out of meat in February 1805 but reported being "at no loss," because they were able to exchange blacksmith work for "large quantities of corn." Thirty years later Maximilian echoed the explorers' dependence on Indian corn: "We subsisted entirely on maize broth and maize bread," he recorded.

Men sometimes helped with the harvest, but farming was overwhelmingly woman's work. Each woman and her daughters cultivated a plot from one-to-three acres, using implements made from wood or animal bones. Their principal tool was the hoe. In early times this implement was made from the shoulder blade of a buffalo or elk. Later they used iron hoes purchased from white traders.

Although the work was arduous, women derived direct benefits. In the nomadic tribes men traded the furs and hides prepared by women, but it was not unusual among the sedentary groups for women to trade corn directly with whites. Lewis and Clark encountered a Mandan woman with a sick child who "offered as much corn as she could carry for some medicine." Fur trader Manuel Lisa recorded women traders among the Arikara. Edwin Denig, who traded among the Upper Missouri tribes for 23 years, described the operations of women traders at an American Fur Company fort:

> This trade (of 500 to 800 bushels in a good season) is carried on by their women who bring the corn by pansful or

Four young women (left side of scene) are allowed to take part in this dance portrayed by Catlin. "Women rarely participated in men's dances...," he wrote in his North American Indians.

> the squashes in strings, and supply themselves by the exchange with knives, hoes, combs, beads, paints, etc., also purchasing ammunition, tobacco, and other useful articles for their husbands. In this way each family is supplied . . . Though the women do all the labor of tilling they are amply compensated by having their full share of the profits thus accruing.

These female farmers controlled the use of the land, and usually enjoyed a relatively high status associated with their crucial economic contributions. Unlike the nomadic tribes, whose rituals centered on the male activities of hunting and warfare, the religious observances of horticultural groups celebrated the importance of women's work. The farming tribes performed rituals at planting and harvesting seasons and made extensive use of corn symbols. Pawnee men even carried an ear of corn as an amulet when they went into battle. Moreover, female deities, especially Bright Star and Mother Corn, were central figures in the religious systems of the settled tribes.

The absence of men at war or on the hunt cannot fully explain why farming was women's work, for

Indian women play and wager in "the game of the plum-stones," a version of rolling dice. Wagstaff and Andrews engraving from Eastman.

CHIPPEWAY SQUAW & CHILD.

"The life of the Indian woman, under the most favorable circumstances, is one of continual labor and unmitigated hardship," said Thomas McKenney and James Hall in their book, Indian Tribes of North America.

Cheyenne woman drying meat. This and the illustration at right from Curtis, North American Indian. *Tasks shown are considered "women's work."*

Wichita woman with braided squash for food use.

women cultivated the land even when men's efforts were not consumed with hunting and warfare. Because women have been and are yet farmers in many lands throughout the world, anthropologists speculate that women probably invented farming as a natural outgrowth of their work as gatherers. Moreover, American Indians believed that women were the better farmers: Their power to reproduce human life was associated with their ability to produce larger and better crops than men. However women came to be farmers, in groups where agriculture was women's work, they not only enjoyed a high place in the culture's value system, but they also exercised power and influence. Europeans observed among the southern Caddos a woman who was "like a queen among them" and reported that the government of the Wichitas was "democratic, without the exclusion of women."

Plains people were also dependent on women to prepare meat, the most favored food. Since the supply of buffalo and other game was not consistent, women's ability to work quickly to preserve it was essential. They produced what white men called "jerky," by thinly slicing the meat and drying it on racks. Pemmican lasted even longer, but required much more labor, as Pretty Shield related:

> We cut good, lean meat into strips and dried it a little; then roasted it until it looked brown. After this was done we pounded the dry meat with stone hammers . . . Next we soaked ripe chokeberries in water, and then used this water to boil crushed bones. When the kettle of boiled bones was cool we skimmed off the grease from the bone marrow, mixed it with the pounded meat, poured this into buffalo heart-skins, and let it get solid.

Such labor, if it were well done, could produce 55 pounds of pemmican and 45 pounds of jerky from a single buffalo cow.

Plains women also had to attend to the hides quickly before they became too stiff. Dressing of skins involved scraping off the tissue and fat, removing the hair, softening the hide, soaking and wringing it out, smoothing or graining it, and pulling it back and forth across a rope or post to soften it. Even though women worked together, it took three days to prepare one buffalo robe, and the average woman produced 18 to 20 of them during a winter.

Although Plains women spun buffalo wool into strands for weaving blankets and ropes, they fashioned most of their furniture and clothing from the hides they had dressed. They adorned many of these articles with quill work, a demanding art which involved softening porcupine quills, pressing, drying and embroidering them onto clothing and other objects. Cheyenne women had a special society which recognized and celebrated women's accomplishment at quill work.

Plains Indian women were literally home-makers, for the sexual division of labor assigned them the work of constructing their families' dwellings. In the roving tribes, women not only made the tepees, which had to be renewed every year or so, but they also were responsible for taking them down and setting them up again each time the family moved. Among the village tribes, women built the earth lodges or grass houses, where they resided during the growing seasons, and the tepees which they erected on more sheltered areas during the winter. Men often helped with the raising of heavy beams, but women did most of the work, and they owned the lodges or tepees. In fact, among the Pawnee and other farming groups, kinship was traced through the female line; a woman headed each household which also contained her husband, their daughters and husbands, and their grandchildren.

Mitigating the arduous features of Indian women's work was its social character. Girls and women worked in groups to gather berries, roots and nuts, often interrupting their harvest for play. Most of the steps in tanning required at least two women who could talk while they worked. Although the farmers cultivated individual plots, they were close enough so that women tilling the fields could enjoy the company of their peers. As they worked, Mandan and Hidatsa women sang songs composed specifically for that occupation. The structure and location of women's work was compatible with their child-rearing duties. Women could count on the help of their daughters, and daughters learned the skills necessary for their own adulthood as they worked with their mothers.

Some women shared their work with co-wives. Polygyny existed among most Plains tribes, but only successful men could afford more than one wife.

Among the Crows, for example, fur trader Edwin Denig estimated that half the men had more than one wife. Especially after possession of horses and guns increased men's capacity for hunting, additional wives reduced the work load for the individual woman. The system was most advantageous for first wives who held the highest status and exercised authority over newer wives. Sororal polygyny was the preferred type and usually worked best; when sisters were co-wives there was less rivalry and greater cooperation. Polygyny distributed the responsibilities of work and childrearing, and it reduced the number of pregnancies for each woman.

The one position in Plains societies which was filled by both men and women was that of shaman, or medicine man or woman. Access to these occupations was not completely equal because many tribes restricted women from various activities during their menstrual periods, and some permitted women to become shamans only after they had completed menopause. Yet in most groups, women as well as men had visions and were considered to possess supernatural powers. A band of Crows, for example, moved camp on the strength of Painted-Woman's dream that predatory bears were foraging in the area. More frequently medicine women operated as doctors, winning both respect and material gain. The woman who assisted Pretty-Shield's first delivery was paid with "one of my father's best horses" and "several fine robes." Some medicine women used natural cures such as herbs and other plant and animal products, while others also employed supernatural means. Although men always outnumbered women as shamans, women occupied these positions in almost all tribes, gaining the status, power, and income that went with the occupation.

While Indian women as farmers, home builders, and healers routinely performed labor considered man's work in other societies, they occasionally breached the sexual division of labor in their own communities. Before horses came to the Great Plains, women participated in the game drives or "surrounds" which were organized communally and on foot. Even after Plains tribes acquired horses in the 18th century, on rare occasions a woman

Another Wichita woman at work with her mortar. From Curtis, North American Indian.

might become a skilled hunter. Certainly women were not encouraged in this manly enterprise, but most tribes displayed considerable tolerance for aggressive and individualistic women.

Women could even become horse-raiders and warriors. Such women were found among the Crows, Mandans, Pawnees and other tribes. Running Eagle was a Blackfeet woman who assumed the warrior's role and became a leader of war parties to avenge her husband's death.

In 1876 Buffalo Calf, a Cheyenne wife and mother, saved her brother's life in the Battle of the Rosebud, and a week later she fought in the Battle of the Little Bighorn. In the Rosebud battle, two other women, the Other Magpie and Finds-Them and Kills-Them, fought with the Crow. In recounting their feats, Pretty-Shield remembered:

> The return of the Crow wolves and these two women to our village was one of the finest sights that I have ever seen. I felt proud of the two women, even the wild one, because she was brave.

But Pretty-Shield also felt that courageous women did not receive appropriate recognition. With some resentment she noted, "All the men saw these things, and yet they have never told you about them."

The pinnacle of masculine status was, of course, that of chief, but a woman occasionally occupied this position. The fur trader Edwin Denig knew the most famous woman chief. A member of the Gros Venture tribe, she was captured by the Crows at about age 10. When her foster father noticed "a disposition in her to assume masculine habits and employments," he encouraged her, and upon his

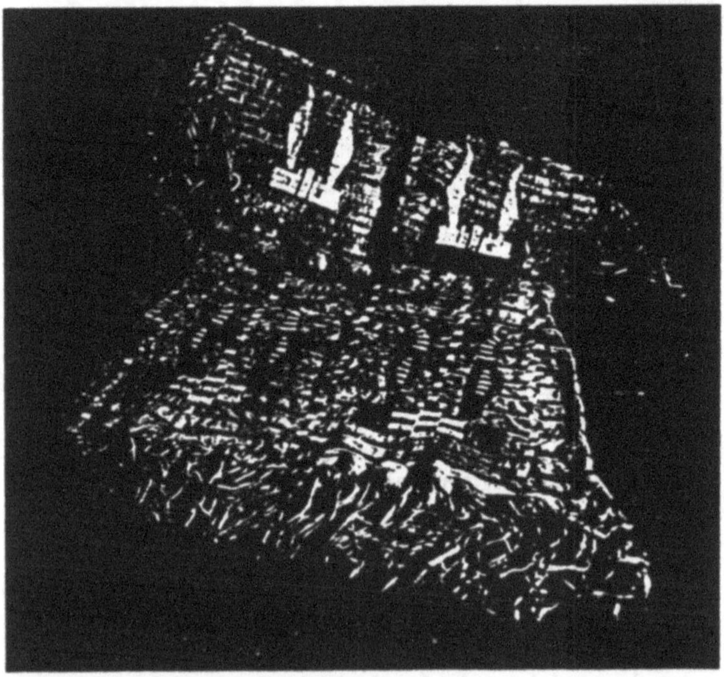

Quill-work Indian dress made by a Plains woman and now in the anthropology collection of the Missouri Historical Society.

death she assumed responsibility for his family. She surpassed most men as a hunter and fighter, and the Crows composed songs celebrating her feats. Woman Chief ranked third of all chiefs in the Crow Nation: According to Denig, "she had fame, standing, honor, riches, and as much influence over the band as anyone except two or three leading chiefs."

Just as women occasionally could fill normally masculine roles, men in many Plains tribes were allowed to perform feminine duties. Among the Dakota Sioux, Cheyennes, Crows, Mandans, Omahas and several other Plains groups, there existed a specific role, status, and name for men who preferred to perform women's work. Whites used the term "berdache" for such a person, although each tribe had its own term. Young men often assumed this role as the result of a vision, and they began to wear women's clothing and to practice female skills. Among the Dakotas, berdaches were thought to excel women in tanning, cooking, bead and quill work.

In most tribes the berdache was accepted without stigma. According to John Fire Lame Deer, a Dakota, "To us a man is what nature, or his dreams, make him. We accept him for what he wants to be." Berdaches often were believed to have supernatural powers, and they frequently performed special roles in rituals. The existence of the berdache role indicates a sophisticated understanding of the complexity of human nature. Moreover, it suggests that since men were not routinely derogated for adopting feminine activities, the occupations of women enjoyed considerable prestige even though they did not match the status of masculine occupations.

The institution of the berdache is just one example of the flexibility and diversity which operated in the structure of work in Plains societies. Plains Indian women in the sedentary tribes contrasted sharply with their white contemporaries who rarely worked in the fields and participated only peripherally in farming, the major enterprise of white Americans. (These native women had more in common with female slaves who routinely did field work, but who, of course, lacked the Indian woman's control over the organization of farming). Women's work varied across tribal lines with the

The two wives, three children and four dogs of a Comanche chief drawn by George Catlin. They were part of a tribal encampment which had 800 teepees and "thousands of inhabitants." From Catlin, North American Indians.

major difference demarcating nomadic women from their village counterparts who practiced farming. Even withing a single group, women's work changed with the seasons, with the peculiarities of nature and with the degree of their men's success on the hunt. In most tribes women's work contained more variety than that of men. Moreover, the division of labor itself manifested some diversity, as tribes allowed exceptional women to perform the masculine occupations of hunting, fighting and leadership and permitted men to take up customarily feminine activities.

Finally, women's work varied in time. The advent of the horse transformed hunting into an overwhelmingly masculine occupation, and it freed women from carrying heavy burdens on their backs. The expanded capacity for hunting along with the growth of trade, increased the amount of labor required of women in processing the furs and hides. Among the nomadic tribes men gained in prestige and power as they provided most of the group's subsistence and controlled the distribution of surplus. Increased warfare, both inter-tribal and between Indians and white imperialists, intensified the numerical imbalance between the sexes. In the mid-19th century, Pierre Jean DeSmet estimated that women composed from two-thirds to three-fourths of the Blackfeet population. Such a ratio gave men an advantage in that potential wives were abundant, and women were put into a poor bargaining position. In all, nomadic women lost some of the power and prestige they had enjoyed during earlier times.

Work in the sedentary tribes changed less dramatically. Although these people suffered from invasions and epidemics, women's position relative to men did not seem to deteriorate. Their produce continued to be valuable and, unlike their nomadic sisters, they participated in its exchange and profits. Women in both roving and village tribes gained access to products such as metal pots and iron hoes which eased some of their labor. In the process they lost traditional crafts: Quill work, for example, was replaced by bead work, and the old skill all but vanished among Indian women. In the end, of course, these changes were but preludes to the mas-

The lives of these three women came together for a historically significant moment in 1879. Indian agent N. S. Meeker of the Ute agency on the White River in Colorado created so much ill will among the tribes that he started a brief uprising. At one point during the disorder, the Utes attacked the agency and carried off three white women. One of them was Josephine Meeker, ***at left above.*** *During the six-day captivity, Chief Ouray's younger sister,* ***Susan, center,*** *befriended the three white women, attempting to ease their conditions. Chief Ouray's wife, Chipeta, shown with her husband, right, helped the women in a different way when she entered the Utes' tribal council (ordinarily composed only of men) to speak on behalf of their release. After the death of her husband, Chipeta assumed the leader's role and became an important Ute chief. Josephine and Susan photographed by W. G. Chamberlain, a Denver photographer. The photo of Chipeta and Ouray used courtesy of the State Historical Society of Colorado, Denver, Colorado.*

sive destruction of native American culture which came with the reservations. Then, both men and women were, in the words of Pretty-Shield, "trying to live a life that I do not understand."

Susan Hartmann is Professor of History and Coordinator of Women's Studies at the University of Missouri-St. Louis. She received her A.B. from Washington University and her Ph.D. from the University of Missouri-Columbia. She is the author of The Marshall Plan, Truman and the 80th Congress, *and* The Home Front and Beyond: American Women in the 1940s, *as well as several articles on women's history. Her interest in native American women grew out of a course she developed, "History of Women in Comparative Cultures."*

The following sources provided most of the information for this essay:

Rosemary Agonito and Joseph Agonito, "Resurrecting History's Forgotten Women: A Case Study from the Cheyenne Indians," *Frontiers: A Journal of Women's Studies* VI (Fall 1981), 8-16

Edwin Thompson Denig, *Five Indian Tribes of the Upper Missouri*. Edited and with an Introduction by John C. Ewers (Norman, Okla., 1961).

Donald G. Forgey, "The Institution of Berdache Among the North American Plains Indians," *Journal of Sex Research* XI (February 1975), 1-15.

Preston Holder, *The Hoe and the Horse on the Plains: A Study of Cultural Development among North American Indians* (Lincoln, Neb., 1970).

Margot Liberty, "Hell Came with Horses: Plains Indian Women in the Equestrian Era," *Montana: The Magazine of Western History* (Summer 1982), 10-19.

Frank B. Linderman, *Pretty-Shield: Medicine Woman of the Crows* (Lincoln, Neb., 1932).

Margaret Mead, *The Changing Culture of an Indian Tribe* (New York 1932).

Carolyn Niethammer, *Daughters of the Earth: The Lives and Legends of American Indian Women* (New York 1977).

John Upton Terrell and Donna M. Terrell, *Indian Women of the Western Morning: Their Life in Early America* (New York 1974).

Katherine M. Weist, "Plains Indian Women: An Assessment," in W. Raymond Wood and Margot Liberty, eds., *Anthropology on the Great Plains* (Lincoln, Neb., 1980), pp. 225-71.

George F. Will and George E. Hyde, *Corn Among the Indians of the Upper Missouri* (Lincoln, Neb., 1964).

American Indian Women and the Catholic Church

by Valerie Sherer Mathes

Katharine Takakwitha, the "Lily of the Mohawks." Her statue stands at St. Joseph's Seminary Hall at Dunwoodie, New York.

— *State Historical Society of North Dakota Collection*

The participation of Indian women in such traditional roles as wife, mother, housekeeper, and less traditional roles of warrior, chief, and medicine women or shaman has been recorded[1] but little has been written of their role in Western religions. Religion has always been important in American Indian cultures and women often assumed positions of importance, particularly in rituals of prayer for food, good health, or other aspects of life in which they were the principal actors. Within the pantheon of Indian religions there are several prominent female spirits, including, for example, Earth Mother. To some cultures the Evening Star was female, as was the Moon; and among the Navajo, the female spirit, Changing Woman, represented fertility and life.[2]

[1]For a general discussion of Indian women, see John Upton Terrell and Donna M. Terrell, *Indian Women of the Western Morning: Their Life in Early America* (New York: The Dial Press, 1974); Carolyn Neithammer, *Daughters of the Earth: The Lives and Legends of American Indian Women* (New York: Collier Books, 1977); and Valerie Sherer Mathes, "A New Look at the Role of Women in Indian Society," *American Indian Quarterly*, (Summer, 1975).

[2]For a general discussion of Indian religions see Ruth M. Underhill, *Red Man's Religion: Beliefs and Practices of the Indians North of Mexico* (Chicago: University of Chicago Press, 1965), pp. 51-61. See also Carolyn Niethammer, "Religion and Spirituality: A Constant Reality," *Daughters of the Earth*, pp. 235-246.

This tradition of successful participation in native religions led some native women to participate in their adopted religions. In this new role they could command respect and could exercise authority at a time when Indians in general were viewed with contempt or possibly pity. One such woman was Katharine Tekakwitha,[3] born at Ossernenon village on the southern bank of the Mohawk River in New York in 1656 to a Christian Algonquin woman and her Mohawk husband. Orphaned in 1660 by the death of her parents from smallpox, she was raised by an uncle. In 1667 when several Jesuits arrived at her village and took lodging in the home of her uncle, Katharine was exposed for the first time to the Catholic faith. But not until 1675, when Father James de Lamberville found her at home with an injured foot while he was visiting the village, was she able to express her desire to become a Roman Catholic. Baptized on Easter Sunday, April 5, 1676, by Father de Lamberville, she moved to St. Francis Xavier mission at Sault St. Louis the following year to be closer to other Christian Indians and to escape criticism from the non-Christian members of her own village.

On Christmas Day, 1677, she participated for the first time in the Holy Eucharist;[4] unable to be as totally devoted as she wanted, Katharine and two friends decided to move to Isle Aux Herones in the St. Lawrence River, to establish a sisterhood, and to devote their lives to teaching children of the Christian village of Caughnawaga; however, Father Fermin, a

[3]No attempt will be made to discuss the life of Katharine in great detail. For accounts by contemporaries see Father Claude Chauchetiere, "The Life of the Good Katharine Tegakouita, Now Known as the Holy Savage" in *The Positio of the Historical Section of the Sacred Congregation of Rites on the Introduction of the Cause for Beatification and Canonization and on the Virtues of the Servant of God: Katharine Tekakwitha: The Lily of the Mohawks* (New York: Fordham University Press, 1940), pp. 111-211. The original can be found in the Archives of St. Mary's College of the Society of Jesus, Montreal, Canada. See also: Father Cholenec, S.J. "The Life of Katharine Tegakouita, First Iroquois Virgin," in *Positio of the Historical Section* pp. 239-335. The original can be found at the Archives of the Hotel Dieu Monastery, Quebec. See also Father Cholenec's letter of August 27, 1715, which contains "A Life of the Servant of God, Katharine," pp. 341-379. Published biographies include Daniel Sargent, *Catherine Tekakawitha* (New York: Longmans, Green and Company, 1936); Marie Cecilia Buehrle, *Kateri of the Mohawks* (Milwaukee: The Bruce Publishing Company, 1954), and Ellen H. Walworth, *The Life and Times of Kateri Tekakwitha: The Lily of the Mohawk* (Buffalo: Peter Paul and Brother, 1891).

[4]*The Positio of the Historical Section*, p. 24; and Walworth, *The Life and Times of Kateri Tekakwitha*, p. 203.

local missionary, dissuaded them because he felt they would be unable to support themselves. Nevertheless, Katharine and one friend chose to live as monastic a way of life as possible, and in March, 1679, she took the first known vow of chastity[5] by a North American Indian woman. As penance, Katharine would often beat herself with a bundle of thorny switches, mix ashes in her food to make it unsavory, walk barefoot over ice and snow, recite her rosary half buried in winter snows, or sleep on a pallet strewn with sharp thorns.[6]

Upon her death on April 17, 1680,[7] at age 24, Katharine's face, once scarred from smallpox, became beautiful; the scars totally disappeared. From then on miraculous cures[8] were attributed to a power located either in the dirt of her tomb or in her crucifix. As a result of these cures, her piousness during her lifetime, and her devotion, the Society of Jesus (Jesuits) forwarded a petition to the Third Plenary Council of the Bishops of the United States in Baltimore in 1884 for her canonization. In 1932 her name was formally presented to the Vatican for consideration, and Pope Pius XII declared her to be "venerable" in 1943.

Although no Western American Indian woman has yet achieved the respect and position accorded Katharine, one of exceptional piety received the careful attention of Jesuit Father Pierre Jean de Smet, founder of the first Catholic mission in the Northwest. This young woman, Louise Sighouin, daughter of a Coeur d'Alene chief in Idaho, met de Smet in April, 1842, when she and a number of other tribal members were baptized. Desiring to devote her life to God, Louise renounced the guidance of her father and decided

> to follow the Black-robes to the end of the World, for fear that death should surprise and strike me far from them, and

[5]Father Cholenec, S.J., "The Life of Katharine Tegakouita, "First Iroquois Virgin," pp. 286-287.

[6]See *The Jesuit Relations and Allied Documents: Travels and Explorations of the Jesuit Missionaries in New France, 1610-1791* (Cleveland: The Burrows Brothers, 1900), Vol. LXII, pp. 177-179 for examples of her penance.

[7]See *The Jesuit Relations,* Vol. LXIII, p. 217 for discussion of her death.

[8]For the miracles and cures attributed to her see: *The Jesuit Relations,* Vol. LXIII, pp. 223, 229-31; and *The Jesuit Relations,* Vol. LXIV, p. 155, for Father Chauchetiere's statement that Katharine saved him when the chapel blew over during a storm. See also Vol. LXV, pp. 31-33 for further discussions of cures from the dirt of her tomb.

thus deprive me of the help of the Holy Sacraments and the salutary counsels of the Fathers.[9]

From then on, Louise lived a life of poverty and devoted herself to helping her people. She continually labored to instruct them in her new found religion despite personal dangers connected with opposing the tribe's powerful medicine men. She entered their lodges, fearing neither sneers nor threats, and spoke to them of the great truths of Catholi-

An oil painting done in 1681 by Claude Chauchetiere, S.J., honors Katharine Takakwitha, the first Indian woman in North America known to have become a Nun.

— *Reproduced from* The Jesuit Relations, *edited by Reuben Gold Thwaites*

[9]Hiram Martin Chittenden and Alfred Talbot Richardson, *Life, Letters and Travels of Father Pierre Jean de Smet, S.J., 1801-1873* (New York: Francis P. Harper, 1905), III, p. 1145. For information on Jesuit activity in the Northwest see Robert Ignatius Burns, S.J., *The Jesuits and the Indian Wars of the Northwest* (New Haven: Yale University Press, 1966), and Nicolas Point, S.J., *Wilderness Kingdom: Indian Life in the Rocky Mountains: 1840-1847: The Journals and Paintings of Nicolas Point, S.J.* (London: Michael Joseph, 1968).

cism. As a result of her efforts, these men lost power and the respect of their people.

According to Father de Smet

> Louise Sighouin . . . was endowed with the noblest qualities of mind and heart, which won her the esteem and respect not only of her nation, but also of the neighboring tribes and all whites who had an opportunity of knowing her . . . She was an oasis amid a sterile waste; she was a light amid the shades of death.[10]

Gaining as much religious instruction as possible and possessed of a remarkable memory, Louise began composing her own short prayers to instruct other women and children. Although having rather delicate health, she never neglected her work nor failed to attend church daily. She also spent hours visiting the sick and dying, often arriving before the priest. Despite her active schedule she still had time to attend to her husband, Adolph, who was crippled. Praising his wife to Father de Smet in February, 1859, after her death, Adolph called her a guardian angel who would carry him to their canoe whenever he was too sick to walk and cut his food and feed him.[11]

During planting season, Louise sowed her seeds in the form of a cross, and while other's corn did not grow, hers was always abundant. But despite the exemplary life she led, Louise nevertheless regarded herself as a sinner, and like Katharine Tekakwitha often subjected herself to public whipping as a form of penance.

During her final illness, Louise's continual prayers seemed to ease her pain and suffering; she did not complain. Learning of her impending death, her people rushed to her lodge and removed the mats to gaze at her for the last time. Father Gregory Gazzoli, superior of the Coeur d'Alene mission, with eyes filled with tears, watched the people assemble for their final act of gratitude and admiration. According to him

> . . . [Louise's] virtues have shown like a brilliant torch amid the Indians . . . Here, amid these isolated mountains, appears a poor Indian woman, whose unsaked faith and firm hope rendered her superior to trials of every kind.[12]

[10]Chittenden, *Life, Letters and Travels of Father Pierre Jean de Smet, S.J.*, III, p. 1143.

[11]*Ibid.*, p. 1172.

[12]*Ibid.*, p. 1166.

Probably the most lasting tribute to this most remarkable woman can be found in the words of Father de Smet:

> The zeal and fervor in the service of God, which she manifested immediately after her baptism, were the unfailing tokens of a predestined soul, filled with extraordinary gifts from heaven. These privileged favors were manifested in all their light by her admirable gentleness, which the greatest opposition could not disturb, by her patience under every trial, by her truly angelic modesty, by her fervent and sustained piety.[13]

Both Katharine and Louise aspired to live a religious life, but were unable to join a religious order; however, during the 19th Century several sisterhoods for Indian women were founded, and from then on Indian women were able to join and even become professed.

The earliest such order was established by Father George Antoine Belcourt, who worked among the Indians of both Manitoba and North Dakota. Born in Quebec Province in 1803, Belcourt attended Nicolet College. Following his ordination in 1827, he held various positions at local missions until finally consenting in 1831 to undertake missionary work at St. Boniface mission in Manitoba. For the next 17 years he labored among Indians and half bloods, accompanying hunters on the trail, compiling a Salteaux dictionary and grammar, and founding missionary stations. However, difficulties with the Hudson's Bay Company caused him to leave the Canadian mission field, and he decided to work among Indians of the United States.

Encouraged in his plans by the Bishop of Dubuque, he gained release from the Bishop of Quebec and in March, 1848, undertook his duties among the Chippewa Indians, half bloods, and settlers of Pembina in what is today northeastern North Dakota.

Following the flooding of the Red River in 1850, Father Belcourt moved his mission to higher ground at St. Joseph (now Walhalla), but retained the Pembina site as a station. As he worked among his new charges, he realized he needed additional help and founded the community of the Sisters of the Propagation of the Faith at St. Joseph. Members of this new community were half-blood women whose sole duty was the care and instruction of Indians and half-bloods. Unfortunately, Father Belcourt's community was short lived; when he departed the Dakota missions in 1859, it ceased to exist. Nevertheless, the sisters had successfully taken complete

[13] *Ibid.*, p. 1146.

charge of the mission schools at Pembina and St. Joseph during their short existence.[14]

One year after Father Belcourt's departure from Pembina, St. Boniface was the scene of the baptism of Anpao (Little Dawn), a small Santee Sioux Indian girl, by the Sisters of Charity (The Grey Nuns) of Montreal. Several months earlier her older brother and sister had been taken to St. Boniface by their parents to be baptized and placed in the care of the sisters. In 1863 Anpao, now Maria Josephine,[15] joined her siblings at the mission. Soon she was attending classes at Tache Academy where she learned cooking, housekeeping, embroidery, mathematics, and languages. However, when she reached the age of 15, according to regulations set up by the Sisters of Charity, she had to leave and choose a life of her own. The eleven years spent at the mission made adjustment to life on the Sioux reservation with her widowed mother extremely difficult; the following Fall, she returned to the academy to continue her studies.

Josephine eventually decided to join the order that had raised and educated her. On October 25, 1884, following her acceptance by the superior general in Montreal, she was clad in the postulant's habit; and following six months of preparation, she received her habit on May 14, 1885. On May 31, 1887, as Sister Maria Josephine Nebraska, she took her final and perpetual vow, becoming the first Sioux nun.

Her entrance into the order sparked the following article in the *Dakota Catholic* in the Summer of 1889.

> An interesting question has been raised as to the full-blood Sioux first admitted to the religious profession. A correspondent at Fort Totten states that this honor is due to a young member of the celebrated Iron-Heart family at that agency, who is now known in religion as Sister Nebraska. Three years ago she entered the novitiate of the Gray Nuns and after spending two years as a novice, according to the rule of the order, she made her religious profession in that community, and is now at St. Boniface, Manitoba. Her excellent qualities as a most

[14]For data about Father Belcourt see Sister Mary Aquinas Norton, "Catholic Missions and Missionaries among the Indians of Dakota," *North Dakota Historical Quarterly*, (April, 1931), pp. 153-158; for a biography of Belcourt see Vernice M. Aldrich, "Father George Antoine Belcourt, Red River Missionary," *North Dakota Historical Quarterly*, (October, 1927), pp. 30-51.

[15]Sister Mary Ione Hilger, O.S.B., *The First Sioux Nun: Sister Maria Josephine Nebraska, S.G.M., 1859-1894* (Milwaukee: The Bruce Publishing Company, 1963).

> efficient religieuse are highly appreciated by her local superiors and by Archbishop Tache. A hope is now entertained that she maybe transferred to the Fort Totten mission, where, as well as at the Sisseton agency, she has many relatives upon whom her good example would have a marked effect.[16]

As a result of failing health, Sister Nebraska was sent to Ste. Anne des Chenes on the open prairie in Manitoba to teach English to French children; however, she remained only six months before she was recalled to St. Boniface. Her health continued to decline; by March, 1894, she was diagnosed as being in the terminal stages of tuberculosis, a disease common to Indians who left their natural environment to live in the white world. As a result of the disease, on April 3 of that year she died.[17]

Sister Nebraska's example would be followed by other Sioux women who joined a community of Indian sisters established by Father Francis Craft, himself a descendant of the New York Mohawk. Sent as a missionary to Standing Rock Reservation to work among the Sioux during the 1880's, Father Craft, like Father Belcourt, became aware that some Indian girls were drawn to religious life; he determined to relieve the shortage of sisters by recruiting candidates from among the promising Indian girls at various reservation schools. He envisioned a native sisterhood and turned for help to the Benedictine sisters who taught at the reservation schools.

Mother Superior M. Gertrude Leupi of the recently established community of Benedictine sisters at Maryville, Missouri, was not at all against Father Craft's idea. One of the co-foundresses of the convent of Maria Rickenback in Switzerland, in 1874 Mother Gertrude had carefully selected members of her community to establish a new community in Missouri[18] to which she herself moved in 1879 to become Mother Superior. Despite difficulties often faced in a new undertaking, Mother Gertrude at the request in 1881 of Bishop Martin Marty accepted the challenge of sending some of her community to Standing Rock Reservation to take over three of the four schools already established there; thus, the education of future Indian sisters was undertaken.

[16] *The Dakota Catholic* (Sioux Falls, South Dakota), July 27, 1889.

[17] *Le Manitoba, Journal Hebdomadaire* (St. Boniface, Manitoba), 4 Avril, 1894, p. 31.

[18] Eventually the Maryville Foundation would evolve into the present day Sacred Heart Convent at Yankton, South Dakota.

Father George A. Belcourt founded the short-lived order, The Sisters of the Propagation of the Faith, at St. Joseph (now Walhalla) in the 1850's.

— *State Historical Society of North Dakota Collection*

To aid Father Craft in his long range plan for an Indian sisterhood, the Maryville community accepted their first Indian candidate in October, 1885. Ellen Clark, a half blood born on Standing Rock Reservation in 1868, was educated at Fort Yates Indian school. Receiving the name Sister M. Gregory Clark, she made her profession in 1886 at Zell, South Dakota, where the Maryville community had recently moved. Shortly thereafter, she began teaching music at St. Lawrence School in Milbank, South Dakota; however in 1891 she withdrew from the community.[19]

[19]*Catalogue* of the Benedictine Sisters, Maryville, Missouri, 1886. Sister M. Claudia Duratschek, O.S.B., *The Beginnings of Catholicism in South Dakota* (Washington, D.C.: The Catholic University of America Press, 1943), p. 108; Sister Mary Claudia Duratschek, *Crusading Along Sioux Trails: A History of the Catholic Indian Missions of South Dakota* (St. Meinrad, Indiana: The Grail, 1947), p. 95; and Sister M. Claudia Duratschek, *Under the Shadow of His Wings* (Aberdeen, South Dakota: North Plains Press, 1971), pp. 91, 124, 137.

The second half-blood Indian woman accepted was Emma Halsey, daughter of William Halsey, a half-blood Sioux interpreter at Fort Yates. Probably also educated at Fort Yates, Emma entered the convent as a candidate in 1885 as Sister M. Christine Halsey. Clothed with the habit on January 17, 1889, she professed her vows on her death bed at Zell on August 20 of the same year.[20]

The most promising Sioux woman and the first full blood to be admitted was Josephine (Sacred White Buffalo), daughter of Hunkpapa chief Joseph Crowfeather.[21] Born in 1872, Josephine was chosen by Craft to become the foundress of his Indian sisterhood because her people revered her. As a baby, she had been carried through a battlefield in her father's arms; because she escaped untouched, the band considered her a sacred virgin with a charmed life. She spent four years as a student of the Benedictine sisters at Fort Yates and later, along with several other Indian girls, studied at the Academy of the Sisters of the Holy Childhood in Avoca, Minnesota. Under Craft's careful direction, she applied to enter the novitiate of the Benedictine Convent at Zell. Receiving her habit on Easter Sunday, 1889, as Sister M. Catherine Crowfeather, she professed her vows in 1890 with Sister M. Bridget Pleets, a half blood, born at Fort Yates in 1873. Both were sent to Immaculate Conception Mission School at Stephen, South Dakota, on the Crow Creek Indian reservation where Sister M. Bridget taught and Sister M. Catherine was assistant cook.[22]

Another pupil at Fort Yates, Theodora Piicagewin, gave all indications to Craft that she had a similar vocation, but

[20]Archival Records of Sacred Heart Convent, Yankton, South Dakota. See also: Duratschek, *Under the Shadow of His Wings*, p. 91; and Duratschek, *Crusading Along Sioux Trails*, p. 76. Information on Emma Halsey was also obtained from a letter to the author from Sister Verena Kaiser, Archivist, Benedictine Sisters, Sacred Heart Convent, Yankton, South Dakota, November 5, 1977.

[21]Josephine was the second child; she was baptized at age 14 at St. Benedict's mission in Kenel, South Dakota, in 1882. The baptismal record gives her Indian name as "Ptesanwanyakapi" translated to "They see a White Buffalo Woman;" Duratschek, *Crusading Along Sioux Trails*, p. 94.

[22]Duratschek, *Crusading Along Sioux Trails*, pp. 94-95; 170; Duratschek, *The Beginnings of Catholicism*, p. 108; Duratschek, *Under the Shadow of His Wings*, p. 91. See also *Catalogue* of the Benedictine Sisters, Zell, South Dakota, for 1890, and the *Catalogue* of Benedictine Sisters of 1892.

Identified only as ''Father Craft's Indian sisters at Elbowoods in the 1890's,'' this is the only known photograph of the Congregation of American Sisters, an order for Native American women founded on the Fort Berthold Reservation in 1891 by Father Francis Craft. The picture was very likely taken before 1893; the individual Nuns are unidentified.

Courtesy Assumption Abbey Archives, Richardton, North Dakota poor health proved an obstacle to entrance into the convent. When her health grew worse, Father Craft decided she should die as a religious:

> Her desire to make religious profession grew stronger, and she begged so earnestly to be allowed to die as a member of the Order of St. Benedict that her request could not be refused. Her death-bed became the scene of her religious profession, and at the hands of the Rev. Father Craft, Martin and Bell, surrounded by the Sisters of the Community there, she received the Holy Habit and made religious profession on May 21st.[23]

The newly professed Sister Mary Gertrude of the Sacred Heart lingered until July, 1889, when she died, also a victim of tuberculosis.[24]

Father Craft, now with three professed women (Sisters M. Catherine Crowfeather, M. Gregory Clark, and M. Bridget Pleets), and several other Indian women candidates at Yankton, decided to establish his sisterhood and invited them all to accompany him to Fort Berthold in North Dakota where he planned to found his community. With the blessing of Bishop John Shanley of Jamestown, North Dakota, authorization was given on November 1, 1891. Sister M. Catherine Crowfeather became Mother M. Catherine Sacred White Buffalo, and was appointed to head the new community, the Congregation of American Sisters (or "Red Sisters"). Other members of the community included Mary Black Eyes and Jane Big Moccasin, both from Cannonball, Susan Bordeaux and Josephine Two Bears from Rosebud reservation, and several girls from Pembina.[25]

The purpose of this new order was to prepare Indians for eventual citizenship, teach them English, and act as directors of Indian societies. Craft taught his community the rudiments of medicine and nursing and soon they began caring for the sick. Unfortunately, Father Craft also forbade the eating of meat by members of his community; because this was the mainstay of the Plains tribes' diet, their health slowly began to deteriorate. Mother M. Catherine Sacred White Buffalo was

[23] *The Dakota Catholic* (Sioux Falls, South Dakota), July 6, 1889.

[24] Duratschek, *Crusading Along Sioux Trails*, p. 95; Duratschek, *The Beginnings of Catholicism*, p. 108.

[25] Duratschek, *Crusading Along Sioux Trails*, pp. 95-96; Duratschek, *Under the Shadow of His Wings*, p. 128; Duratschek, *The Beginnings of Catholicism*, p. 109; Robert I. Burns, S.J., "Americane Indiane, Suore," *Dizionario enciclopedico dei religiosi e degli instituti secolari*, ed. by Giancarlo Rocca (Rome: Edizioni Paoline, 1974-), Vol. VI. pp. 575-576.

the first victim, dying at age 26 on May 3, 1893, of tuberculosis after having received Holy Communion.[26]

By 1894 the community numbered only five: Mother Ligouri Sound-of-the-Flying-Lance, successor to Mother Sacred White Buffalo; Mother Frances White Eagle, a relative of Brule Chief Spotted Tail; Mother Gertrude Brings Forth Holiness; Sister Anthony Cloud Robe; and Sister Aloysia Black Eyes. Sisters M. Bridget Pleets, M. Gregory, and several others had already left the community.[27]

When the Spanish-American War broke out in 1898, Father Craft offered the services of his community to the War Department. He requested that they be sent to the front to care for wounded under fire because their frontier experience fitted them for such a dangerous task. And to remain with his sisters, he enlisted as hospital steward. Subsequently, the War Department commended several of the community for their work at Camp Libre, Jacksonville, Florida, and later in Savannah, Georgia, and Havana, Cuba.[28]

Following the war, Father Craft and the women returned home to find the rest of their community dispersed during their absence. Unable to obtain full ecclesiastical recognition for so few members, he gave up his plan and returned East. Although most of the community members abandoned religious life; a few continued to work as lay religious among their people, and as recently as 1942 three of the group were still alive.[29]

Despite the failure of both Belcourt's and Craft's religious communities, the idea of using Indian women as nuns to aid in the acculturation process of their people still had merit for Father Sylvester Eisenman, O.S.B. A graduate of St. Meinrad's Preparatory Seminary in Indiana and the Novitiate at the Abbey, Father Sylvester was assigned to St. Paul's mission in Marty, South Dakota. As he worked among the Sioux, he, like his predecessors, still believed a solution to improving the condition of the Indians was to have them

[26]Duratschek, *Crusading Along Sioux Trails,* p. 96; Duratschek, *The Beginnings of Catholicism,* pp. 109-110.

[27]Duratschek, *Crusading Along Sioux Trails,* pp. 96-97; Duratschek, *The Beginnings of Catholicism,* p. 110.

[28]Duratschek, *Crusading Along Sioux Trails,* p. 97; Duratschek, *The Beginniings of Catholicism,* p. 110.

[29]Duratschek, *The Beginnings of Catholicism,* p. 111; Duratschek, *Crusading Along Sioux Trails,* p. 98.

taught and cared for by members of their tribe. He began consulting mothers superior of various religious communities about their experiences with Indian women who aspired to join their orders and found all in agreement that possibilities of Indian women fitting within an established community were not particularly good.

Not easily discouraged, Father Sylvester presented his plan to Mother Katherine Drexel, Superior General of the Sisters of the Blessed Sacrament; she consented to have her group "mother" the proposed foundation and selected two sisters who opened a novitiate at Marty to begin the training of Indian women candidates. Rules different from those of white religious communities were drawn up to fit best the conditions at Marty. The Indian sisters, following a two year novitiate, would take vows for a year at a time; and at the end of that year, they were free to leave if religious life did not suit them. A practical habit made of a simple grey dress with a black cape and simple headdress was designed. Preliminary approval came from Rome, and on October 6, 1935, seven Indian girls from the mission high school were admitted as postulants to the sisterhood, known as the Oblate Sisters of the Blessed Sacrament, the only novitiate at that time exclusively for Indian girls.[30]

The daily activities of these young Indian women included supervising playgrounds, acting as teachers' assistants, helping in the kitchen, infirmary, sewing room and laundry, and serving as sacristans and secretaries, as well as caring for the sick, distributing food and clothing to needy, teaching catechism to the children, and eventually actually teaching.

During the 1960's the Oblate Sisters of the Blessed Sacrament began to admit women who were not of Indian blood.[31] As of the Summer of 1978, the order had a total of 15 members, six of whom are of Indian descent[32] and all of whom

[30]"Oblate Sisters of the Blessed Sacrament: A Sisterhood for Indian Girls Only," *The Catholic Indian Herald*, Vol. IX, No. VII (April 1, 1940), pp. 1-8. See also Duratschek, *Crusading Along Sioux Trails*, pp. 307-310; and "Reservation and School Notes," *The Catholic Sioux Herald* (Marty, South Dakota), English Section, June 5, 1936, p. 5 and *America: A Catholic Review of the Week*, November 30, 1935, p. 173.

[31]Letter dated 5/5/78 to the author from Louis J. Delahoyde, Chancellor, Catholic Chancery Office, Sioux Falls, South Dakota.

[32]Sister Inez Jetty, St. Sylvester's Convent, Marty, South Dakota, in a January 15, 1978, letter to the author listed the following sisters of Indian descent: Sister Lillian Dubois, Sister Anthony Davis, Sister Francis Poitra, Sister Christine Hudson, Sister Madeleine LeCompte, and Sister Inez Jetty.

are teaching.[33] Although today there is no one single order open only to Indian women, women of many different tribes have been professed into various religious orders[34] and are continuing to work among their people and communities as a whole.

While the religious role of American Indian women within the Catholic Church has not been extensive, they were nevertheless able to gain respect not only from their peers but from the white communities as a whole. And the self inflicted pain endured, for example, by Katharine and Louise was not inconsistent with Indian cultures. Among certain tribes, women were required to gash themselves or even cut off part of a finger at the death of relatives — all part of organized mourning traditions. In addition, the vision quest in which both boys and girls participated found young Indian girls totally on their own for days without food and water as a means of gaining a vision that would guide them the remainder of their life.

Although few Indian women did achieve exaulted positions like that of Katharine and Louise, many did have the opportunity, and still do, to serve as members of Fathers Belcourt's, Craft's, and Eisenman's communities as well as present day communities. They thus form a unique group among the native peoples of North America.

[33]Brother Paul Nyquist, Librarian, Assumption Abbey, Richardton, North Dakota, in letter to Larry Remele, State Historical Society of North Dakota, dated April 21, 1978, and xeroxed and sent to the author states that the Oblate Sisters of the Blessed Sacrament has 15 members and all of them are teaching.

[34]No attempt has been made in this article to discuss all orders that include Indian women, but to present to the reading public the three main orders established by Belcourt, Craft, and Eisenman.

Racial Ethnic Women's Labor: The Intersection of Race, Gender and Class Oppression

EVELYN NAKANO GLENN

ABSTRACT: A colonial labor system and other forms of racial oppression shaped the productive and reproductive labor of racial ethnic women in ways that made their experiences fundamentally different from those underlying the construction of feminist analyses of women's oppression. For black, Mexican-American and Chinese-American women, key concepts such as the private-public dichotomy, gender conflict within the family and the division of reproductive labor need to be reformulated. This study examines the historical evidence on black, Mexican-American and Chinese-American women's work from the mid-nineteenth century to the present in light of contemporary Marxist-feminist and colonial labor system theories. Thus, the author begins to reformulate and synthesize key concepts in these contemporary theories to explain the experiences of racial ethnic women.

INTRODUCTION

The failure of the feminist movement to address the concerns of black, Hispanic and Asian-American women is currently engendering widespread discussion in white women's organizations. Paralleling this discussion is a growing interest among racial ethnic women[1] in articulating aspects of their experiences that have been ignored in feminist analyses of women's oppression (e.g., oral histories by Sterling 1979; Elessar, MacKenzie and Tixier y Vigil 1980; Kim 1983; and social and historical studies by Dill 1979; Mirande and Enriquez 1979; Davis 1981; Hooks 1981; Jones 1984).[2]

As an initial corrective, racial ethnic scholars have begun research on racial ethnic women in relation to employment, the family and the ethnic community, both historically and contemporarily (e.g., Acosta-Belen 1979; Mora and Del Castillo 1980; Melville 1980; Rodgers-Rose 1980; Tsuchida 1982). The most interesting of these studies describe the social world and day-to-day struggles of racial ethnic women, making visible what has up to now been invisible in the social sciences and humanities. These concrete data constitute the first step toward understanding the effects of race and gender oppression in the lives of racial ethnic women.

Department of Sociology, Florida State University, Tallahassee, FL 32306.
This paper grew out of studying with members of the Inter-University Group Researching the Intersection of Race and Gender: Bonnie Dill, Cheryl Gilkes, Elizabeth Higginbotham and Ruth Zambrana. I am also grateful to members of the Women and Work Study Group for their contributions to my thinking: Carole Turbin, Natalie Sokoloff, Susan Lehrer, Amy Kesselman, Amy Srebnick, Myra Ferree, Nadine Felton, Roz Feldberg, Peggy Crull, Carol Brown and Chris Bose. Finally, I thank Nancy Breen, Gary Dymski, Betsy Jameson, Bill James and Laurie Nisonoff for their careful critiques even though I was unable to incorporate all their suggestions. An early version was presented at the Meetings of the American Association for the Advancement of Science, Washington, D.C., January 1982. This is a substantially revised version of a paper published in the proceedings volume and is reprinted by permission of Westview Press from *Social Power and Influence of Women*, Liesa Stamm and Carol D. Ryff (eds.) Westview Press, 1985.
Copyright © 1984 by the American Association for the Advancement of Science.

A necessary next step is the development of theoretical and conceptual frameworks for analyzing the interaction of race and gender stratification. Separate models exist for analyzing race, ethnic or gender stratification. Although the "double" (race, gender) and "triple" (race, gender, class) oppression of racial ethnic women are widely acknowledged, no satisfactory theory has been developed to analyze what happens when these systems of oppression intersect. A starting point for developing such a theory would appear to lie in those models which view race and gender stratification as part of a larger system of institutionalized inequality. During the 1970s two models which view race and gender divisions as embedded in and helping to maintain an overall system of class exploitation came to the fore: the *patriarchy* model developed by Marxist-feminists to explain the subordination of women (e.g., Weinbaum and Bridges 1979; Sokoloff 1980; Brown 1981; and Hartmann 1981a) and the *internal colonialism* model developed by activists and scholars to explain the historic subordination of blacks, Hispanics, Asian-Americans and other people of color in the United States (e.g., Clark 1965; Carmichael and Hamilton 1967; Moore 1970; Barrera, Muñoz and Ornelas 1972; and Blauner 1972).

At the center of the Marxist-feminist analysis is the concept of patriarchy, which may be defined as a hierarchical system of power which enables men as a class to have authority and power over women (Hartmann 1976; Sokoloff 1980). In this model the main mechanism by which control is achieved and maintained by men is the *sexual division of labor,* which places men in positions of authority over women and permits them to reap disproportionate benefits. Similarly, at the center of the internal colonialism model is a system of power relations by which subordinate minorities are kept politically and economically weak so they can be more easily exploited as workers. The main mechanism by which economic dependency is maintained is a *colonial labor system,* characterized by a segmented labor market, discriminatory barriers and separate wage scales. This system ensures that people of color are relegated to the worst jobs, i.e. insecure, low-paying, dangerous, dirty and dead-end.

Neither model explicitly recognizes the specific situation of racial ethnic women. The patriarchy model ignores differences among women based on race. When race is discussed, it is treated as a parallel system of stratification: an analogy is often made between "women" and "minorities," an analogy that involves comparison of the subordinate status of white women and minority men. Minority women are left in limbo. Similarly, the internal colonialism model ignores gender by treating members of colonized minorities as undifferentiated with respect to gender. Analyses of racial ethnic labor have generally focused only on male workers. Yet, these studies also assume that the detrimental impacts of the labor system on men is synonymous with the impacts on the group as a whole, men and women alike.

Despite the focus on only one axis of stratification, the patriarchy and internal colonialism models have some important commonalities. Each focuses on explaining the persistence of inequality and sees gender/race stratification as dynamically related to the organization of the economy. Thus, each implies an historical perspective, one that traces changes in the relations between dominant and subordinate groups in relation to the development of capitalism. Each emphasizes institutional arrangements that ensure control by the dominant group over the labor of the subordinate group. There thus seems to be some common ground for developing a more integrated framework by combining insights from the two perspectives.

This paper is a preliminary effort to identify aspects of the two models that might contribute to an integrated framework. I will start by briefly reviewing the Marxist-feminist analysis of women's subordination. I will then review racial ethnic women's experience as members of colonized minorities in the United States. In light of this experience, I will examine the paid and unpaid work of Chinese, Mexican-American and black women from the mid-nineteenth century to the present, showing how they diverge from those presumed to be typical of white women. In the concluding section, suggestions are made for revision of Marxist-feminist theory to be more inclusive of the race-gender interaction.

MARXIST-FEMINIST ANALYSIS

The Marxist-feminist perspective views women's subordination as a product of two interacting systems: patriarchy and capitalism. While generally adhering to the Marxist analysis of class exploitation, Marxist-feminists diverge by giving equal importance to patriarchy, which, they argue, existed prior to capitalism, though interacting with it as capitalism developed. According to this analysis, the main mechanism by which patriarchy was established and is maintained today is the sexual division of labor. The assignment of certain tasks (usually the more onerous and/or less valued) to women, and others (usually the more highly valued) to men, is considered more or less universal.

Under capitalism the sexual division of labor takes a particular form due to the separation of production of goods, and then services, from the household. As production was industrialized the household became increasingly privatized, and its functions reduced to consumption, which includes shopping and negotiating for services (Weinbaum and Bridges 1979) and biological and social reproduction, including child care, cleaning, preparing food and providing emotional support for the breadwinner. As capital took over production, thus households became increasingly dependent on the market for goods and, therefore, on wages to purchase goods and services needed for survival. During the nineteenth century — in part because men could be more intensively exploited as wage laborers, while women could benefit capital as full-time consumers and reproducers — a specialization developed, whereby women were assigned almost exclusive responsibility for household consumption and reproduction and men were allocated responsibility for publicly organized production. This division became prescribed in the mid-nineteenth century with the development of the cult of domesticity, which idealized the woman as the center of home and hearth (Welter 1966). This division of labor contributed to the subordination of women by making them economically dependent on a male wage earner. Simultaneously the domestic code controlled women's behavior by threatening those who deviated from it with the loss of their feminine identity.

The ideal of separate spheres was, of course, unattainable for many women whose fathers or husbands were unable to earn a family wage and who therefore had to engage in income producing activities to support themselves and their families (Lerner 1969; Easton 1976). Yet the conception of women as consumers and reproducers affected them too, depressing their position in the labor market. Women were defined as secondary workers, a status maintained by a sexual division in the labor market, i.e. occupational segregation. Jobs allocated to women were typically at the bottom of the authority hierarchy, low in wages, dead-end and frequently insecure. The secondary position of women in the labor force meant that women had little leverage to shift the burden of household work onto husbands, so they continued to be responsible for the domestic sphere. Moreover, because of low wages and insecure jobs, even when employed, women remained dependent on the additional wages of the male earner (Hartmann 1976; Kessler-Harris 1982).

This analysis has much to offer: it permits us to view women's subordination as part of a larger framework of economic exploitation. It also draws connections between women's domestic work and their work in the labor force, and shows how subordination in one sphere reinforces subordination in the other. It is intended as a general analysis that encompasses all women. Yet, it is built on class- and race-bounded experiences. To what extent do the concepts developed in the Marxist-feminist model apply to the experience of racial ethnic women? To what extent does the private-public split and women's association with the domestic sphere exist for racial ethnic women? To what extent has economic dependence on men been an important basis for racial ethnic women's subordination? To what extent do struggles over allocation of household labor create gender conflict in racial ethnic households?

In order to begin addressing these questions we need to examine the impacts of race stratification on racial ethnic women's work, both paid and unpaid. For this, I draw on both earlier and more recent research on the labor histories of "colonized minorities." Because histories of the various peoples in different regions of the country vary and because of the limited size and scope of this paper, I will limit my examination to three case studies for which there is comparable information from the mid-nineteenth century to the present: Mexican-Americans in the Southwest, Chinese in California and blacks in the South.

COLONIZED MINORITIES IN INDUSTRIALIZING AMERICA

The United States started out as a colonial economy which offered raw resources and land to European and American capitalists. In order to develop the economic infrastructure and extract resources, capitalists needed labor, which was always in short supply. The presence of racial ethnic groups in this country is tied to this demand for labor. Most were brought to this country for the express purpose of providing cheap and malleable labor (Cheng and Bonacich 1984).

Although European immigrants were also welcomed as a source of low-wage labor, they were incorporated into the urban economies of the north. Racial ethnics were recruited primarily to fill labor needs in economically backward regions: the West, Southwest and South (Blauner 1972). In the late nineteenth and early twentieth century, Chinese men constituted from a quarter to a third of the work force (reclaiming agricultural lands, building railroads, and working in mines), and 90 percent of the domestic and laundry workers in California (Saxton 1971). During this same period, native Chicanos and Mexican immigrants (Mexicanos) were employed as miners, railroad hands and agricultural laborers in the western states (Barrera 1979). In the years following emancipation blacks were concentrated in agriculture, as well as in heavy labor in construction and domestic service in the South (Cheng and Bonacich 1984). All three groups helped build the agricultural and industrial base on which subsequent industrial development rested, but were excluded from the industrial jobs that resulted.

Racial ethnic labor was cheaper for infrastructure building in two senses: racial ethnics were paid less (including lower benefits) and provided a reserve army to be drawn in when the economy expanded or labor was needed for a short-term project, and pushed out when the economy contracted or the particular project ended. Their cheapness was ensured by institutional barriers that undercut their ability to compete in the labor market. The labor market itself was stratified into separate tiers for whites and racial ethnics. The better paying, more skilled, cleaner and secure jobs in highly capitalized industries were reserved for white workers, leaving the low paying, insecure, dangerous, seasonal and dead-end jobs in competitive industries for people of color. A dual wage system was also characteristic of the colonial labor system; wages for racial ethnics were always lower than for whites in comparable jobs (Barrera 1979). White workers benefitted because better jobs were reserved for them. The dual labor system also buffered them from the effects of periodic depressions, since racial ethnics took the brunt of layoffs and unemployment.

Further, racial ethnics were prevented from competing for better work and improved conditions by legal and administrative restrictions. Restrictions on their rights and freedoms began right at the time of entry or incorporation into the United States. While the exact form of entry for the three groups differed, in all cases an element of subordination was involved. The most striking instance of forced entry was that of blacks, who were captured, torn from their homelands, transported against their will and sold into slavery. This institution so structured their lives that even after emancipation former slaves were held in debt bondage by the southern sharecropping system (Painter 1976). Equally involuntary was the incorporation of Mexicans residing in territories taken over by United States military conquest. Anglo settlers invaded what is now California, Texas, Arizona, New Mexico and Colorado. When the United States seized the land, native Mexicans living in those areas were reduced to agricultural peons or wage laborers (Barrera 1979). An intermediate case between forced and free entry was that of the Chinese. Their immigration was the result of the economic and political chaos engendered, at least in part, by western colonial intrusion into China (Lyman 1974). Many Chinese men entered the United States as contract laborers so they could support destitute kin in their villages. Under the credit ticket system they signed away seven years of labor in exchange for their passage (Ling 1912).

These unfree conditions of entry imposed special liabilities on racial ethnics. Blacks were not citizens and counted in the census as only three-fifths of a person, Mexicans were defined as second-class citizens, and Chinese were aliens, ineligible for citizenship. All three groups were placed in separate legal categories, denied basic rights and protections and barred from political participation. Thus, they could be coerced, intimidated and restricted to the least desirable jobs, where they were especially vulnerable to exploitation.

The process of incorporation and entry into the labor system in turn had profound effects on the culture and family systems of racial ethnics. Native languages, religion and other ways of life were constrained, destroyed or transformed and kin ties and family authority undermined. As Blauner (1972:66) notes:

> The labor system through which people of color became Americans tended to destroy or weaken their cultures and communal ties. Regrouping and new institutional forms developed, but in situations with extremely limited possibilities.

We are most familiar with assaults on family ties of blacks under slavery due to sale of individuals regardless of kin ties, slave master control over marriage and reproduction, and the brutal conditions of life. Scholars and policy analysts in the past argued that slavery permanantly weakened kin ties and undermined the conjugal household, thereby creating a legacy of family pathology (Frazier 1939; Moynihan 1965). More recently, revisionist historians have argued that slaves resisted assaults on family integrity and managed to maintain conjugal and kin ties to a greater extent than previously believed (Blassingame 1972; Fogel and Engerman 1974; and Gutman 1976). Gutman (1975) found that a large proportion of slave marriages were of long standing and many couples legalized their marriages when given the opportunity to do so after emancipation. Black families showed great strength in the face of assaults on kin networks, though their survival required great struggle and exacted great costs.

Less well known are the assaults on the culture and family lives of Chicanos and Chinese-Americans. In both groups households were broken apart by the demand for male labor. Many Mexican-American men were employed in mining camps and on railroad gangs which required them to live apart from wives and children (Barrera 1979). This was also true for male migrant agricultural workers until the 1880s when the family labor system became the preferred mode (Camarillo 1979). In the case of the Chinese, only prime age males were recruited as workers, and wives and children had to be left behind (Coolidge 1909). The Chinese Exclusion Act of 1882 not only prohibited further entry of Chinese laborers, it also barred resident laborers from bringing in wives and children (Wu 1972; Lyman 1974). This policy was aimed at preventing the Chinese from settling permanently, once their labor was no longer needed.

Given these conditions, what was the work of racial ethnic women in the nineteenth and early twentieth centuries?

RACIAL ETHNIC WOMEN'S WORK IN INDUSTRIALIZING AMERICA

The specific conditions of life experienced by the three groups of women differed. However, the women shared some common circumstances due to their similar positions in the colonial labor system and the similar difficulties the system created for their families. All three groups of women had to engage in constant struggle for both immediate survival and the long term continuation of the family and community. Because men of their groups were generally unable to earn a family wage, women had to engage in subsistence and income producing activities both in and out of the household. In addition they had to work hard to keep their families together in the face of outside forces that threatened their integrity.

Chinese-American Women

Perhaps the least is known about Chinese-American women in the nineteenth and early twentieth centuries. This may be due to the fact that very few working class Chinese women actually resided in the United States then. For most of the period from 1860 to 1920 the ratio of men to women ranged from 13 to 20 males for every female. As late as 1930 there were only 9,742 females aged 10 or over in a population that included 53,650 males of the same age (Glenn 1983). It is estimated that over half of the men had left wives behind in China (Coolidge 1909). Although most of these wives never came to the United States, their lives must be considered as part of the experience of American racial ethnics, for they raised subsequent generations of sojourners who went to America, often with false papers. Little research has been done on what women did in their home villages or how they survived. The available evidence, based partly on some family history interviews I conducted and partly on other sources (Kingston 1977; Hirata 1979), suggests the following: the wife often resided with the husbands' parents or other kin, who received remittances from the husband, acted on his behalf and oversaw the household. Wives took care of children, performed household work under the direction of the mother-in-law, and helped in subsistence farming. Her sexual chastity was carefully guarded, as was her overall behavior. She might never see her husband again or, if lucky, see him once or twice over the course of 20 or 30 years during his rare visits home.

In the late nineteenth century, aside from wives of merchants who were still allowed entry into the United States, the only notable group of Chinese women were prostitutes (Hirata 1979; Goldman 1981). The imbalanced sex ratio created a demand for sexual services. Except for a few years when some women were able to immigrate on their own as free entrepreneurs, Chinese prostitutes were either indentured servants or outright slaves controlled by Chinese tongs or business associations. They had been sold by their parents or kidnapped and involuntarily transported. The controllers of the trade reaped huge profits from buying and selling women and hiring out their services. Women who ran away were hunted down and returned to their captors, usually with the collusion of the police and courts. Unable to speak English and without allies, the women could not defend themselves.

Initially the Chinese were dispersed throughout the West in mining towns, railroad camps and agricultural fields. They were subjected to special penalties, such as a foreign miner's tax in California that rendered it difficult for them to make a living. Finally, during the economic depression of the 1870s the Chinese were forcibly driven out of many areas (Nee and Nee 1972). They congregated in urban Chinatowns, so that by the 1880s the Chinese were a largely urban population. In place of households, the men formed clan and regional associations for mutual welfare and protection (Lyman 1977). By the early 1900s some Chinese men were able, with minimal capital, to establish laundries, restaurants and stores, thereby qualifying as merchants eligible to bring over wives (Lyman 1968). These small businesses were a form of self-exploitation; they were profitable only because all members of the family contributed their labor and worked long hours. Living quarters were often in back of the shop or adjacent to it, so that work and family life were completely integrated. Work in the family enterprise went on simultaneously with household maintenance and child care. First up and last to bed, women had even less leisure than the rest of the family. Long work hours in crowded and rundown conditions took its toll on the whole family. Chinatowns had abnormally high rates of tuberculosis and other diseases (Lee, Lim and Wong 1969).

It is unclear what proportion of women laboring in family laundries and shops were counted as gainfully employed in the census. They were undoubtedly severely undercounted. In any case some sizable proportion of women were employed as independent wage workers. As employees, Chinese women were concentrated in ethnic enterprises because of color bars in white-owned businesses. Nearly half of all gainfully employed women in 1930 worked in jobs that were typical of Chinese enterprise. Out of a work force of 1559, garment operatives and seamstresses accounted for 11.7 percent, sales and trade for 10.6 percent, laundry operatives for 7.3 percent, waitresses for 8.2 percent, and clerical workers for 11.2 percent. The only major form of employment outside the ethnic community was private household service, which accounted for 11.7 percent of Chinese women (U.S. Census 1933; for broad occupational distributions, see Table 1).

Table 1
Occupational Distribution of Employed Black, Chinese-American, Mexican-American and White Women, 10 Years of Age and Over, 1930

Occupation	Black	Chinese	Mexican	White
Professional	3.4	11.3	3.0	16.5
Trade	0.8	15.3	9.0	10.7
Public Service	0.1	0.0	0.1	0.2
Clerical	0.6	11.2	2.6	22.4
Manufacturing	5.5	20.4	19.3	20.0
Transportation	0.1	1.1	0.5	3.1
Agriculture	26.9	1.5	21.2	4.5
Service, (excluding Servants and Laundresses)	35.4	27.6	13.5	20.1
Servants/Laundresses	27.2	11.7	30.8	2.5
Total	100.0	100.1	100.0	100.0

Source: U.S. Bureau of the Census, *Fifteen Census of the United States: 1930, Population*, Volume 5, General Report on Occupations, Chapter 3, Color and Nativity of Gainful Workers. (Washington, D.C.: U.S. Government Printing Office, 1933), Tables 2, 4, and 6.

Mexican-American Women

The information on the work of Chicanas in the late nineteenth century is also sparse. Barrera (1979) suggests that prior to the 1870s Chicano families followed the traditional division of labor, with women responsible for household work and child care. Thus, Mexican-American women worked largely in the home. Under the conditions of life among working class and agricultural families this work was extensive and arduous (Jensen 1981). In rural areas the household work included tending gardens and caring for domestic animals. Many Chicano men were employed in extracting industries which required them to live in work camps and company towns in unsettled territories. If a wife remained behind with the children in the home village, she had to engage in subsistence farming and raise children on her own. If she joined her husband in camp, she had to carry on domestic chores and child rearing under frontier conditions, forced to buy necessities in company stores that quickly used up meager wages. Even in the city the barrios often had no running water, and unsanitary conditions added to women's burdens of nursing the sick (Garcia 1980).

By the 1880s Mexican-American women were increasingly being brought into the labor force. In cities such as Los Angeles, Santa Barbara and El Paso, Chicanas were employed as servants, cooks and laundresses (Camarillo 1979; Garcia 1980). An economic depression in the 1880s forced more women to seek outside wage work, not only in private households, but also as washerwomen in commercial laundries, and as cooks, dishwashers, maids and waitresses in hotels and other public establishments. In this same period women entered the agricultural labor market. Prior to that time prime-age male workers were preferred for seasonal and migratory field work. In the 1880s whole families began to be used, a pattern that accelerated during World War I (Camarillo 1979:91). By the 1920s family labor was common throughout the Southwest. Describing the situation in Colorado, Taylor (1929) noted that landowners felt that families, despite their lower productivity per unit, were preferable because they were a more stable work force that could be counted on to return year after year.

These trends are reflected in occupational patterns of Chicana women. Between 1880 and 1930, they tended to be employed in two main types of situations. A large part of the Chicana work force, 20 percent officially, were employed as farm laborers (Barrera 1979). Many of these were employed as part of the piece rate system in which entire families worked and moved with the crops (Taylor 1937; Fisher 1953; McWilliams 1971). Under this system women had to bear and raise children, cook and keep house, while also working long hours in the field or packing house. Infants accompanied their parents to the fields, and children started working from an early age. Living conditions in migrant camps were extremely harsh. Adults rarely lived past 55 and infant and child mortality was high. Children had no regular schooling because of constant movement and the need for their labor. Schools were geared to fit agricultural schedules and provided minimal training (Taylor 1929). Once into the migrant pattern it was almost impossible for families or individuals to break out.

The second type of employment for Chicanas, primarily those in cities and towns, was in unskilled and semi-skilled "female" jobs. The distribution of jobs varied in different areas of the Southwest, but the most common occupations in all areas were service positions (household servants, waitresses, maids, cooks, and laundry operatives), which accounted for 44.3 percent of all employed Chicanas in 1930, and operatives in garment factories and food processing plants, which together employed 19.3 percent in 1930 (Table 1). The latter industries also employed Anglo women, but Chicanas were given the worst jobs and the lowest pay. They were victims of both occupational stratification and a dual wage system. Their plight was revealed in testimony by employers before the Texas Industrial Welfare System in El Paso in 1919. For example, F. B. Fletcher, a laundry owner representing the owners of the four largest laundries in El Paso testified that almost all the unskilled labor was performed by Mexican women, while the skilled positions as markers, sorters, checkers, supervisors and office assistants went to Anglo women. Further, Mexican women were paid an average of $6.00 a week while Anglo women received $16.55. Fletcher argued that:

> This difference indicates that in this industry, the minimum wage can be fairly fixed for Mexican female help and for the American entirely different and distinct (Garcia 1981:91).

Only by combining their wages with those of husbands and older children could Mexican-American women survive.

Whether engaged in subsistence farming, seasonal migratory labor, agricultural packing, laundry work, domestic service or garment manufacturing, Chicanas had to raise their children under colonized conditions. As part of the continued legal and illegal takeover of land by Anglos in Texas and Colorado from 1848 to 1900, the Chicanos became a conquered people (McLemore 1973, 1980). Defined and treated as inferior, their language and culture became badges of second class status. Through their daily reproductive activities and work women played a critical role not only in maintaining the family, but also in sustaining Mexican-American ways of life.

Black Women

Perhaps more than any other group of women, black women were from the start exempted from the myth of female disability. To be sure, they were exploited on the basis of their gender as breeders and raisers of slaves for plantation owners (Genovese 1974). Their gender also made them liable to a special form of oppression, sexual assault. Nevertheless, their gender did not spare them from hard physical labor in the field (Jones 1984). Hooks (1981) claims plantation owners often preferred women for the hardest field work because they were the more reliable workers. In addition black women did the heavy housework and child care for white women; in that role they were subject to abuse and even physical beatings at the hands of their mistresses. As Angela Davis (1971) notes, under conditions of plantation slavery, staying alive, raising children, and maintaining some semblance of community were forms of resistance.

After emancipation, life for rural blacks remained harsh under the sharecropping system; blacks found themselves held in debt bondage. Hooks (1981) suggests that landowners preferred sharecropping to hiring labor because black women were unwilling to be employed in the fields once slavery was abolished. With sharecropping women's labor could be exploited intensively, since women had to work hard alongside the men in order to pay off the ever-mounting debt to the owner. One observer of black farmers noted that these women:

> . . . do double duty, a man's share in the field, and a woman's part at home. they do any kind of field work, even ploughing, and at home the cooking, washing, milling and gardening (Lerner 1973).

Although there were some independent black farmers, it became increasingly difficult for them to make a living. Jim Crow laws deprived blacks of legal rights and protections, while national farm policies favored large landowners. Independent black farmers were increasingly impoverished and finally driven off the land (Painter 1976).

Aside from farming, the next largest group of black women were employed as laundresses and domestic servants. Black women constituted an exclusive servant caste in the South, since whites refused to enter a field associated with blacks from slave times (Katzman 1978). As servants, black women often worked a 14 to 16 hour day and were on-call round the clock (Brown 1938). They were allowed little time off to carry out their own domestic responsibilities, despite the fact that the majority of black domestics had children of their own. A married domestic might see her children once every two weeks, while devoting night and day to the care of her mistress's children. Her own children were left in the care of husband or older siblings (Katzman 1978). Low wages were endemic. They had to be supplemented by children taking in laundry or doing odd jobs. Many black women testified that they could only survive through the tradition of the service pan — the term for leftover food that was left at the disposal of the colored cook (Lerner 1973: 18).

Manufacturing and white collar jobs were closed to black women, though some of the dirtiest jobs in industry were offered to them. They were particularly conspicuous in southern tobacco factories and to some extent in cotton mills and flour manufacturing. In the cotton mills black women were employed as common laborers in the yards, as waste gatherers and as scrubbers of machinery. The actual manufacturing jobs were reserved for white women (Foner and Lewis 1981). Regarding black women in the tobacco industry, Emma Shields noted in a pamphlet she prepared for the Women's Bureau in 1922:

> Conditions of employment throughout the tobacco industry are deplorably wretched, and yet conditions for Negro women workers are very much worse than those for white women workers... Negro women are employed exclusively in the rehandling of tobacco, preparatory to its actual manufacture. Operations in the manufacture of cigars and cigarettes are performed exclusively by white women workers. Negro women workers are absolutely barred from any opportunity for employment in the manufacturing operations.... It is not unusual to find the white women workers occupying the new modern sanitary parts of the factory, and the Negro women workers in the old sections which management has decided to be beyond any hope of improvement (Quoted in Lerner 1969).

World War I saw increasing migration of blacks to the urban North and, simultaneously, the entrance of blacks into factory employment there. As late as 1910, 90.5 percent of all black women were farm laborers and servants, but between 1910 and 1920, 48,000 black women entered factory work (Lerner 1969). Most were employed in steam laundries, the rest in unmechanized jobs in industry as sweepers, cleaners and ragpickers (Foner and Lewis 1981).

During the entire period from 1870 to 1930 black women, regardless of rural or urban residence, were notable for their high rates of labor force participation, particularly among married women. In 1900, 26.0 percent of married black women were in the labor force compared to 3.8 percent of married white women (Pleck 1979). They thus had to contend with the double day long before this became an issue for a majority of white women. Moreover, although their wages were consistently lower than those of white women, their earnings constituted a larger share of total family income, due to the marginal and low wage employment of black men (Byington 1974). Finally, they had to perform their double duty in the face of poor and crowded living conditions, an educational system that provided inferior schooling for their children, uncertain income and other trials.

RACIAL ETHNIC WOMEN'S WORK IN THE CONTEMPORARY PERIOD

All three groups are predominately urban today, a process that began in the late nineteenth century for the Chinese, during World War I for blacks and after World War II for Chicanos. All have also experienced dramatic changes in occupational distributions since 1930.

Chinese Women Since World War II

The main change in circumstance is for Chinese women is that they were allowed entry to the United States in large numbers for the first time after World War II. Many separated wives were able to join their spouses under the provisions of the Walter-McCarran Act of 1953, and whole family units were able to enter after passage of the liberalized 1965 immigration law (Li 1977; U.S. Department of Justice 1977). Since World War II female immigrants outnumbered males, and the sex ratio of the Chinese population now approaches equality, with the remaining imbalance existing only in the older age categories (U.S. Bureau of the Census 1973). Women who have rejoined spouses or arrived with husbands are adapting to the post-war urban economy by entering the paid labor force. Handicapped by language, by family responsibilities and gender and race discrimination in the skilled trades, both husbands and wives are employed in the secondary labor market — in low wage service and competitive manufacturing sectors. The most typical constellation among immigrant families is a husband employed as a restaurant worker, store helper or janitor and a wife employed as an operative in a small garment shop. The shops are located in, or close to, Chinatowns and are typically subcontracting firms run by Chinese. They often evade minimum wage laws by using an unofficial piece rate system (Nee and Nee 1972).

An examination of the occupational distribution of Chinese-American women reveals a bimodal pattern. In 1970 (Table 2) Chinese women were concentrated in clerical (31.8 percent) and professional white collar work (19.4 percent), and in the operative category (22.5 percent). While the high proportion in white collar fields indicates considerable success by second, third and fourth generation women, generational mobility may be less than these figures suggest, since many professionals are actually recent immigrants of gentry origin rather than working class Chinese-Americans who have moved up. Working class Chinese women continue to be relegated to operative jobs in the garment trade. What Chinese women of all classes share is a higher than average rate of labor force participation (U.S. Bureau of the Census 1973).

Table 2
Occupational Distribution of Black, Chinese-American, Mexican-American and White Women in the United States, 1970

Occupation	Black	Chinese-American	Mexican-American	White*
Professional	11.3	19.4	6.4	16.6
Managerial	1.4	3.8	1.9	4.0
Sales	2.6	5.1	5.7	8.1
Clerical	20.7	31.8	25.9	37.0
Craft	1.4	1.2	2.3	1.8
Operative	16.5	22.5	25.8	13.7
Laborers (excluding farm)	1.5	0.9	1.8	0.9
Farming (including farm labor)	1.2	0.5	4.0	0.7
Service	25.5	12.8	20.6	15.3
Private Household Workers	17.8	2.0	5.5	1.9
TOTAL	99.9%	100.0%	99.9%	100.0%

*Category comprised of all women minus black and Spanish origin.

Sources: U.S. Bureau of Census, *Subject Reports of the 1970 Census:* PC (2)-1B, *Negro Population,* Table 7; PC (2)-1C, *Persons of Spanish Origin,* Table 8; PC (2)-1F, *Japanese, Chinese, and Filipinos in the United States,* Table 22 (Washington, D.C.: U.S. Government Printing Office, 1973) and U.S. Bureau of the Census, Census of the Population: 1970, *Detailed Characteristics of the Population,* Final Report, PC (1)-D1, *U.S. Summary,* Table 226, (Washington, D.C.: U.S. Government Printing Office, 1973).

Post-war economic changes have undercut family enterprises such as laundries and small stores, so that working class families today typically engage in dual wage earning. They encounter difficulties due to the long work hours of parents and crowded and run-down housing. Working mothers are responsible for not only the lion's share of domestic chores, but often raise their children almost single-handedly. Husbands are frequently employed in the restaurant trade, which requires them to be at work from 11 in the morning until 10 in the evening or even midnight. Thus, they are rarely around while their children are awake. The women's own work hours are often prolonged because they leave work during the day to cook meals or pick up children. They make up the time by returning to the shop for evening work or by taking materials home to sew at night (Ikels and Shang 1979). Their energy is entirely absorbed by paid employment and domestic responsibilities. The one ray of light is their hope for their children's future.

Mexican-American Women

The Chicano population is still characterized by continued migration back and forth between Mexico and the United States. In 1970, 16 percent of the resident population in the United States was foreign-born (Massey 1982:10). Not surprisingly, Chicanos remain concentrated in the Southwest, with 78 percent residing in California and Texas in 1979 (Pachon and Moore 1981). Contrary to their image as rural people, four out of five (79 percent) resided in metropolitan areas. In line with the urban shift has been a sharp reduction in the percentage of men and women engaged in agriculture. The proportion of women employed as farm workers fell from 21.2 percent in 1930 to 2.4 percent by 1979 (Tables 1 and 3). Due to the mechanization of agriculture which caused a sharp decline in the total number of farm workers, however, Chicana women constituted a higher *proportion* of women in agricultural labor in 1979 than they did in 1930. For those still involved in migrant labor, conditions remain harsh, with extensive exploitation of children, despite child labor laws (Taylor 1976).

Table 3
Occupational Distribution of Employed Black, Mexican-American and White Women, 16 Years Old and Over, 1979

Occupation	Black*	Mexican-American	White
Professional	14.2	6.4	16.4
Managerial	3.4	3.5	6.8
Sales	3.1	5.1	7.4
Clerical	29.0	31.1	35.9
Crafts	1.2	1.8	1.9
Operatives	15.3	25.0	11.0
Laborer (excluding farm)	1.6	1.3	1.3
Farming (including farm labor)	0.8	2.4	1.3
Service (including private household)	31.5	23.4	18.1
TOTAL	100.1	100.0	100.1

*Category consists of "black and other."

Source: U.S. Bureau of the Census, *Current Population Reports*, Series P-20, No. 354, *Persons of Spanish Origin in the United States: March 1979* (Washington, D.C.: U.S. Government Printing Office, 1980), Table 10. U.S. Bureau of Labor Statistics, *Employment and Earnings*, 27, No. 1 (1980), Table 22.

The period from 1930 to the present saw a steady rise in the occupational status of Mexican-Americans. As with other racial ethnic groups the occupational dispersion of Chicanos is related to labor shortages during wars, especially World War II. In the post-war period, rising numbers of Chicanas found employment in clerical and sales jobs, though they still lagged behind white women, especially in sales. The lower rates in white collar jobs were matched by over-representation in blue collar and service occupations. Mexican-American women were concentrated in operative jobs, principally in garment factories, laundries and food processing plants, which together accounted for 25.0 percent of their employment in 1979 (Table 3). These enterprises tended to be small competitive firms that paid minimum wages and were often seasonal. Another 23.4 percent of all employed Chicanas were in service jobs, including private household work.

Mexican-American women have traditionally had among the lowest rates of labor force participation among racial ethnic women (Almquist and Wehrle-Einhorn 1978). However, in the 1970s Chicanas rapidly entered the labor market, so that by 1980 their rates were similar to that of whites, though lower than those for black and Asian-American women (Massey 1982). The lower rates may be related to two other circumstances which usually depress employment: education and family size. Chicanas have the lowest education levels of the three groups and also have the largest number of children. These factors in turn mean that when Chicanas are in the labor force, they are at a great disadvantage. In 1976 nearly one-third (31. 5 percent) of all employed Chicanas had 8 years of education or less; comparable figures for blacks was 14.1 percent and for whites 7.6 percent (U.S. Department of Labor 1977).

In short, though Mexican-American women have achieved greater employment parity with Anglo women, they continue to have lower educational levels and heavier family burdens. In addition, they encounter racial barriers to white collar employment.

Black Women

Black women have also experienced shifts in employment since World War II. The post war period saw a great decline in domestic service as a major category of women's work. Because black women were so concentrated in it they have shown the most dramatic decline. Whereas in 1940, three out of five (59.5 percent) employed black females were in domestic service, by 1960 that proportion had dropped to a little over a third (36.2 percent), and by 1980 to one out of fourteen (7.4 percent) (U.S. Census 1943, 1973; Westcott 1982). Partially replacing service in private households has been service employment in public establishments, particularly in food service and health care, where the number of low level jobs has proliferated. These jobs accounted for 25.4 percent of black female employment in 1980, compared to 16.0 percent of white women (Westcott 1982).

U.S. Census data (Table 3) show that black women are over-represented in the operatives category, where 15.3 percent were employed in 1979, in contrast to 11.0 percent of whites. As in the past, there is a stratified labor market and a dual wage system. Baker and Levenson (1975a) examined the careers of black, Hispanic and white graduates of a New York City vocational high school, and found that black and Hispanic women were disproportionately tracked into lower paying operative jobs in the garment industry, while better paying jobs outside the garment industry were reserved for white graduates. Years later the difference in pay and mobility was even greater as black and Hispanic women were progressively disadvantaged (Baker and Levenson 1975b).

The last barrier to fall was white collar employment. A dramatic increase in professional-technical, clerical and sales employment took place after 1950. By 1979, the former accounted for 14.2 percent of black female employment, the latter two together for 32.1 percent. Differences remained, however, in that white collar employment accounted for over two-thirds of white women's jobs, but less than half of black women's employment. In addition, within white collar jobs, black women were concentrated in lower level jobs. For example, in 1980 black women constituted 10.8 percent of all clerical workers, but they made up over 15 percent of such lower level positions as file clerks, mail handlers, key punchers and office machine operators, and less than 6 percent of more skilled positions as secretaries, bank tellers and bookkeepers (Glenn and Tolbert 1985). In effect, though black women have experienced desegregation at the level of broad occupations, they have been re-segregated at the finer level of detailed job categories.

Other measures also show continued disadvantage for black women. They have a 50 percent higher unemployment rate and somewhat lower earnings (U.S. Department of Labor 1977). The largest gap is in terms of median family income, due to discrimination against black men. Even with the mother in the labor force, the median family income for black families with children under 18 years old was $14,461 in 1975 compared to $17,588 for similar white families (U.S. Department of Labor 1977). Even though they could not raise family income to white levels by being employed, black women's wages made a bigger difference to overall family income. The gap between blacks and whites was even greater if the mother was not employed: the median for black families without mothers in the labor force was $8,912 compared to $14,796 for whites (U.S. Department of Labor 1977). Regardless of income level, the economic fate of the black conjugal family rested on an economic partnership between men and women. Moreover, even among relatively affluent black families, the need to combat racism was a theme that infused daily life and absorbed the energy of parents in socializing their children (Willie 1981). Women's role as nurturers required them to combat the daily assaults on their children's self-esteem and to be vigilant in protecting them from psychic injury.

IMPLICATIONS FOR FEMINIST ANALYSIS

The history of racial-ethnic women's work in the United States reveals their oppression not just as women, but also as members of colonized minorities. As members of colonized minorities, their experiences differed fundamentally from those used to construct Marxist-feminist theory. Thus, concepts within that framework require reformulation if it is to generate analyses that are inclusive of racial ethnic women. I will briefly examine three concepts in Marxist-feminist theory that need to be redefined to take into account the interaction of race and gender. These are the separation between private and public spheres, the primacy of gender conflict as a feature of the family, and the gender-based assignment of reproductive labor.

The growing separation of public and private spheres with industrialization was central to early Marxist-feminist analyses of women's oppression under capitalism. However, recent historical and comparative research has called into question the extent to which private and public constituted separate and bounded spheres for all classes and groups. Scholars note that in industrializing societies working class women engage in many income-earning activities, such as doing piece-work at home, taking in boarders, or trading on the informal market, which cannot be easily categorized as private or public (Jensen 1980). Moreover, industrial wage work and family life have been found to interact in complex ways, so that, for example, women's family roles may include and overlap with their roles as workers (Harevan 1977). The examination of racial ethnic women's work adds to the critiques growing out of this research.

The nature of the split, and the extent to which women are identified with the public sphere, seems to vary by class and ethnicity, and differences among groups in women's relationship to public and private spheres needs to be examined. Like many other working class women, racial ethnic women were never out of public production. They were integrated into production in varying ways. Black women were involved in agriculture and waged domestic service from the time of slavery. Chinese-American women frequently engaged in unpaid labor in family enterprises, where there was little separation between public and private life. Mexican-American women were initially more confined to household based labor than the other groups, but this labor included a great deal of actual production, since men's wages were insufficient to purchase the necessities of life. Thus, a definition of womanhood exclusively in terms of domesticity never applied to racial ethnic women, as it did not to many working class women.

Where racial ethnic women diverge from other working class women is that, as members of colonized minorities, their definition as laborers in production took precedence over their domestic roles. Whereas the wife-mother roles of white working class women were recognized and accorded respect by the larger society, the maternal and reproductive roles of racial ethnic women were ignored in favor of their roles as workers. The lack of consideration for their domestic functions is poignantly revealed in the testimony of black domestics cited earlier, who were expected to leave their children and home cares behind while devoting full-time to the care of the white employer's home and children. Similarly, Chinese and Mexican-American women and children were treated as units of labor, capable of toiling long hours without regard to their need for private life. This is not to say that racial ethnic women themselves did not see themselves in terms of their family identities, but that they were not so defined by the larger society, which was interested in them only as workers.

Another area of divergence is in the scope of what is included in the so-called private sphere. For racial ethnic women the domestic encompasses a broad range of kin and community relations beyond the nuclear family. Under conditions of economic insecurity, scarce resources and cultural assault, the conjugal household was not self-sufficient. Racial and ethnic peoples have historically relied on a larger network of extended kin, including fictive relatives and clan associations, for goods and services. This means that women's reproductive work in the "private" sphere included contributions to this larger circle, within which women took care of each others' children, loaned each other goods, and helped nurse the sick. Beyond the kin network women's work extended to the ethnic community, with much effort being expended in support of the church, political organizing and other activities on behalf of "the race" (*la raza*). Women are often the core of community organizations, and their involvement is often spurred by a desire to defend their children, their families and their ways of life (Ellesar et al 1980; Gilkes 1981; Yap 1983). In short, race, as organized within a colonial labor system, interacted with gender (patriarchy) and class (capitalism) to determine the structure of private and public spheres and women's relationship to these spheres.

A second aspect of Marxist-feminist theory that requires reformulation in light of race is the concept of the family as a locus of gender conflict. The Marxist-feminist analysis of the family is a response to traditional approaches that treat the family as an entity with unitary interests; in particular, it challenges the functionalist view of the division of labor as complementary rather than exploitative. By focusing on inequality — the economic dependence of women and the inequitable division of labor — some Marxist-feminists see members of the family as divided in their interests, with conflict manifested in a struggle over resources and housework (e.g. Hartmann 1981b; Thorne 1982; for a contrasting view, see Humphries 1977). In this view the conjugal family oppresses women; the liberation of women requires freeing them from familial authority and prescribed roles.

Examination of racial ethnic women's experiences draws attention to the other side of the coin — the family as a source of resistance to oppression from outside institutions.[3] The colonial labor system made it impossible for men of color to support their families with their labor alone and therefore ruled out economic dependence for women. The issue for racial ethnic women was not so much economic equality with husbands, but rather the adequacy of overall family income. Because racial ethnic men earned less, women's wages comprised a larger share of total family income in dual wage-earner families. In the case of family enterprises, common among Asian-Americans, family income depended on the labor of men and women equally. Thus, in both dual wage-earner and small business families, men and women were mutually dependent; dependence rarely ran in one direction.

As for the division of household labor, Marxist-feminist analysis sees it as benefitting men, who receive a greater share of services while contributing less labor. In the racial ethnic family, conflict over the division of labor is muted by the fact that institutions outside the family are hostile to it. The family is a bulwark against the atomizing effects of poverty and legal and political constraints. By transmitting folkways and language, socializing children into an alternative value system, and providing a base for self-identity and esteem, the family helps to maintain racial ethnic culture. Women do a great deal of the work of keeping the family together and teaching children survival skills. This work is experienced as a form of resistance to oppression rather than as a form of exploitation by men. In the colonial situation the common interest of family members in survival, the maintenance of family authority, and the continuation of cultural traditions are emphasized. This is not to say that there are no conflicts over the division of labor but struggles against outside forces take precedence over struggles within the family. Thus, the racial stratification system shapes the forms of intra-familial and extra-familial conflict, and determines the arenas in which struggle occurs.

A third concept in Marxist-feminist theory that would benefit from consideration of race oppression is the very useful notion of reproductive labor. Following an early brief formulation by Marx, Marxist-feminists identified two distinct forms of labor, production and reproduction (Sokoloff 1980). Reproduction refers to activities that recreate the labor force: the physical and emotional maintenance of current workers and the nurturing and socializing of future workers. In other words, people as well as things have to be produced. Although both men and women engage in production, women are still the ones who carry out most of the reproduction. In large part this is because much reproductive work remains at the household level, which is women's domain. In considering the situation of racial ethnic women, it is useful to recognize the existence of a racial as well as a sexual division of reproductive labor. Historically, racial ethnic women have been assigned distinct responsibilities for reproductive labor.

In the early industrial period racial ethnic and immigrant women were employed as household servants, thereby performing reproductive labor for white native families. The labor of black and immigrant servants made possible the woman belle ideal for white middle class women. Even where white immigrant domestics were employed, the dirtiest and most arduous tasks, laundering and heavy cleaning — were often assigned to black servants. There was a three-way division of labor in the home, with white middle class women at the top of the hierarchy, followed by white immigrants, with racial ethnics at the bottom. In the late industrial period, as capital took over more areas of life, reproductive activities also were increasingly taken out of the household and turned into paid services which yielded profits (Braverman 1974). Today, such activities as caring for the elderly (old age homes) preparing food (restaurants and fast food stands) and providing emotional support (counselling services) have been brought into the cash nexus. As this has happened, women have been incorporated into the labor force to perform these tasks for wages. Within this female-typed public reproduction work, however, there is further stratification by race. Racial ethnic women perform the more menial, less desirable tasks. They prepare and serve food, clean rooms and change bed pans, while white women, employed as semi-professionals and white collar workers, perform the more skilled and administrative tasks. The stratification is visible in hospitals, where whites predominate among registered nurses, while the majority of health care aides and housekeeping staff are blacks and latinas. Just as white women in tobacco manufacturing benefitted by getting cleaner and more mechanized jobs by dint of the dirty preparation work done by black women, so white women professionals enjoy more desirable working conditions because racial ethnic women perform the less desirable service tasks. The better pay white women receive also allows them to purchase services and goods that ease their reproductive labor at home.

This point leads to a final consideration. It may be tempting to conclude that racial ethnic women differ from white women simply by the addition of a second axis of oppression, namely race. It would be a mistake though, not to recognize the dialectical relation between white and racial ethnic women. Race, gender and class interact in such a way that the histories of white and racial ethnic women are intertwined. Whether one considers the split between public and private spheres, conflict within the family and between the family and outside institutions or productive and reproductive labor, the situation of white women has depended on the situation of women of color. White women have gained advantages from the exploitation of racial ethnic women, and the definition of white womanhood has to a large extent been cast in opposition to the definition of racial ethnic women (Palmer 1983). Marxist-feminist theory and the internal colonialism model both recognize white men as the dominant exploiting group; however it is equally important to emphasize the involvement of white women in the exploitation of racial ethnic people and the ways in which racial ethnic men have benefitted from the even greater exploitation of racial ethnic women.

NOTES

1. The term racial ethnic designates groups that are simultaneously racial and ethnic minorities. It is used here to refer collectively to blacks, latinos and Asian-Americans, groups that share a legacy of labor exploitation and special forms of oppression described in the body of this paper. It is offered as an alternative to more commonly used designations, viz. minority groups, people of color and Third World minorities, each of which is problematic at some level.
2. Sokoloff (1980) points out that whereas earlier Marxist feminists viewed gender oppression as a by-product of capitalism, what she calls "later" Marxists feminists developed the concept of patriarchy as a separate system that pre-dated capitalism and that interacts with class exploitation under capitalism.
3. This general line of argument may also apply to white working class families. However, I would assert that there were crucial differences in the historical experiences of white working class and racial ethnic families. The family system of the white working class was not subject to institutional attacks (such as forced separation) directed against black, Chicano and Chinese families. Moreover white working class women were accorded some respect for their domestic roles.

REFERENCES

Acosta-Belen, Edna (ed.). 1979. *The Puerto Rican Woman*. New York: Praeger.

Almquist, Elizabeth M. 1979. *Minorities, Gender and Work*. Lexington, MA: D.C. Heath.

Almquist, Elizabeth M. and Juanita L. Weherle-Einhorn. 1978. The Doubly Disadvantaged: Minority Women in the Labor Force. In, *Women Working*, Ann H. Stromberg and Shirley Harkess (eds.). pp. 63–88. Palo Alto, CA: Mayfield Publishing.

Baca-Zinn, Maxine. 1982. Review Essay: Mexican American Women in the Social Sciences. *Signs* 8:259–272.

Baker, Sally Hillsman and Bernard Levenson. 1975a. Job Opportunities of Black and White Working-Class Women. *Social Problems* 22:510–532.

______ 1975b. Earnings Prospects of Black and White Working Class Women. Unpublished Paper.

Barrera, Mario. 1979. *Race and Class in the Southwest*. Notre Dame, IN: University of Notre Dame Press.

Barrera, Mario, Carlos Muñoz and Charles Ornelas. 1972. The Barrio as an Internal Colony. In, *Urban Affairs Annual Review* 6, Harlan Hahn (ed.).

Blassingame, John. 1972. *The Slave Community*. New York: Oxford University Press.

Blauner, Robert. 1972. *Racial Oppression in America*. New York: Harper and Row.

Braverman, Harry. 1974. *Labor and Monopoly Capital*. New York: Monthly Review Press.

Brown, Carol. 1981. Mothers, Fathers and Children: From Private to Public Patriarchy. In, *Women and Revolution: A Discussion of the Unhappy Marriage of Marxism and Feminism*, Lydia Sargent (ed.). pp. 239–269. Boston: South End Press.
Brown, Jean Collier. 1938. *The Negro Woman Worker*. Women's Bureau Bulletin 165. U.S. Department of Labor. Washington, D.C.: U.S. Government Printing Office.
Byington, Margaret. 1974. *Homestead: The Households of a Milltown*. Pittsburgh, PA: University of Pittsburgh Press.
Camarillo, Albert. 1979. *Chicanos in a Changing Society*. Cambridge, MA: Harvard University Press.
Carmichael, Stokely and Charles V. Hamilton. 1967. *Black Power: The Politics of Liberation in America*. New York: Vintage.
Cheng, Lucie and Edna Bonacich. 1984. *Labor Immigration Under Capitalism: Asian Immigrant Workers in the United States Before World War II*. Berkeley, CA: University of California Press.
Clark, Kenneth. 1965. *Dark Ghetto*. New York: Harper and Row.
Coolidge, Mary. 1909. *Chinese Immigration*. New York: Henry Holt.
Davis, Angela Y. 1971. Reflections on the Black Woman's Place in the Community of Slaves. *The Black Scholar* 2:3–15.
———. 1981. *Women, Race and Class*. New York: Random House.
Dill, Bonnie Thornton. 1979. The Dialectics of Black Womanhood. *Signs* 4:543-555.
Easton, Barbara. 1976. Industrialization and Femininity: A Case Study of Nineteenth-Century New England. *Social Problems* 23:389–401.
Elesser, Nan, Kyle MacKenzie and Yvonne Tixier y Vigil. 1980. *Las Mujeres: Conversations from a Hispanic Community*. Old Westbury, NY: The Feminist Press.
Fisher, Lloyd. 1953. *The Harvest Labor Market in California*. Cambridge, MA: Harvard University Press.
Fogel, William and Stanley Engerman. 1974. *Time on the Cross*. Boston: Little Brown.
Foner, Philip S. and Ronald L. Lewis. 1981. *The Black Worker: A Documentary History From Colonial Times to the Present*, Vol. VI, *The Era of Post-War Prosperity and the Great Depression, 1920–1936*. Philadelphia: Temple University Press.
Frazier, E. Franklin. 1939. *The Negro Family in the United States*. Chicago: University of Chicago Press.
Garcia, Mario T. 1980. The Chicana in American History: The Mexican Women of El Paso, 1880–1920 — A Case Study. *Pacific Historical Review* 49:315–337.
———. 1981. *Desert Immigrants: The Mexicans of El Paso, 1880–1920*. New Haven: Yale University Press.
Genovese, Eugene. 1974. *Roll, Jordan, Roll*. New York: Pantheon.
Gilkes, Cheryl. 1982. Successful Rebellious Professionals: The Black Woman's Professional Identity and Community Commitment. *Psychology of Women Quarterly* 6:289–311.
Glenn, Evelyn Nakano. 1983. Split Household, Small Producer and Dual Wage Earner: An Analysis of Chinese American Family Strategies. *Journal of Marriage and the Family* 45:35–46.
Glenn, Evelyn Nakano and Charles M. Tolbert II. 1985. Technology and Emerging Patterns of Stratification for Women of Color: Race and Gender Segregation of Computer Occupations. Revised version of a paper presented at the Women, Work and Technology Conference, University of Connecticut.
Goldman, Marion. 1981. *Goldiggers and Silverminers*. Ann Arbor, MI: University of Michigan Press.
Gutman, Herbert G. 1975. Persistent Myths About the Afro-American Family. *Journal of Interdisciplinary History* 6:181-210.
———. 1976. *The Black Family in Slavery and Freedom*. New York: Pantheon.
Harevan, Tamara. 1977. Family Time and Industrial Time: Family and Work in a Planned Corporation Town, 1900–1924. In, *Family and Kin in Urban Communities: 1900–1930*. New York: New Viewpoints.
Hartmann, Heidi. 1976. Capitalism, Patriarchy and Job Segregation by Sex. *Signs* 1:137–169.
———. 1981a. The Unhappy Marriage of Marxism and Feminism: Towards a More Progressive Union. In, *Women and Revolution: A Discussion of the Unhappy Marriage of Marxism and Feminism*, Lydia Sargent (ed.). pp. 1–41. Boston: South End Press.

_____. 1981b. The Family as a Locus for Gender, Class and Political Struggle: The Example of Housework. *Signs* 6(5):366–394.

Hirata, Lucie Cheng. 1979. Free, Indentured and Enslaved: Chinese Prostitutes in Nineteenth Century America. *Signs* 5:3–29.

Hooks, Bell. 1981. *Ain't I a Woman: Black Women and Feminism*. Boston: South End Press.

Humphries, Jane. 1977. Class Struggle and the Persistence of the Working Class Family. *Cambridge Journal of Economics* 1:241–258.

Ikels, Charlotte and Julia Shang. 1979. The Chinese in Greater Boston. Interim Report to the National Institute of Aging.

Jensen, Joan M. 1980. Cloth, Butter and Boarders: Women's Household Production for the Market. *Review of Radical Political Economics* 12(2):14–24.

_____. 1981. *With These Hands: Women Working on the Land*. Old Westbury, NY: Feminist Press.

Jones, Jacqueline. 1984. *Labor of Love, Labor of Sorrow: Black Women, Work and the Family from Slavery to the Present*. New York: Basic Books.

Katzman, David. 1978. *Seven Days a Week: Women and Domestic Service in Industrializing America*. New York: Oxford University Press.

Kessler-Harris, Alice. 1982. *Out to Work*. New York: Oxford University Press.

Kim, Elaine. 1983. *With Silk Wings: Asian American Women at Work*. San Francisco: Asian Women United of California.

Kingston, Maxine Hong. 1977. *The Woman Warrior*. New York: Vintage.

Lee, L. P., A. Lim and H. K. Wong. 1969. *Report of the San Francisco Chinese Community Citizens' Survey and Fact Finding Committee*. (Abridged Edition). San Francisco: Chinese Community Citizens' Survey and Fact Finding Committee.

Lerner, Gerda. 1969. The Lady and the Mill Girl: Changes in the Status of Women in the Age of Jackson. *American Studies* 10:5–14.

_____. 1973. *Black Women in White America: A Documentary History*. New York: Vintage.

Li, Peter S. 1977. Fictive Kinship, Conjugal Ties and Kinship Claim Among Chinese Immigrants in the United States. *Journal of Comparative Family Studies* 8(1):47–64.

Ling, Pyan. 1912. The Causes of Chinese Immigration. *Annals of the American Academy of Political and Social Sciences* 39:74–82.

Lyman, Stanford. 1968. Marriage and Family Among Chinese Immigrants to America, 1850–1960. *Phylon* 29(4):321–330.

_____. 1974. *Chinese Americans*. New York: Random House.

_____ 1977. Strangers in the City: The Chinese in the Urban Frontier. In, *The Asian in North America*. Santa Barbara, CA: ABC Clio Press.

Massey, Douglas S. 1982. *The Demographic and Economic Position of Hispanics in the United States: 1980*. Report to the National Commission for Employment Policy. Philadelphia: Population Studies Center, University of Pennsylvania.

McLemore, Dale. 1973. The Origins of Mexican American Subordination in Texas. *Social Science Quarterly* 53:656-670.

_____. 1980. *Racial and Ethnic Relations in America*. Boston: Allyn Bacon.

McWilliams, Carey. 1971. *Factories in the Field*. Santa Barbara, CA: Peregrine Publishers.

Melville, Margarita B. (ed.). 1980. *Twice a Minority: Mexican American Women*. St. Louis: C. V. Mosby.

Mirande, Alfredo and Evangelina Enriquez. 1979. *La Chicana: The Mexican American Woman*. Chicago: University of Chicago Press.

Mora, Magdelina and Adelaida R. Del Castillo (eds.). 1980. *Mexican Women in the United States: Struggles Past and Present*. Los Angeles: Chicano Studies Publications.

Moore, Joan W. 1970. Colonialism: The Case of Mexican Americans. *Social Problems* 17:463–472.

Moynihan, Daniel Patrick. 1965. The Negro Family: The Case for National Action. Washington, D.C.: U.S. Government Printing Office. Prepared for the Office of Policy Planning and Research.

Nee, Victor and Brett deBary Nee. 1972. *Long Time Californ'*. New York: Pantheon Books.

Pachon, Harry P. and Joan W. Moore. 1981. Mexican Americans. *Annals, American Academy of Political and Social Science* 454:111–124.

Painter, Nell Irvin. 1976. *Exodusters: Black Migration to Kansas After the Reconstruction*. New York: Norton.
Palmer, Phyllis Marynick. 1983. White Women/Black Women: The Dualism of Female Identity and Experience in the United States. *Feminist Studies* 9:151–170.
Pleck, Elizabeth H. 1979. A Mother's Wages: Income Earning Among Married Italian and Black Women, 1896–1911. In, *A Heritage of Her Own: Toward a New Social History of American Women*, Nancy F. Cott and Elizabeth H. Pleck (eds.). pp. 367–392.
Rodgers-Rose, La Frances (ed.). 1980. *The Black Woman*. Beverly Hills, CA: Sage Publications.
Saxton, Alexander. 1971. *The Indispensable Enemy: Labor and the Anti-Chinese Movement in California*. Berkeley: University of California Press.
Sokoloff, Natalie. 1980. *Between Money and Love*. New York: Praeger.
Sterling, Dorothy. 1979. *Black Foremothers: Three Lives*. Old Westbury, NY: The Feminist Press.
Taylor, Paul S. 1929. Mexican Labor in the United States: Valley of the South Platte, Colorado. *University of California Publications in Economics* 6(2):95–235.
———. 1937. Migratory Farm Labor in the United States. *Monthly Labor Review* (March): 537–549.
Taylor, Ronald. 1976. *Sweatshops in the Sun*. Boston: Beacon Press.
Thorne, Barrie. 1982. Feminist Rethinking of the Family: An Overview. In, *Rethinking the Family: Some Feminist Questions*, Barrie Thorne and Marilyn Yalom (eds.). pp. 1–24. New York: Longman.
Tsuchida, Nobuya (ed.). 1982. *Asian and Pacific American Experiences: Women's Perspectives*. Minneapolis: Asian/Pacific American Learning Resource Center.
U.S. Bureau of the Census. 1933. Fifteenth Census of the United States:1930, *Population*, vol. 5: *General Report on Occupations*, Chapter 3, Color and Nativity of Gainful Workers. Washington, D.C.: U.S. Government Printing Office.
———. 1973. *Census of the Population: 1970*. Subject Reports, Final Report PC(2)1G. *Japanese, Chinese, and Filipinos in the United States*. Washington, D.C.: U.S. Government Printing Office.
———. 1933. *Fifteenth Census of the United States: 1980*. Population, Volume II: General Report, *Statistics by Subject*. Washington, D.C.: U.S. Government Printing Office.
U.S. Department of Justice. 1977. *Immigration and Naturalization Service Annual Report*. Washington, D.C.: U.S. Department of Justice.
U.S. Department of Labor. 1977. *U.S. Working Women: A Databook*. Bureau of Labor Statistics, Bulletin 1977. Washington, D.C.: U.S. Government Printing Office.
Weinbaum, Batya and Amy Bridges. 1979. The Other Side of the Paycheck: Monopoly Capital and the Structure of Consumption. In, *Capitalist Patriarchy and the Case for Socialist Feminism*, Zillah R. Eisenstein (ed.). New York: Monthly Review Press.
Welter, Barbara. 1966. The Cult of True Womanhood: 1820–1860. *American Quarterly* (Summer):151–174.
Westcott, Diane Nilsen. 1982. Blacks in the 1970's: Did They Scale the Job Ladder? *Monthly Labor Review* (June):29–32.
Willie, Charles. 1981. *A New Look at Black Families*. Bayview, NY: General Hall.
Wu, C. 1972. *"Chink": A Documentary History of Anti-Chinese Prejudice in America*. New York: Meridian.
Yap, Stacey G. Y. 1983. *Gather Your Strength Sisters: The Careers of Chinese American Women Community Workers*. Unpublished Ph.D. Dissertation, Boston University.

Accepted 15 September 1985

Doing "Women's Work": The Grey Nuns at Fort Totten Indian Reservation, 1874-1900

by Susan C. Peterson*

One day in 1872, two women dressed in somber black and grey garments and dark-colored cloaks got off the train in Jamestown, Dakota Territory. These women were sisters Charlebois and Rose Clapin, Sisters of Charity, more commonly known as the Grey Nuns, from Montreal. Their community had been approached by Major William Forbes, Indian Agent at the recently established Devils Lake agency, to assist in operating a school for the reservation inhabitants. After being refused by several American religious orders, Forbes had turned to the Canadian congregation because he was somewhat familiar with their activities; he had two cousins who were members. In 1871, Forbes had visited the motherhouse in Montreal and asked Superior General Elizabeth Dupuis to send some Sisters to Dakota Territory to start a school among the Indians of the Devils Lake reservation.[1]

Because Mother Dupuis was reluctant to agree with Forbes' request without more information about the location, she decided to have two Sisters, who were already planning an official visit to Grey Nuns at St. Boniface, Manitoba, take the train from St. Paul to Jamestown, where the railroad ended. She assumed that Forbes would have the Sisters escorted the remaining ninety

* The author thanks the University of North Dakota Faculty Research Committee for support during the preparation of this article. A different version of this paper was presented at the 19th Annual Northern Great Plains History Conference at Bismarck, ND, on September 28, 1984.

[1] *St. Michael's Indian Mission, 1874-1974* (Martin, SD: Blue Cloud Mission Press, 1974), n.p.

miles to the agency. Unfortunately, communication was poor, and the agent did not prepare for the Sisters' intended arrival in Jamestown because he was unaware of their plans.[2] After they realized that nobody was to accompany them to the reservation, Sisters Charlebois and Clapin tried to hire transport from Jamestown; nobody would help them. People in the frontier settlement feared the Indians because warriors were rumored to go outside the reservation and kill anyone they might chance to meet. Thus, the two Sisters had no alternative other than to return to Montreal, unable to make their visit to inspect the location of the school.[3]

In spite of this inauspicious beginning, two years later the Grey Nuns did accept Major Forbes' invitation. A small party left the Motherhouse in the summer of 1874, but this time it was larger and included Father Louis Bonin of Montreal as escort. Others in the group were Sister Clapin, who would serve as Superior; Sister Auxelie Lajemmerais, Assistant; Sister Celene Allard; Sister Philomene Drapeau; and Miss Rose Labelle, a Franciscan novice who joined the group to assist the Grey Nuns with their work on the reservation. The Sisters had letters of instruction from Forbes, who planned to meet them in St. Paul and guide them to the Agency.[4] After the Grey Nuns arrived in St. Paul, they spent more than a month waiting for their quarters at the agency to be completed and receiving rudimentary instruction in the Sioux language. They departed for Jamestown in late October and were met this time by Major James McLaughlin, assistant to Forbes. An early winter snow storm slowed the group's progress, but they finally arrived at the agency on November 2.

The mission was located six miles from the Agency headquarters, and the convent/school building was still uncompleted. The Sisters saw bags of grain on the kitchen floor, dust, and scraps of lumber everywhere; but they immediately cleaned the structure. They next prepared their school for the opening of classes.[5]

[2] Sister Celine Allard, "Chronicles, Our Lady of Sorrows Mission, Fort Totten, ND," 1874-1882, p. 2, Grey Nuns Provincial House Archives, St. Boniface, Manitoba (hereafter cited GNPA).

[3] *St. Michael's Indian Mission*; "Chronicles," p. 2.

[4] "Chronicles," pp. 3, 4.

[5] *Ibid.*, pp. 5-14.

The story of the Grey Nuns at Fort Totten Indian Reservation illustrates several elements in Indian policy and women's history. The Sisters were agents of the government "Peace Policy" and its attempt to assimilate Indians into white society; the policy was strongly supported by Office of Indian Affairs leaders in the la: quarter of the nineteenth century. The nuns' work as teachers and health care providers on the reservation also demonstrates that turn-of-the-century society identified separate spheres for men and women. The Sisters' work among the Devils Lake Sioux was accepted, even encouraged, as long as it fell within the two categories traditionally associated with "women's work": nurturing of children and caring for the sick. Within this larger role, however, the Sisters did engage in activities not generally associated with women and especially not associated with Catholic Sisterhoods.

President Ulysses S. Grant is credited with the creation of the government Peace Policy toward Native Americans in the 1870's. This program started with placing the government's Office of Indian Affairs in cooperation with the private Board of Indian Commissioners. This board, made up of Protestant denominational leaders, hoped that its religious orientation would combat abuses and corruption long associated with reservation administration.[6] The Board and the Office of Indian Affairs together accelerated their attempts to move Indian people toward the goal of assimilation into white society during the early years of the decade; the two groups planned together to replace Indian culture and beliefs with "American" religion (Christianity), "American" language (English), and "American" occupations (Farming). These reformers identified a system of reservation schools that combined religious, linguistic, and vocational training as the best possible place to begin the assimilation process, and as a result the mission schools received additional government funding in order to expand their in-

[6] Francis Paul Prucha, *American Indian Policy in Crisis: Christian Reformers and the Indians, 1865-1900* (Norman: University of Oklahoma Press, 1976), pp. 31-46.

The Grey Nuns served the people of the Fort Totten Reservation without fail after establishing a school in 1875. Due to the remote location of their institution and the characteristic modesty of the order, the nuns were rarely photographed. This picture, however, apparently depicts the "Sisters' school" in the old Indian Agency buildings near Fort Totten; the photograph was probably taken in 1883 or 1884 after fire destroyed the original school at St. Michael's mission. Though the people are not identified, the nun at the center of the group of children is thought to be Sister Rose Clapin, who was Mother Superior of the mission from the time of its establishment. Note the uniform worn by the children attending the school.

—*State Historical Society of North Dakota Collection*

fluence on already existing reservations and on new reservations in the West.[7]

In order to eliminate denominational feuding, the Board assigned specific churches to specific reservations and asked the appropriate religious organizations to nominate agents and missionaries to oversee operations. There was apparent favoritism displayed in the assignments, however, and several denominations complained. For example, among the reservations located in Dakota Territory, only Standing Rock and Devils Lake were allocated to the Catholic Church. The agents on both reservations set about bringing in Catholic missionaries to cooperate in the assimilation of tribal members. For this reason Major Forbes was anxious to bring the Grey Nuns to Devils Lake agency.[8]

The school that the Sisters opened on the Devils Lake reservation in February 1875 was a manual labor facility that combined the rudiments of reading, writing, and arithmetic with training in manual or industrial vocations for boys and in the domestic arts for girls. This course of study, it was believed, provided more successful assimilation than would one stressing only academic subjects; moreover, supervision by missionaries would ensure a widescale conversion to Christianity by reservation-dwellers. The school was a boarding school because reformers assumed that students needed extended separation from their families and camp life in order for assimilation to take hold. Another reason for designation as a boarding school was the long distances between settlements and the mission headquarters.[9]

The curriculum followed at the Grey Nuns' industrial boarding school in the early years consisted of academic classes in reading, writing, spelling, and arithmetic. The manual labor courses included gardening, milking, and care of stock for boys; girls learned cooking, sewing,

[7] *Ibid.*, p. 53.

[8] Roy Meyer, *History of the Santee Sioux* (Lincoln: University of Nebraska Press, 1967), p. 228; Prucha, *Indian Policy in Crisis*, p. 53. The Peace Policy was in effect until 1881 when reservations were opened to all denominations.

[9] Prucha, *Indian Policy in Crisis*, pp. 265-270.

laundry, and general housekeeping.[10] Students were examined at the end of the school year by the agent, and the Sisters received favorable comments about their students' progress from his reports.[11]

Good relations with the agent were essential to the Sisters' welfare at the mission school, and they were fortunate to enjoy excellent cooperation from Major Forbes. After Forbes' death in 1875, Major James McLaughlin served as agent until his transfer to Standing Rock Indian Reservation in 1881. McLaughlin was instrumental in continuing the school in spite of low enrollments during the facility's first years, and he wrangled with Office of Indian Affairs officials in Washington on the Sisters' behalf. McLaughlin's successor, Major John Cramsie, ably guided the Sisters' activities until his resignation in the 1890's.[12]

The problems that the Sisters confronted from the start of their first school had to do with language, educating the older boys, and agency rations. Because the Sisters were not well versed in the Sioux language, or even English for that matter (some Sisters only spoke French), they required an interpreter during the first year of school operation. They hired a mixed-blood female to help with the classes and also to instruct the Sisters in the Sioux language. They hoped that an ability to speak Sioux would attract more Indians to Mass as well as facilitate instruction in the school.[13]

Schooling for adolescent boys was a thorny question for the Sisters. In their agreement with Agent Forbes they promised to operate a school for girls of all ages and for boys up to age twelve. This meant that almost from the school's first year a sizeable segment of the reservation's male population did not have access to schooling. Because the Sisters firmly refused to accept older boys as students, Agent Forbes asked Father Bonin, the Sisters' confessor, to handle that age group; he also refused. In

[10] Eccole St. Michel, ND Historique, GNPA; "Chronicles," p. 33, 34.

[11] "Chronicles," p. 33.

[12] Meyer, pp. 231-244; "Chronicles," pp. 45-52. Also see Louis Pfaller, OSB, "Forging of an Indian Agent," *North Dakota History*, 34-1 (Winter, 1967), pp. 62-76.

[13] "Chronicles," pp. 20, 21.

Fort Totten dominated the reservation that the Grey Nuns served. Established in 1867, the post presented a serene, whitewashed appearance by 1878. Troops from the fort patrolled the reservation and the International boundary area.

—*State Historical Society of North Dakota Collection*

1878 Agent McLaughlin solved the problem by securing the services of Benedictine monks Father Claude Ebner and Brother John Apke through the assistance of Abbot Martin Marty, OSB, who had been assigned to oversee operations on both Catholic reservations in Dakota Territory by the Bureau of Catholic Indian Missions. The Benedictines took over the manual training and academic classes for the older boys in a separate school built near the mission church and the Grey Nuns' school.[14]

A third problem that the Sisters encountered early in their school's operations concerned the issuing of rations. They subsisted on rations from agency supplies from the beginning of their stay on the reservation, and it was with dismay that Mother Clapin read a notice from the Office of Indian Affairs in 1877 that this practice must not continue. Because their funds were so low and because she did not know how her community could pay for the rations they received, Mother Clapin considered ending the Sisters' relationship with the mission school and returning to Montreal. Fortunately Agent McLaughlin interceded on the Sisters' behalf with government officials, and a compromise was reached. Subsequently, the government deducted the cost of rations from the Sisters' wages, but at the same time their pay was increased enough to cover the added expense.[15]

In spite of the uncertainties and difficulties of the Grey Nuns' early years at the St. Michael's Mission school, by the early 1880's they entered what appeared a period of stability for their facility. They had solved immediate problems, and they had seen enrollment rise to nearly one hundred students by 1880. The number of Sisters at the mission had increased from five to eight, and the new agent, Major Cramsie, seemed cooperative. The Sisters were entitled to look to the future with satis-

[14] *St. Michael's Indian Mission;* "Historique;" "Chronicles," p. 57. Abbot Martin Marty became Bishop of Dakota Territory in 1879.

[15] Meyer, p. 233; "Chronicles," p. 33; Letter from Rev. J.B.A. Brouillet to Major John McLaughlin, Agent, Devils Lake, January 6, 1880, Bureau of Catholic Indian Missions, Archives, Memorial Library, Marquette University, Milwaukee, Wis. (hereafter cited BCIM), Series 1, Box 3, Folder 10.

faction, but their optimism did not last long. Disaster struck on March 16, 1883, when their entire two-story convent/school building was completely destroyed by fire.[16]

After the catastrophe, the Sisters and their students set up temporary quarters in the recently completed older boys' new school, while the Brothers and their charges returned to the old log building that had been their first quarters. This temporary arrangement lasted for two years until the Sisters' new convent/school was completed in 1885.[17]

Aside from serving as teachers, the Grey Nuns also provided essential health care to reservation dwellers. They opened their convent/school to ailing Indians and operated an infirmary under the direction of Sister Auxelie Lajemmerais. Lajermmerais was recognized as Agency Physician because the agency was without medical services other than those of the doctor employed at the nearby fort. The government sent medicines directly to the mission so that Lajammerais could dispense them and compile reports for the Indian office. She provided this service entirely without remuneration. In fact, the agent and the Bureau of Catholic Indian Missions director both recognized Lajemmerais' service as a financial savings to the government. Because an Agency Physician was entitled to a salary of $1,400 per year the Bureau of Catholic Indian Missions intended to "keep Sister Lajemmerais in charge of the Medical Department and thus save the agency the doctor's pay, which, with proper approval, could be used to build and support a hospital."[18]

Although a hospital was not constructed, the Sisters cared for the sick, treated accident victims, and dispensed medicines in their infirmary which occupied the entire

[16] "Chronicles," pp. 66, 125; "Index Alphabetique," GNPA.

[17] "Chronicles," pp. 125-134; *St. Michael's Indian Mission*. The old log building had originally served as part of the first Fort Totten military post.

[18] "Chronicles," pp. 21, 35-38, 54, 59, 61, 71; letter from Agent Paul Beckwith to Commissioner of Indian Affairs E.P. Smith, December 30, 1875, BCIM, Series 1, Box 3, Folder 8; letter from Rev. J.B.A. Brouillet, Catholic Commissioner of Indian Missions, to Agent Beckwith, Nov. 19, 1875, BCIM, Series 1, Box 3, Folder 8.

The first military post at Fort Totten served the Indian agency and religious schools after it was abandoned by the army. In the years 1883-1885, it became a school for older boys while buildings were constructed to replace the original mission at St. Michael. This school was operated by Benedictine monks.

—*State Historical Society of North Dakota Collection*

first floor under the convent/school building. As the years passed, Sister Lajemmerais found it difficult to care for both out-patients and patients staying at the infirmary; she suggested to agent Cramsie in the early 1880's that he retain a physician for the Indians. Lajemmerais reasoned that the agency had access to the military doctor only for emergencies, and she wished to close the infirmary because the Sisters who worked there were not being paid for this assistance. Furthermore, the infirmary was especially time-consuming. Not wanting to lose Lajemmerais' services for reservation-dwellers, Cramsie left the decision up to them. Their deliberations proved unnecessary, however, because the fire in 1883 destroyed the entire building, thus abolishing the infirmary and the medicines it held.[19] The agency thereby lost not only its school, but its "hospital" as well.

The second school that the Grey Nuns operated on the Devils Lake reservation was completed in 1885, was located approximately a mile from the fort, and was overcrowded from the first.[20] When the School Inspector made his annual visit in 1886, he informed Agent Cramsie that the school needed to be enlarged. Cramsie got permission to add two wings and thus expand facilities for the school's manual training curriculum.[21] Other than this comment about overcrowding, subsequent inspectors gave the Sisters' operation high evaluations. However, such was not always the case for the older boys' school which moved from the old log structure into its new building when the Sisters' school was completed.[22]

Curriculum and instruction expanded in the years that the Sisters' school was located in the new building. In her annual report to Agent Cramsie, Mother Clapin described the students' schedule as follows: class hours went from 8:00 a.m. to 10:30 a.m., and from 1:30 p.m. to

[19] "Chronicles," pp. 21, 80, 81.
[20] Sister Philomene Drapeau, "Chronicles," pp. 181-210. Sister Drapeau took over writing the Chronicles from Sister Allard in 1883.
[21] *Ibid.*, p. 214.
[22] *Ibid.*, p. 159, 162, 166.

4:00 p.m., with classes in vocal music three times a week. She listed five grades studying reading, spelling, multiplication, geography, and grammar in the morning, as well as catechism, writing, and arithmetic in the afternoon. For manual labor the larger girls worked in the laundry two days a week and in the kitchen a week at a time. In sewing, several of the girls were "quite proficient at making and mending clothing. . . and very good at 'fancy work.'"[23] Because boys only stayed at the Sisters' school until they were twelve years old, their manual training was not very extensive until they transferred to the Benedictine priests' school. The Sisters did supervise the young boys in simple tasks like carrying wood and water, driving cattle, and working in the garden. Until the building's second wing was added in the late 1880's, conditions remained crowded. There were ninety children studying in a building that was only comfortable for fifty, and Mother Clapin enlisted aid from the Bureau of Catholic Indian Missions in getting the second addition built.[24]

After the older boys moved into their new building in 1885, Agent Cramsie and Father Jerome Hunt appealed to the Sisters to open a second infirmary in the industrial school located near the site of the Sisters' first school for students and reservation-dwellers. In 1887 Sister Lajemmerais and two other Sisters agreed to operate the infirmary as well as cook and clean for students at the school and care for the nearby church. Unfortunately, this second infirmary operated for little more than two years as a result of a misunderstanding about the Sisters' duties between Father Hunt, Superintendent of the boys' school, and the Grey Nuns. He wanted the Sisters to devote less time to visiting the sick and dispensing medicines and more time to domestic chores at the school. Because relations between the Sisters and Father Hunt were strained, Major Cramsie offered a solution whereby the overcrowding at the Sisters' school and the need for medical services could be addressed. He proposed that

[23] Letter from Mother Clapin to Agent Cramsie, August 1884, "Ft. Totten Correspondence, 1871-1897, 1901," GNPA.

[24] *Ibid.*

the office of Indian Affairs build a new, larger, government boarding school for students of both schools and that the current boys' school building be remodeled into a hospital.[25]

Agent Cramsie's plan to build a school large enough to accommodate older boys and their industrial training requirements included provisions for the Sisters to continue teaching the female students and younger boys, as they had been doing since 1875. Thus he discharged the Grey Nuns from responsibility for the infirmary at the boys' school and invited them to open an infirmary in the new government school; but Sister Lajemmerais refused. Because the new school and infirmary would be closely supervised by the government, she feared that she would lose too much autonomy. The Sisters closed their infirmary at St. Michaels in August of 1889, thus ending their fifteen years as health care providers on the reservation.[26] However, their activities in education continued for many years.

By the 1880's, Grant's Peace Policy and the practice of awarding government contracts to religious denominations entrusted with educating and assimilating Indian children were under attack from several Protestant groups; the Grey Nuns' school, being a Catholic operation, underwent intense scrutiny from government officials as a result. Their contract was administered by the Bureau of Catholic Indian Missions, an agency founded to supervise Catholic mission work on the reservations and to lobby in Washington, D.C., for mission interests,[27] but correspondence between the Bureau and the Grey Nuns seldom refers to the controversy raging between Protestant and Catholic groups in the nation's capital. The upshot, however, was that the system of contract schools on reservations was phased out in favor of government-operated boarding schools. On the Devils

[25] "Chronicles," pp. 181-210.
[26] *Ibid.*, p. 214.
[27] Prucha, *Indian Policy in Crisis*, p. 57. See Francis Paul Prucha, *The Churches and the Indian Schools* (Lincoln: University of Nebraska Press, 1979) for a detailed treatment of the contract controversy.

Lake reservation, Fort Totten was abandoned by the military in 1890 and its buildings were turned over to the Indian Service for operation of a school. The Grey Nuns were retained as civil service employees, and they continued to hold classes for female students and young boys in their building located a mile from the fort.[28]

The Sisters' day-to-day life altered very little when they became government workers, and the minor changes had little impact on the school. Girls of all ages and boys under twelve years old continued to receive instruction from the Grey Nuns, and older boys were taught by government employees transferred to the school from assignments elsewhere. The new school was supervised by William Canfield,[29] who instituted the Indian Department course of study and oversaw frequent examinations of the school by the Indian Department School Inspector. The Sisters' *Chronicle* noted that the school was found to be satisfactory "each time,"[30] and the Sisters were praised for their efforts. Superintendent Canfield wrote, in a letter to Bishop John Shanley of Fargo in 1897, that "the Sisters are doing well and are held in high regard by the Indians of the reservation." He also commented that it "would be difficult to procure the services of workers who would do as well" as they did.[31]

As government employees, the Grey Nuns did see some changes. For example, they received the same wage scale as workers at other federal Indian boarding schools. The following chart lists the positions that the Sisters

[28] Francis Paul Prucha, *The Churches and the Indian Schools*, pp. 3-8, 26, 27; letter from Sister Margaret Page to Joseph Stephen, BCIM, Series 1, Box 28, Folder 19; letter from Bishop John Shanley to John Noble, Secretary of the Interior, June 12, 1890, BCIM, Series 1, Box 28, Folder 19; Letter from Archbishop John Ireland to John Noble, Secretary of the Interior, September 11, 1890, BCIM, Series 1, Box 28, Folder 19. U.S. Department of Interior, Office of Indian Affairs. *Annual Report of Commissioner of Indian Affairs to the Secretary of the Department of Interior, 1892*, p. 686.

[29] Meyer, p. 240; "Historique;" letter from William Canfield to Acting Commissioner of Indian Affairs R.V. Belt, October 21, 1890, "Ft. Totten Correspondence, 1871-1897, 1901," GNPA, p. 3.

[30] "Chronicles," p. 219.

[31] Letter from William Canfield to Bishop John Shanley, February, 1897, "Ft. Totten Correspondence, 1871-1897, 1901," GNPA.

filled and their salaries for the years 1890 and 1900, the last year of this study:

Position	Name	1890 Salary	1900 Salary
1 principal teacher	Sr. Margaret Page	$1000.00	600.00
2 teachers	Sr. Mary Hart, Mary Franklin	1200.00	980.00
1 matron	Sr. Celine Allard	720.00	500.00
1 assistant matron	Sr. Mary Dorsey	300.00	400.00
1 seamstress	Sr. Mary Tiffault	500.00	400.00
1 cook	Sr. Alodia Arsennault	500.00	400.00
1 assistant cook	Sr. Mary Jeanotte	300.00	
1 laundress	Sr. Mary Renaud	540.00	480.00

For the most part, the Grey Nuns' school continued as it had previously; the Sisters performed tasks assigned by the Superintendent in much the same manner as prior to the time when the government assumed control of the school. The Sisters were expected to conform to the Rules for Indian Schools and follow the Course of Study prescribed by the Indian office, using textbooks furnished by the government. However, Superintendent Canfield and Agent Cramsie were careful to protect the Grey Nuns' community privacy as a religious order, and the Sisters successfully adapted to the minor changes in their situation.[32]

There were, nevertheless, some difficulties. Due to the continuing debate in Washington, D.C., about Catholic workers in Indian boarding schools, questions were raised about the Sisters' language and citizenship. In the early 1890's, Commissioner of Indian Affairs T.J. Morgan sent a letter to Superintendent of Indian Schools Daniel Dorchester in which he stressed the need to ascertain whether or not teachers at government schools spoke English at all

[32] "Chronicles," pp. 219, 220; "List of Authorized Positions, Grey Nuns School: Sept., 1890," GNPA; "Indian Industrial School, Fort Totten, 1900," GNPA; letter from Acting Commissioner R.V. Belt to William Canfield, October 21, 1890, "Ft. Totten Correspondence, 1871-1897, 1901," GNPA, pp. 1, 2. US Department of Interior, Office of Indian Affairs, *Annual Report of the Commissioner of Indian Affairs to the Secretary of the Department of Interior, 1900*, p. 713.

The Grey Nuns' church and school complex at Fort Totten eventually developed into a substantial establishment. The large brick school buildings were constructed in phases after 1885 and stood until 1926, when fire destroyed the school.

—*Courtesy Archives of the Grey Nuns, Winnipeg, Manitoba*

times,[33] and Dorchester's School Inspector was careful to observe the language used by the Grey Nuns at Fort Totten. While two of the nine Sisters employed spoke English poorly, neither was directly involved with students; but Major Cramsie's and the School Inspector's correspondence showed concern that the nuns "murder the language."[34] Cramsie encouraged the Sisters to improve their English and thereby dispense with the need for an interpreter. This was the Inspector's only complaint about the school; in fact, he commented that the school seemed to run well, had good attendance, and had students who profited from a good education.[35]

As the tension between Protestant and Catholic groups in Washington, D.C., continued, the subject of religious groups' citizenship received much attention; the Grey Nuns' origin as a Canadian Sisterhood thus became another possible problem for the Order's members who were civil service employees. In April 1899, Father Hunt received a letter from Rev. Joseph Stephan of the Bureau of Catholic Indian Missions that advised of potential trouble if the Grey Nuns' citizenship came under scrutiny. He suggested that the Sisters apply for naturalization papers without waiting for permission from their Motherhouse; he reasoned that this declared intention to become citizens would avert any threat to the Sisters' positions as civil servants. Stephan further stated that the Grey Nuns would be dismissed if they failed to give notice of their intention to become American citizens.[36]

From the time of their arrival in Dakota Territory in 1874, the Grey Nuns had felt no compunction to become naturalized; however, Mother Clapin and Sister Lajemmerais had individually received citizenship papers in case it might become necessary for them as representatives of the Order. As a result of Rev. Stephan's letter, all Sisters who were Canadian began the process of natur-

[33] Prucha, *Churches and Indian Schools*, p. 8; letter from T.J. Morgan, Commissioner of Indian Affairs, to Daniel Dorchester, Superintendent of Indian Schools, October 12, 1891, "Ft. Totten Correspondence, 1871-1897, 1901," GNPA.

[34] "Chronicles," p. 216.

[35] *Ibid.*

[36] Letter from Father Joseph Stephan of BCIM to Father Jerome Hunt, May 17, 1899, BCIM, Series 1, Box 39, Folder 7.

A priest, Father Louis Bonin, accompanied the Grey Nuns to Fort Totten. Although he left in 1878, other priests continued to teach on the reservation. Though this photograph is unidentified as to place or date, it reveals a scene familiar to those who attended schools operated by religious orders on the reservations; the priest is Father Paul, longtime instructor at St. Michael's Mission.

—*Courtesy Archives of the Grey Nuns, Winnipeg, Manitoba*

The Sisters of Charity (The Grey Nuns) taught, nursed, and served the people of the Fort Totten Reservation for many decades. This portrait, taken about 1920, represents the latter-day successors to the small band led by Sister Rose Clapin who came to work on the reservation in 1874.

—*Courtesy Archives of the Grey Nuns, Winnipeg, Manitoba*

alization. Three Sisters were from the eastern United States and were exempt from possible dismissal. The Grey Nuns applied for citizenship in nearby Devils Lake and thereby weathered this last storm over their status as government employees.[37]

By 1900 the Grey Nuns of Fort Totten Indian Reservation had experienced a quarter-century of change and growth in their position as agents of federal Indian education policy. Their first appearance on the reservation in 1874 came about because President Grant's Peace Policy assigned Devils Lake to the Catholic Church. As the Peace Policy was modified in the 1880's, the Sisters continued as contract mission school teachers and as health care providers. In 1890 they became government school employees, and once again their position altered. Through all of these changes, however, the Grey Nuns remained faithful to their primary purpose as agents of assimilation. They offered a Christian example and education in practical industrial and domestic arts along with operating infirmaries for reservation inhabitants. Their response to the challenge of educating children of a different culture was admirable in the face of official apprehension about Catholic religious practices. They performed as teachers and nurses with determination and flexibility despite the common belief that Catholic Sisterhoods lived cloistered, sheltered, or suspicious lives. The Grey Nuns' labors fell within the nineteenth century view of women's work; nevertheless, their early years on the Dakota frontier present a story of adaptability and persistence not generally associated with that history. Their early success portended well for the next seventy-five years of the history of the Grey Nuns at Fort Totten Indian Reservation.

[37] "Chronicles," pp. 73, 265, "List of Naturalized Sisters," GNPA.

Crossing Ethnic Barriers in the Southwest: Women's Agricultural Extension Education, 1914–1940

JOAN M. JENSEN

The educational programs of the Agricultural Extension Service were, inevitably, reflective of the public policies and practices of the various agencies involved in delivering those programs. Created in 1914 as part of the progressive reform movement in the United States, the Agricultural Extension Service (AES) was involved in both the idealism of that movement and the realities of American life that committed it in most areas to rigid gender and ethnic segregation. Because AES was both national and local, it became the crossroads where public policies of various levels of government met, clashed, and changed. At the national level, officials attempted to maintain systematic policies; at the local level agents attempted to adapt them to local conditions. The success of these programs must, in the last analysis, be judged by how they worked at the local level, educating the poorest, female ethnic women. Educating ethnic women and girls in rural communities in New Mexico, the focus of this paper, can thus be seen as more than just an isolated example of how public policy was implemented. How well agents crossed the ethnic barriers in the Southwest as well as other areas of the country

JOAN M. JENSEN is Professor of History and head of the History Department at New Mexico State University.

is one key to judging how well agricultural policy functioned in the United States.

This paper looks at the way in which the New Mexico AES (NMAES) dealt with the question of ethnicity in its educational programs for women during its first twenty-six years, from 1914 to 1940. I use the counties of Doña Ana in southern New Mexico and Santa Fe in northern New Mexico to test the success of AES in delivering educational programs to non-English speaking, Hispanic communities. My criteria for success are: involvement of ethnic women in the program, ability to adapt national and state programs to local economic and social conditions and needs of these constituents, the amount and quality of transfer of technology occurring, and number of rural people able to remain on the land. Measured by these criteria, despite the ethnic and gender discrimination inherent in the program, agents were quite successful in Santa Fe in delivering an educational program to Hispanic constituents. In Doña Ana agents were almost totally unsuccessful.

All New Mexico counties shared certain geographical and demographic characteristics that made educational programs difficult to implement. The region in 1914, indeed to a great extent today, is large, sparcely populated, and divided by mountains and deserts that are practically impassable during parts of the summer and winter. While much of the farming population was, and is, concentrated in the valley of the Rio Grande, a fertile swath that cuts through the center of the state from north to south, other rural communities are scattered along the Pecos and Gila Rivers as well as numerous smaller rivers, in mountain valleys, and on the eastern plains. In 1910, a few years before the AES began, over 80 percent of New Mexico women were living in these rural areas, on farms or ranches. In 1940, almost 70 percent still lived there.[1]

Economically, most rural women in New Mexico were poor. Some were so poor they could not afford the few cents necessary to buy commercial patterns or material necessary for clothing proj-

1. For a more detailed study of the demographic changes between 1900 and 1940 see Joan Jensen, "New Mexico Farm Women, 1900–1940," in Robert Kern, ed., *Labor in New Mexico: Strikes, Unions and Social History Since 1881* (Albuquerque: University of New Mexico Press, 1983), 61–81.

ects. In 1940 almost half of the state's eighty-four thousand farm women lived on farms under fifty acres and over three-fifths on farms under 175 acres worth just over four thousand dollars each. Over one-third lived on subsistence farms producing primarily for their own use and almost three-forths lived on farms that produced less than one thousand dollars worth of products to use or sell.[2]

In 1914 at least 60 percent of all rural women were Hispanic. Most read and spoke only Spanish. By 1940 the number of rural women who spoke and read English was greatly increased but most women still were not completely comfortable using English literary sources. Moreover, Hispanic women had their own separate cultural traditions. Their strongest ties were to kin and village community. Mother-daughter and neighbor ties were particularly strong. Public activities usually revolved around religious holidays and there were few nonreligious, community-based, public activities. Women did not often accompany men on trips to town, nor did they migrate to work there. Women took care of the small subsistence farms while men and children, usually boys, worked off farm to bring in a cash income. There was, however, a tradition of village cooperation, frequently kin-based, with labor exchange among women common.[3]

The Hispanic culture was well-adapted to deal with changing conditions. Communities had successfully adapted to major economic and political changes since their arrival as colonists in the late-seventeenth and early-eighteenth centuries, primarily through family-based change. There was also a tradition of distrust of outsiders, developed over several centuries. Some outsiders thought they understood the problems of rural people and wanted to help; others wanted to exploit. Sometimes the difference between the two types seemed minor as rural people attempted to develop survival strategies that would allow their families to remain on the land.

2. Ibid., 74–75.

3. These generalizations are drawn specifically from the annual reports of Fabiola Cabeza De Baca for 1930 to 1940 for Rio Arriba and Santa Fe counties. New Mexico College of Agriculture and Mechanical Arts, State College, Agricultural Extension Service, Annual Reports, New Mexico, National Archives, Microcopy, Reels 12–18, 20–22, 25 (NMCAAES, Annual Reports). Hispanic families in southern New Mexico probably differed in some respects but there are no similarly detailed reports for them.

Staff officials recognized the need to recruit bilingual agents early in the new program. Few Americans knew Spanish, however, and administrators had no strategy for training Spanish-speaking agents except through the regular college agricultural and home economics programs. Few rural people had the necessary education to complete these programs nor the economic and social support necessary to do so. The early home demonstration staff was small, underpaid, and undervalued. Men assumed that agricultural agents could organize home demonstration activities but that home demonstration agents could not organize agricultural activities; that if only one agent could be funded, that one should be a male agricultural agent. On this premise, both the AES administrators at the land grant college and the county officials agreed. If the population was mixed, the agent was almost always Anglo. Only in overwhelmingly Spanish-speaking counties, where county commissioners stipulated that a Hispanic agent be supplied in their funding agreements, were agents Spanish-speaking. Before 1929, except for World War I, home demonstration agents served in only two to four of the state's thirty-one counties. From 1929 to 1937, only eight to sixteen home demonstration agents served and not until 1938–1940 were there seventeen to twenty agents in the state. Of these, only one Hispanic agent, Fabiola Cabeza de Baca, was employed for any length of time, from 1929 to 1940.[4]

World War I provided a small exception to this poor record of support for home demonstration agents before 1929. The state voted emergency funds during the war and these, together with expanded federal funds, allowed the AES to hire extra home demonstration agents. During 1917 Gertrude Espinosa was hired with emergency funds, and in February 1918 a Spanish-speaking Anglo agent was added. Espinoza began to translate bulletins on cooking, sewing, and poultry raising into Spanish. She spoke to parents before organizing children, something she knew was absolutely necessary. During 1918 these two agents gave 162 demonstrations in Spanish in seven counties and visited over three

4. For the early period see Joan M. Jensen, "Canning Comes to New Mexico: Women and Agricultural Extension, 1914–1919," *New Mexico Historical Review* 57 (October 1982): 351–86.

hundred homes of Hispanic women. Informal canning demonstrations went on in the homes of women where, as one agent wrote: "the native women come with black shawls over their heads, roll their cigarettes and smoke as they stand about the table where the demonstrator is working." The first statewide Mother-Daughter Congress, held during the war, featured demonstrations in Spanish as well as English. Only a miniscule part of the Hispanic majority was reached, however, and after the war funds for Spanish educational programs for women were dropped. The few male Hispanic agents retained after the war provided some guidance, primarily for girls and boys in clubs. The female Hispanic majority was largely unreached during the 1920s even in the few counties that did retain a demonstration agent.[5]

The assumption that agricultural agents were more important than home demonstration agents, and that no one person could be trained to perform both tasks led to instability that greatly weakened the home demonstration program. Sarah Van Vleck, the only Spanish-speaking agent, took over Doña Ana county in 1918 at the end of the war. She stayed for seven years but after her term, neither a permanent nor a Spanish-speaking agent replaced her. The next agent stayed for only two years. Her successor stayed for over four years but when she left in June 1932, she was not replaced until June 1937. During these five years, no work was done with women. Girls were enrolled in cooking or clothing clubs but little attention given to their work. It took the new agent over a year to reorganize the women, and then in two years, she left. Thus, the program suffered from the lack of an ongoing program for English-speaking women as well as for the Spanish-speaking majority.[6]

With the exception of Van Vleck, none of the agents spoke Spanish or gave much time to organizing the Spanish-speaking majority. A few girls had been organized into clubs since World War I. At least one woman in San Miguel, Señora Rodriguez, described by the agent as the "most cultured and influential lady in the town," became a club leader. In Old Mesilla an Anglo

5. Ibid.
6. Information from NMCAAES, Annual Reports, NA T876, Reels 4–19, 21–22, 24.

teacher organized Hispanic girls there into an award-winning club that canned, did needlework, and gave concerts. When it came to organizing women during the 1920s, however, the agents chose to work primarily through the local Farm Bureau rather than directly with farm families, and the Farm Bureau was organized primarily of Anglo agricultural developers. As Van Vleck explained in 1924, "While natives and Mexicans make up about 50 percent of the population, the American people take the lead in all agricultural affairs, and determine the policies to be pursued."[7]

Doña Ana County had a Hispanic majority but not as large a majority as in the northern counties. Hispanics had lost political control in Doña Ana by the late nineteenth century and they had lost much of their land as well. The census of 1910 showed that two-thirds of the farm families were still Spanish surnamed, however, almost one-half of them born in New Mexico, another one quarter naturalized citizens who had immigrated from Mexico, and one quarter Mexican aliens who frequently rented land and worked as farm laborers. Most of the Anglo minority were citizens but almost all had migrated to the county from other parts of the United States. This Anglo rural minority had successfully engineered the development of Elephant Butte Dam in the early twentieth century. When it was completed in 1915, it resulted in high water assessments that many poor Hispanic farm families could not pay. Anglos also successfully pushed for other public projects in the county that raised the tax base on land. The state land grant college and thus the state AES was located in Doña Ana County, but the college, the AES, and the Farm Bureau were dominated by Anglos. All three groups considered Anglo male farmers with their agricultural development projects as their primary constituents.[8]

The decision to work through the Farm Bureau simplified the work of the overworked, underpaid, HDAs. It also meant, how-

7. Annual Report for 1924, NMCAAES, Annual Reports, NA T876, Reel 6.

8. U.S., Manuscript Census for 1910. Based on a systematic random sample of the farms in the county. For a more detailed account of the effect of the Elephant Butte Dam project on loss of land by Hispanics see Joan M. Jensen, "Farm Families Organize Their Work: New Mexico, 1900–1940," (Unpublished paper presented at the New Mexico Family and Community History conference, Albuquerque, New Mexico, July 14–16, 1983).

ever, that they would spend most of their time working with the Anglo women already organized in the Farm Bureau, most of whom assumed their roles to be narrowly domestic. No complete records of the county Farm Bureau exist for the period after 1917, when it was formed. A liberal and quite progressive Jewish–New Mexican businessman headed the Farm Bureau during these years. He lobbied successfully for federal projects favorable to western farmers, including irrigation. However, no Spanish surnames appear on county lists of male or female officers. Only once do the records of the agent note meeting at the home of a Hispanic woman for a demonstration. One meeting was held with blacks in Vado in 1927, and a food preservation meeting for "colored girls" took place in 1937, but except for these references, one would not know that the rural majority was Hispanic or that there was at Vado a vigorous community of black farmers who would later organize a branch of the Southern Farm Tenants Union. There seemed to be a total lack of understanding of Hispanic women and what was needed to engage them in the programs. As the agent reported in 1927: "There are a great many Mexicans in the valley but little work has been done with them, tho they are always invited to the meetings."[9]

One agent did initiate an outreach program in the northern part of the county in 1922. With the help of the state Director of Child Welfare, Dr. Janet Reid, Van Vleck began a study of nutrition of Hispanic children. A state nurse spent six months surveying health conditions with Van Vleck and they found an appallingly high infant mortality rate—an estimated 50 percent in the village of Salem—and widespread malnutrition. Few families had cows and adults fed children what they ate—tortillas, beans, and chili. The two women took action at once. A dairy donated goats that they loaned to the mothers of the most malnourished children. With the aid of the Red Cross the women obtained milk supplements for the schools. They organized clubs to can food and cook

9. Meeting at home of a "Mexican who could not even speak English," and with blacks at Vado noted in Annual Report for 1927 and "Colored girls" mentioned in Annual Report for 1937, NMCAAES, Annual Reports, NA T876, Reels 9 and 19. The only known Farm Bureau records are in the Freudenthal Family Papers, Box 10, Folders 2, 3, Rio Grande Historical Collections, New Mexico State University Library.

school lunches. They also succeeded in getting the county to hire a full-time health physician and a nurse. The nurse then took over the health work in rural areas.[10]

These projects, however, were undertaken for the poorest rural population, those who lived in *jacals* (chinked wood huts) in the *bosque* (brush around the river), and who were really below subsistence. As for those Hispanic farm women who were struggling to continue subsistence farming, or to improve their farms, there was no explicit mention of attempting to reach them. The strict gender segregation of clubs may have contributed to this lack of contact. Poorer families needed to have projects that contributed to the income of the family. Most Anglo farmers, as the HDAs repeatedly noted, were well educated and fairly prosperous. While the prosperity of Anglo farmers was probably exaggerated by agents, the comments did reflect the fact that those women and children who were organized into clubs had different interests from poorer Hispanic farm women and daughters. Anglo daughters could afford material for sewing and cooking projects; many Hispanic daughters could not. The agent did not encourage mixed vegetable or poultry clubs, thus girls tended to be organized only in cooking and sewing clubs. When the new agent arrived in 1940, she noted that at Mesquite "the Anglo and Spanish-American girls were separated because they did not work well together." When this new agent tried to visit the Hispanic Club, she drove all over Mesquite before finally giving up. "We have hopes of locating the girls and their leader early and really doing some work with them next year," she reported. The old agent had managed to work with one group of Hispanic women on sewing for three months but when few women showed up during the summer the new agent disbanded the group. The new agent apparently did not understand why these women might not be attending during the summer and abandoned further attempts at education.[11]

Late in the 1930s the agent reported that the Hispanic boys could not afford livestock projects and thus were being organized into handcraft groups. Nowhere was there discussion of organiz-

10. Annual report for 1922 and 1923, NMCAAES, Annual Reports, NA T876, Reels 5 and 6.
11. Annual Report for 1940, NMCAAES, Annual Reports, NA T876, Reel 24.

ing girls into vegetable or poultry groups, or of helping to provide livestock to children who might develop projects. Goats were loaned to starving families but little was done to help other families improve their situation. The gender segregation both reflected and increased the ethnic segregation already institutionalized in the county AES program.[12]

As a result of the indifference of the agents and their lack of understanding, there was little help in countering the drastic economic influences of agricultural development on Hispanic farm families. Most families turned to farm labor and housework to survive. When the New Deal came into the county, agents worked with federal representatives but they opposed programs that might have helped the poorer farmers. The Farm Bureau blocked an attempt to establish a migrant camp in Doña Ana because farm owners feared it might become a center for farm worker to organize. The agricultural agent also opposed resettling poor share-cropper families on land of their own under the rehabilitation program of 1935. He believed that people were rehabilitated if they were placed back in their former status of farm laborers or share croppers. "It is doubtful," he wrote, "if it is possible to rehabilitate most of these clients beyond the point where they were at the time of the beginning of the depression." In fact, most New Deal programs in the Mesilla Valley benefited middling families or wealthy farmers.[13]

The situation in Santa Fe County was a direct contrast to that in Doña Ana County. Stability was the most important factor. There was no HDA in the 1920s but from the time that Fabiola Cabeza de Baca was appointed in 1929, the program grew steadily under her guidance. From 1929 to 1932, De Baca served both Santa Fe and Rio Arriba Counties; from 1932 through 1940 she worked in Santa Fe County alone. Except for a period of hospitalization and recovery from an automobile accident, between December 1932 and September 1934, and relatively short vacations, De Baca devoted her full energy and time to serving the Hispanic, Anglo, and

12. Annual Report for 1922, NMCAAES, Annual Reports, NA T876, Reel 5.

13. Agricultural Agent's Annual Report for Doña Ana for 1935, NMCAAES, Annual Reports, NA T876, Reel 17. See also Jensen, "New Mexico Farm Women, 1900–1940," p. 73.

Indian women of the county. The women's support for her was so firm that even during her illness, the women continued their organizations. When De Baca returned, she was able to rebuild momentum swiftly. This decade of stability was a very important factor in building rapport and trust within the Hispanic community. The agricultural agents also remained the same in both counties for the entire period, both welcomed her work, and found that her organizing of women assisted them in organizing the men. As the agent in Rio Arriba reported, his organizing among the men was much easier after De Baca arrived: "She has helped materially in establishing much better cooperation among farm homes, with the results that men farmers have reacted more readily to better farming practices."[14]

Thus much of the credit for success among both men and women belongs to this unique woman who pioneered agricultural extension among Hispanic farm families. De Baca had grown up on her grandparents ranch near Las Vegas, New Mexico, after her mother died when she was five. She studied with the Sisters of Loretto, then taught in a rural school before receiving her degree in Home Economics from the agricultural college at Las Cruces. Her clearly written reports provide an extraordinary record of how AES educational programs were implemented at the local level.[15]

In some ways, the lack of organization by a Farm Bureau or similar organization was an advantage to De Baca. It enabled her to organize new groups in communities of Anglos and Indians, as well as Hispanics. By 1938, she had helped organize thirteen adult clubs, and estimated that she was reaching 80 percent of the farm families. De Baca also organized women to act as volunteers for children's clubs, both Anglo and Hispanic, teachers and farm women. She did not encourage strict gender segregation in children's clubs. By 1937, for example, she had organized some 373 children, 112 boys and 261 girls. Of the girls a majority, 191, were in traditional food and clothing clubs but an additional 70 were in

14. Agricultural Agent's Annual Report for Rio Arriba for 1931, NMCAAES, Annual Reports, NA T876, Reel 13.

15. For more details on De Baca see Joan M. Jensen, " 'I've Worked, I'm Not Afraid of Work': Farm Women in New Mexico, 1920–1940," in Joan M. Jensen and Darlis A. Miller, *New Mexico Women: Intercultural Perspectives* (Albuquerque: University of New Mexico Press, 1986), 227–55.

agricultural clubs with the 112 boys. Many girls were in home gardening and poultry clubs. De Baca began by encouraging women to undertake gardens and can or sell surplus, to learn nutrition as an adjunct to preparing this surplus, to exchange field labor with neighbors to obtain the foods they needed for their food preservation projects, to engage in poultry raising, to learn handicrafts to sell as well as to improve their homes, to sew better constructed garments, and to undertake home repairs. For those she could not reach directly, with group demonstrations or individual home visits, she provided a "Ciencia Domestica" column in the weekly newspaper *El Nuevo Mexicano* and bulletins in Spanish.[16]

De Baca also encouraged transfer of technology among poor Hispanic women. During the early 1930s, she helped them obtain—both cooperatively and through family-saving projects—canning equipment such as pressure cookers, tin can sealers, jars, and second stoves that could be placed outdoors where it was cooler. Later, she helped them obtain sewing machines, purchased patterns for collective use (fifty to sixty women used each of the patterns collected in her office), taught them how to repair their sewing machines, and how to modify the commercial patterns. She encouraged the women to barter labor for material and sewing supplies, shop for inexpensive yardage, and encouraged their efforts to improve the appearance of their children and themselves. By the late 1930s, 95 percent of the women had home gardens and 90 percent had sewing machines. The children were well nourished and well dressed.[17]

By this time women were also redirecting savings into the appearance of their homes. De Baca reported in 1938, "Nearly every woman in club work has carried on some repair work in her home." New Deal projects were bringing in cash to the families through husbands, and children and women were saving this cash income to purchase needed building materials. This pattern had been established long before, however, for even in hard

16. Ibid., and Annual Reports for Santa Fe for 1930–1940 in NMCAAES, Annual Reports, NA T876, Reels 12–18, 20–22, 25.

17. Percentages given in Annual Reports for Santa Fe for 1936 and 1938, NMCAAES, Annual Reports, NA T876, Reels 18, 21.

times of the drought, she had encouraged men and children to pool family resources to help the women buy pressure cookers to improve the family food supply. Then families had helped with the purchase of sewing machines to be better dressed. Now women planned and organized more elaborate building projects. Women usually depended on men for adobe brick-making, carpentry, and putting up walls, but they assumed responsibility for plastering, painting, and finishing houses, additions, and storage rooms.[18]

Women also began to take a new interest in the interiors of their houses. De Baca encouraged this first through the development of handicrafts, which she hoped would supplement family incomes. Outlets for crafts had been established in Santa Fe for native crafts during the 1920s, and De Baca encouraged women to supply articles directly to these stores. She noted that although women usually had good taste in selecting material and colors, when purchasing ready-made items they often selected garishly colored items because they wanted to be up to date. De Baca told women to trust their own traditions, to produce products of hand-dyed and woven materials, and to continue to do their traditional *colcha* wool embroidery.[19]

The work of De Baca is a good example of what could be done with extension education when agents successfully crossed ethnic barriers. Her ethnicity allowed her to know how to work with Hispanic women as well as Anglo women. She worked to decrease ethnic and gender segregation. She encouraged women in their traditional farm work, labor exchanges, and handcrafts, at the same time that she introduced new technology. She began with what people wanted most and then introduced other programs as they saw their relevance to their survival and prosperity.

When the depression of 1932–1933 and the drought of 1933–1934 hit Santa Fe farm communities, the work of De Baca bore fruit. Although there were few federal programs in existence at the time, families were already expanding family gardens and knew how to can. When the federal government finally arrived

18. Annual Report for Santa Fe for 1938, NMCAAES, Annual Reports, NA T876, Reel 21.
19. Annual Report for Rio Arriba and Santa Fe for 1932, NMCAAES, Annual Reports, NA T876, Reel 14.

with its program to purchase cattle, the families were able to butcher and can the healthiest animals. In 1935, over 90 percent of the farm families preserved enough food for the following year. They also canned large amounts of food cooperatively for families unable to do so. Through educational work, De Baca helped change attitudes and practices while retaining much of the fabric of Hispanic culture. She kept families on the farms for a decade, thus enabling families to remain on the farm through the severest drought and depression in New Mexican history. Once established, the pattern continued through World War II, with cash from soldiers going directly to the women who maintained the family farms. Ultimately, the war did cause disruption of rural communities. It brought heavy casualties of New Mexican men and few rural jobs for those men who returned. With the post war, New Mexican women entered a new phase of the struggle to remain on the land. That struggle has still not ended.

NEWCOMERS TO NAVAJOLAND: TRANSCULTURATION IN THE MEMOIRS OF ANGLO WOMEN, 1900–1945

HELEN M. BANNAN

CULTURAL HISTORIANS have long regarded narratives of captivity among the Indians as rich sources of America's myth structure. Scholars have convincingly argued that the basic plot of the captivity narrative, with its reenactment of the universal pattern of the Hero's separation, transformation, and triumphant return, has helped shape our national self-concept.[1] The standard cast of characters and dramatic embellishments of the narratives, with savage Indians violating and torturing helpless women, have strongly affected our images of Native Americans and led to the assumption of an especially intense, specifically female fear of Indians.[2]

The dominance of this mythic heritage has prompted its attack from several different perspectives. Historians have analyzed evidence of a variety of Indian-white interaction patterns, drawn from frontier letters, diaries, and other documents. Anthropologists have described Native American cultures in rich detail. Native Americans themselves, in oral histories, autobiographies, tribal and general historical accounts, have presented their side of the story. And, Americans who have lived among various tribes have published their versions of "my life among the Indians," seeking to capitalize upon the international fascination with Indian lore while undercutting its stereotypic content.

This article examines nine such works, produced in the twentieth century by Anglo women who had lived on the Navajo reservation prior to the end of World War II. These books were selected because they were written when most Americans believed Indians belonged in the past or in the movies, in dramatic contrast to an

0028-6206/84/0400-0165 $2.10
© Regents, University of New Mexico

earlier time, in which many readers of captivity narratives expected to experience a vicarious thrill of a possible danger. The Navajo reservation seemed an especially appropriate setting for several reasons: since continuous Navajo contact with Anglos began later than elsewhere, and since the reservation in the years prior to World War II was generally isolated from profound American influences, the experiences of "voluntary exiles" living there might be quite comparable to protagonists in captivity narratives. Also, focusing on Anglo residents among a single cultural group would highlight differences among individual responses, and selecting the Navajo, whose culture was distinctly different from the Plains stereotype that too many Americans define as Indian, would likely ensure that authors might elaborate more on details of tribal customs they found particularly striking. Moreover, the sample was limited to women's autobiographical works to draw again the parallel with women writers of captivity narratives and to test the longevity of the allegedly intense female fear of Indians. In addition, the author wished to explore interaction patterns among women of different cultures and the effect of reservation work roles upon the newcomers' attitudes toward their Navajo neighbors.

Once these criteria were established, the sample included all books a thorough searching produced, with the exception of anthropologist Gladys Reichard's *Spider Woman*.[3] A professional participant observer who studied with the noted relativist scholar Franz Boas at Columbia, Reichard and the account of her experiences seemed qualitatively different from those of the other women, whose roles generally emphasized the qualities of an emissary of American culture rather than those of a student of Navajo culture. While a comparison of trained field workers to those filling other reservation roles is a significant topic, that subject is not covered here. On the other hand, the nine remaining autobiographies, written by female traders, teachers, and the wife of a government employee, provided a wealth of information for my purposes.

Although these nine writers should not be regarded as creators of great literature, their works go beyond the usual travelogue in presenting a view of self-growth through experience, an approach strikingly similar to the pattern of the Hero's initiation journey evoked in the captivity narratives, although secularized and stripped of ethnocentric emphasis on Indian barbarism. While these works include little deep introspection into the total content and meaning of life, a clear and consistent self-concept emerges in them: the self as exile and initiate, attempting to understand a different cultural environment, and to find a place for the self in these surroundings. The title of Ruth Werner's book, *Novice in Navajoland,* could fit any of these autobiographies, since it concisely expresses the dominant self-concept each contains.

These twentieth-century women shared with protagonists in captivity narratives the experience of transculturation, which anthropologist A. Irving Hallowell defined as "the process whereby individuals under a variety of circumstances are temporarily or permanently detached from one group, enter the web of social relations that constitute another society, and come under the influence of its customs, ideas, and values to a greater or lesser degree."[4] As this definition indicates, the process includes the stages found in any initiation experience: separation and transition. Whether the final stage, incorporation,[5] will mean return to the original "home" society, as for the mythic Hero, or absorption into the different "host" society, as for some "White Indian" captives,[6] depends upon the degree of transculturation achieved. This, Hallowell reminds us, depends likewise on several variables, among them the person's age when the process begins, initial attitudes toward people of the second culture, length of residence among them, roles the initiate plays in the second society, and personal motivational factors.[7]

Using this model to analyze the experiences presented in these autobiographies of newcomers to Navajoland, this essay will highlight the part these women played in the ongoing social history of Indian-white relations. By allowing readers to take seriously the anthropological truism, "Cultures don't meet, people do," these works offer an opportunity to explore the ways in which nine American women, each a unique configuration of culturally normal and deviant traits, interacted with equally unique representatives of Navajo tradition. None of these writers should be labeled a "typical" American woman, or a "typical" reservation resident; such creatures probably do not exist. Yet the fact that these nine women produced books about their Navajo years separates them from the majority

The Newcomb Trading Post at Blue Mesa, located on the Navajo Reservation, from *Navajo Neighbors*, p. 29.

Elizabeth Hegemann with John and Louisa Wade Wetherill, from *Navajo Trading Days*, p. 243.

of those who shared a reservation experience. Also, in writing about herself, each woman created a persona: the person she wished readers to believe her to be. She chose those aspects of her personality to stress or downplay, those incidents to include or omit. This autobiographical angle provides an intensely personal view of each writer but also a limited, one-sided perspective. Still, analyzing several such works and placing individual differences within a common framework should illuminate the specific and general aspects of the authors' transculturation and thus enhance one's understanding of this important process in intercultural relations.

Although all the writers studied here were adults when they entered Navajoland, each had individual reasons for moving to the reservation. The four women who were single when they arrived came for teaching jobs, which they needed for their self-support, but their reasons for accepting these particularly strenuous positions varied.

Minnie Braithewaite Jenkins, who titled herself *The Girl from Williamsburg*, had dreamed of becoming a medical missionary to China, but changed her plans when she was denied entrance to the nearby College of William and Mary because of her sex. She taught school in Virginia for several years before seeking more adventuresome employment in the Indian Service. Minnie's mother attempted to use political influence to block her daughter's new dream by encouraging Indian Service officials to appoint her daughter to "'a school that no one . . . [would] accept.'" Minnie surprised her mother by accepting that assignment to remote Blue Canyon, Arizona. In 1900, she "left home promptly, although dutiful daughters weren't ever supposed to be so independent."[8] After a year in Navajoland, she accepted a transfer to a boarding school at Fort Mohave, Arizona, declining a post in Wisconsin because she loved the desert, but believing that her health demanded a less rigorous situation than Blue Canyon.

Health was also a concern of Franc Johnson Newcomb, but her persistent cough led her to request a transfer from the Menominee Indian School in Wisconsin to the drier climate of Fort Defiance, Arizona, in 1912. Perhaps her memories of Winnebago playmates during her Wisconsin childhood led Franc to join Indian Service

Minnie Braithwaite, 1901, from *Girl from Williamsburg*, frontispiece.

after six years of teaching in district schools. After two years teaching at Fort Defiance, she married Arthur J. Newcomb, a trader, and spent twenty-one more years getting to know her *Navaho Neighbors* at the Blue Mesa Trading post in New Mexico. In 1935, she moved to Albuquerque so that her daughters could attend school, and she began writing about her reservation experiences.[9]

Dorothy Dykhuizen began teaching at the Christian Reformed Church mission school at Rehoboth, New Mexico, in 1938, and she was still teaching there when she published *Go Quickly and Tell* in 1946. Much of her book is a general description of the work of the mission; even in its autobiographical sections, Dykhuizen referred to herself as the Teacher in self-detached third person. Presumably, the Teacher shared the motivation of other mission workers, who, Dykhuizen stated, had "assumed their duties not for personal gain but to express their love for the Master and for the people who need their help."[10]

Ruth Werner shared an ideal of service, but in a secular context. Her first dream was to be a cowgirl, but since her rural Iowa high school offered girls only a Normal Training course, she became a teacher. Before she entered Indian Service in 1941, she had taught in rural schools in Iowa, Wyoming, and Missouri. After her first eighteen months as a *Novice in Navajoland* at Red Rock, Arizona, she volunteered for service as a WAC for the duration of World War II. Three years later, she returned to the reservation for twenty-four years of work as a teacher, supervisor, and principal until her retirement.[11]

While all of the single women thus made independent decisions to move to Navajoland, most of the women who were married before they arrived reported that they followed their husbands, with varying degrees of enthusiasm. Economic motivation was again primary in each case, but other factors determined the choice of the reservation as the place to earn a livelihood.

Louisa Wade Wetherill and John, her husband of four years, had several disappointing seasons farming in Colorado's Mancos valley when they decided in 1900 to move with their two small children to accept a job managing a trading post at Ojo Alamo, New Mexico. John had already developed his interest in ancient Indian ruins and decided to follow his brother to Navajo country, where he could combine his archaeological explorations with making a living as *Traders to the Navajos*. Louisa, fascinated by stories of Navajo life since her youth on the Ute frontier, willingly made the journey and spent the rest of her life on the reservation. Her coauthor, Frances Gillmor, reported that Wetherill was buried near her home at Kayenta, Arizona, in 1945, next to her husband who died the year before.[12]

Another trader's wife, Mary Jeanette Kennedy, was more apprehensive about her husband George's plans to enter the trading business, but "after a great deal of persuasion, . . . finally consented to go" to Salina Springs, Arizona, in 1913, accompanied by her sister and two sons under four. A native of a southern city, Kennedy had misgivings about the isolation, but she and her family stayed on the reservation for twenty-five years, the last fourteen in Rock Springs, New Mexico, near enough to Gallup for her sons to attend school there. In 1938, her husband accepted a job as an oil company agent in Gallup, and they settled in town, where Mary Jeanette wrote *Tales of a Trader's Wife*, and celebrated her fiftieth wedding anniversary in 1959.[13]

In seven years of marriage, Hilda Faunce and her husband Ken had moved from Colorado cattle country to the Oregon coast, where a bank failure in 1914 prompted Ken's urge to return to the life of a Navajo trader that he had known in his youth. Hilda "had been willing to go anywhere, anyhow—with Ken—and I still was," so they decided to "turn toward the Southwest and go until we found work,—work that meant food and clothes and a new start." They found a trading post they could afford to buy at Covered Water, Arizona, and for four years Hilda was a *Desert Wife*. By 1918, the couple had saved enough money to buy a farm, and they left the reservation.[14]

Elizabeth Compton Hegemann had driven through Navajo country as a tourist several times before she settled there in 1925, when she married Mike Harrison, a park ranger at the Grand Canyon. When that marriage ended in 1928, she went to live with friends at the trading post at Tuba City, Arizona, beginning what she saw as her "transition period" toward "the free, simpler life of the vast Navaho Reservation." In 1929, she remarried, and with her second husband, Harry Rorick, began her *Navaho Trading Days* at a post in Shonto, Arizona, "not only to make our living, but because we liked being among Navahos and a part of the Reservation life." In 1939, Hegemann sold her half-interest in the trading post to her husband and left him and the reservation, citing "personal reasons, of which my mother was one" as the cause of this sudden change in her life.[15]

Elizabeth Ward's life also changed drastically in this period; her first marriage to a rich Texas oil man, which had produced two children, ended after the stock market crash in 1929. Elizabeth then married a cowboy, Dan Ward, who soon lost his job when the boss of his ranch declared against employing hands with families. His next position at a dude ranch was tedious for a serious cowboy, and in the mid-thirties, Dan gladly accepted a job as a "range rider" on the Navajo reservation since the position offered him a chance to continue in his chosen profession, although it entailed enforcing the BIA's controversial stock reduction program. Elizabeth left her children at schools in Tucson and followed her husband to Sheep Springs, New Mexico, where she found *No Dudes, Few Women*, a title that raises questions about her views of Navajo females. She and her husband remained on the reservation until 1943, when Elizabeth could no longer endure feeling that "everyone but myself had a constructive job. . . . I simply had to leave. I had to find a part in the war, somewhere." Dan was able to arrange his transfer to the Southern Arizona Reservation near Tucson, where Elizabeth could work in an aircraft factory.[16]

These brief sketches enable us to analyze these nine women in terms of some of the variables Hallowell identified as affecting transculturation. All were adults at the time they entered Navajoland and thus fully socialized into American culture before their arrival. Although all expressed curiosity and eagerness to learn about Navajo society, only Newcomb, Wetherill, and Hegemann had had any previous experience with Native Americans, and even these had only brief encounters, mostly with non-Navajos. Their initial attitudes were thus not strongly formed by experience, and most seemed determined to be open-minded about cultural differences. Still, each had been influenced to some degree by attitudes prevailing in the American culture of their time. In the early twentieth century, these views depicted Indians as a wronged, perhaps latently violent, but now vanishing race, with some romanticism about the noble values of Indian cultures.[17] None of the writers dwelled upon her preconceptions in her memoirs, so the level of influence these ideas had on each person cannot be accurately determined.

More obvious is the variation among the women in the length of their reservation residence, which ranged from Jenkins's single year, to Wetherill's entire remaining lifespan of forty-five years. One can reasonably expect that those who lived in Navajoland less than a decade, Jenkins, Faunce, Ward, and Dykhuizen, would be influenced less strongly by Navajo lifeways than those who remained longer, Hegemann, Newcomb, Kennedy, Werner, and Wetherill, in order of increasing years' seniority.

These introductory sketches also indicate that each woman's motivation for moving to the reservation was very closely tied to the role that she would play there. Hegemann alone voiced a genuine interest in following a Navajo lifestyle, but she chose to pursue this interest by becoming a trader. It is important to remember that Navajos before World War II defined the roles of schoolteacher and trader, which most of these women filled, as belonging to outsiders, so the possibilities of their complete acceptance into Navajo society were virtually eliminated. The role of teacher, particularly missionary teacher, involved a conscious intent to be a carrier of American culture. The role of trader also involved bringing American material culture to the Navajos, though traders were perhaps not always so conscious of themselves as agents of change. Acculturation is a two-way process, however, and these roles were flexible enough to allow some degree of transculturation to occur, if the individual's attitudes and inclinations permitted. Each role included a "constellation of behaviors appropriate to particular situations," but such requirements should not be viewed as totally determining individual action, "but rather as imposing some kind of limits on possible action, which the actors can manipulate in order to achieve their ends."[18] The next section will concentrate on the variations in the ways each woman played her role, as she responded to the stages of her initiation into Navajo life. Understanding the range of reactions to separation from Anglo society and transition into reservation lifestyles will help one appreciate the kinds of circumstances and attitudes that promoted and prohibited these women's increasing participation in and absorption of Navajo culture.

The isolation of the reservation and the strength of Navajo traditional culture in the first half of the twentieth century helped dramatize the "separation" phase these women experienced.[19] The geography of the reservation, its vast distances, arid climate, and stark desert beauty, sets it apart from most other American landscapes. Many of the women's memoirs include long passages detailing their sense of shock and isolation upon arrival. These reactions were heightened for Jenkins, Wetherill, and Faunce by long and difficult wagon journeys to their reservation destinations. The advent of the automobile made travel somewhat easier for the later arrivals, but the unimproved roads and suddenly treacherous weather continued to present challenges.

Responses to the landscape varied somewhat according to the environment to which each woman had been accustomed. Wetherill, from southern Colorado, was the least upset. Jenkins, from Virginia, thought the "stark barren desolation" of her school and its surroundings "might have been on the moon. Such a spot surely did not belong to our earth."[20] The Iowan Werner, on her first day in Navajoland, "began to wonder if I would ever adjust to this country of vast horizons, towering distant mountains, mesas, eroded wasteland and a myriad of black, gray and red rocks."[21] Ward, originally from Texas and immediately from the Tucson area, should have been more accustomed to open spaces and arid lands, but she thought the reservation "stretched in a dreary waste to every side," and stated, "It seemed incredible that people lived here, or at least existed, for three hundred and sixty-five days of the year. But here were the homes of the Navahos, and if they could stand it for always, I could stand it for a little while."[22] Faunce, transplanted from the rainy Northwest, expressed her reaction in terms of fear: "The emptiness, the barrenness, the vastness threatened me. . . . I could not face life in a country without one spear of green grass, with nothing but rocks and bare dirt, with never a human being in sight."[23]

When human beings were sighted, in the form of traditional Navajos, responses were mixed. Newcomb, "thrilled with my first glimpse of Navaho people engaged in their normal pursuits," described in detail the dress of the people she saw at a trading post on the way to Fort Defiance. Particularly taken by a woman swinging a baby on a cradleboard across her shoulders as she mounted a horse, Newcomb summarized her first impression of Navajo life as "a gay and colorful pageant."[24] When Kennedy awoke her first morning in her trading post, a Navajo man who had walked in without knocking was standing, smiling, at the foot of her sister's bed. Kennedy described this scene as "the first of many humorous, and some frightening, incidents for us."[25] Jenkins's reaction was similarly mixed; she noted the "bright, intelligent faces" of her students, as they "gazed at me fearfully. Actually, I was as much afraid as they were."[26] Ward, in contrast, was "frankly curious" about the Navajos and "watched them with honest interest, knowing that we had come to live among these people, wondering how one ever came to know them, when they showed not the slightest interest in us. . . . Navahos, I decided, were not friendly people."[27] Since none of the writers dwells upon any specifically female fear of rape or captivity, their fears generally can be classified as self-doubts, questioning their personal adequacy for their tasks and their adjustment to reservation settings and lifestyles. These fears are usually mixed with other emotions, notably excitement and curiosity, that new situations often arouse. Since all of the women realized what Hegemann expressed, "The Reservation was their home and our home, and we depended upon each other,"[28] all made efforts to get to know the Navajo people, beginning their transitional phase.

Communication difficulties complicated the process. Ward, who had no official function on the reservation, never learned to speak Navajo, which increased and prolonged her sense of isolation: "It seemed to me that I was the only white person living."[29] She finally established a friendship with an English-speaking Navajo woman, who explained Indian ways to Ward and eased her loneliness. English speakers were few, however, when Wetherill arrived, and her husband immediately left her to mind the trading post while he went exploring. Louisa's younger brother became desperately ill, and she could speak to no one to ask for help. When he recovered, she decided that "never again must she be so helpless. She resolved to learn the language of the desert people, to make them her friends."[30]

Wetherill and the other traders felt a most pressing need to learn to communicate with their Navajo customers; all learned at least enough Navajo for rudimentary business conversations. As Faunce explained, "of necessity, I learned rapidly the Navajo words for articles in the store. Our customers enjoyed teaching me and would point to sugar, coffee, tobacco, pants and repeat endlessly, . . . until I could say [the Navajo words for] them with some shadow of the correct accent."[31] The teachers, whose role emphasized training Navajos to speak English, had mixed attitudes about the possible effects of their own bilingualism. Jenkins refused to learn Navajo, "in order to help the progress of the children" in learning English.[32] Newcomb, on the other hand, believed that "it was not until I asked them, one and all, to teach me the Navaho language, that I made any headway" with the students.[33]

The functions each woman served on the reservation affected more than their attitudes towards language skills. Teachers and traders did not complain of the "monotony" the unemployed Ward experienced,[34] but then, neither did Hegemann, who, in her pre-trading days, held a similar position as wife of a government employee. Hegemann from the first had a strong interest in the Navajos who lived near the Grand Canyon and frequently visited their hogans, preferring their company to that of the families of Park Service employees, whom she found rather stuffy. Hegemann decided to learn to weave and received pieces of the necessary equipment from Navajo friends who

> showed their interest in the Belecana (any white-skinned person) woman who wanted to work as they did, by parting with their treasures. . . . To set up a Navaho loom in our Park Service headquarters was a project in itself. . . . As my work progressed and I continued to wear Navaho dress with more and heavier pieces of old pawn silver, I became rather well known in the El Tovar lobby.[35]

Hegemann was called "the woman who weaves," and Ward, "Dan's wife," by local Navajos; these descriptive names reveal Navajo appreciation of each woman's response to her situation.[36] Ward spent much of her time, while her husband was riding the range, with a local trader's family "because they understood the homesickness and the emptiness. The days went by, more or less alike, depending on the weather."[37]

Trader Kennedy held a nearly opposite view. "People were always asking if we didn't get very lonely living so far away from other white people. Each day seemed to be an adventure in itself for we never knew who would come or what would happen before the day was over."[38] Living in outlying posts near Navajo communities, traders became closely involved with the daily and the ceremonial life of the people. Their memoirs are filled with interesting stories of their interactions with their neighbors and often emphasize incidents that show their appreciation of Navajo beliefs and customs. Since Navajos avoided the dead, traders were often called upon in times of grief, and each of the traders' books includes some discussion of insights into Navajo family life gained through care of the dead and dying. Although traders' trips around the reservation were limited in length and duration because of the literal need to mind the store, they frequently attended nearby sings and ceremonies, and most regularly visited the homes of their customers. Newcomb, who married a trader after two years as a teacher, appreciated the widened opportunity her new role afforded to learn about "the lives, ambitions, projects . . . [and] problems of the individual Navajo."[39]

The teachers grew to know and like their students, but their confinement in school compounds isolated them from the full round of Navajo life. Much of Jenkins's book, for example, concerns her problems with an obnoxious and overbearing couple, the teacher-in-charge and his wife, the matron running the dormitory, who burdened her with unnecessary chores and made her adjustment as difficult as they could. Jenkins got along much better with her students, who called her "beautiful teacher," and with a Navajo woman who lived near the school, with whom she communicated in gestures and through the children's interpretation.[40] Forty years later, the car and school bus gave Werner greater mobility to attend ceremonies with the Navajo employees of her school and to visit the homes of her day school students. On one school bus run, Werner stopped to visit and was invited to help her female students complete their after-school job of grinding corn. Her inexpert efforts created a small explosion of corn, laughter for everyone, and greater understanding of her students' daily lives.[41] At a mission boarding school, Dykhuizen was farther removed from the homes of most of her students, but she particularly enjoyed the Saturday visits of children to her classroom. Then, "they talked at length of their home life, their ideas, and their reactions. In short, they revealed so much of their character and personality that their Teacher was able to come to a much better understanding of them through these conversations than the limited contacts which the school room permitted."[42]

Limited or extensive, such contacts led to friendships with Navajo families, relationships that taught the newcomers much about Navajo culture through their new friends. Interestingly, friendships reported in the autobiographies do not fit feminist expectations of women bonding across cultural boundaries. Although Ward and Jenkins emphasized their friendships with Navajo women, their closest female friends were other reservation Anglos. Several of the other authors mentioned especially close relationships with Navajo family groups, including men and women, with whom they interacted according to patterns of fictive kinship, informally "adopting" the newcomer as daughter or sister. An act of service often cemented these friendships. Faunce, for example, altered a man-sized coat to fit a small boy, although she worried as she sewed: "I was never much of a seamstress . . . but I worked and prayed the coat would please them. If it did, we had made not one friend, but many; if it did not, I had perhaps destroyed their slight confidence in us." The tailoring was a success, and Faunce heard a Navajo customer say to the boy's father, "'She is a grandmother to your small boy, my friend.'"[43]

Newcomb, whose Navajo name was medicine woman, earned her reputation and the friendship of noted medicine man Hosteen Klah when she bravely volunteered to assist in the cure of his nephew. Dressed Navajo-style, Newcomb entered the medicine lodge and asked the healer performing the rite if she could use her medicine to help; perhaps since Billy Yazzi was near death, the singer accepted. Newcomb lanced Yazzi's infected arm, drained and cleaned the wound, and instructed the patient's wife to continue to apply clean compresses. If the man had died, Newcomb would have been blamed for interrupting the ceremony and destroying its efficacy. Fortunately for her, Yazzi recovered, and the native healer was given full credit for the cure. "In discussing the affair, the Navahos agreed that I had done no harm in adding my assistance to the ceremony, as I had acted with a friendly purpose. Any of his friends would be willing to do as much. This attitude we were very happy to accept, as it assured us of a continued cordial relationship with our Navaho neighbors."[44] Hosteen Klah, the uncle, became Newcomb's close friend, and, in her biography of him, she states, "It was through his influence that I was able to attend Navaho religious ceremonies, and it was with his permission that I started making sketches of his sacred sand paintings."[45] This friendship was a most interesting one, revealing a great deal of intercultural exchange. Newcomb learned much about Navajo religion and curing from Klah, and encouraged by her enthusiasm, he began to weave sandpainting rugs, a breach of tradition that others with less power feared. Neither partner in this relationship was "typical," yet each learned much of the other's culture in the exchange.

Louisa Wetherill provides the strongest example of the power of friendship to overcome cultural boundaries. Wetherill learned to speak Navajo so well and became close to so many Navajo families through her medical assistance, listening, and arbitration of disputes that she was not viewed as a true "belecana." Since a Navajo woman the Utes captured long ago had never returned and since Wetherill came from the Ute country, it was assumed that she was a descendant of the captive, whose clan adopted the trader, bringing her fully into the Navajo kinship web of rights and responsibilities. She, for instance, was asked by Hoskinini, a Navajo head man who accepted "slim woman" as his grand-daughter, to dispose of his property and care for his slaves after his death, which she did. Also, with the help of friends in California, Wetherill provided her Navajo friends with ocean water needed to purify ceremonial objects.[46]

No other Anglo woman of this group reached this level of incorporation. Werner expressed most clearly the feeling that emerges from the works of all the others: "In general we lived in the Navajo world, enjoying our experiences but never quite becoming an intimate part of their unique existence."[47] Some of this distance resulted from the newcomers' inability to change culturally induced attitudes. For instance, to Ward hogans seemed smelly, crowded hovels, while to Faunce they seemed spacious and clean. Hegemann found them home-like and architecturally suited to the environment; she had several built at her trading post to house Navajo and Anglo guests alike.[48] Clearly, these attitudes affected these women's behavior while visiting Navajo homes, affecting in turn their relationships with the inhabitants.

Religion and traditional beliefs that governed much of Navajo life drew similarly different responses from these women, according to the degree of cultural relativism each achieved and conversely the degree of cultural distance each maintained. Newcomb, Wetherill, and Hegemann were very observant of Navajo customs and diligently tried to adapt their own behavior to avoid affronting their neighbors. Even when Newcomb acted against tradition, as in her intervention in Billy Yazzi's cure, she used her knowledge of tradition to mitigate novelty: in that case, she hummed a Navajo song while working and followed proper protocol in entering and leaving the medicine lodge, attempting to become a part of the ceremony. Such knowledge was not easily acquired; as Hegemann wrote, "Sometimes at Shonto I felt that the Navahos we knew well, often dropped little kernels of truth in a casual way, but never in answer to direct questions."[49] Those who lived long among the Navajo and respected their traditions learned to listen well, and trust and friendship brought understanding.

Some of the women never learned to appreciate the religious aspects of Navajo culture. Kennedy, Jenkins, and Dykhuizen did not mention attending Navajo ceremonies in their memoirs. Dykhuizen, as a missionary, might not have wanted to appear supportive of native religious beliefs; her book includes instead a chapter on a mission-sponsored harvest festival.[50] Faunce, Ward, and Werner did attend ceremonies, but had mixed reactions to them. Faunce was impressed by the ritual and sense of earnestness at Navajo sings, yet found the social "squaw dance" boring and called Navajo patients "victims" of their cures.[51] Werner attended a fire dance and a yeibichai dance, and although she felt "fortunate" to have had these opportunities, she could not appreciate the harmony of the singers and found the clowns more obscene than funny.[52] Ward was interested in learning about Navajo religion and was determined not to "scoff," since she "always felt that sincere belief merits respect, and the Navajos were sincere." Nevertheless, the fire dance severely taxed her intellectual commitment to a relativist position; she found the dance "completely savage," which verified her sense of cultural distance: "I knew that this was their world, and we were interlopers."[53]

Interlopers seems too strong a word to use to describe all of the women in this group. Certainly, each of these women had learned through personal contact something of what it means to be Navajo. Only Wetherill can be considered to have experienced fully transculturation, but many of the others, particularly Hegemann and Newcomb, were deeply affected by their Navajo experience. Werner expressed an idea that echoes throughout all their books: "How much more the Navajos had taught me that I had taught them!"[54] Not all of the lessons so taught were actually learned and accepted; none of the women acknowledged personal belief in witchcraft or relied totally on Navajo medicine, although they respected Navajos who did. Still, those who left the reservation did so with a sense of some regret, appreciating the broader awareness of life their years in Navajoland had given them. Unlike their antecedents, the authors of the captivity narratives, they did not emphasize their return to "civilization" as triumphant. The mood of Faunce's final page epitomized what most of these writers seemed to experience: "I had not realized that we had woven so many threads of friendship that it hurt to break them. I stopped often to think that in all my life these . . . years were the most isolated and the most colorful."[55] What their Navajo years had taught them, essentially, was to understand and respect a different way of life and the people who lived it.

These works will never have the impact on American culture that the captivity narratives have had, but they do include valuable insights for those who wish to understand intercultural relations. They are particularly useful for those who study the social history of acculturation from the other direction, emphasizing the transculturation of Native Americans in Anglo society. Many early teachers and missionaries, convinced of the superiority of American culture, were thoroughly disappointed when Indian students returning from boarding schools resumed their native way of life. These twentieth-century Anglo women similarly accepted permanently few Navajo traits, and most left the reservation, again to live like and among their own people, although they valued their Navajo experience. "Cultures don't meet, people do," and both change very slowly.

NOTES

1. Roy Harvey Pearce, "The Significance of the Captivity Narrative," *American Literature* 19 (March 1947): 1–20; Richard VanDerBeets, "The Indian Captivity Narrative as Ritual," *American Literature* 43 (January 1972): 548–62; Richard Slotkin, *Regeneration Through Violence: The Mythology of the American Frontier, 1600–1860* (Middletown, Conn.: Wesleyan University Press, 1973).
2. The roots of this assumption are ably discussed in Sandra L. Myres, *Westering Women and the Frontier Experience, 1800–1915* (Albuquerque: University of New Mexico [UNM] Press, 1982), chapter 3. Myres questions the assumption and presents convincing evidence to refute it.
3. Gladys A. Reichard, *Spider Woman: A Story of Navajo Weavers and Chanters* (1934; reprint ed., Glorieta, N. Mex.: Rio Grande Press, 1976).
4. A. Irving Hallowell, "American Indians, White and Black: The Phenomenon of Transculturation," *Current Anthropology* 4 (December 1963): 523.
5. Arnold L. Van Gennep, *The Rites of Passage* (1909; reprint ed., Chicago: University of Chicago Press, 1960).
6. James Axtell, "The White Indians of Colonial America," *William and Mary Quarterly* 32 (January 1975): 55–88.
7. Hallowell, "American Indians," p. 523.
8. Minnie Braithewaite Jenkins, *The Girl from Williamsburg* (Richmond, Va.: Dietz Press, 1951), pp. 4, 252, 255.
9. Franc Johnson Newcomb, *Navaho Neighbors* (Norman: University of Oklahoma Press, 1966), pp. 8, 229. Also, typescript ms., "Autobiography of Franc Johnson Newcomb," Newcomb Papers, Maxwell Museum of Anthropology, University of New Mexico, Albuquerque.
10. Dorothy Dykhuizen, *Go Quickly and Tell* (Grand Rapids, Mich.: William B. Eerdmans Publishing Company, 1946), p. 196. See also J. C. DeKorne, *Navaho and Zuni for Christ: Fifty Years of Indian Missions* (Grand Rapids, Mich.: Christian Reformed Board of Missions, 1947), p. 47.

11. Ruth E. Werner, *Novice in Navajoland* (Scottsdale, Ariz.: Southwest Book Service, 1972), biographical statement as preface to text, unpaged.

12. Frances Gillmor and Louisa Wade Wetherill, *Traders to the Navajos: The Story of the Wetherills of Kayenta* (1934; reprint ed., Albuquerque: UNM Press, 1953), pp. 46–49; foreword by F. G., unpaged.

13. Mary Jeanette Kennedy, *Tales of a Trader's Wife (Life on the Navajo Indian Reservation), 1913–1938* (Albuquerque: Valliant Company, 1965), pp. 12, 16, 27–28, 60.

14. Hilda Faunce, *Desert Wife* (1934; reprint ed., Lincoln: University of Nebraska Press, 1981), pp. 9, 7.

15. Elizabeth Compton Hegemann, *Navaho Trading Days* (Albuquerque: UNM Press, 1963), pp. 59, 115, 383.

16. Elizabeth Ward, *No Dudes, Few Women: Life with a Navajo Range Rider* (Albuquerque: UNM Press, 1951), pp. 244, 1, 12, 14, 16, 27, 32.

17. American attitudes toward Indians are much more complex than any brief statement can express; see especially Robert F. Berkhofer, Jr., *The White Man's Indian: Images of the American Indian from Columbus to the Present* (New York: Alfred A. Knopf, 1978).

18. H. G. Barnet, Leonard Broom, Bernard J. Siegel, Evon Z. Vogt, and James B. Watson, "Acculturation: An Exploratory Formulation" in Deward E. Walker, Jr., editor, *The Emergent Native Americans: A Reader in Culture Contact* (Boston: Little, Brown and Company, 1972), p. 27; Frederick George Bailey, *Tribe, Caste and Nation*, quoted by James A. Henretta, "Social History as Lived and Written," *American Historical Review* 84 (December 1979): 1301.

19. For anthropological analyses of Navajo culture in the period, see Clyde Kluckhohn and Dorothea Leighton, *The Navaho* (Cambridge: Harvard University Press, 1946); Gladys A. Reichard, *Dezba: Woman of the Desert* (New York: J. J. Augustin, 1939); and Ruth M. Underhill, *Here Come the Navaho!*, ed. by Willard W. Beatty (Kansas: Haskell Institute, 1953). For Navajo accounts of their life in this period, see Left Handed, *Son of Old Man Hat: A Navaho Autobiography*, recorded by Walter Dyk (Lincoln: University of Nebraska Press, 1938), and Kay Bennett, *Kaibah: Recollections of a Navajo Girlhood* (the author, 1975).

20. Jenkins, *Girl from Williamsburg*, p. 29.

21. Werner, *Novice in Navajoland*, p. 4.

22. Ward, *No Dudes*, p. 20.

23. Faunce, *Desert Wife*, p. 58.

24. Newcomb, *Navaho Neighbors*, p. 6.

25. Kennedy, *Tales of a Trader's Wife*, p. 4.

26. Jenkins, *Girl from Williamsburg*, p. 33.

27. Ward, *No Dudes*, p. 18.

28. Hegemann, *Navaho Trading Days*, p. 64.

29. Ward, *No Dudes*, p. 105.

30. Gillmor and Wetherill, *Traders to the Navajos*, p. 51.

31. Faunce, *Desert Wife*, p. 98.

32. Jenkins, *Girl from Williamsburg*, p. 96.
33. Newcomb, *Navaho Neighbors*, p. 7.
34. Ward, *No Dudes*, p. 96.
35. Hegemann, *Navaho Trading Days*, p. 37.
36. Hegemann, *Navaho Trading Days*, p. 38; Ward, *No Dudes*, p. 29.
37. Ward, *No Dudes*, p. 66.
38. Kennedy, *Tales of a Trader's Wife*, p. 43. For descriptions of traders, see Frank McNitt, *The Indian Traders* (Norman: University of Oklahoma Press, 1962), and Robert M. Utley, "The Reservation Trader in Navajo History," *El Palacio* 68 (Spring 1961): 5–27.
39. Newcomb, *Navaho Neighbors*, p. 18.
40. Jenkins, *Girl from Williamsburg*, pp. 55, 61–72, 228–35. For a history of Navajo schools and teachers in the period, see Hildegard Thompson, *The Navajos' Long Walk for Education: A History of Navajo Education* (Tsaile, Ariz.: Navajo Community College Press, 1975).
41. Werner, *Novice in Navajoland*, p. 17.
42. Dykhuizen, *Go Quickly*, p. 136.
43. Faunce, *Desert Wife*, p. 104.
44. Newcomb, *Navaho Neighbors*, p. 56.
45. Franc Johnson Newcomb, *Hosteen Klah: Navaho Medicine Man and Sand Painter* (Norman: University of Oklahoma Press, 1964), Introduction, p. xv.
46. Gillmor and Wetnerill, *Traders to the Navajos*, pp. 107–11, 173, 195.
47. Werner, *Novice in Navajoland*, p. 131.
48. Ward, *No Dudes*, pp. 51–52; Faunce, *Desert Wife*, p. 91; Hegemann, *Navaho Trading Days*, p. 292.
49. Hegemann, *Navaho Trading Days*, p. 93.
50. Dykhuizen, *Go Quickly*, chapter 9.
51. Faunce, *Desert Wife*, pp. 168–72, 208.
52. Werner, *Novice in Navajoland*, pp. 49, 23, 48.
53. Ward, *No Dudes*, pp. 38, 224.
54. Werner, *Notice in Navajoland*, p. 169.
55. Faunce, *Desert Wife*, p. 305.

WOMEN AND INTERCULTURAL RELATIONS: THE CASE OF HISPANIC NEW MEXICO AND COLORADO

SARAH DEUTSCH

At the turn of the century, the part women played in intercultural relations—in assimilation, acculturation, or resistance—was perfectly obvious to those who studied the question with an eye to Americanization. Women ruled the home. They governed a private world to which they gave outside forces, in this case Americanizers, only limited access. In addition, the women alone, in the eyes of these officials, cared for the young children and shaped the values, habits, and desires of the next generation. In the twin temporal kingdoms of present and future, as guardians of the present home and as mothers of the future generation, they held the primary power to influence their cultural complex.[1]

Many current scholars, like their predecessors, have seen women as crucial to intercultural relations chiefly in their capacity as mothers and guardians of the hereditary culture.[2] Some historians depict women as

[1] See, e.g., George Sanchez, "'Go After the Women': Americanization and the Mexican Immigrant Woman, 1915–1929," Working Paper no. 6 (Stanford, Calif.: Stanford University, Stanford Center for Chicano Research, n.d.); and Maxine Seller, "The Education of the Immigrant Woman, 1900–1945," *Journal of Urban History* 4 (May 1978): 307–30.

[2] Richard Griswold del Castillo, *La Familia: Chicano Families in the Urban Southwest, 1848 to the Present* (Notre Dame, Ind.: University of Notre Dame Press, 1984); Virginia Yans McLaughlin, *Family and Community: Italian Immigrants in Buffalo, 1880–1930* (Ithaca,

[*Signs: Journal of Women in Culture and Society* 1987, vol. 12, no. 4]
© 1987 by The University of Chicago. All rights reserved. 0097-9740/87/1204-0012$01.00

builders of cultural bridges either between generations or between ethnic groups. Alternatively, women are portrayed as barriers, resisting Americanization, or even as burdens on their own ethnic groups, preventing rapid assimilation and upward mobility as defined by the dominant culture.[3] Other historians have abandoned the traditional attempt to define women in these terms and, instead, look more closely at women's economic activities.[4] These historians describe women's work patterns as part of a family economy and strategy but usually stop short of examining the implications that changes in those patterns had for women and for the group as a whole as it struggled to survive in an intercultural arena.[5]

This article reassesses women's part in the dynamics of cultural interaction, focusing on Hispanic women in Colorado and northern New Mexico. Written histories of village Hispanic women or rural Chicanas are still rare, and of Chicanas or Hispanic women in Colorado virtually nonexistent.[6] The

---

N.Y.: Cornell University Press, 1977); Miriam Cohen, "Italian-American Women in New York City, 1900–1950: Work and School," in *Class, Sex and the Woman Worker*, ed. Milton Cantor and Bruce Laurie (Westport, Conn.: Greenwood Press, 1977), 120–43; Judith E. Smith, "Italian Mothers, American Daughters: Changes in Work and Family Roles," in *The Italian Immigrant Woman in North America*, ed. Betty Boyd Caroli et al. (Toronto: Proceedings of the Tenth Annual Conference of the American Italian Historical Association, 1978), 206–21; Charlotte Baum, Paula Hyman, and Sonya Michel, *The Jewish Woman in America* (New York: Dial Press, 1976); Corinne Krause, "Urbanization without Breakdown: Italian, Jewish, and Slavic Women in Pittsburgh, 1900 to 1945," *Journal of Urban History* 4 (May 1978): 291–306.

[3] Seller.

[4] For example, Elizabeth Pleck, "A Mother's Wages: Income Earning among Married Italian and Black Women, 1896–1911," in *A Heritage of Her Own: Toward a New Social History of American Women*, ed. Nancy Cott and Elizabeth Pleck (New York: Simon & Schuster, 1979), 367–92; Julia Kirk Blackwelder, "Women in the Work Force: Atlanta, New Orleans, and San Antonio, 1930–1940," *Journal of Urban History* 4 (May 1978): 331–58, and *Women of the Depression: Caste and Culture in San Antonio, 1929–1939* (College Station: Texas A&M University Press, 1984); Mario T. García, "The Chicana in American History: The Mexican Women of El Paso, 1880–1920," *Pacific Historical Review* 49 (May 1980): 315–37; Albert Camarillo, *Chicanos in a Changing Society: From Mexican Pueblos to American Barrios in Santa Barbara and Southern California, 1848–1940* (Cambridge, Mass.: Harvard University Press, 1979).

[5] Exceptions include Tamara Hareven, "Family Time and Industrial Time: Family Work in a Planned Corporation Town, 1900–1924," *Journal of Urban History* 1 (May 1975): 365–89, and "The Laborers of Manchester, New Hampshire, 1912–1922: The Role of Family and Ethnicity in Adjustments to Industrial Life," *Labor History* 16 (Spring 1975): 249–65; Judith E. Smith, "Our Own Kind: Family and Community Networks in Providence," in Cott and Pleck, eds., 393–411; Hasia Diner, *Erin's Daughters in America: Irish Immigrant Women in the Nineteenth Century* (Baltimore: Johns Hopkins University Press, 1983).

[6] "Hispanic" and "Spanish American" refer to Spanish-speaking, Spanish-surnamed, and/or Spanish-heritage people whose ancestors had settled in Colorado and New Mexico before the U.S. conquest. "Chicanos" and "Chicanas" encompass as well the more recent Mexican migrants and immigrants. Recent work on village women includes Janet LeCompte, "The Independent Women of Hispanic New Mexico, 1821–1846," *Western Historical*

mushrooming contemporary scholarship on Chicanos concentrates instead on the urban experience from 1850 to 1930. It indicates that many urban Chicanas worked for wages and headed households, but it assumes that this pattern of activity—outside the home and with some measure of autonomy—stands in contrast to women's lives in the villages.[7] My research on Hispanic-Anglo relations in northern New Mexico and Colorado from 1880 to 1940 undermines the assumptions that Hispanic village women were more subordinated in the village than outside it and that they found the move north to Anglo areas and cities a liberating experience. In other words, the common wisdom will not do. A better understanding of Hispanic women's experience in the village is central, it turns out, to our understanding of the Hispanic experience in Hispanic-Anglo relations anywhere.[8]

In the Hispanic world of northern New Mexico's communal villages, a sexual division of labor and production laid the foundation on which villagers built their strategies for interaction with the Anglo world that surrounded them by the end of the nineteenth century. In the villages, women's activities regarding community networks, land, and production grew in importance as male migration out of the villages for wage work became increasingly vital to village survival. But when entire Hispanic families migrated and settled in enclaves away from the villages, the balance between women's and men's activities shifted. The process by

---

Quarterly 12 (January 1981): 17–35; Marcela Trujillo, "The Colorado Spanish Surnamed Woman of Yesteryear," in *Hispanic Colorado: Four Centuries' History and Heritage*, ed. Evelio Echevarría and José Otero (Fort Collins, Colo.: Centennial Publications, 1976), 90–94; Joan Jensen, "Canning Comes to New Mexico: Women and the Agricultural Extension Service, 1914–1919," *New Mexico Historical Review* (hereafter *NMHR*) 57 (October 1982): 361–86, and "'I've Worked, I'm Not Afraid of Work': Farm Women in New Mexico, 1920–1940," *NMHR* 61 (January 1986): 27–52; Frances Swadesh, *Los Primeros Pobladores: Hispanic Americans of the Ute Frontier* (Notre Dame, Ind.: University of Notre Dame Press, 1974).

[7] On the dangers of accepting the common wisdom, cf. Elinor Lerner, "Into the Melting-Pot," *Women's Review of Books* 3 (June 1986): 12. See also, Rosalinda M. Gonzalez, "Chicanas and Mexican Immigrant Families, 1920–1940: Women's Subordination and Family Exploitation," in *Decades of Discontent: The Women's Movement, 1920–1940*, ed. Joan Jensen and Lois Scharf (Westport, Conn.: Greenwood Press, 1983), 59–84; Blackwelder, *Women of the Depression*, 102, 162; Alfredo Mirandé and Evangelina Enríquez, *La Chicana: The Mexican American Woman* (Chicago: University of Chicago Press, 1979); Maxine Baca Zinn, "Gender and Ethnic Identity among Chicanos," *Frontiers* 5 (Summer 1980), 18–24. On urban Chicanas, see Ricardo Romo, *East Los Angeles: History of a Barrio* (Austin: University of Texas Press, 1983); Richard Griswold del Castillo, *The Los Angeles Barrio, 1850–1880: A Social History* (Berkeley: University of California Press, 1979), and *La Familia* (n. 2 above); García (n. 4 above); and Mario T. García, *Desert Immigrants: The Mexicans of El Paso, 1880–1920* (New Haven, Conn.: Yale University Press, 1981); Camarillo (n. 4 above).

[8] For a more extended and detailed treatment of this thesis, see Sarah Deutsch, *No Separate Refuge: Culture, Class, and Gender on an Anglo-Hispanic Frontier in the American Southwest, 1880–1940* (New York: Oxford University Press, in press).

which women's experiences, so central to village life, became isolated and peripheral the closer women moved to Anglo towns and farms, is inextricably bound to the transformation of social and economic relationships wrought by Anglo-Hispanic contact. Taken together, the changes in those relations across time and space tell us much about how village households could and could not use their production patterns to maintain some cultural autonomy while at the same time taking advantage of economic opportunities offered by a rival culture.

* * *

Looking back on a New Mexico village of the early twentieth century, Luisa Torres recalled: "I watched my maternal grandparents a lot. . . . On the day that my grandmother was seventy, I saw her open the doors of her little adobe house. It was a spring day and there were millions of orange and black butterflies around the corn plants; my grandmother ran towards the butterflies and gathered so many of them in her apron that she flew up in the air, while she laughed contentedly. I wanted to know all that my grandmother knew." Like many grandmothers of the time, Luisa's grandmother knew particularly about medicinal plants, "remedios," but in wanting to know all that her grandmother knew, Luisa was expressing more than a desire to share in the knowledge of herbal medicine.[9] In the Hispanic heartland's communal villages, women had their own world in addition to the one they shared with men. They had realms of expertise that served the entire village, and a society and economy of their own.

Nestled among relatively inaccessible mountains, northern New Mexico's villages seemed to many changeless and idyllic. Yet as mines, railroads, and commercial agricultural enterprises encompassed the region in the 1880s, as Anglo courts legalized the dispossession of villages in the loss of communal lands, and as taxes and cash demands rose, increasingly men migrated seasonally out of the villages in search of wage work. Through at least the 1930s, these migrants provided the majority of Spanish-speaking labor for the mines, railroads, and farms of Colorado and New Mexico.[10]

[9] Luisa Torres, "Palabres de Una Viejita/the Words of an Old One," *El Palacio* 84 (Fall 1978): 12. See also Annette Thorp, "Vicenta," Works Progress Administration (hereafter WPA) 5.5.53, no. 1, New Mexico Historical Library, Sante Fe, New Mexico (hereafter NMHL).

[10] Sarah Deutsch, "Culture, Class, and Gender: Chicanas and Chicanos in Colorado and New Mexico, 1900–1940" (Ph.D. diss., Yale University, 1985), 4–61; William deBuys, *Enchantment and Exploitation: The Life and Hard Times of a New Mexico Mountain Range* (Albuquerque: University of New Mexico Press, 1985); Swadesh (n. 6 above); Paul A. F. Walter, "A Study of Isolation and Social Change in Three Spanish Speaking Villages of New Mexico" (Ph.D. diss., Stanford University, 1938); Victor Clark, *Mexican Labor in the United States*, U.S. Labor Bureau Bulletin no. 78 (Washington, D.C.: Government Printing Office, 1908).

Despite the migration and the increasing Anglo presence in the region, the villages remained distinctively Hispanic. The social organization of the villages and, in particular, the activities of women, help explain this resilience. For as the men migrated, their participation in the village began to shrink until the women's world and the world of the village began to merge.

Women in the villages had a panoply of responsibilities. They led church services and gained authority as healers, mothers, and midwives. The activities covered here—community networking, property ownership, production, and work—are not comprehensive, microcosmic, or unique, but they best illustrate the trends imposed by geographic and economic change.[11]

Northern New Mexico's Hispanic villages had long survived by a mixture of pastoral and irrigated agricultural activities, along with a modest but absolutely essential amount of external trade that was gradually replaced by seasonal wage labor as barriers to trade rose. This was an economy, in the arid mountains, requiring a substantial amount of communal labor—for both agricultural and stock production—and an economy also dependent on communal rights regarding pasturage and water.[12]

The norm among village households was a complete or extended family headed by a married couple. Unless one was caring for an elderly relative, marriage was the assumed destiny of all young people. One Hispanic woman, unhappy in her childhood and her married home, could see no alternative. "Where else could I have gone?" she asked.[13] Marriage and child rearing performed the important function of creating households varied by sex and age and closely connected to other village households, welding the small communities together. Marriage integrated the individual once more into this essential communal group, and children per-

[11] Deutsch, "Culture, Class, and Gender," 62–102, treats midwifery, the family, and religion in greater detail, though these and other facets of village women's lives still bear further investigation.

[12] See, e.g., Jerold Widdison, "Historical Geography of the Middle Rio Puerco Valley, New Mexico," *NMHR* 34 (October 1959): 264; John Van Ness, "Hispanic Village Organization in Northern New Mexico: Corporate Community Structure in Historical and Comparative Perspective," in *The Survival of Spanish American Villages*, ed. Paul Kutsche, Colorado College Studies no. 15 (Colorado Springs: Colorado College Studies, 1979), 38; Allan Harper et al., *Man and Resources in the Middle Rio Grande Valley* (Albuquerque: University of New Mexico Press, 1943), 18–19

[13] Luisa Vigil in Nan Elsasser, Kyle MacKenzie, and Yvonne Tixier y Vigil, *Las Mujeres: Conversations from a Hispanic Community* (Old Westbury, N.Y.: Feminist Press, 1979), 13; U.S. Department of Commerce, Manuscript Census, Rio Arriba County, New Mexico, 1880, 1900, 1910, National Archives, Washington, D.C. For example, of El Rito's 117 households in 1880, only nine were headed by women. In 1900, sixteen of 120, and in 1910, eighteen of 164 were headed by women. Six, sixteen, and seventeen of these, respectively, were widows; two, one, and three were single women; and one, one, and none were divorcees. See also Annette Thorp, "Chana," WPA 5.5.52, no. 71, NMHL.

petuated that integration. For every child, the parents selected a *comadre* and a *copadre*, terms for which coparent is a better translation than godparent. And as more children arrived, the networks of coparents spread.[14]

In a household with adult men and women, men earned some cash through trade or seasonal labor and raised grain crops and livestock, while women raised produce, including cash-earning items such as chili and eggs. When one or other of the partners was missing, whether through divorce, death, or desertion, the household became lopsided and difficult to keep afloat. Men and women both owned property, inheriting it equally; community property in marriage was the rule, and husbands left property to wives, not eldest sons. Yet widows and widowers remarried at about the same high rates.[15] As heads of households, single men appeared no more frequently than single women. Single heads of household of either sex tended to live with siblings or nieces or nephews given to them by generous relatives to redress the imbalance of age and sex in their household.

While women and men both demonstrated this desire to multiply attachments to the group, for women there were particular and increasing hazards in remaining unattached. Despite the fact that Hispanic women bought and sold property, homesteaded, conducted business, and let sheep out on shares independently, men had greater access to the cash economy: they could migrate out of the village in search of seasonal labor in local mining ventures, on railroad tracks, or herding other peoples' sheep or cattle.[16] Not one of these cash-earning jobs in the Anglo sector was open to women.

[14] See, e.g., Antonio Goubaud-Carrera, "Food Patterns and Nutrition in Two Spanish-American Communities" (Master's thesis, University of Chicago, 1943), 59; Fran Leeper Buss, *La Partera: Story of a Midwife* (Ann Arbor: University of Michigan Press, 1980), 27. Annette Thorp, "Vicenta" (n. 9 above), "Lina," WPA 5.5.52, no. 74, NMHL, and "Weddings," WPA 5.5.52, no. 67; NMHL. Coparents were usually close relatives, partly because one could not marry coparents, so they were taken from among already ineligible mates of the small villages. See Swadesh (n. 6 above), 189. Widowhood, remarriage, and large families were all common. To contrast with practices in Los Angeles in naming coparents, see Griswold del Castillo, *Los Angeles* (n. 7 above), 97.

[15] Wayne Moquin and Charles Van Doren, eds., *A Documentary History of the Mexican Americans* (New York: Praeger Publishers, 1971), 268; Olen Leonard, *The Role of the Land Grant in the Social Organization and Social Processes of a Spanish American Village in New Mexico* (1943; reprint, Albuquerque: Calvin Horn Publishers, 1970), 119. Mrs. J. B. Martinez to J. U. Vigil, January 24, 1900, Vigil Papers, Box 1, Western Historical Collection, University of Colorado, Boulder, Colorado (hereafter WHC). On Hispanic vs. Anglo marital property law, see Joan Jensen's warning against romanticizing this community property practice in "I've Worked" (n. 6 above), 30.

[16] On women's property management, see John Lawrence Diary, November 5, 1901, and October 27, 1901, WHC; Cleofas Jaramillo, *Romance of a Little Village Girl* (San Antonio, Texas: Naylor, 1955), 125–37; Case 337, Lujan v. Lujan, Catron Papers, archive 29, box

Households required both the cash and the produce, but, limited as most women were to such low-paying professions as sewing and taking in laundry, women who were left without sufficient property or sufficient numbers of male wage earners in their household had a far lower earning potential than did men. Men could, through their earnings, buy those items a wife would have produced, but few women could earn enough to substitute for a man's grain and sheep, and his wages. If widowed or divorced women owned their own property and had grown sons to help work it, they could sustain themselves as heads of families, but divorced or widowed women with young children seldom could sustain an independent existence. They relied on exchange with and the kindness of relatives and neighbors.[17]

It is possible to see, in the light of their greater vulnerability to poverty and their greater stake in supportive networks outside marriage, women's particular part in constructing the sense of community so vital to the survival of the Hispanic villages. They did have, after all, and always have had a hand even in the literal construction of the community. Men made the adobes and built basic structures, but women did all the plastering, inside and out, for their homes and for common buildings, and they built adobe ovens and fireplaces.[18] This was a community service that not only echoed the mutually supportive pattern of production but also took women outside the home and gave them some power over the actual physical shaping of their environment.

201:10, folder 1, Special Collections, University of New Mexico; 1896 Juez de Paz Record Book, Abiquiu, June 15, 1905, and Reception Book, 1887–1912, New Mexico State Records Center and Archives, Santa Fe (hereafter NMSRCA); Louis Sporleder, *The Romance of the Spanish Peaks* (n.p., 1960), 16. On business, see Ruth Laughlin Barker, *Caballeros* (New York: D. Appleton, 1931), 177; Case 253, Maria Rita M. De Montoya v. Juan Sanchez and Mrs. Remedio de Sanchez, 1915, Santa Fe, Catron Papers, box 201:8, folder 15. Anaria Margarita Vasquez to Vigil, November 24, 1912; Mrs. Eva Montoya to Vigil, March 19, 1913; and Mrs. J. B. Martinez to Vigil, April 11, 1913, Notary's Record 1906, and file 19, Vigil Papers.

[17] Manuscript Census, Rio Arriba County, 1910, e.g., Chama: nine women did washing, three did odd-job labor, three took in lodgers, and six did housework. According to the census, almost each village had at least one divorced person, usually female, and frequently more. Also see "Tia Lupe," pp. 96–102, WPA files, no. 20, NMSRCA. Case 337 Lujan v. Lujan, *New Mexico Penitentiary Records*, reel 1, NMSRCA. Women and men without ties to the village were also vulnerable to charges of witchcraft. See, e.g., Marc Simmons, *Witchcraft in the Southwest* (Flagstaff, Ariz.: Northland Press, 1974); Marta Weigle, *Spiders and Spinsters: Women and Mythology* (Albuquerque: University of New Mexico Press, 1982), esp. 41–42.

[18] Plastering was usually a communal event. For example, Alice Blake in *Home Mission Monthly* (hereafter *HMM*) 27 (November 1912): 18; Leva Granger in *HMM* 16 (November 1901): 16; *HMM* 26 (1911): 14; HMM 19 (November 1904): 4; and A. Thorp, "Chana" (n. 13 above); Sister M. Lucia Van der Eerden, *Maternity Care in a Spanish-American Community* (Washington, D.C.: Catholic University of America Press, 1948), 34.

Women, also, to a greater extent than did men, nurtured the human networks of the village. Often fourteen different visitors would come to one home, some returning three or four times in a single afternoon. Women also maintained the links with kin in other villages, sometimes journeying with the whole family, sometimes alone, sometimes for several weeks at a time.[19] These links maintained connections with coparents, grandparents, or trustworthy foster parents for the children in case of economic disaster. They provided farm labor in old age, widowhood, or illness, and employment (usually for payment in goods rather than cash). The maintenance of community ties thus became a means to ensure the welfare of oneself and one's family.[20]

Perhaps the most fundamental work of women was one more obviously allied to maintenance and to women's place in Hispanic society; it centered around food. Hispanic women were responsible for the "garden," a plot of irrigated land usually closer to the house than were the fields of grain. This garden produced more and more of the food consumed by the family as Anglo and Hispanic speculators, railroads, and national parks acquired the grazing lands necessary for livestock production. Women controlled this garden land totally. It provided them with an autonomous base, a source of subsistence independent of but not in competition with men.[21]

The effort and time involved in processing food, a love for the land that had produced it for generations, and its life-giving properties imbued food with a symbolic significance. Sociologists have explained that the borrowing and sharing of food among members of the extended family and friends are important means of fostering social cohesion.[22] In these villages the significance went even further, as illustrated by one Hispanic midwife's story.

[19] Compare Nancy Grey Osterud, "Strategies of Mutuality: Relations among Women and Men in an Agricultural Community" (Ph.D. diss., Brown University, 1984); Leonard, 75–76 133; Prudence Clark in *HMM* 24 (November 1909): 5; Harriet Benham in *HMM* 16 (November 1901): 8; Elsasser, MacKenzie, and Tixier y Vigil: Vigil, 14; John Lawrence Diary, throughout. See also Griswold del Castillo, *La Familia* (n. 2 above), 42–43.

[20] A. Thorp, "Chana"; Charles Hayden MS, 66, WHC, *HMM* 19 (November 1904): 13; C. Jimenez. Oral History 72, March 31, 1969, Denver Public Library, Denver, Colorado (hereafter DPL); "Alita," *HMM* 14 (November 1899): 8; Carolyn Atkins, ed., *Los Tres Campos—the Three Fields* (Albuquerque, N.M.: Menaul Historical Library of the Southwest, 1978), 18, 48.

[21] A. Thorp, "Chana"; Flora Lucero Garcia, "Margarita Ruyball Lucero," *San Luis Valley Historian* (hereafter *SLVH*) 8 (1976): 3–5; Matilda Allison in *HMM* 23 (November 1908): 9, Manuscript Census, Rio Arriba County, 1880, 1900, 1910. On women's participation in food processing—butchering, rendering lard, drying meat, shelling, toasting, sifting, and sometimes harvesting grains—see P. Clark in *HMM* 15 (March 1901): 104–5, Victoria MacArthur in *HMM* 24 (November 1909): 16; Jensen, "Canning" (n. 6 above), 365; Hayden MS, 69, WHC.

[22] A. Thorp, "Vicenta"; Leonard (n. 15 above), 71; Goubaud-Carrera (N. 14 above), 64. Compare George Foster, "The Dyadic Contract: A Model for the Social Structure of a Mexican Peasant Village," in *Peasant Society: A Reader*, ed. Jack M. Potter et al. (Boston: Little, Brown & Co., 1967), 218–20.

The midwife had come to deliver a child and found the labor lasting an unusually long time. Exhausted, she went to borrow something from a neighbor and there discovered the apparent reason for the difficult birth. It seemed the woman ate her meals standing in her doorway but gave nothing away. Children who were hungry asked for bread and stood watching her eat, but to no avail. The midwife concluded that the woman was so stingy the child did not want to be born to her, so the midwife took the woman's wheat flour (considered a luxury and kept for feast days) and made a large number of tortillas. Then she had the mother-to-be call in all the children she could find and dispense the tortillas with her own hands. The child was finally born, and the new mother became very generous.[23]

Food, as a woman's own product to dispose of as she wished, became intimately bound to her virtue, and a woman's treatment of it defined her character both as a woman (one worthy to be a mother) and as a member of a communal village. Women did not belong to the community simply as dependents whose place there was determined by the behavior of their nearest male relative. They belonged as producers, and it was in part through the distribution of their own produce that they held a place in their own right.[24]

Women also produced food for exchange. For example, one woman "sold" her cheese "to the village people who did not have cows or goats of their own." But she sold it within an informal women's exchange network, bartering cornmeal, flour, or homemade soap for the cheese.[25] Women would also pay church dues with hens and the children's school fees with their produce.[26] Any cash they earned from their own products women usually obtained through men's marketing their crops. Trading for cash—outside the village almost by definition since there was virtually no cash in circulation there, and certainly outside a woman's network of community and kin—usually remained in the hands of either husbands or male relatives. This delegation of the cash nexus to men would acquire new meaning when whole families migrated to Anglo areas.

Meanwhile, food remained distinct from other products women and men produced, and there were separate peripheries to its legitimate sale. It was more like village land, whose preferred buyers were always relatives, than like, for example, weavings or sheep. A woman from Cordova rejected the opportunity to sell her homemade ice cream through a local

[23] "Parteras," WPA 5.5.53, no. 8, NMHL.

[24] On distribution norms, e.g., Buss (n. 14 above), 21; Leonard, 80; and Olen Leonard and C. P. Loomis, *Culture of a Contemporary Rural Community* (Washington, D.C.: Government Printing Office, 1941), 19.

[25] Thorp, "Vicenta." See also Ann Lucero, "Memories of Mr. Abel Chavez," *SLVH* 8 (1976): 23–24.

[26] For example, Ruth Barber, Oral History TC 35C, Menaul Historical Library of the Southwest, Albuquerque, New Mexico (hereafter MHL), and various issues of Home Mission Monthly.

merchant. "It would be dishonest to sell food you make in your home for profit at a store," she explained. Her husband concurred, "She is right, because to make food is part of our life as a family and to start selling that is to say that we have nothing that is *ours* . . . better to have less money and feel we own ourselves, than more and feel at the mercy of so many strangers."[27] Exchange for trade, even cash sales if sold by the producer, retained the intimate connection between producer and subsistence product and retained the producer's control over that product. By introducing a middleman, one lost control of one's virtue. Women's production of food, like women's creation of neighborhood, was thus both imbued with the communalism of the village and vital to it.

Much of this women's economy of production and exchange, like its role in the Hispanic-Anglo frontier, has remained invisible to historians, made so less by its unsalaried and often informal nature than by the dominance of Anglos and males among record and census takers. In the 1910 census for Rio Arriba County, for example, male and Anglo female enumerators listed ten females with occupations for every one hundred males in communities they covered. Sophie Archuleta, however, a Hispanic public school teacher in Truchas whose father was a general farmer, whose mother was a seamstress, and whose sister and brother performed labor on the home farm, listed seventy-nine females with occupations for every one hundred males.[28] Seventy-nine, not ten—this statistic argues for a different interpretation of the value and centrality of women's work.

Even the basic outlines of acceptable women's work had always depended more on the composition of the family than on sexual norms. Anthropologists Paul Kutsche and John Van Ness noted that within the household, tasks were divided by sex and age "in a marked but not rigid fashion," adding that "the division of labor is not absolute. If age and sex distribution in a family, or illness, or jobs away from home, makes it inconvenient to go by custom, then anyone does anything without stigma."[29] Men could wash, cook, and iron; women could build fences, hoe corn, plant fields, and herd and shear sheep.[30] In Chimayo, the men usually

[27] Quoted in Robert Coles, *The Old Ones of New Mexico* (Albuquerque: University of New Mexico Press, 1973), 25.

[28] Manuscript Census, Rio Arriba County, 1910. Other examples of obscured female activities occur in Leonard, 80; Goubaud-Carrera (n. 14 above), 60; Margaret Mead, ed., *Cultural Patterns and Technical Change* (Paris: Unesco, 1953), 182. Anthropologist Beverly Brown tells the story of a man filming an African village while questioning a man on what women did. As women erected a house in the background, the man, after a long pause, responded, "Well, they take care of the children, yes, that's what they do; they take care of the children." Conversation at sixth Berkshire Conference on the History of Women, Northampton, Mass., 1984.

[29] Paul Kutsche and John Van Ness, *Cañones: Values, Crisis and Survival in a Northern New Mexico Village* (Albuquerque: University of New Mexico Press, 1981), 35.

[30] Men: *HMM* 19 (November 1904): 11; William Parish, ed., "Sheep Husbandry in New Mexico, 1902–1903," *NMHR* 37 (October 1962): 263. Women: "Manuela," 275–76, WPA

did the carding of wool, the women spun, and both wove. Prudence Clark recalled visiting a house in Chimayo in 1903 where, while twelve women sat spinning, in the adjoining room the men smoked, gossiped, and looked after "the little people." The women, too, would stop occasionally "and have a smoke."[31] As more and more men migrated for longer and longer seasons of wage work to earn the cash essential to village survival, women's work load increased, and the communities' already malleable division of labor flexed to accommodate the new circumstances. The traditional lack of rigidity about the sexual division of labor eased the transition to a migratory community, whether or not ideological norms changed.

Both Anglos and Hispanics noted the relatively rapid spread of "American" bedsteads, tables, chairs, sewing machines, and cooking stoves into Hispanic homes after 1880, paid for by the men's earnings from newly available wage jobs.[32] They noted this technological cross-cultural contact, but they gave less notice to the concommitant extension of women's work in the village. That women often enjoyed the new technology, in particular the cookstoves, is not in dispute. In 1901 two women were sufficiently attached to the same cookstove to bring a case to court.[33] But the changes in women's labor were not limited to their work within the home. When men left the village for wage work each spring, the women were left with the care of the men's crops. The women were moving from a shared position at the village center as village producer to sole tenancy.

As witnesses at the time observed, "There was no abandonment of the land; rather a new order saw the women taking charge of the planting of crops aided in part by their children and men too old to seek work outside the valley."[34] The cash the migrants brought home to the villages paid taxes and permitted such modern necessities as gable or corrugated iron roofs and school supplies despite depleted resources.[35] Without the work of the

files, no. 11, NMSRCA; Parish, 285; A. Thorp, "Chana" and "Vicenta"; M. K. Marquez, "Juanita Ortega de Gomez," *SLVH* 8 (1976): 19–23; Juanita sheared and butchered her own sheep on her homestead after her husband died in 1908 and was also a *curandera* (herbal doctor); Jesusita herded and sheared sheep as her father had no sons and found no stigma attached to attending village dances in jeans: "Not like a girl, like a boy. And nobody bothers me, no. Everybody likes me" (Buss, 23–25).

[31] *HMM* 18 (November 1903): 10.

[32] For example, V. Clark (n. 10 above), 498, 501, 504. Sue Zuver, quoted in Alice Blake, "Presbyterian Mission Work in New Mexico" (unpublished manuscript, MHL, 1935), 122; Brengle in *HMM* 25 (November 1910): 15.

[33] Case 598, Rio Arriba County Court Records, District Court, 1895–1905, Docket Book D, NMSRCA.

[34] "Deep Village," WPA files, 220, Rio Arriba County History, NMSRCA; and see Leonard (n. 15 above), 27, 29; Juan B. Rael et al., "Arroyo Hondo. . . ," *El Palacio* 81 (Spring 1975): 8, 10.

[35] Buss, 29, 50; N. Howard Thorp, "Rio Arriba County History," 3, WPA files, 220, NMSRCA; Mary A. Steer, "A Journey Abroad at Home," *Women and Missions* 2 (May 1925): 48; Ivie Jones, Home Demonstration Agent, San Miguel County, 13, "New Mexico Agricul-

women in the villages, however, without adapting the sexual division of labor to new strategies made necessary by cross-cultural contact, the Hispanic villages, as such, could not have survived.

Anthropologist Alice Schlegel has pointed out that "division of function . . . does not necessarily lead to stratification."[36] In the northern New Mexico villages, Hispanic men and women worked on and off the land and in their communities not competitively but, instead, in a mutually supporting way. Individuals were not as effective economically on their own as they were in a unit; but neither were they powerless or completely dependent. As women's work was not limited to hidden and reproductive work in the household, the work of both sexes remained visibly essential to subsistence itself.

In a village increasingly divided into village women and migrant men, women's activities sustained the community physically and spiritually. The integrative function of women grew in importance, and increasingly women provided the ongoing principle, the continuity for the village. Through the work of women, Hispanics could maintain an area where they retained control over the development of their own culture, selected artifacts from the Anglo world, and continued their patterns of communal networking and exchange outside of direct Anglo contact, despite loss of overall economic and political dominance. So completely, in fact, had village life come to devolve on these women by the end of the 1920s that one Hispanic male recalled, "When the men came back, they were kind of like guests."[37]

---

tural Extension Service Report," T876-10-1928, National Archives, Washington, D.C.; Dora Ortiz y Vasquez, *The Enchanted Dialogue of Loma Parda and Canada Bonita* (n.p., 1983), 10; Lyle Saunders, "The Social History of the Spanish-speaking People in Southwestern United States since 1846" (paper read at First Conference of Historians of the United States and Mexico, Monterrey, 1949), 8, Community Relations Papers, box 2, Western History Department, DPL; Elsasser et al. (n. 13 above): Ida Gutierrez, 67. Barker (n. 16 above), 303; Jensen, "Canning" (n. 6 above), 362. Where men did not migrate and opportunity permitted, women in increasing numbers performed wage work for Anglos, usually laundry or domestic service, to provide the necessary cash. See "Home Economics Evening School Classes for Spanish American Women," *New Mexico School Review* 4 (April 1925): 15; Buss (n. 14 above), 32. Ruth Barber, "Financial Independence Increasing," *Women and Missions* 40 (May 1924): 68. The female wage workers, like the males, tended to view wage work as peripheral to their main object, the continuity of village life. As such, the village accepted both the day work of the women and the sorties of girls to Santa Fe and Albuquerque with, as one male Chimayo inhabitant remembered, "a great pride" (interview with John Trujillo, Chimayo, New Mexico, November 12, 1983); Charles Briggs, "'Our Strength Is in the Land'" (Ph.D. diss., University of Chicago, 1981), 312.

[36] Alice Schlegel, "An Overview," in *Sexual Stratification: A Cross-cultural View*, ed. Alice Schlegel (New York: Columbia University Press, 1977), 355–56. Compare Eleanor Leacock, *Myths of Male Dominance* (New York: Monthly Review Press, 1981), 144.

[37] Interview with Arthur Maes, Denver, Colorado, September 12, 1983. (Names of most interviewees have been changed to protect their privacy.) Interview with John Trujillo, Chimayo, New Mexico, November 12, 1983.

This tightly bound economic balancing act worked for the villages and their migrant men, but it would fall apart when whole families moved to the Anglo-dominated city or the Anglo rural north, to Denver or northern Colorado's beet fields, as they did increasingly during the 1920s. In these northern Anglo areas, Hispanic women experienced a new marginality. Differences in the social structure of Anglo communities and restrictions on Hispanic landowning there inhibited the ability of women to play the same vital economic role they had played in the village.

Hispanics in sugar beet growing areas of northern Colorado found it difficult if not impossible to make the traditional progression from laborer to tenant to farm owner. Landowners hesitated to lease farms to Hispanics. Largely restricted, as a result, to seasonal beet labor, the migrants arrived at a time when land values had escalated while wages had not and when the move to ownership by anyone had generally dwindled. Yet without owning productive land, it would be difficult for Hispanics to convert new settlements in the north into stable villages. Even town lots were not easily acquired. Restrictive covenants and low wages kept Hispanics on the margins in northern towns. The state's largest beet sugar company, Great Western Sugar, with its company-financed colonies for Hispanic labor, did not discourage this state of affairs. Rather, the colonies epitomized the effort to preserve a system that identified Hispanics as a perpetual and distinct laboring force. Their one- or two-room distinctive adobe structures stood on lots devoid of shade, sufficient water, or farmland, a mile or two outside Anglo towns, or literally across the tracks.[38]

Women in this setting could not produce enough food to feed their families. Hispanic women in northern Colorado planted gardens when they could, but with over half the women working in the beet fields, even in the relatively rare instances when they had suitable land and water, they did not have the time to tend vegetables, so often they planted flowers instead. Fewer than 2 percent of Hispanic families working in the beet fields in northern Colorado produced a major part of their own food, and at least 33 percent had no gardens at all.[39]

[38] See, e.g., Paul S. Taylor, *Mexican Labor in the United States Valley of the South Platte, Colorado* (Los Angeles: University of California Publications in Economics, 1929), 6:54, 117–18, 136, 138, 171, 185, 186, 189, 191, 209; Sara Brown et al., *Children Working in the Sugar Beet Fields of Certain Districts of the South Platte Valley, Colorado* (New York: National Child Labor Committee, 1925), 64; Charles Timberlake, U.S. Congress, House of Representatives, Committee on Immigration and Naturalization, *Hearings: Immigration from Countries of the Western Hemisphere*, 70th Cong., 1st sess. (Washington, D.C.: Government Printing Office, 1928), 701; Robert McLean and Charles Thomson, *Spanish and Mexican in Colorado* (New York: Board of National Missions of the Presbyterian Church in the U.S.A., 1924), 34; Great Western Sugar Company property records, 1920–40, Great Western Sugar Building, Denver; *Through the Leaves* (Denver: Great Western Sugar Company, 1913–35), monthly publication available in Great Western Sugar Company Papers, WHC.

[39] U.S. Department of Labor, Children's Bureau, *Child Labor and the Work of Mothers in*

Hispanic women in northern Colorado, as in the villages, inherited and controlled property when the family had any property. But food had to be purchased; preparation was not shared among the community.[40] In the Hispanic villages, women had measured their value by their ability to provide and prepare food, both for their own and for neighboring families. As in other societies, food was more than sustenance; it carried emotional freight, bound villagers to one another, and defined their relations. Change in this arena would eventually shake all others.[41] Women would have to find new ways to measure their value. As with the men, their relationship to the land and to what it produced, a relationship that had provided the key to village membership, had changed. Membership in the community, like women's own value, would have to be defined in other ways.

The community itself was none too easy for women to find. Its elusiveness became most evident at childbirth. Midwives, essential and respected members of villages, moved north in the same way other women did, as members of beet-working families. But as such, they, too, became highly transient, here one year, gone the next. Some Hispanic women turned instead to free county clinics when they opened in the 1930s, but they found them a mixed blessing. It was "much better" during birth because they had ether for the pain, but much harder afterward. In New Mexico, relatives and neighbors had gathered round. All helped. In the north, remembered one mother, "we didn't have nobody to do anything for us so we had to work up to the minute we had kids and then up immediately, no women around to help."[42]

There were rare stories of interethnic friendship and even intimacy among women. At least one Hispanic mother learned English in an informal group of women beet workers, including Japanese and German-Russian, that met in each other's kitchens and exchanged ways of cooking. She learned to make German bread and other German dishes and cried when her German friend moved away. Maria Chavez remembered that though "neighbors" never visited each other, "white and brown" came to

---

the Beet Fields of Colorado and Michigan, Bureau Publication no. 115 (Washington, D.C.: Government Publications Office, 1923), 25–26, 54–55; B. F. Coen et al., *Children Working Farms in Certain Sections of Northern Colorado*, Bulletin no. 2 (Fort Collins: Colorado Agricultural Department, 1926), 99; interview with Rose Lopez, Española, Greeley, Colorado, September 26, 1983, who had a vegetable garden and did not work beets, and with Juan Gonzales, Española, Greeley, September 26, 1983, whose mother had a garden and did canning as did "lots of families" in the colony.

[40] Interview with Margarita Garcia, Windsor, Colorado, October 12, 1983. For property owning, see, e.g., Great Western Sugar Company property records.

[41] Brown et al., 102–4; Coen et al., 95–100. Mead, ed. (n. 28 above), 213.

[42] Interviews with Arthur Maes, with Rose Lopez, with Juan Gonzales, with Margarita Garcia, and with Lucy Romero, Greeley, Colorado, October 12, 1983.

dances on the farms.[43] Observer Paul Taylor related an incident of a woman farm operator who cared for the baby of the Spanish Americans working on her farm for three months when the mother went to the hospital with blood poisoning. There were even a few intermarriages: five in Weld County in 1926, or 8.6 percent of Hispanic and .9 percent of all marriages in the county that year.[44]

For many Hispanic women, however, the loneliness and isolation experienced in a childbirth unattended by women relatives and neighbors permeated their lives. They could remember a life in New Mexico where families always got together, one night at one house, one night at another, and now they spent months on isolated farms, scattered across the valley.[45] Amelia Cordova's mother liked to melt the snow that piled in corners and wash her hair with it. When one night a chemical in the snow blinded her mother, Amelia had to quit school to take care of her.[46] No community of women had arisen to replace the one they left in New Mexico.

Without the communal and exchanged labor of the village, the comradeship of women in childbirth, the power bases of the garden and of the village itself, Hispanic women in northern Colorado found their place in society altered indeed. Thoroughly dependent on a money economy, Chicanas in northern Colorado did not find in wage labor, when they could get it, a satisfactory replacement for their gardens as a means, or for their villages as an end. Performing agricultural labor for wages, unlike the nonwage labor in the garden or the village fields, provided neither the status of ownership nor even necessarily control of income produced. The farmer contracted with and paid the husband and not the wife for the family's labor.[47]

[43] Interview with Maria Chavez, Greeley, Colorado, October 12, 1983; Taylor revealed that in smaller rural communities in the eastern part of the South Platte Valley where there were fewest Mexicans, there was occasional social mingling at dances; and Margarita Garcia's father learned German from his association with the German Russian beet families and gave German square dancing calls (Taylor [n. 38 above], 228).

[44] Interview with Margarita Garcia: one owner's wife, a Swede, was friendly, the other did not want much to do with them. See also Taylor, 155. There were three intermarriages in 1920 and one in 1922; compare to seventeen in 1926 in Las Animas County (13.9 percent of Hispanic and 3.8 percent of all registered marriages) and seven in Rio Arriba County (10 percent of all marriages) (Weld County Marriage-Registers, Greeley, Colorado).

[45] Interview with Lucy Romero; Coen et al., 131–34.

[46] Interview with Amelia Cordova, Evans, Colorado, October 12, 1983. Theodore Rice, "Some Contributing Factors in Determining the Social Adjustment of the Spanish Speaking in Denver and Vicinity" (Master's thesis, University of Denver, 1932), 62. Coen et al., 107–8, 135–36; Brown et al. (n. 38 above), 60–61, 109. Language was a factor: in 1920, only 17 percent of Mexican and just over half of Spanish-American mothers knew enough English to make themselves understood, whereas 42 percent of the Mexican and almost all of the Spanish-American fathers did, a legacy of dealing with external affairs. But even within groups, many families had no visiting contacts at all (U.S. Department of Labor [n. 39 above], 17–18).

[47] Note that, as family labor, the labor of the 60 percent of Chicanas in the beet fields tended not to be recorded by the Anglo census takers, so that, e.g., only approximately 9.5

Moreover, there was little in the off-season jobs available to them that would advance the status of Hispanic women in either the Hispanic or the Anglo society. The winter occupations open to the women were even more limited and poorly paid than those open to Hispanic men. Only about one-tenth of the Chicanos with winter wage work were mothers, and while the men with winter employment averaged sixty dollars a month income, the women averaged half of that.[48] Domestic service, the largest category of jobs open to Chicanas, paid as much as ten or twelve dollars per week in Denver, but Maria Chavez remembered cleaning houses for fifty cents a day in the beet areas of Wyoming.[49] And not all employers looked kindly on Chicana domestics, as one Spanish American girl, a U.S. citizen working her way through school, recalled: "A woman to whom I applied for work when I first came to x—— said, 'People of your nationality are just terrible; I can't stand them, they're so crude, lazy, and so uncultured.'"[50]

---

percent of Chicanas in Colorado were recorded as gainfully occupied in 1930, the lowest proportion of any racial or ethnic group listed, whereas beet labor studies showed that 60 percent of Chicana mothers worked in beets (*Fifteenth Census of the United States, 1930 Population* [Washington, D.C.: Government Printing Office, 1933], 4:238). Also note that Hispanic men were recorded as gainfully employed at 74.1 percent, only slightly higher than the native Anglo (73.8 percent) and lower than black and foreign born, which may have been due to the time of year when the census was taken, to the reluctance of census takers to enter the barrios, or to their inability to communicate once they did (interview with Arthur Maes). See Mario Barrera, *Race and Class in the Southwest* (Notre Dame, Ind.: University of Notre Dame Press, 1979), 98, on agricultural *wage* as new to Chicanas.

[48] Brown et al., 83; Greeley Salvation Army report, January–March 1930, cited in Rice, 76. In Greeley no Hispanic clerked in a store until after World War II; Chicanas who obtained teachers' certificates found the north an uncongenial environment for job seeking, and even Denver lacked the Hispanic infrastructure necessary to provide more than a handful of clerical jobs; Helen Salazar, Colorado Board of Charities and Corrections, Colorado State Archives, box 66927; interviews with Rev. Alfonso Esquibel, Santa Fe, November 9, 1983, and Juan Gonzales (n. 42 above). In 1926 Reyes Gutierrez became the only Hispanic teacher in Weld County (Weld County School Records, box 13361, Colorado State Archives, Denver).

[49] "Survey of Employed Women in Denver, Colorado" (August 1920), 7, YWCA Records, Denver; Colorado Industrial Commission, *Annual Report* (1930), 29, on women's wages. Born in 1913 in New Mexico, Maria Chavez completed only the third grade because she "topped," or harvested, beets in December and cleaned houses in winter. She learned English through her contact with Anglos as a domestic worker (interview, n. 43 above).

[50] Quoted in Taylor, 225. Despite the tendency of the men I interviewed to be unable at first to recall many Hispanic domestic workers, at least one had a mother who had taken in laundry, and over half of the women interviewees had either themselves done domestic work or had mothers or sisters who did domestic work of some kind in northern Colorado. Margarita Garcia's mother took in laundry, as did Arthur Maes's mother (a widow). Maes commented, "That was how they made extra . . . not a lot of women, those who had to do it, had to because of the kids." Maes also remembered girls who went out and did day work in Denver. Rose Lopez continued to do domestic work, principally child care (live-in) after she was married. See also Timberlake (n. 38 above), 699. In the 1930 census, 41.6 percent of gainfully employed "Mexicans" were listed under domestic service and 41.5 percent under farm labor (Barrera, 97).

Hispanic women in Anglo areas virtually were left, of the entire panoply of their village activities, with the home alone. In contrast, the male realm of wage earning and external relations took on an ever-increasing importance. Hispanic men in the Anglo north, too, faced limited opportunities and options, and male/female relations in terms of decision-making and respect within marriage did not necessarily change, at least not immediately.[51] But the Hispanic women had lost ground within the Hispanic community as well as in the larger community, for they continued, after all, as inferior wage earners, and now wage earning had become the only means to an autonomous base. The balance within the Hispanic community had altered.[52]

Anglo women, too, had a role to play in this intercultural equation. Both in the villages and in the northern communities in Anglo areas, Anglo social service workers reached out particularly to Hispanic women. They adopted the prevalent assumption that women functioned as cultural bridges, that "mothers frequently furnish the key to the situation" and so shape the terms of cultural survival or acculturation.[53] Over 200 unaccompanied Anglo women missionaries had come to claim the Hispanic villages for Protestant America between 1900 and 1914 alone, and in the Anglo north, social workers and settlement house residents were simply missionaries by another name.[54]

Anglo women, like Anglo men, sought to fit Hispanic women into roles Anglos had designed for them. They envisioned them not as semiautonomous property owners who worked outside the house as well as within it and who lived with a relatively flexible sexual division of labor. Instead, they saw Hispanic women either as women thrust by circumstance and improvident men outside their true role (in the home), or as martyrs to domestic ignorance, their bad housekeeping making them slovenly and

[51] On decision making, see interviews with Margarita Garcia (n. 40 above), with Maria Chavez (n. 43 above); Reyes Ramos, "Movidas: The Methodological and Theoretical Relevance of Interactional Strategies," *Studies in Symbolic Interaction* 2 (1979): 141–65, and "Discovering the Production of Mexican American Family Structure," *De Colores* 6 (1982): 1–19 (typescript version); Helen Walker, "Mexican Immigrant and American Citizenship," *Sociology and Social Research* 13 (May–June 1929): 469; Roland Tharp et al., "Changes in Marriage Roles Accompanying the Acculturation of the Mexican-American Wife," *Journal of Marriage and the Family* 30 (August 1968): 404–12, esp. 409; Miguel Montiel, "The Social Science Myth of the Mexican American Family," *El Grito* 3 (Summer 1970): 56–63, esp. 56, 61–62; Mirandé and Enríquez (n. 7 above), 116.

[52] Interview with Arthur Maes (n. 37 above); Tharp, 409; McLean and Thomson (n. 38 above), 4; *Colorado Latin American Personalities* (n.p., 1959), 32. Compare Laila Shukry Hamamsy, "The Role of Women in a Changing Navaho Society," *American Anthropologist* 59 (1957): 109.

[53] Robert McLean, "Getting God Counted among the Mexicans," *Missionary Review of the World* 46 (May 1928): 362.

[54] For more information on these missionaries, see Deutsch, "Culture, Class, and Gender" (n. 10 above), 105–77.

impoverished. From the missionaries in the village to social workers in Denver, these middle-class Anglo women sought to transform Hispanic women into ideal domestic servants and proper housewives capable of Americanizing Hispanic men.[55]

As increasing numbers of women entered the labor force throughout the country, they experienced the same sort of segmentation of their labor market as had men. Different jobs held different status, and access to education coupled with discriminatory hiring practices could divide the female labor force along ethnic and racial lines.[56] Middle-class Anglo Americanizers in northern Colorado as elsewhere participated in this division by seeing Chicanas as they had for years seen "dependent" and other "inferior" females of any race, as the ideal solution to the "one phase of woman's work we seem incapable of handling, that of the large class of women, who, as domestic workers are in our homes."[57] These Americanizers, like social workers with other immigrant groups, displayed a desire to mold the behavior of women from another culture into standards acceptable to but not identical with their own middle-class "American" standards and aspirations. Often themselves professional social workers and teachers, they trained Chicanas to be solely domestic servants and "mothers." They continued to believe that mothers held "the channel through which to raise the standard of community along all lines."[58] And

[55] Flora Leavitt, "Our Spanish-speaking Neighbours," First City Conference on Denver's Social Problems, *Report* (June 1928), Community Relations Papers, box 2, DPL; Mrs. Clara Gard, "The Schools and Our Spanish Speaking Neighbours," Community Relations Papers, box 2, DPL. And see, e.g., Merton Hill, "The Development of an Americanization Program" (1928), reprinted in *Aspects of the Mexican American Experience* (New York: Arno Press, 1976), 93, 103; Anne Reynolds, *The Education of Spanish-speaking Children in Five Southwestern States*, Bulletin no. 1 (Washington, D.C.: Department of Interior, Office of Education, 1933), 17. Camarillo (n. 4 above), 177–79, 221; García, *Desert Immigrants* (n. 7 above), 77, 253; and Blackwelder, *Women of the Depression* (n. 4 above).

[56] Alice Kessler-Harris, "Stratifying by Sex: Understanding the History of Working Women," in *Labor Market Segmentation*, ed. Richard Edwards et al. (Lexington, Mass: D. C. Heath & Co., 1975), 231.

[57] W. H. Slingerland, *Child Welfare Work in Colorado*, University of Colorado Bulletin, vol. 20, no. 10 (Boulder: University of Colorado, 1920); Report of Industrial Committee, Colorado State Federation of Woman's Clubs, *Yearbook* (1914), 54; Dorothy Overstreet, "Problems and Progress among Mexicans of Our Own Southwest," *HMM* 32 (November 1917): 6; Grace Farrell, "Homemaking with the 'Other Half' along Our International Border," *Journal of Home Economics* 21 (June 1929): 413–18, esp. 418.

[58] Sarah B. Sutherland, *HMM* 35 (May 1921): 68. See also Maxine Seller, "Beyond the Stereotype—a New Look at the Immigrant Woman, 1880–1924," *Journal of Ethnic Studies* 3 (Spring 1975): 59–70, esp. 59, "The Education of the Immigrant Woman, 1900–1945" (n. 1 above), and "Protestant Evangelism and the Italian Immigrant Woman," in Caroli, ed. (n. 2 above), 128–29; Rudolf Glanz, *The Jewish Woman in America* (New York: Ktav Publishing House, 1976), 20; Emory Bogardus, *Essentials of Americanization*, 3d rev. ed. (Los Angeles: University of Southern California Press, 1923), 354.

they could imagine no better way to train Chicanas in "American" mothering than by encouraging them to meet the demand for domestic servants.[59]

The assumption on the part of Americanizers that women functioned as cultural guardians ensured women, both Anglo and Chicana, a central role in the process of Americanization. They would comprise both teacher and pupil. Such Americanization, however, was limited in what it offered Chicanas. Improved domestic care and the ability to speak English in and of themselves would not move Chicanas from margin to center in Anglo society and would certainly not return them to the center of Hispanic society. Even their job of cultural transmission was work on the margin of both cultures, at the boundary between them, and so provided them with a central place in neither.[60]

* * *

Increasingly at the center of village life, Hispanic women found the move north anything but liberating. Both men and women settling permanently in the Anglo north suffered from narrowed opportunities, but among Hispanics in the north, women found that their activities declined in significance relative to the men's.[61] Contrary to what many sociologists and other observers believed, this marginality of Hispanic women in the north was not something carried with them from the villages, but the result of adapting to life in a new, an Anglo, setting.[62] In a sense, this development was an Americanization of gender roles. It echoed the experiences of U.S. women during nineteenth-century industrialization as well as those of immigrant groups at the turn of the century. Arenas of female authority—such as food production, nonwage work, and kin and community affairs—for Chicanas became as they were in Anglo society, increasingly peripheral to the main concerns of subsistence in a centralized, male-dominated, and cash economy. For Hispanic women and men alike, a move into Anglo areas to the north afforded a loss of status, but for the women, full integration into the Anglo community would not remedy that loss.

The world from which these Hispanic women came—that of their village lives—has scarcely appeared in the historical literature of Chicanos except as overgeneralized and stereotyped in images of submissive, clois-

[59] Emory Bogardus, *The Mexican in the United States*, no. 5 (Los Angeles: School of Research Studies, 1934), 43.

[60] McLean (n. 53 above), 362.

[61] Maxine Baca Zinn, "Mexican-American Women in the Social Sciences," *Signs* 8, no. 2 (Winter 1982): 272.

[62] On the erection of "the hypothetical traditional family," something evident in master's theses of the 1930s and 1940s at the University of New Mexico and elsewhere, see Miguel Montiel, "The Chicano Family: A Review of Research," *Social Work* 18 (March 1973): 22–31, esp. 25.

tered, and powerless women. The focus has been on the rigidly patriarchal ideology articulated by those peripheral to or outside this world, by the Hispanic elite or Anglo observers of the time, or by later authors imposing views derived from other sites and times. Indeed, the accumulated weight of such stereotypes led some propagators to refute even firsthand testimony confronting them. Americanization teacher Alfred White insisted in 1923, "Mexican men like to refer to their wives as having influence and wisdom although they know such has never been the case."[63]

The relationship between ideology and practical life is more complex than White's claim suggests. A few authors have lately cited Hispanic women's activities in urban areas and even in the villages to cast doubt on the stereotypical ideology.[64] Other work suggests that women's daily activities in some contexts are not necessarily related to ideology; departures from the norm can be justified as emergencies. Frontiers—and in many respects this region encompassed an enduring Anglo-Hispanic frontier—could, in this view, perpetuate emergencies from generation to generation. Some recent historians of Hispanic ideology seem to support this view. They argue that despite differences between ideology and practice, a patriarchal ideal of unlimited male authority persisted in the upper and middle classes and was probably imitated by the lower classes and villagers, presumably male and female.[65] Yet a male villager himself recently rejected such a formulation, casting doubt on the wisdom of assuming that an ideology articulated by one class was consumed by all.[66]

In any case, the concentration on ideology and the confusion of it with practical life has distorted our view of village life and marred our understanding of the dynamics of intercultural relations, both rural and urban. It is against a more concrete, village background that the developments of this region and the Chicanas' and Chicanos' experiences as they moved into Anglo enclaves must be judged. Only by examining the gender structure of the village as it was lived can the impact of cross-cultural relations in the village and outside it be understood.

[63] Alfred White, *The Apperceptive Mass of Foreigners as Applied to Americanization, the Mexican Group* (1923; reprint, R&E Research Associates, 1971), 31.

[64] See, e.g., Swadesh (n. 6 above); and LeCompte (n. 6 above). For protests and summaries of relevant literature, see Baca Zinn, "Gender and Ethnic Identity among Chicanos" (n. 7 above), and "Mexican-American Women in the Social Sciences" (n. 61 above); Mirandé and Enríquez (n. 7 above), 108–17; and Griswold del Castillo, *La Familia* (n. 2 above).

[65] Laurel Ulrich, *Goodwives: Image and Reality in the Lives of Women in Northern New England, 1650–1750* (New York: Alfred A. Knopf, 1982), 8, 36, 50; Ramon Gutierrez, "Marriage, Sex, and the Family: Social Change in Colonial New Mexico, 1660–1846" (Ph.D. diss., University of Wisconsin—Madison, 1980); Griswold del Castillo, *La Familia* (n. 2 above).

[66] Facundo Valdez, "Vergüenza," in Kutsche, ed. (n. 12 above), 99–106. The impact of class differences among Hispanics on female behavior and the ideology of gender bears further exploration.

The changes in the balance between women's and men's activities brought about by cross-cultural relations affected not only the Hispanic women or the nature of the Hispanic family, for the village's sexual division of labor had sustained the entire group and their cultural autonomy. As varied sources of income diminished, as Hispanics came to rely solely on the men's wages, the autonomy of the community diminished also. Bereft of their autonomous base, Hispanic women in the north could not provide the stability that permitted forays into the cash economy to coexist with an autonomous cultural base. In Hispanic villages, the autonomy of women and the autonomy of the community had depended on each other. It was the work of the village women that made it possible for a time to exploit the exchange between Anglo and Hispanic economies. The Hispanic settlements in Anglo areas could not recreate this system.[67]

History Faculty
Massachusetts Institute of Technology

[67] For a discussion of the failed 1932 beet workers' strike in Colorado, see Deutsch, *Culture, Class, and Gender* (n. 10 above), 362–451, esp. 389–92.

Quiet Suffering: Atlanta Women in the 1930s

Julia Kirk Blackwelder*

ON April 28, 1934 a hotel maid in Atlanta, Georgia was making her rounds when she discovered a 24-year-old mother near death and her infant daughter, already dead, huddled in their bed. The mother recovered to testify that she had poisoned the baby and herself because she was destitute and could neither give the child up nor watch her starve. While this young mother's reaction was far from typical, it was symptomatic of the despair of many women in this city who suffered quietly through poverty and unemployment during the Great Depression. In April of 1931 an Atlanta woman wrote a local newspaper columnist that "trusting Jesus" was helping her cope with unemployment, but that religion held no cure for her problems. She warned of dire possibilities for the future: "If work cannot be gotten soon, numbers will have to be obliterated in some way."[1]

During the 1930s women's place in the Atlanta work force grew larger, but the expansion in jobs did not keep pace with the rapid flow of women into the labor market. Women who had been employed at the time of the Great Crash lost positions during the thirties and many more new job seekers were unsuccessful in securing work. New workers and older women found it harder to compete for employment than younger but experienced women. The new jobs created during the 1930s were concentrated in the clerical services and other low level white collar areas. Census figures as well as the reports of welfare workers indicate that black women did not share in the expanding women's labor market and that unemployment was higher among blacks than among whites. Throughout the Depression decade race was the primary determinant of a woman's

*Professor of History, The University of North Carolina at Charlotte.

place in the work force and of her access to public and private relief.

In placing Atlanta women in a larger perspective, some demographic patterns emerge which coincide with regional or national trends, but in other respects the city's women were exceptional. Atlanta women differed from their southern sisters in being urban. Although the percentage of black women in Atlanta was higher than in most American cities, it was only slightly higher than in the state as a whole. In 1930 total employment levels in Atlanta were three per cent higher than in Georgia as a whole, but for women only the Atlanta figure was twelve percent higher than state-wide employment.[2]

The pattern of female employment in Atlanta and in the state is more fully comprehended with reference to racial groups. In 1930 fifty-seven per cent of Atlanta black females of ten years of age and over were employed while forty-two percent of Georgia black females were employed. For white women the percentages were twenty for Atlanta and eighteen for the state. Not only was employment higher among black women throughout the state, but residence in Atlanta was a significant factor in raising employment among black women while it had little effect among white women.

In focusing on female employment in Atlanta in 1930, it also becomes apparent that the effect of marital status on women's employment varied according to race. Among single women fifteen years of age and older race was not a significant factor in the decision to enter the job market. Marriage, widowing, and divorce, however, affected the two racial groups in differing degrees. Seventeen percent of married white women worked while forty-seven percent of married black women were employed. Loss of spouse through death or divorce increased the employment of white women to thirty-seven percent, but of widowed and divorced black women seventy-seven percent worked, nearly the same ratio as among males. The Fifteenth Census also reveals that black women as well as black men went to work at an earlier age and worked later in life than whites.

Black and white women in Atlanta faced some hostility to their employment, but unlike other Depression cities Atlanta did not legislate restrictions against the hiring of married women and state efforts in this direction failed. In 1931 a bill to end night work for women in Georgia textile mills was submitted to the state legislature. As capital of the state, Atlanta was the center of controversy over passage of the bill. Although Georgia mill operators had terminated women's night shifts for economic reasons, they opposed and defeated the measure. Although the bill covered all female textile workers, the major argument for the measure was that night labor was dangerous to mothers and their children. The supporters of the bill were the Atlanta Federation of Trades, the Georgia Federation of Trades, and the Southern Council on Women and Children in Industry. Southern Council spokesman Lucy Randolph Mason contended that children of working mothers were more sickly and were poorer students than children of non-working mothers.[3]

In 1932 and 1935 members of the Atlanta Board of Education proposed a ban on female teachers' marrying and the hiring of married women teachers. Unlike the textile workers bill which was humanitarian in appeal, the resolutions on teacher hiring were directly related to the economy, their intent being to limit families to a single income. Newspaper accounts indicate that support for the resolutions was negligible and that they were swiftly killed. The Woman's Chamber of Commerce and the *Journal of Labor*, official voice of the Atlanta Federation of Trades, were immediate and unequivocal in their denunciation of any restrictive policy on teachers' marital status.[4]

The problem of employment discrimination against married women as a policy of employers or an attitude of the community is difficult to assess. A 1933 study of business women conducted by the U. S. Women's Bureau concluded that there was less job discrimination against married women in Atlanta than in northern cities. Atlanta also had a long history of inexpensive day care centers for children of both races, which indicates a measure of community support for working mothers. There is evidence, however, that married women did feel prejudice against their working. One Atlanta woman requested of a local journalist, "Please say something in favor of married women working. This is important to thousands."[5]

During the Depression many Atlantans, mostly whites, sought advice on employment problems from Mildred Seydell, a columnist for the Atlanta *Georgian*. The letters which Seydell received expressed the views of women in varying economic situations and revealed the particular handicaps which the youngest and oldest members of the work force faced in competing for jobs. A 20-year-old woman with college and secretarial training who had been seeking work for a year worried that her unemployment reflected personal inadequacy. "Is something wrong with me?" she wrote. "Please, what is wrong when a girl as young as I is unable to find work and relieve her family?" A correspondent describing herself as an "elderly business woman" complained, "When registering at the Post Office, Community Employment Bureau and the regular business employment bureaus, they require you to give your age. As soon as you give it, if you are honest, that is the end for you, as all calls for office help of any kind are for 'Young girls about 25 years of age, college education, five or six years experience, etc.' " Among Seydell's correspondents the lowest employment aspirations came from older women. A 77-year-old woman wrote her in search of domestic work.[6]

Older women, many of whom had never worked, seemed the least able to cope with the Depression. Women who had relied on savings or pensions felt victimized and helpless. One woman wrote to Seydell, ". . . all this talk about what men & man is to get . . . but we women has nothing to get it seems. . . . I am thinking of all the old girls who are as it seems on the rocks thanks to these noble sons operating banks and investment companies. Our savings are gone and no sign of a chance to make money." Older women also wrote Seydell in hopes that she could help them sell their belongings or items of their handiwork.[7]

While a woman's age affected her chances of finding employment, sex and race were the significant factors in fixing the type of job she might hope to gain. Inspection of the 1930 Census of Occupations reveals a pervasive caste system by race and sex in the distribution of jobs in Atlanta. In 1930 one-fourth of the labor force or 32,734 persons were domestic workers, only slightly fewer than the 36,345 persons employed in all manufacturing and mechanical industries combined. Three-fourths (74%) of Atlanta domestics were female, more than four-fifths (84%) were black, and two-thirds (66%) were black females. Of black female workers in Atlanta in 1930, 21,869 or ninety percent were employed as domestics.

In the Fifteenth Census nearly all service jobs were classified as domestic work. Within the category of domestic work there were also significant differences by race in the distribution of jobs. There were 12,980 black female servants in Atlanta in 1930. This figure does not include untrained nurses and laundresses employed outside commercial laundries who totaled over 6,000. The employment of white domestics followed quite another pattern. Only 275 or twelve percent of white domestics were classed as servants. The remainder included housekeepers and boardinghouse keepers, waitresses, hairdressers, and manicurists. Not only were the majority of black female workers domestics, but among female domestics the more desirable jobs were dominated by whites.

Among white women the largest occupational category was clerical work. In 1930 there were 9,333 clerical positions held by Atlanta women, but only 180 of these jobs were filled by blacks. Indicative of the unbending institution of segregation, a federal study revealed that all black clerical workers in Atlanta were employed by black-owned businesses.[8] While the vast majority of laundry operatives were black females, white women dominated female jobs in the manufacturing and mechanical industries, in transportation and communication, and in sales.

Women appeared in the skilled trades and crafts in token numbers only.[9]

A summary of the employment of female professionals confirms that black women, regardless of training, had a more difficult time securing work than whites. The habit as well as the legal status of segregation ensured a place for the black professional person, but segregation also held down salary and advancement possibilities for blacks. Black women were underrepresented relative to white women in professional ranks both with respect to their place in the population and their place in the work force. The greatest number of female professionals were teachers of whom 488 or twenty-nine percent were blacks employed under a separate pay scale from that applying to whites.[10] Black women were best represented proportionally among college presidents, professors, and instructors. Although the Census Bureau noted that some secondary personnel may have been included with college teachers, the existence of Atlanta's black college undoubtedly had a positive effect on the position of black women in higher education. However, among social and welfare workers, racial discrimination erased the advantages Atlanta blacks secured through their educational institutions. Although the predominantly black Atlanta School of Social Work conducted one of the few recognized training programs in social work in the nation and the only one in the area, there were thirteen black women as opposed to seventy-seven white women in welfare positions in Atlanta.

The story of employment during the 1930s is primarily one of losses, but when the Atlanta work force is broken down into four groups by race and sex, it can be seen that over the ten-year period employment did not decline in a real sense for all four groups. Excepting emergency work, the number of jobs held by black males decreased between 1930 and 1940 and the increase in jobs held by white males did not keep pace with population growth. Black women lost more than 900 jobs during the decade while white women gained approximately 4,000 jobs. The employment of white women aged fourteen and over held steady at thirty-one percent while the employment of black women decreased from fifty-eight percent to forty-seven percent. If emergency jobs for women are included in the 1940 employment figures, white women are seen to have increased their employment by nearly two percent. White women shifted from the minority to the majority of the female work force and for black women employment became the exception rather than the rule.[11]

In addition to shifting female employment levels during the 1930s, there were important changes in the nature and status of women's work. Overall occupational statistics indicate that during the Depression women maintained or improved their status in professional positions relative to men; the number of men in eighteen professions enumerated in the Census decreased by 302 between 1930 and 1940 while the number of women increased by 20. However, examination of the areas in which job gains were achieved reveals that men gained 125 jobs in professions dominated by males and 216 jobs in categories dominated previously or concurrently by women. In contrast women gained only twenty-six jobs in categories where men had predominated in 1930 and 174 jobs in professions which women had dominated in 1930. In 1930 women comprised fifty percent of the city's professionals, but they accounted for fifty-four percent of unemployed professionals and seventy-five percent of professionals on layoff. In 1940 women comprised sixty-two percent of Atlanta's unemployed professionals. The decline in the status of professional women was paralled by a decrease in the number of women in managerial and supervisory positions.[12]

Although women lost status in professional and supervisory areas during the Depression, new employment options for women were opening in the blue collar crafts and trades. Women were token representatives in each of the following occupations in 1940, but there had been no women in these trades in 1930. New occupations included machinist, stone cutter, auto mechanic, plumber, plasterer, sheet metal worker, shoemaker, cabinetmaker, lineman, welder, and furnaceman. In other jobs such as repairman, chauffeur, deliveryman, and mason, women increased their representation during the 1930s. Women lost jobs in construction, but overall gains far outweighed the losses. While World War II is generally credited with drawing women into the blue collar trades, Atlanta in 1940 showed no sign of the defense build-up which followed.[13]

While the employment record of white women during the thirties reveals an expanding job market partially offset by declining job status, black women lost ground in both respects. Black women not only suffered higher unemployment than white women, but they also found it more difficult to obtain public or private relief than did men or white women. In the early years of the Depression the particular needs of women were largely disregarded by Atlanta's relief agencies and throughout the 1930s the burden of black Atlantans was made heavier by racial discrimination. In 1930 Atlanta had few facilities for the care of indigents and public charity homes and hospitals were not expanded to meet increased Depression needs. The governments of the city and county subsidized Community Chest agencies including the Florence Crittenton Home, the Salvation Army, and the Home for Old Women, all of which offered at least temporary shelter to women but none of which accepted blacks. The Salvation Army Emergency Lodge offered housing to pregnant women without the restrictions imposed by the Crittenton Foundation. The Lodge greatly enlarged its facilities during the 1930s, but it took no steps to aid black women.[14]

The hard times of 1930 and 1931 prompted the opening of soup kitchens and relief centers, but inadequate private and public funding doomed these projects to a short life. The Atlanta Urban League, which had provided food for many black families, was forced to close its kitchen late in 1931. The City Relief Center which was open from November, 1931 to June, 1932 made food available to all needy people, but it provided beds for white males only. The same pattern was initially followed by the Atlanta Transient Bureau which operated from 1933 until 1935 when it was replaced by other FERA programs.

Although the Federal Transient Service eventually provided housing for black men, women of either race were offered housing only when there were funds to rent private rooms.[15]

Throughout the 1930s the Atlanta Police Department provided relief to women of both races who had nowhere else to turn. Women were allowed to sleep at the jail although stays were generally limited to twenty-four hours. Statistics of the Woman's Bureau of the Atlanta Police Department indicate that in 1931 five times as many white women as black women were given shelter by the Department. The Woman's Bureau also attempted to aid female refugees in finding employment or locating families who would take them in.[16]

Needy Atlantans who were unable to secure relief formed a corps of intra-urban transients who lived in the streets and in abandoned buildings. An official of the Community Chest described one of these persons who was later aided by the Chest:

> Some days ago, I noticed an old negro woman sitting at a window of a good but vacant house. I stopped to learn why she was there. I found this old negro, about seventy years old with a leg so badly infected that she could hardly walk across the room, had been in this house absolutely bare of bed or other furniture, for weeks and had been fed by the neighborhood. The case had been reported to the police and she was taken to the station only to be released the next day to return to the house. She was reported to county authorities and an effort made to get her in the Alms House. This failed because there was no place for her and her leg was merely dressed and she was returned to the house.[17]

Atlanta welfare workers were aware of the desperate conditions in the black community. Reports issued by the federal government indicated that blacks constituted sixty percent of the city's relief load. A resident of Atlanta's west side black community described the fruits of depression during the winter of 1931 to 1932:

> Crime was hand in hand with want. Coal was stolen by the ton from peoples' coal houses. The act of tearing down vacant houses for fuel became so acute [that the city passed special

> legislation to prevent it.] Families moved every month rather than try to pay rent. Thugs struck down and robbed men, women, and children of food, money, and even clothing was taken from peoples' backs.

Conditions continued to worsen through 1934 when black Atlantans demanded increased police protection because "women and girls were being attacked on their return from work, and their money being taken and themselves beaten."[18]

Despite the disproportionate suffering of blacks, rampant discrimination in per capita relief allocations and in the distribution of emergency jobs went largely uncriticized by white leaders. Following its study of relief applicants in 1935 the FERA published a survey of relief cases which had been dropped because of inadequate funding. A random sample of closed cases in Atlanta revealed that only thirteen of 102 families dropped were white and that sixty-five of eighty-nine black families dropped were headed by females. Despite higher unemployment among black women, white women received the majority of female emergency jobs. The unemployment census of 1937 reported that white women held 1,225 emergency jobs while only 447 positions were secured by black women.[19]

For many white women in Atlanta the Depression brought discomfort as opposed to despair. The Depression fostered new family tensions and wives were not always sympathetic with the difficulties faced by husband-providers. Several wives wrote Mildred Seydell that their husbands made comfortable incomes, but that they squandered their funds on themselves while their families suffered. Most of Seydell's female correspondents who complained of unhappy marriages were reluctant to divorce because they felt they could not survive financially outside marriage. One Atlanta wife wrote that she wished to leave her husband but that she had no relatives who could support herself and her children. A childless wife stated that she was "bored" with her husband but that she feared the "notoreity" of divorce and knew that she "couldn't earn a decent living."[20]

There are many facets of women's suffering during the 1930s, but the effects of the Depression on Atlanta women differed most according to race. Although it is commonly known that black females in America have worked at the least desirable jobs for the lowest wages, the magnitude of the disparity between black and white women in Atlanta and the strictness of the caste system of employment are surprising. For the vast majority of black women domestic work was the only employment option. The number of domestic jobs declined during the decade and other types of jobs were not opening for blacks. Overall, white women were enlarging their place in the work force although they were not advancing in positions of high status. The presence of women in unusual blue collar occupations and evidence of qualified support for working mothers in Depression Atlanta point up the need for reevaluation of women's roles in the South. Although there is much to be learned about the effects of cloistering on women's perceptions of the world outside the home, it appears that women's understanding of the Depression were highly dependent upon the degree to which they were involved in the economy.

NOTES

[1]Atlanta *Journal*, June 12, 1934, p. 1; Atlanta *Constitution*, June 13, 1934, p. 5; letter to Mildred Seydell, April 20, 1931, Seydell Papers, Emory University.

[2]William F. Ogburn, *Social Characteristics of Cities* (Chicago, 1937), p. 2 Unless otherwise cited, all statistics in the essay were computed from U. S. Department of Commerce, Bureau of the Census, *Fifteenth Census of the United States*, 1930 (Washington, G. P. O., 1932), Population, III; *ibid.* (Washington, 1933), Occupations, IV; *ibid.* (Washington, 1931), Unemployment, I; Bureau of the Census, *Census of Partial Employment, Unemployment , and Occupations, 1937*, (Washington, 1938); Bureau of the Census, *Sixteenth Census of the United States, 1940*, (Washington, 1943), Population, II-III.

[3]*Journal of the House of Representatives of the State of Georgia*, 1931 (Atlanta, 1931), pp. 299, 612; Georgia Federation of Labor, *Proceedings of the Thirty-Third Annual Convention* (n. p., 1931), pp. 9, 30, 34; Atlanta *Constitution*, July 1, 2, 17, 1931; Lucy Randolph Mason, *To Win These Rights: A Personal Story of the CIO in the South* (New York, 1952), p. 8; Mason, *Standards for Workers in Southern Industry*, printed by the National Consumers' League (New York, 1931), pp. 26-28.

[4]Atlanta *Constitution*, April 7, 10, 1935 *Journal of Labor*, May 3, 1935; letter to the Atlanta Board of Education from the Woman's Division, Atlanta Chamber of Commerce, April 8, 1935. Additional information on married teachers in Atlanta is contained in the Tommie Dora Barker Papers, Emory University.

[5]U. S. Department of Labor, Women's Bureau, Bulletin no. 120, *The Employment of Women in Offices* (Washington, G. P. O., 1934), p. 63; Sheltering Arms Day Nursery Association Papers, Atlanta Historical Society; letter to Mildred Seydell, October 17, 1930.

[6]Letters to Mildred Seydell, March 3, 1936; August 9, 1934; January 13, 1937.

[7]Letter to Mildred Seydell, December, 1933; May 15, 1931; September 24, 1933; October 26, 1935; May 31, 1936.

[8]*The Employment of Women in Offices*, 56.

[9]In 1930 there were thirteen black women employed overall in transportation and communication, none of whom were telephone or telegraph operators. Black and white women together held thiry-three construction jobs and seven laborers positions in the rail industry. There were two female sheriffs, seven policemen, two detectives, eighteen city or county inspectors, one contractor, one carpenter, and four undertakers. Of 1,100 trained female nurses, 200 were black. There were thirty-six black and fifty-six white women enumerated as college faculty members.

[10]Black teachers in the Atlanta Public Schools pressed a suit for equal pay in 1947, Barker Papers.

[11]The ratio of jobs to population in 1930 and 1940 apparently conflicts with unemployment statistics gathered by the Census Bureau in the same years. Among Atlantans the Census Bureau reported that unemployment in 1930 was lowest among white females, followed by black females, then white males, and finally black males. In 1940 white males were reported to have the lowest unemployment, followed by white females who were followed by black females with black males again having the highest unemployment. Since white males replaced white females as the group with the lowest unemployment, it appears the white women did not hold their own in the labor market respective to white men. However, white women were entering the job market at a faster rate than men so that unemployment *rates* were growing at the same time that real employment was increasing. According to the Census Bureau unemployment among black women rose by only eight percent between 1930 and 1940, but it has already been seen that the ratio of employed to total population decreased from fifty-eight percent to forty-seven percent. Apparently many black women no longer reported themselves as seeking work and are therefore not represented in 1940 unemployment figures. Rupert B. Vance and Nadia Danilevsky, "Population and the Pattern of Unemployment in the Southeast 1930-1937," *Southern Economic Journal*, VII (October, 1940), p. 196.

[12]The largest gains in any professional category were in teaching where men gained 173 jobs between 1930 and 1940, an increase of sixty percent, and women gained 101 jobs, an increase of six percent. Men gained thirty-two social and welfare positions while women gained fifty-five. Areas where women gained positions at the same time that men lost jobs were engineering, medicine, and the writing professions where women gained a total of seventeen (5, 3, 9) jobs while men lost a total of 161 (68, 52, 41) jobs.

[13]Social Planning Council, *A Report on Health and Welfare in DeKalb and Fulton Counties* (Atlanta, 1943), p. 87.

[14]Department of Public Welfare of the Board of Control of Eleemosynary Institutions, *Directory of Georgia Social Agencies and Institutions* (Atlanta, 1932), p. 11; J. Arthur Flynn, "Transients in Georgia; Report of the Transient Committee," *Georgia Conference on Social Work* (Atlanta, 1933), p. 9; *Community Life*, I (July, 1931), 4.

[15]Dixie Brooks Jones, "A Study of Twenty Boys Registered in the Atlanta Transient Bureau May and June, 1935," (M. A. thesis, Emory University, 1935), pp. 45-50.

[16]*Fiftieth Annual Report of the Chief of Police of the City of Atlanta, Georgia, 1931*, pp. 6, 30.

[17]Comer McDonald Woodward, "The Community Chest," typescript, n. d., Woodward Papers, Emory University.

[18]*Community Life*, II (July 20, 1932), p. 3; U. S., Federal Emergency Relief Administration, Research Bulletin, I, 5, *The Relief Turnover in Thirteen Cities* (Washington, G. P. O., 1935), p. 7; Mrs. L. D. Shivery, "How the Union Handled the Unemployment Crisis, 1931-1932," Neighborhood Union Papers, box 3, Atlanta University; Minutes of the Executive Committee of the Neighborhood Union, May 9, 1934, Neighborhood Union Papers.

[19]F. E. R. A., Research Bulletin, I, 11, *Survey of Cases Removed from Relief Rolls for Administrative Reasons in June, 1935 in Atlanta, Georgia* (Washington, G. P. O., 1935), p. 3.

[20]Letters to Mildred Seydell, August 14, 1930; n. d., ca. 1931; February 15, 1930; June 19, 1931.

RACE, SEX, AND CLASS: BLACK FEMALE TOBACCO WORKERS IN DURHAM, NORTH CAROLINA, 1920-1940, AND THE DEVELOPMENT OF FEMALE CONSCIOUSNESS

BEVERLY W. JONES

This article examines how race, sex, and class affected the lives and consciousness of black female tobacco workers in Durham, North Carolina, and how they conceptualized work and its meaning in their lives. The research was based on fifteen interviews. The interviewees fall into three broad age categories: five were born before 1908, seven between 1908 and 1916, and three between 1916 and 1930. All were born in the rural South. The majority migrated to Durham in the 1920s, subsequently entering the labor force.

Historically, black labor of both females and males has been critical to the tobacco manufacturing industry. As cigarette manufacture became mechanized, blacks were hired as stemmers, sorters, hangers, and pullers. These "dirty" jobs were seen as an extension of field labor and therefore as "Negro work" for which whites would not compete.[1] The rapidly expanding number of tobacco factories employed the thousands of black females and males migrating from the rural South. The pull of better paying jobs and the push of falling farm prices, perennial pests, and hazardous weather induced a substantial number of black sharecroppers, renters, and landowners to seek refuge in Durham.

Charlie Necoda Mack, the father of three future female tobacco workers, remembered the difficulties of making an adequate living out of farming in Manning, South Carolina. "I was a big cotton farmer; I made nine bales of cotton one year. Next year I made, I think, one or two, and the next year I didn't make none. I left in July, I had to leave. I borrowed money to get up here—

Feminist Studies 10, no. 3 (Fall 1984). © by Feminist Studies, Inc.

Durham. I had six children and I know no jobs available. Well, then I came up here in July in 1922 and got a job at the factory. And by Christmas I had all my children with clothes and everything." Unlike the Mack family who were pushed out of South Carolina, others were pulled into the city. Dora Miller, after marrying in 1925, left Apex, North Carolina, because she heard of the "better paying jobs in Durham." Mary Dove, at age ten and accompanied by her family, left Roxboro, North Carolina, because a "Duke agent told us that a job in the factory at Liggett Myers was waiting for my daddy." Rosetta Branch, age eighteen and single, left Wilmington, North Carolina, because her mother had died, and "there were no other kinfolks."[2]

Thus, Durham's gainfully employed black population swelled from 6,869 in 1910 to 12,402 in 1930. (The city's total black population in 1930 was 23,481.) According to the census, the number of black female tobacco workers in 1930 was 1,979 out of a total black female population of 12,388. (See table 1.)

TABLE 1 Tobacco Industry Employment by Race and Gender

	White		Negro	
Durham County: 1930	Male	Female	Male	Female
	2,511	2,932	1,336	1,979
North Carolina: 1940	Male	Female	Male	Female
	6,517	3,175	5,899	5,898

Source: U.S. Bureau of the Census, *Population: 1930* (Washington, D.C.: GPO), vol. 3, pt. 2, pp. 355, 378; *Labor Force: 1940* (Washington, D.C.: GPO, 1940), vol. 3, pt. 4, p. 566.

Durham and Winston Salem tobacco factories employed more black females than other cities: one-half of the number of women employed in tobacco factories in 1930 in these cities were black compared with the 19.7 in Petersburg and Richmond in Virginia.[3]

Upon disembarking the central train station, the newly arrived southern migrants were immediately faced with race restrictions. Rigidly segregated communities were the dominant feature of

Durham's black life. Many of the migrants settled in the dilapidated housing in the larger communities of East End and Hayti, a bustling commercial district of black businesses, and in the smaller areas of Buggy Bottom and Hickstown. Almost all black workers rented either from the company and white landlords or from black real estate agents. The comments of Annie Barbee, the daughter of Necoda Mack, reflect her first impressions of Durham.

> We were renting in the Southern part of Durham—the Negro section—on Popular Street, second house from the corner, across the railroad tracks. The house was small, two rooms, but somehow we managed. The street was not paved and when it rained it got muddy and in the fall, the wind blew all the dust into your eyes and face. There were no private family bathrooms. But it was an exciting life. See, in the country things were so dull—no movie houses. . . . Up here people were always fighting and going on all the time.[4]

Despite the exploitive living conditions described by Barbee, urban employment did have some liberating consequences for rural daughters.

Race restricted the black population to segregated neighborhoods and also determined the kinds of jobs black females could get. Black female tobacco workers also faced discrimination as poor people and as females. Although class and sex restraints punctuated the lives of white female tobacco workers, their impact was reinforced by management policies. Although white females' wages were a fraction of white males' and inadequate to support a family, black females' wages were even lower. According to some black female tobacco workers, the wage inequity led many white women to consider black women inferior. This in turn led to an atmosphere of mistrust between black and white females. Management strengthened racial and class inequities in hiring practices, working conditions, and spatial organization of the factory, and therefore impeded the formation of gender bonds among working-class women.

Black females were usually hired as if they were on an auction block. "Foremen lined us up against the walls," one worker stated, "and chose the sturdy robust ones." Mary Dove recalled that she had "to hold up one leg at a time and then bend each backwards and forwards."[5] Once hired, black and white women were separated on different floors at the American Tobacco Company and in entirely different buildings at the Liggett Myers Tobacco Company. In the 1920s and 1930s, according to a report by the Women's Bureau (the federal agency created in 1920), and confirmed by my interviews, 98 percent of these black females were confined to the prefabrication department where they performed the "dirty" jobs—sorting, cleaning, and stemming tobacco.[6] White females had the "cleaner" jobs in the manufacturing and packing department as they caught, inspected, and packed the tobacco. However, both jobs were defined by the sex division of labor—jobs to be performed by women. Black men moved between the areas pushing 500-lb hogsheads of tobacco while white men worked as inspectors, safeguarding the sanctity of class and sex segregation.[7]

Reflecting on these blatant differences in the working conditions, some fifty years later, many black women expressed anger at their injustice. Annie Barbee recalled: "You're over here doing all the nasty dirty work. And over there on the cigarette side white women over there wore white uniforms. . . . You're over here handling all the old sweaty tobacco. There is a large difference. It ain't right!" Rosetta Branch spoke of her experience with anger. "They did not treat us Black folks right. They worked us like dogs. Put us in separate buildings. . . thinking maybe we were going to hurt those white women. Dirty work, dirty work we had to do. Them white women think they something working doing the lighter jobs."[8] These comments reflect both the effectiveness of management policies to aggravate racial and sexual differences in order to preclude any possible bonds of gender, but also illustrate the unhealthy working conditions to which black women were exposed.

In fact, the interviews indicate that the health of some black women suffered in the factories. Pansy Cheatham, another daughter of Necoda Mack, maintained that the Georgia leaf-tobacco "was so dusty that I had to go to the tub every night after work. There was only one window and it got so hot that some women just fainted. The heat and smell was quite potent." Mary Dove recounted one of her fainting spells. "You know on the floor there was a salt dispenser, because it would get so hot. I did not feel so well when I came to work but I had to work. After about two hours standing on my feet, I got so dizzy—I fell out. My clothes was soaking wet from my head to my feet. When I woke up I was in the dispensary."[9]

Blanche Scott and another worker were forced to quit for health reasons. Scott, who began working for Liggett Myers in 1919, quit four years later. "When I left the factory, it became difficult for me to breathe. The dust and fumes of the burly tobacco made me cough. The burly tobacco from Georgia had chicken feathers and even manure in it. Sometimes I would put an orange in my mouth to keep from throwing up. I knew some women who died of TB." The other worker had miscarried twice. Pregnant again, she decided not to return to the American Tobacco Company. "I felt that all that standing while I stemmed tobacco," she stated, "was the reason I lost my two children." Some women found momentary relief from the dust by retreating outside the confines of the factory complex to breathe the fresh air while sitting under trees or on the sidewalk during lunch.[10]

These comments on the poor, unhealthy, working conditions were verified by research on Durham's death records between 1911 and 1930. In many instances, the records were imprecise and failed to provide information about race and occupation. Of the 105 certificates that identified black women as tobacco workers, who died between 1911 and 1920, 48 (about 46 percent) died of tuberculosis, sometimes listed as phthisis and consumption. Of the 134 recorded deaths of black female tobacco workers between 1920 and 1930, 86 (64.5 percent) died of tuberculosis. Because tuberculosis is a bacteria that can be transmitted by a tubercular person through the cough, it is likely that poorly ventilated rooms and incessant coughing by workers, possibly by a carrier, made some workers susceptible to the disease, although deplorable living conditions of workers cannot be dismissed as a contributing factor.[11]

As studies have found in other cities, black females in Durham were more likely to work than white females.[12] Black females also earned lower wages than white females. In the early 1900s, wages for black tobacco workers, both female and male, ranked the lowest in the nation. In 1930, 45.5 percent of native-born white women in Durham were gainfully employed—27.7 percent in tobacco. While 44 percent of black women were working, 36.2 percent were employed in tobacco. From 1920 to 1930, Durham's white female tobacco workers averaged about 29 cents per hour, while black female hand stemmers earned about 11.9 cents an hour. However, black men, as well as black women who stemmed tobacco by machine, averaged about 27 cents an hour, still less than white women.[13]

Wage differential continued and worsened throughout the 1930s. By the eve of the New Deal, a Women's Bureau survey reported figures for North Carolina which revealed an even higher wage discrepancy. White women working in the making and packing departments reported a median weekly wage of $15.35. Wages ranged from $14.10 earned as catchers to $20.50 on older packing machines. On the newest packing machines, the median wage was $18.15. Black women, working in the leaf department, reported a median weekly wage of $7.95. Hand stemmers earned a median wage of $6.50.[14]

The low wage was itself demeaning to black female workers. But the inadequate wages also forced many into the labor force at an early age. Black women thus worked for a longer part of their lives, and henceforth were more vulnerable to diseases and other health problems. Blanche Scott, for example, began working at the age of twelve. "Since my mother stayed so sick, I had to go to work. I worked at Liggett Myers after school got out. I attended West End School. I'd normally get out at 1:30 and worked from two o'clock to 6 p.m. I was just twelve years old. In the summer, they're let children come and work all day until four o'clock." Pansy Cheatham began working at age thirteen. "My father talked to the foreman," she stated, "I worked because my sisters Mae and Annie worked; I stemmed tobacco by hand. But Papa did collect the money and use it for food and clothing." Cheatham's statement would indicate that the gender hierarchy of the black family resided in the father who controlled the daughter's wages.[15]

Many women saw their employment as a means of "helping out the family." Better stated in the words of Margaret Turner, "that's what a family is all about, when we—the children—can help out our parents."[16] Out of the fifteen interviewees, the ten women who entered the work force at an early age all conceptualized the central meaning of their work in relation to their families.

By the late 1920s and early 1930s, the enforcement of the Child Labor Law of 1917 arrested the practice of employing children under the age of sixteen. "They began to ask for your birth certificate," one worker stated. A study done by Hugh Penn Brinton, substantiated the decrease of child labor employment in Durham's factories. Brinton found that from 1919 to 1930 the percentage of black laboring-class households sending children into the labor force had decreased from 35 to 14 percent.[17]

However, the legislation against child labor did not force the wages up for black tobacco workers, and the constant low earning power of both female and male breadwinners continued to affect the lives of black female workers psychologically. Many women submitted to the demands of the foreman and other company officials. Viewed as short-term cheap labor, some females submitted to physical and verbal harassment, because in many instances defiance would have certainly resulted in the loss of jobs. Dora Miller asserted that "since the foreman knew you needed the job, you obeyed all of his demands without question. He called you dirty names and used foul language but you took it." Mary Dove recalled what it was like to work under one "of the toughest bosses." "Our foreman was a one-eyed fella named George Hill. He was tight! He was out of South Carolina, and he was tight. I mean tight! He'd get on top of them machines—they had a machine that altered the tobacco—he'd get on top of that machine and watch you, see if you was working all right and holler down and curse. Holler down and say, "GD. . . get to work! GD. . . go to work there you ain't doin' nothin." Janie Mae Lyons remembered one who walked in on her while she "was in the sitting position on the stool" and told her "that if you ain't finished then you can pack up and leave. I was so embarrassed and that's what I did."[18]

Lyons's departure from the factory represented a form of militancy—a definitive stance against further harassment. Other women resisted verbally. Annie Barbee publicly castigated "women who allowed the foreman to fumble their behind" and further stated that if "one did that to me he would be six feet under." She indicated no one ever did. One worker resisted "by playing the fool." "The foreman thought I was crazy and left me alone."[19]

Constantly resisting physical and verbal abuse and trying to maintain their jobs, the workers were further threatened by increased mechanization. "I don't think it is right," one woman stated, "to put them machines to take away from us poor people." "Because of the strain we work under," another maintained, "they don't care nothing for us." One woman recalled crying at the machines because she could not quit in the face of high unemployment. "With them machines you have to thread the tobacco in. Them machines run so fast that after you put in one leaf you got to be ready to thread the other. If you can't keep pace the foreman will fire you right on the spot. Sometimes I get so nervous but I keep on goin'."[20]

The increased mechanization of the tobacco factories resulting in physical hardships of female workers can to some degree be attributed to Franklin D. Roosevelt's National Industrial Recovery

Acts of 1933 and 1934. On the one hand, President Roosevelt's New Deal measure fostered economic stability for many black families by establishing standard minimum wages and maximum hours. On the other hand, this standardization exacerbated the job insecurity of black workers by indirectly catalyzing many companies to maximize profits by replacing hand labor with technology. During the latter part of the 1930s, Liggett Myers closed its green leaf department that had employed the majority of black women.[21]

The long-term insecurities of their jobs led black female stemmers to organize Local 194. The limited success of the union was reflected in the decline of its membership of two thousand in January 1935 to less than two hundred by May 1935. Black female union members found little support from either Local 208, black controlled, or Local 176, white controlled. In the eyes of the male unionists, the temporary nature of women's jobs excluded them from any serious consideration by the locals.[22] Conscious of their auxiliary position and the lack of support from male-led unions, black females chose not to support the April 16, 1939, strike at Liggett Myers. Reporting for work on that day, they were turned away as management had no other recourse but to close the factory. Dora Miller recalled that the black stemmery workers "were never involved in the strike because demands for wage increases did not include us."[23] On April 26, 1939, the company capitulated. The contract indeed reaffirmed Miller's assessment because the stemmery workers were not mentioned.[24]

The factory policies of hiring, wages, working conditions, and spatial segregation, inherently reinforced by racism, the "cult of true white womanhood," and the inadvertent effect of New Deal governmental measures, all came together to touch the lives of black women tobacco workers, with sex, race, and class exploitation. These practices further dissipated any possible gender bonds between black women and white women workers. As a race, black female tobacco workers were confined to unhealthy segregated areas either in separate buildings or on separate floors. As a working class, they were paid inadequate wages. As a sex, they were relegated to the worst, lowest paid, black women's jobs.

Black females conceptualized work as a means of "helping out the family." Denied self-respect and dignity in the factory, black female tobacco workers felt a need to validate themselves in other spheres. Victimized by their working conditions, female tobacco workers looked to the home as a preferred if not powerful arena. The home became the inner world that countered the factory control over their physical well-being. The duality of their lives—workers of production and nurturers of the family—could be assessed as a form of double jeopardy. But it was their role as nurturers, despite the hardship of work, that provided them with a sense of purpose and "joy." As Pansy Cheatham described her daily routine, "I get up at 5:30 a.m. I feed, clothe, and kiss my children. They stay with my sister while I work. At 7 a.m. I am on the job. A half-hour for lunch at about twelve noon. At 4 p.m. I quit work. At home about 4:30 then I cook, sometimes mend and wash clothes before I retire. About 11:30 I go to bed with joy in my heart for my children are safe and I love them so."[25]

Black females who worked together in the tobacco factories also had the positive experience of creating networks of solidarity. Viewing their plight as one, black females referred to one another as "sisters." This sisterhood was displayed in the collection of money during sickness and death and celebration of birthdays. The networks established in the factory overlapped into the community and church. Many of these workers belonged to the same churches—Mount Vernon, Mt. Gilead, and White Rock Baptist Church—and functioned as leaders of the usher boards, missionary circles, and Sunday School programs. These bonds were enhanced in the community by the development of clubs. These church groups and female's clubs overlapped the factory support networks and functioned in similar ways.

Finally, the resistance to the physical and verbal abuse that was a constant in the work lives of black women fostered among some a sense of autonomy, strength, and self-respect. Annie Barbee was one of those women. The assertiveness, dignity, and strength she developed through work became an intricate part of her private life. At age forty and pregnant, she decided to obtain private medical assistance despite her husband's resistance. "When you know things ain't right God gave you a head and some sense. That's my body. I knew I wasn't going to Duke Clinic. And I was working and making my own money, I went where I wanted to go. You see, being married don't mean that your husband controls your life. That was my life and I was carrying his child, it's true, but I was going to look after myself."[26]

Although the work experience of black women tobacco workers was one of racial, sex, and class oppression, the early advent into the labor force, the resistance to exploitation, and the longevity of work created a consciousness that fostered a sense of strength and dignity among some women in this working class. Management tactics of wage inequity, hiring practices, and racial-sexual division of labor pitted black women against white women economically as workers, and made the formation of gender bonds across race lines all but impossible. Yet among black women, the linkages of sisterhood engendered a consciousness of female strength, if not feminism.

NOTES

I am deeply grateful to North Carolina Central University for a Faculty Research Grant and for the excellent editorial comments of the *Feminist Studies* editors.

1. For discussion of the historical involvement of black labor in tobacco manufacturing, see Joseph C. Robert, *The Tobacco Kingdom* (North Carolina: Duke University Press, 1938).
2. Charlie Necoda Mack, interview with author, 22 May 1979, on file in the Southern Oral History Program, University of North Carolina, Chapel Hill, hereafter cited as SOHP/UNC. Dora Miller, interview with author, 6 June 1979, SOHP/UNC; Mary Dove, interview with author, 7 July 1979, SOHP/UNC; Rosetta Branch, interview with author, 15 Aug. 1981.
3. The 1940 labor force figures do not include information for Durham County. U.S. Bureau of the Census, *Population: 1930* (Washington, D.C.: GPO, 1930), 3:341. In 1900, the major tobacco industries in the South were the American Tobacco Company and Liggett Myers in Durham; R.J. Reynolds in Winston Salem; and P. Lorillard in Richmond, Virginia.
4. Annie Barbee, interview, 28 May 1979, SOHP/UNC.
5. Interview, 30 May 1981; Mary Dove, interview.
6. Women's Bureau, *The Effects of Changing Conditions in the Cigar and Cigarette Industries*, Bulletin no. 110 (Washington, D.C.: GPO, 1932), 774-75. The Women's Bureau was established by Congress in 1920 under the aegis of the United States Department of Labor. Its purpose was to gather information and to provide advice to working women.
7. Mary Dove, interview; interviews, 15 and 28 Aug. 1981.
8. Annie Barbee and Rosetta Branch, interviews.
9. Pansy Cheatham, interview with author, 9 July 1979, SOHP/UNC; Mary Dove, interview.
10. Blanche Scott, interview with author, 11 July 1979, SOHP/UNC; interviews, 8, 15 June, 1981; Mary Dove, Annie Barbee interviews.
11. Death Certificates, 1911-1930, Durham County Health Department, Vital Records, Durham, North Carolina. I was also interested in the correlation of working conditions and female-related maladies such as stillbirths, miscarriages, and uterine disorders. Further perusal of death certificates of stillbirths were less valuable for there were no indications of mothers' occupations. Even hospital statistics lacked occupational data. This area of inquiry as it relates to the health of black female workers and working conditions needs further research. Further questions that will have to be explored include: Was there a higher percentage of female tobacco workers dying of

tuberculosis than non-female tobacco workers? How long were stricken female workers employed in the factory? How much weight must be given to the working environment over that of home environs? Despite the lack of solid data on these questions, the interviews and death records clearly indicate that racial division of labor negatively impacted upon the health of many black female tobacco workers.

12. Elizabeth H. Pleck, "A Mother's Wage: Income Earning among Married Italian and Black Women, 1896-1911," in *The American Family in Social-Historical Perspective*, 2d ed, ed. Michael Gordon (New York: St. Martin's Press, 1978), 490-510; "Culture, Class, and Family Life among Low-Income Urban Negroes," in *Employment, Race, and Poverty*, ed. Arthur M. Ross and Herbert Hill (New York: Harcourt, Brace and World, 1967), 149-72; "The Kindred of Veola Jackson: Residence and Family Organization of an Urban Black American Family," in *Afro-American Anthropology: Contemporary Perspective*, ed. Norman E. Whitten, Jr., and John F. Szwed (New York: Free Press, 1970), chapt. 16.

13. U.S. Bureau of the Census, *Population: 1930*, vols. 3 and 4; U.S. Department of Labor, Women's Bureau, *Hours and Earning in Tobacco Stemmeries*, Bulletin no. 127 (Washington, D.C.: GPO, 1934).

14. Women's Bureau, *Effects of Changing Conditions*, 172-75.

15. Blanche Scott and Pansy Cheatham, interviews.

16. Margaret Turner, interview with author, 25 Sept. 1979, SOHP/UNC.

17. Interview, 8 June 1981; Hugh Penn Brinton, "The Negro in Durham: A Study in Adjustment to Town Life" (Ph.D. diss., University of North Carolina, Chapel Hill, 1930).

18. Dora Miller, and Mary Dove, interviews; Janie Mae Lyons, interview with author, 4 Aug. 1981.

19. Annie Barbee, interview; interview, 10 July 1981.

20. Interviews, 4 and 15 June 1981.

21. For the best discussions of the National Industrial Recovery Acts' impact on blacks, see Raymond Wolters, *Negroes and the Great Depression: The Problem of Economic Recovery*, ed. Stanley E. Kutler (Westport, Conn.: Greenwood Publishing Co., 1970); and Bernard Sternsher, ed., *The Negro in the Depression and War: Prelude to Revolution, 1930-45* (Chicago, Ill.: Quadrangle Books, 1969). Also see Dolores Janiewski, "From Field to Factory: Race, Class, and Sex and the Woman Worker in Durham, 1880-1940" (Ph.D. diss., Duke University, Durham, North Carolina, 1979).

22. *Durham* (N.C.) *Morning Herald*, 17, 18 Apr. 1939, p. 1; Janiewski.

23. Dora Miller, interview.

24. For terms of contract, see *Durham* (N.C.) *Morning Herald* and *Durham* (N.C.) *Sun*, 27 Apr. 1939, pp. 1, 2; Janiewski.

25. Pansy Cheatham, interview.

26. Annie Barbee, interview.

The Role of Women in a Changing Navaho Society

LAILA SHUKRY HAMAMSY*
American University at Cairo

INTRODUCTION

MOST of the work on which this paper is based was done in 1951–52 in the Fruitland Irrigation Project in San Juan County, at the northwestern corner of New Mexico.[1] The project area has a thirteen-mile boundary along the southern bank of the river, which is settled on the north by Mormons and other white farmers. The area at that time included 2,500 acres of irrigated land divided into 205 farms and assigned to 191 family units (Sasaki 1950). The nearest urban center is the predominantly white town of Farmington, just off the reservation.

Although the area has long been inhabited by Navaho farmers and owners of livestock, the development of the irrigation project dates from 1933 when the land was surveyed for the purpose of establishing farm tracts. These tracts were assigned in ten-acre lots to original residents and to applicants from other parts of the reservation.

Particular aspects of Fruitland's position made it useful for the purposes of this study. There is directed social change in the form of government programs, including the irrigation project itself. Further, Fruitland is on the edge of the reservation and is in continuous interaction with the neighboring white society. It is also a well-defined geographic and social unit. Finally, there was available a great deal of data gathered by the research team of the Cornell University Southwest Project which had been working in the area since 1948.

Data for the present study were gathered by the author during a 17-week residence in the Fruitland area in 1951 and 1952, and preceding that, during a three-week residence at Navaho Mountain, a more traditional settlement than that represented by Fruitland. Methods of collecting data were primarily those of participant observation and informal open-ended interviews. They were chosen because of the limited time of residence and because the relationship between the author and the residents rapidly became one of friendship, which seemed to make difficult the role of formal interviewer. Additional sources of data were the field notes of other research workers of the Southwest Project, Indian Service reports and documents, and anthropological literature on the Navaho.

TRADITIONAL ECONOMIC AND SOCIAL ORGANIZATION

The economic and social organization here termed traditional is that which developed after 1868 when the Navaho returned to the southwestern location after a four-year forced exile. It is informal and loosely knit in comparison to that of many other Indians, for example, the Pueblo; and there are local variations due to differing degrees of contact with other groups, historical accidents, and geographic conditions. A general pattern, however, is fairly evident and tions due to differing degrees of contact with other groups, historical accidents, and geographic conditions. A general pattern, however, is fairly evident and

* Prepared with the assistance of Mrs. Alice Longaker, professional editor.

even today many conform to it. Kluckhohn and Leighton (1946) estimate conformity in live-stock regions at 85 percent.

The Navaho traditionally live in widely scattered matrilocal family groups (extended families). Within each group, each nuclear family lives in a separate hogan. The extended family is usually composed of an older woman, her husband, her unmarried children, her married daughters, and the daughters' husbands and children. Some families have additional but secondary shelters at summer pasture lands.

Raising livestock and subsistence farming are the major economic activities. In these, and in the management of the hogan, there is a division of labor between men and women, each assuming significant functions. Men are generally responsible for the horses and cattle, women for the sheep and goats. Women carry the main burden in the running of the hogan, including the making of clothing, but men are responsible for the leather and silver work. Blanket weaving is a common pursuit of the women, and baskets and pottery are made by a few.

The smallest and most important unit of social and economic co-operation is the nuclear family, but in the frequent times of heightened activity such as harvest and planting, all members of the group in an area may help each other. On the other hand, in some regions the extended family operates as a unit. The sheep of all members of the family will be pooled under the direction of the matron of the household, and are herded by the group's young men and women.

The ownership and use of property and livestock is generally subject to control by the extended family, although individuals and nuclear families may be owners in fact. Only personal property such as jewelry and cash is not under such control. Economically, the women fare equally with or better than the men, since they are the usual owners of sheep, a major property, and since they can earn cash through their weaving. In addition, inheritance is through the women, and daughters and nieces often receive the same as or more than the male relatives.

The father is the formal head of the family, but the mother and children make up its stable core. The man moves frequently between his family of orientation and his family of procreation, since he has obligations to both. In contrast, the woman remains with her family of orientation, in her own extended family group. Within this group, and in her own nuclear family, she usually has as much or more influence than her husband. She often makes the decisions in the family's financial affairs, even if the goods involved were originally the husband's individual property. "The general tendency, even in spite of the theoretical power of the avunculate, is for sons, brothers and husbands to consult the maternal head of the house and to respect her opinion" (Reichard 1928:53). Children count descent through the mother and are considered to belong to her and her clan.

The one social function of the family that is usually left to the men is that of relations with the world outside the group, but here too, women can play a part if they choose.

All members of the extended family participate in the raising and training of children. The mother has the day-to-day responsibility for their care and discipline. Maternal uncles have important teaching and disciplinary functions. The father's relationship to the children, on the other hand, is mainly affectional. As the young grow into adult life, they remain under the social control of the family, since they are dependent on the goodwill of parents and relatives for their economic survival and social acceptance.

Marriages are usually arranged by parents and relatives, most importantly the maternal uncles, and are frequently made for economic and social reasons. The groom provides a bridal gift, often livestock and household utensils, and these become the property of the bride. Newly wed couples live near the wife's family, and there is constant visiting of the young woman and her children with the family matron. The husband is excluded from such contact by a taboo forbidding a man to look upon his mother-in-law. The son-in-law's position is a subordinate one in the extended family household and he is closely supervised by his father-in-law. One groom was told: "Your folks have turned you over to us. You don't belong over there any more. You are here now, to take care of the bride's property" (Dyk 1947:109–110). The young married woman, on the other hand, enjoys security and assistance with her household and family tasks from the close relatives surrounding her. Her family protects her if her husband is abusive, and she retains her property and her children in case the marriage fails.

If the marriage is successful and productive, the husband and wife may establish a more independent hogan and may separate their flocks from the family herd, thus becoming the nucleus of a new extended family group. If the marriage dissolves, as is frequent, it is the husband who suffers dislocation and financial loss. Leighton and Kluckhohn (1947:83) estimate that only one woman in four reaches old age with her original husband. Desertion is the most common cause of family dissolution, more frequent even than death. The husband is forced out of his home, to return to his family of orientation or to a new wife's hogan, and his property usually remains with his former wife.

Beyond the extended family, the next unit of social organization is the outfit: a group of related extended families who co-operate in larger economic, social, and religious functions. Groups of outfits occupying specific localities are organized into bands with recognized leaders. There is also a clan organization which is chiefly important as a regulator of marriage choices. There is no indigenous centralized tribal organization.

NEW ECONOMIC POSITION

The drastic changes introduced into the traditional Navaho economic pattern within the last twenty-odd years have had direct effects on women's economic position and on the value of their work, and are, we suggest, important among the forces that are redefining the role of Navaho women today.

Most Navaho have been subject to a slow economic decline and to the accompanying need for new sources of income, notably wage work. In Fruitland the economic picture is particularly sharp. It is an area in which the greatest changes have been made in traditional agriculture and herding patterns. Being a border community, the residents are nearer to work opportunities and more enticed than Indians in the interior by employment opportunities in the white world "outside." Both of these factors have direct effects on the Navaho woman's economic position.

Two aspects of the land policy initiated in 1933 are relevant. First, only married men were originally eligible for land, and only on the condition that they made proper use of it. Women and children, traditionally important owners of land, were thus barred in the beginning from ownership. They could become owners only through inheritance or other transfer from the male assignees. Further, the threat that the government might "take away" the land if it were used improperly introduced an uncertainty not existing in traditional ownership patterns.

The second aspect of the changing economy is less direct. It is that few families manage to make a living from farming alone, or even in combined farming and livestock operations. Most of them are forced to seek additional income. The most available source is in the white communities at Fruitland's border. The economic result of this is that the Navaho woman's family may have more "cash" than formerly, but it is provided by the man of the house. Both of these are elements foreign to traditional organization, and their effect will be discussed in some detail later.

The extent to which this new economic picture applies in Fruitland can be indicated briefly. Crop report estimates obtained from the Farm Management Supervisor of the Fruitland Project reveal that in the summer of 1951 about 69 percent of 191 families had under assignment between six and fifteen acres, and earned a generously estimated yearly income of less than $900. Only nine families owned between 25 and 33 acres (the maximum holding) and averaged $1,774. Livestock holdings are limited by government regulation and by the lack of good range vegetation. In 1952, 69 individuals held sheep-permits, but they stocked only 61 percent of the sheep their permits allowed them.

On the other hand, the dependence of the Fruitlanders on wage work has increased. In 1952, the author interviewed 38 families and found that of the 32 men in these, all but two had at some time engaged in off-reservation or government work. The two exceptions are men who have large acreages and are successful farmers. There were 43 able-bodied women in this same group of families, but only 11 of them had ever engaged in wage work. Of these, only four were married women living with their husbands. The others were widowed or divorced.

When the women do find work, they are usually poorly paid in comparison with the men. There are a few openings in government institutions such as schools and hospitals, but the major sources of employment are in such areas as seasonal agricultural work, restaurants, and domestic service. The men, on the other hand, find their major employment opportunities in such relatively better paid fields as railroads, agriculture, lumbering, construction and road work, and oil, military, and mining operations, in that order of importance.

SOME EFFECTS OF NEW ECONOMIC POSITION ON SOCIAL PATTERNS

All of the traditional units of Navaho social organization still function in Fruitland, but significant changes are taking place in the relative importance of family units. The importance of the independent biological family is increasing, while the influence of the extended family and of larger units lessens. There is also a strong tendency away from matrilocality. Some men and women still share farm and home tasks and the responsibility for children, but many men are frequently not at home to do their share. Finally, the economic responsibilities of the family fall less on the family as a unit, and more on the male head of the independent nuclear family.

Fruitland residence patterns in 1952 show a trend away from matrilocality. Of 36 families studied, there were only five older families acting as heads of extended family units. There were 13 younger couples living as part of these extended groups, but 12 of these were in patrilocal residence. The remaining 18 families lived independently on their own plots; five of them near, but not as part of the husband's family; five near the wife's family, and eight not near families of either spouse. The five families living near the wife's family were cases in which daughters had married outsiders.

In families where subsistence farming and herding are still major occupations, men and women share the tasks. But many women have been forced by their husbands' absences in wage work to take over many of the farm chores that traditionally belong to men. Thus:

> In the summer time [according to one informant] she comes and stays at Fruitland in order to take care of the farm. Her husband stays at Shiprock and visits on weekends. Her husband helps on the farm, does the carrying of heavy things, while she does all the rest.

Women without husbands and living away from an extended family find it difficult to maintain their farms. One woman told an interviewer:

> My boy has been working outside and I have to irrigate my farm all by myself. Sometimes my neighbors, who belong to the same clan come and help, but most of the time I work it all myself.

Some in this position give up their land:

> After her husband's death, she found that she could not take care of the farm, so she gave it to her son and moved next to her daughter.

Women still have major responsibility for housework and the care of children, but housework takes little time. Laundry is meagre and cooking has become simplified and less time-consuming as the women adopt processed foods. Care of the children is less demanding since only the preschool children are constantly at home. The older children are in school, some in day schools and some in off-reservation boarding schools. The traditional craft of weaving has become impossible with the decline of sheep flocks.

This changing pattern toward independent families and less housework affects the women in a number of ways. Mothers of preschool children, while usually not over-worked, lack the support that other members of the extended family could provide. They have the continuous care of the children and if they leave home to visit or shop, must either take the children with them or hire a baby-sitter. Many complain that they feel tied down. They also lack the guidance and assistance in training and discipline that older members of the family could provide.

The women who have no children, or only older children, have little to do. Many are bored or restless:

Before getting married, Elizabeth worked in a cafe in town. She had stopped "to have a rest." She is bored with home, however, and would like to go back to work again. "I hate to stay at home. There isn't much to do."

A few of the women do try to find wage work; many seek diversion in the near-by town, and others in visiting friends and relatives:

I asked: "What does Mary do all day?" Her aunt said, "Nothing. She just takes care of her baby. She comes to visit me and she goes to visit my mother, that's all."

Economically, the wives are generally dependent on their husbands, but the men are often erratic and irresponsible providers. Cash, as was noted above, traditionally the property of an individual owner, is still considered by many men to belong solely to them, with the result that many women are frequently without economic support. One old man told an interviewer:

The Navaho people who work for wages don't put any money in the bank. They spend everything and at the end, they don't have any money to take care of the needs of other members of the family. They will spend all their money on cars sometimes, but they won't have enough money to eat and buy clothes for the children.

Some women do manage to get part of their husbands' earnings. The following comment by one who does, suggests that she feels her husband to be an exceptionally considerate provider:

My husband give me money. Sometimes he cash check and give me money. Many times he give me all of it. . . . He is good that way. He don't go and spend all his money like some do.

In a few families interviewed by the author, both husband and wife have wage work. In most of these, however, each pays his own way, even in recreational expenses such as an evening in town.

The poorest women in Fruitland are generally the middle-aged and old women who have no male providers. They frequently have no economic support except the relatively inadequate welfare aid. Under traditional conditions these women would be well off; they might be managers of large extended family units, or at least respected female relatives with secure positions within the family group.

"OUTSIDE" INFLUENCES ON TRADITIONAL SOCIAL PATTERNS

Through increasing contact with the white world, the Navaho have become familiar with new goods, new ways of doing things, new forms of recreation, and a number of new problems. Many Navaho now own cars, radios, stoves, washing machines, and other modern durable goods. Some build frame or stone houses to replace the traditional and inexpensive hogans. The desire for these new things makes many women urge their men to greater effort in finding wage work, often with the result that the women become still more alone on the farm and in the home. In addition, these new products and ways are rapidly replacing traditional bases for determining prestige and standards of living. The direct effect of this on the women is that they become less important for the family standards and prestige, while the men, as the wage earners, become much more so.

Traditionally, religious ceremonies, dances, fairs, family visiting, and family parties were major forms of recreation. Women, it may be noted, have important functions in most of these. The frequency of these events, particularly the larger and more organized forms, is now diminishing, and no new forms of recreation have developed on the reservation to replace them. Instead, there is an increasing tendency, especially among younger Navahos, to seek amusement in the urban white center off the reservation. To get there, however, the women usually have to depend on the men—for the ride to town and the money to spend. Once in town, men and women frequently seek separate entertainment. For the women this may be going to the movies, eating in restaurants, drinking, shopping, meeting friends, and window-shopping. One man described his family's trip to town: "I'm happy, and my family is happy. I take a couple of drinks, my wife goes shopping."

"Outside" educational patterns are replacing the traditional home education in the skills of home-making, farming, and herding. While this newer education, which is under government direction, is available to both boys and girls, it is frequently the boys of the family who receive the better and longer training. Many girls are taken out of school early to help at home. Since school-learned skills and the ability to speak English are important factors in earning and social abilities, the girls are often disadvantaged. The author found only a few families in which the wife was better educated than her husband, and in some of these families she was a strong member and family spokesman, a position roughly comparable to that of the wife in a traditional family group.

Many of these new ways can be further traced for their effect on family relationships and family harmony. Differences in education, of course, are an important source of conflict between generations of a family, as well as between members of a single generation. The increasing amount of disposable income and the increasing desire for purchased goods means increasing occasions for family conflict over how wages will be used. For example: "M. B. was reported to the police by his wife who is having a difficult time because M. B. does not bring home his checks" (Field Notes). Drunkenness, wife-beating, infidelity, and jealousy are marked causes of discord in the Fruitland area. Drunkenness is reported to be the most common cause of friction, and it is often a contributing factor in other conflicts: "Suspicion of infidelity of marital partners appears to be especially marked at Fruitland because of easy access to town and liquor. Whenever men or women are away over night they are immediately suspected of having had an affair" (Sasaki 1950:89).

CHANGING SOCIAL ORGANIZATION OF THE FAMILY

Relationships within the family are changing. The father, because of his importance as breadwinner, and because of the change from matrilocal to neolocal or patrilocal residence arrangements, is becoming more indispensable to the family for its economic and social well-being, and at the same time he is frequently away from home. The wife, therefore, still has the daily responsibility for running the house and for the care and training of the younger children.

Both mother and father lose influence, however, as the children grow and undertake school education. Frequently the parents find themselves in an ambivalent position toward these children. Many favor white education, and want their children to embrace white ways:

> The son told me that his father . . . [felt] the main thing was to get an education, so the white man could not cheat him.

Another father told an interviewer that:

> He was anxious for them [the children] to learn a little English and a trade because things were going to get tougher for the Navahos if they don't have a trade.

At the same time, parents find themselves ineffectual in the face of their children's greater education and rejection of traditional customs. Lacking economic and social control, they have little effect against rebellion. Girls frequently express revolt through sexual adventures, which result in the further problem of illegitimate children. Traditionally such children were absorbed into the large, loose framework of the extended family, but today both the unmarried mother and her children may be without economic or social support.

The growing independence of the young carries over to marriage customs, and increasingly marriages are contracted without parental consent. The author knew twelve Fruitland couples who had married within the last ten years. Eight of these married through personal choice and only four through parental arrangement. All of the women in the first group were educated to the extent that they spoke English, and seven of them had worked for wages before marriage. Of the four in the latter group, only one was sufficiently educated to speak English. Even in traditionally arranged marriages, the groom's gift has undergone a change. Frequently, he no longer gives livestock or household utensils, but instead a cash payment.

The position of the daughter-in-law in a patrilocal extended family unit (and to some extent in an independent nuclear family) needs special mention for the marked contrast it provides with that of the daughter-in-law in the traditional matrilocal residence. In a patrilocal unit, the young married woman has to live closely and interact frequently with people who do not embrace her as one of them. Her mother-in-law, the head of the woman's division of the extended family, exercises authority over her without at the same time offering her protection and emotional security. A possessive mother-in-law is in fact often a rival for the young husband's attention. In such rivalry, the daughter-in-law is in a weak position, and even lacks the protection provided by a mother-in-law taboo. The young woman's main, and possibly only, defense in such rivalry lies in her personal influence over the husband.

Conflicts occur frequently in such situations. When mild, they take the form of verbal battles, with gossip a strong weapon. In more serious cases, the young woman can be forced from her home alone, or with her husband if her influence over him is strong. In either case, she suffers dislocation and the loss of economic security and opportunity that she may have enjoyed as part of the extended family. When there is a marked degree of difference in the education of the older and younger women, there are occasions for additional and serious conflicts. Again, it is a struggle which the daughter-in-law, alone in the family group, is likely to lose. Such conflicts arise over education of the children, health measures, the family's manner of living, recreation, and related matters.

In virtually every kind of family organization today, most conflicts that result in divorce or desertion by the husband mean economic and social disorganization and loss of prestige for the women and children. If the family has been in patrilocal residence, the woman and children are frequently forced to leave their homes. In neolocal residence, deserted wives, while possibly retaining their houses, lose economic support. They sometimes return to the wife's family, but this often imposes an economic burden on her people. Other solutions are the finding of a new husband, or moving to town in search of employment. This move is likely to result in minimal economic security, at best, and more often in unemployment, drunkenness, and sexual promiscuity.

The nine cases of divorce known to the author in Fruitland suggest the extent to which women's position in broken marriages has changed. Six of the nine cases resulted in the woman's leaving home. Only two of these women returned to live with their own relatives; the other four left Fruitland and went to the nearby urban white center. In three cases the men left the family. Two of these were families in matrilocal residence and the wives, although not suffering dislocation, did suffer economic hardship, since they had been economically dependent on their husbands' wages.

CONCLUSION—EVALUATION OF THE NEW POSITION OF NAVAHO WOMEN

The preceding summary of life in Fruitland today suggests that there are three aspects of the woman's role that have been adversely affected by the recent social and economic changes there: her economic position, the significance of her function within the family, and her sense of security and bargaining position in family interaction. The last of these is largely a result of the first two.

Although the Fruitland society, in gross calculation, has gained economically from the recent industrial development in the San Juan Valley, a close examination shows that while the men have been compensated for the loss of their traditional sources of livelihood, the women have not been directly compensated in any way. In wage work most men find an adequate substitute for the declining livestock economy. As far as women are concerned, in losing their sheep, they have lost their economic independence. There are few job opportunities for them, and their duties in the home make it impossible for most of them to seek work outside.

This economic dependence of woman is aggravated by the fact that the wants of their families have increased considerably. To obtain the goods and services of white society, the women have to depend upon the industry and good-will of the wage earners—the men. Some women do benefit from what their husbands earn, for there is beginning to develop a definition of the husband's role as economic provider. But there are many instances in which the traditional attitude toward cash is still operative and is applied with a vengeance. Middle age bestows prestige and wealth on the Navaho woman of traditional society, especially if she is fortunate enough to have a large female progeny. In contrast, the poorest category of women in Fruitland are the middle-aged women without male providers.

In assessing the significance of woman's functions in Fruitland today as against those of traditional society, the following questions may be asked: How valuable are her social and economic activities, and how personally rewarding? Can the performance of these be a means for the attainment of status in the prestige hierarchy of society?

Traditionally, every member of the family performs significant tasks that contribute to the survival of the whole unit. The woman, as the central figure in the home, assumes functions there that are indispensable to the economic and social well-being of her family. She is also well equipped to handle most phases of an important economic activity—sheep-raising. The accumulation of wealth is possible for both men and women. As wealth spells prestige among the Navaho, this means that woman's labor and industry are important in determining the status of the family on the prestige ladder of the community.

In Fruitland, the division of labor still follows convenience, and convenience decrees that women perform most of the tasks in and around the house. But the home has been shorn of much of its economic and social significance, and has been largely deserted by the men and older children. The importance of women's functions has declined accordingly. Wage employment is for most families the only means for acquiring processed goods and the newer prestige symbols such as cars and modern homes. It is the men who make these acquisitions possible, and who are therefore mainly responsible for determining the social and economic status and the prestige of the family.

Although women no longer have equal economic opportunities and rewards, they still have the traditional functions of child-bearing and rearing. Are these personally satisfying? Many younger women express dissatisfaction. Mothers in independent residence complain of being tied down by their children, and school-trained women who worked prior to marriage describe home life as confining and dull. In addition, children are no longer social and economic assets. For women who have no children, homemaking offers unproductive leisure, boredom, and restlessness. Farm work is seasonal, and housekeeping takes little time. Weaving is no longer a possible leisure-time activity.

The woman's sense of security and her position within the family have been affected by these changes. The absence of the support of close relatives and the lack of economic opportunities that traditional organization provides, have threatened her sense of economic and social security. And the very facts of her dependence and the diminished significance of her functions have greatly lowered her bargaining position in family interaction. The pertinent questions here are: Which marriage partner can function more adequately without the other? And, who suffers most in case of disagreement that breaks up the family?

When we compare the traditional economic organization to that which is evolving in Fruitland, we find that the woman has become more dependent on the man for her economic and social well-being, and correspondingly, she is much less indispensable to her husband for his well-being. In case of a disagreement that results in a split of the family, she is the one who suffers most, both economically and socially. Thus, the majority of women find themselves relegated to a very minor position of power in the family arena, unless they manage through some personal influence or advantage to counteract the disadvantages of the weak bargaining position offered by the emerging culture.

We conclude, then, that the changing economic position and social organization of the Navaho today are adversely affecting the women. They are losing their economic independence, the satisfactions and rewards that accompany their functioning, and their security and power within the family.

Navaho men are adjusting to the changing conditions by increasingly adopting the life and culture of the white world, but the women are being left stranded on the reservation. Much that was economically and socially important there has become out-moded and discarded, and little has so far evolved to fill the void resulting in the lives of the women. We cannot assume that this is a final, stable position. What direction the women's lives will take depends on where the women see their opportunities; whether life on the reservation can be revitalized and made more satisfactory, or whether the women will follow their men into the world outside. Many of the forces that have helped to shape the changes outlined in this paper continue to be effective and will continue to influence the role of women: government agricultural and service programs, the continually emerging cash economy, school education, and, not least, the continuing culture of the Navaho, which acts as a sieve through which other forces must pass.

NOTE

[1] This paper has its origin in the Cornell Southwest Project, which in turn is part of the Cornell Program for Research and Training in Culture and Applied Science. The total Program is directed by Lauriston Sharp. The Southwest Project is under the general supervision of Alexander H. Leighton; John Adair is former Field Director, and Tom T. Sasaki, is the current Field Director. The research, supported primarily by the Carnegie Corporation of New York, was done by Hamamsy.

REFERENCES CITED

DYK, WALTER

1947 A Navaho autobiography. New York, Viking Fund Publications in Anthropology, No. 8.

KLUCKHOHN, CLYDE and DOROTHEA LEIGHTON

1946 The Navaho. Cambridge, Harvard University Press.

LEIGHTON, DOROTHEA and CLYDE KLUCKHOHN

1947 Children of the people. Cambridge, Harvard University Press

REICHARD, GLADYS

1928 Social life of the Navajo Indians with some attention to minor ceremonies. New York, Columbia University Press.

SASAKI, TOM T.

MS Technological change in a Navaho farming community: a study of social and psychological change. Thesis: Cornell University, 1950.

Copyright Information

Van Kirk, Sylvia. "The Role of Native Women in the Creation of Fur Trade Society in Western Canada, 1670–1830." In *The Women's West*, edited by Susan Armitage and Elizabeth Jameson (Norman, Oklahoma: University of Oklahoma Press, Norman 1987): 53-62. "From *The Women's West*, Edited and With Introductions by Susan Armitage and Elizabeth Jameson. Copyright ©1987 by the University of Oklahoma Press." Also reprinted with permission of the author. Photograph on page 4 is in the public domain. Article first appeared in *Frontiers: a journal of women's studies* 7:3 (1984): 9-13, Women's Studies Program, University of Colorado at Boulder, Boulder, Colorado, USA.

Gutiérrez, Ramón A. "Honor Ideology, Marriage Negotiation, and Class-Gender Domination in New Mexico, 1670-1846." *Latin American Perspectives*, Issue 44, 12:1 (Winter 1985): 81-104. "Ramón Gutiérrez, 'Honor Ideology, Marriage Negotiation and Class-Gender Domination in New Mexico, 1670-1846,' (12:1), pp. 81-104, copyright © by *Latin American Perspectives*. Reprinted by permission of Sage Publications, Inc.," Newbury Park, California, USA.

Miller, Darlis A. "Cross-Cultural Marriages in the Southwest: The New Mexico Experience, 1846-1900." *New Mexico Historical Review* 57 (October 1982): 336-359. ©Regents, University of New Mexico, Albuquerque, New Mexico, USA.

de Graaf, Lawrence B. "Race, Sex, and Region: Black Women in the American West, 1850-1920," *Pacific Historical Review* 49:2 (May 1980): 285-313. ©1980, by The Pacific Coast Branch, American Historical Association, reprinted by permission, Berkeley, California, USA.

Riley, Glenda. "Frontierswomen's Changing Views of Indians in the Trans-Mississipi West." *Montana The Magazine of Western History* 34 (Winter 1984): 20-35. ©Montana Historical Society, Helena, Montana, USA.

Tucker, Susan. "A Complex Bond: Southern Black Domestic Workers and Their White Employers." *Frontiers* 9:3 (1987): 6-13. ©1987 Frontiers Editorial Collective, Women's Studies Program, University of Colorado at Boulder, Boulder, Colorado, USA. Reprinted with permission of the journal and the author.

Green, Rayna. "The Pocahontas Perplex: The Image of Indian Women in American Culture." *The Massachusetts Review* 16:4 (Autumn 1975): 698-714. "Reprinted from *The Massachusetts Review*, ©1976, The Massachusetts Review, Inc.," Amherst, Masschusetts, USA.

Dysart, Jane. "Mexican Women in San Antonio, 1830-1860: The Assimilation Process." *The Western Historical Quarterly* 7:4 (October 1976): 365-375. ©*The Western Historical Quarterly, Journal of the Western History Association*, Utah State University, Logan, Utah, USA.

Armitage, Sue, Theresa Banfield, and Sarah Jacobus. "Black Women and Their Communities in Colorado." *Frontiers* 2:2 (Summer 1977): 45-51. ©1977 Frontiers Editorial Collective, Women's Studies Program, University of Colorado at Boulder, Boulder, Colorado, USA. Reprinted with permission of the journal and the author.

Lerner, Gerda. "Black and White Women in Interaction and Confrontation." *Prospects: An Annual of American Cultural Studies* 2 (1976): 193-208. Copyright ©1976 by Gerda Lerner. "Reprinted with the permission of the Cambridge University Press and the author," New York, New York, USA.

Johnson, Susan L. "Sharing Bed and Board: Cohabitation and Cultural Difference in Central Arizona Mining Towns: 1863–1873." In *The Women's West*, edited by Susan Armitage and Elizabeth Jameson (Norman, Oklahoma: University of Oklahoma Press, Norman 1987): 77-91. "From *The Women's West*, Edited and With Introductions by Susan Armitage and Elizabeth Jameson. Copyright ©1987 by the University of Oklahoma Press." Also reprinted with permission of the author. Article first appeared in *Frontiers: a journal of women's studies* 7:3 (1984): 36-42. Women's Studies Program, University of Oklahoma at Boulder, Boulder, Colorado, USA.

Hurtado, Albert L. "'Hardly a Farm House--A Kitchen without Them': Indian and White Households on the California Borderland Frontier in 1860." *The Western Historical Quarterly* 13:3 (July 1982): 245-270. ©*The Western Historical Quarterly, Journal of the Western History Association*, Utah State University, Logan, Utah, USA.

Hartmann, Susan M. "Women's Work among the Plains Indians." *Gateway Heritage* 3:4 (Spring 1983): 2-9. ©Missouri Historical Society, St. Louis, Missouri, USA.

Mathes, Valerie Sherer. "American Indian Women and the Catholic Church." *North Dakota History: Journal of the Northern Plains* 47:4 (Fall 1980): 20-25. "Originally published 'American Indian Women and the Catholic Church,' *North Dakota History*, 47 (Fall 1980), pp. 20-25, Copyright ©1980, State Historical Society of North Dakota. Used by permission," Bismark, North Dakota, USA.

Glenn, Evelyn Nakano. "Racial Ethnic Women's Labor: The Intersection of Race, Gender and Class Oppression." *Review of Radical Political Economics* 17:3 (Fall 1985): 86-108. ©Union for Radical Political Economics, New York, New York, USA.

Peterson, Susan C. "Doing 'Women's Work': The Grey Nuns at Fort Totten Indian Reservation, 1874-1900." *North Dakota History* 52:2 (Spring 1985): 18-25. "Originally published 'Doing 'Women's Work': The Grey Nuns at Fort Totten Indian Reservation, 1874-1900.' *North Dakota History*, 52 (Spring 1985), pp. 18-25, Copyright ©1980, State Historical Society of North Dakota. Used by permission," Bismark, North Dakota, USA.

Jensen, Joan M. "Crossing Ethnic Barriers in the Southwest: Women's Agricultural Extension Education, 1914–1940." *Agricultural History* 60:2 (Spring 1986): 169-181. ©Agricultural History Society, Washington D. C. and Davis, California, USA.

Bannan, Helen M. "Newcomers to Navajoland: Transculturation in the Memoirs of Anglo Women, 1900–1945." *New Mexico Historical Review* 59 (April 1984): 165-185. © Regents, University of New Mexico, Albuquerque, New Mexico, USA.

Deutsch, Sarah. "Women and Intercultural Relations: The Case of Hispanic New Mexico and Colorado." *Signs: Journal of Women in Culture and Society* 12:4 (Summer 1987): 719-739. "©1987 by The University of Chicago. All rights reserved." Chicago, Illinois, USA.

Blackwelder, Julia Kirk. "Quiet Suffering: Atlanta Women in the 1930s." *The Georgia Historical Quarterly* 61:2 (Summer 1977): 112-124. ©*The Georgia Historical Quarterly*, The University of Georgia, Athens, Georgia, USA.

Jones, Beverly W. "Race, Sex, and Class: Black Female Tobacco Workers in Durham, North Carolina, 1920-1940, and the Development of Female Consciousness." *Feminist Studies* 10:3 (Fall 1984): 441-52. ©by Feminist Studies, Inc., Women's Studies Program, University of Maryland, College Park, Maryland, USA.

Hamamsy, Laila Shukry. "The Role of Women in a Changing Navaho Society." *American Anthropologist* 59 (1957): 101-11. "Reproduced by permission of the American Anthropological Association from *American Anthropologist* 59:1, 1957. Not for further reproduction," Arlington, Virgina, USA.

Index

Bei Fragen zur Produktsicherheit wenden Sie sich bitte an:
If you have any questions regarding product safety,
please contact:

Walter de Gruyter GmbH
Genthiner Straße 13
10785 Berlin
productsafety@degruyterbrill.com